www. cs. orst. edu /~budd

www. awl. com/corp

Search for "Timothy Budd"

Data Structures in C++
Using the Standard
Template Library

Data Structures in C++ Using the Standard Template Library

Timothy Budd

Oregon State University

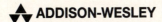 ADDISON-WESLEY

An imprint of Addison Wesley Longman, Inc.

Reading, Massachusetts • Harlow, England • Menlo Park, California
Berkeley, California • Don Mills, Ontario • Sydney
Bonn • Amsterdam • Tokyo • Mexico City

Acquisitions Editor: Susan Hartman
Associate Editor: Deborah Lafferty
Production Editor: Amy Willcutt
Production Assistant: Molly Taylor
Compositor: Windfall Software, Paul C. Anagnostopoulos & Jacqui Scarlott
Artist: George Nichols
Cover Designer: Diana Coe

The procedures and applications presented in this book have been included for their instructional value. They have been tested with care but are not guaranteed for any purpose. The publisher and author do not offer any warranties or representations, nor do they accept any liabilities with respect to the programs and applications.

Many of the designations used by manufacturers and sellers to distinguish their products are claimed as trademarks. Where those designations appear in this book, and Addison-Wesley was aware of a trademark claim, the designations have been printed in initial caps or all caps.

Library of Congress Cataloging-in-Publication Data

Budd, Timothy.
    Data structures in C++ using the standard template library /
Timothy A. Budd.
        p.   cm.
    Includes bibliographical references and index.
    ISBN 0-201-30879-7
    1. C++ (Computer program language)   2. Data structures (Computer science)   3. Standard template library.   I. Title.
QA76.73.C15B8   1998
005.13′3—DC21   97-8477
                                                                    CIP
                                                                    AC

Cover image © Jose Ortega / SIS

Access the latest information about Addison-Wesley titles from our World Wide Web site at http://www.awl.com/cseng

1 2 3 4 5 6 7 8 9 10—MA—01 00 99 98 97

PREFACE

For the past several years, a joint committee of ANSI and ISO (the American National Standards Institute and the International Standards Organization) has been working to develop a formal definition of the C++ programming language. Although at the time of this writing the final document has not yet been approved, the major features of the standard have been disseminated and discussed, and compiler vendors are starting to market products that match the standard.

The Standard Template Library (STL)

One of the largest and most significant changes to have come out of this process is the creation of the *Standard Template Library*, or STL. The intent of the STL is to provide a set of container classes that are both efficient and functional. The presence of such a library will simplify the creation of complex programs, and because the library is standard the resulting programs ultimately will have a high degree of portability.

The design of the Standard Template Library (STL) is the result of many years of research conducted by Alexander Stepanov and Meng Lee of Hewlett-Packard, and David Musser of Rensselaer Polytechnic Institute. STL development drew inspiration both from previous object-oriented libraries and the creators' many years of experience in functional and imperative programming languages such as Scheme and Ada.

In the past decade there have been many different collection classes described in the literature, both as commercial products and as containers developed in conjuction with textbooks. An example of the latter is the set of C++ classes I designed in conjuction with my own earlier textbook on data structures. One of the most interesting aspects of the STL is the way it radically departs in structure from almost all earlier libraries. Because C++ is an object-oriented language, these earlier libraries, such as my own, have tended to rely heavily on object-oriented techniques, such as inheritance. The STL, in contrast, uses almost no inheritance. In many ways, in fact, the STL is almost anti-object-oriented.

To see this non-object-oriented perspective, consider that object-oriented programming holds *encapsulation* as a primary ideal. A well-designed object will try to encapsulate all the state and behavior necessary to perform the task for which it is designed, and, at the same time, hide as many of the internal implementation details as possible. In almost all previous object-oriented container class libraries, such as my own, this philosophical approach was manifested by collection classes with exceedingly rich functionality and, consequently, with large interfaces and complex implementations.

The designers of STL moved in an entirely different direction. The behaviors provided in their standard components are minimal, almost spartan. Instead, each component is designed to operate in conjunction with a rich collection of *generic algorithms*, also provided. These generic algorithms are independent of the containers and can therefore operate with many different container types.

By separating the functionality of the generic algorithms from the container classes themselves, the STL realizes a great savings in size, in both the library and the generated code. Instead of duplication of algorithms in each of the dozen or so different container classes, a single definition of a library function can be used with any container. Furthermore, the definition of these functions is so general that they can be used with ordinary C-style arrays and pointers, as well as with other data types.

AN EXAMPLE

An example will illustrate some of the basic features of the standard template library. A generic algorithm, named find, finds the first occurrence of a given value in a collection. An *iterator* is a pointer-like object in the standard library, used to denote a specific value in a collection. A pair of iterators are used to mark the beginning and end of a structure. The find algorithm takes such an iterator pair and searches for the first occurrence of a specific value. It is defined as follows:

```
template<class InputIterator, class T >
InputIterator
    find (InputIterator first, InputIterator last, T& value)
{
    while (first != last && *first != value)
        ++first;
    return first;
}
```

The algorithm will work with any type of structure, even regular C-style arrays. To find the location of the first 7 value in an array of integers, for example, the user executes the following:

```
int data[100];
    .
    .
    .
int * where;
where = find(data, data+100, 7);
```

However, finding the first value in any of the standard containers, such as a list, is hardly more difficult:

```
list<int> aList;
    .
    .
    .
list<int>::iterator where;
where = find(aList.begin(), aList.end(), 7);
```

The key idea is developing a set of container classes that have simple and standard interfaces, and creating a set of generic algorithms that can be used not only with these containers, but with ordinary C++ arrays as well as with containers of a programmer's own development. All this despite the differences in the internal representation of the different collections.

Differences from my Earlier Book

As I noted already, only a few years ago I wrote an earlier book, entitled *Classic Data Structures in C++*, that explored the structure and implementation of a wide variety of data structures in the C++ programming language. Although not technically obsolete, the presence of the standard template library now requires that I update that earlier work. Using the STL as a vehicle has many distinct advantages:

▲ It gets authors out of the software support business. Like most authors of data structures textbooks, in my previous textbook I developed an entirely new set of container classes. About once or twice a month I would get requests asking, "Have you ported your classes to the FrozelBrod-2000?", where the reference was usually to a machine or operating system I had never encountered. Because the STL is a standard, it will be up to the compiler vendors to provide support.

▲ Because the STL is standard, it gives the book a greater degree of platform independence.

▲ Finally, because students are learning a standard library, they can carry their knowledge about the data structures to later classes, even if they use different platforms.

Readers familiar with my earlier book will note many similarities, as well as a multitude of differences. Although the major topics have remained the same (with some slight changes in ordering), the implementations have been totally changed. More importantly, because the data structures are assumed to exist in the programming environment from the start, the presence of the STL permits within each chapter a different order of presentation of the material. Rather than first going through the implementation at the introduction of each new data structure, as was done by my earlier book and by almost all similar data structures textbooks, I now begin by describing a typical use of the data structure. Next, I typically overview all the operations of the data structure, and lastly present an implementation. The implementations are in most cases simplified from the standard library versions.

The increased emphasis on the use of standard components and decreased emphasis on implementation represents an important shift in perspective, and is indicative of the maturation of the field of computer science. Many authors have predicted that in the future most programs will be constructed by piecing together off-the-shelf components, and the percentage of programs that are developed entirely from scratch will diminish considerably. Therefore, although it may be important for students to know how to construct a linked list, it will be much more important to know how to use the list container in the standard library.

Preface to "Classic Data Structures" Book

A programming language is usually envisioned merely as a notational tool to be used in the description of computer programs. In his 1979 lecture given upon the receipt of the annual Association for Computing Machinery Alan Turing Award, the computer scientist Kenneth E. Iverson[1] discussed computer languages in a talk entitled "Notation as a Tool of Thought." I enjoyed the title (as well as the paper), because I have always held to the idea that computer languages are not simply a mechanism of description, but also a vehicle of conception, cogitation, and analysis.

The field of computer science exists because there are problems that, for one reason or another, are best addressed using the mechanism of an electronic computer. A few of the reasons for using computers include the necessity of speed (the reason computers are used in the electronic ignition of your automobile), accuracy (the reason computers are used in bookkeeping or in the generation of mathematical tables), ease of adaptability (the reason why computers are used to create spreadsheets and wordprocessors), environment conditions (the reason why computers are used on unmanned space probes), and the quantity of data involved (the reason why computers are used in graphics and in large simulations, such as weather models), among others. But in each case, problems arise out of *human* experience. Problems are originated, conceived, analyzed, and developed in the way that human beings deal with problems. This is often a complex combination of intuition, pattern matching, guesswork, heuristics, sweat, and good luck.

An electronic computer, on the other hand, is a true *idiot savant*. It is a machine capable of doing only very simple things, but able to do them quickly. To be processed using such a machine, problem solutions must be

---

1. Kenneth E. Iverson, "Notation as a Tool of Thought," reprinted in [Aschenhurst 87].

expressed in terms the machine can understand — a combination of simple logical, arithmetic, and symbolic instructions.

Thus, a major problem in computer science is to bridge the gap between *problems*, which are developed in characteristically human terms, and solutions in the form of *programs* that can be executed by a computer. The mechanism we use to bridge this chasm is the computer language, and, more specifically, the creation of high-level tools expressed in that computer language.

The first computers, developed in the 1940s and early 1950s, required programmers to work directly in the basic machine code of the device. Thus, the programmer was responsible for making the transition from problem to program. Usually far more time was spent on trivial coding details — such as remembering how certain registers were being used or what values were associated with specific memory locations — than was spent actually thinking about the problem to be solved.

In response to the frustrations generated by the difficulty of programming, high-level languages, beginning with Fortran, Cobol, and Algol-60, were developed in the late 1950s and early 1960s to try to free the computer user from some of the tedium involved in coding computer programs. The key insight here was that the computer itself was capable — indeed more capable than the human programmer — of performing many of the bookkeeping tasks involved in coding computer programs. Using high-level languages, programmers could be less concerned with *how* a specific task was to be accomplished and more concerned with *what* task was to be performed. The computer itself could perform a translation from the high-level language to machine language, and then execute the machine language program.

Since then, the development of computer languages has been largely driven by the competing goals of creating language features that are more expressive, in which complex ideas can be more easily and correctly described, and creating language features that can be easily and efficiently translated into forms the computer itself can understand. The goal of expressiveness is moving the language toward the human side of the bridge, while the emphasis on efficient translation is moving the language toward the computer side of the bridge.

A recent development in programming language design has been the concept of object-oriented programming. I fully believe that object-oriented programming is popular because the metaphor on which it is based — a universe of interacting but largely autonomous objects — is similar to the way people view the real world. In this way, programming in an object-oriented language is closer to the human experience side of the bridge, and programmers can bring to bear real-world experience in the solution of software problems (something not always possible with other programming paradigms). The C++ language is by far the most popular object-oriented language developed to date.

In addition to more closely matching a common way of viewing problems, object-oriented programming also provides a number of mechanisms for the reuse of existing software components. We are beginning to realize the possibility that in the future a program will not be laboriously hand crafted from the first line to the last, but will instead be developed largely out of off-the-shelf standard components. Software reuse is emphasized, and object-oriented concepts are used, throughout this book.

Because the goals of ease of use and efficient translation are almost necessarily antithetical, programming languages almost always represent a technical compromise. The C++ language is no exception. It is often criticized as being large and complex, and for forcing programmers to work at a low level of abstraction (closer to the machine side than to the human side of the abstraction bridge). The language is indeed large, but the features of the language are all useful in solving common problems. An understanding of the problems a language feature is used to solve is thus a requirement in learning how to make effective use of the language. As for working at too low a level of abstraction, here, too, the criticism is misplaced. It is true that the C++ language *permits* the programmer to work at a very low level of abstraction. But the C++ language is preeminently a *tool-building* language. By developing a repertoire of useful and reusable abstractions, programmers can raise the level of abstraction in their problem solutions. This book is foremost about the development of useful programming abstractions.

Background Assumed

The primary intent of this book is not to teach C++. I do not, however, assume that the student will have had prior experience with the language before embarking into the material presented here. It is sufficient for the student to have had exposure to concepts such as statements, expressions, and functions in some language, such as C or Pascal. At Oregon State University, where this book was developed, students will have started to learn C, but will not even have encountered arrays or structures before they reach the point where this book picks up.

Having said that prior C++ experience is not required, it is my sincere hope that having studied the material in the book the student will, by the end, be reasonably proficient in the language. So, somewhere along the line I assume the student will be learning about programming in C++. However, for our purposes the acquisition of this skill is secondary to the development of an understanding of the process of solving problems on the computer, and in particular to an approach to problem solving that emphasizes the creation and utilization of reusable software tools, use of good software engineering principles (including object-oriented programming techniques), a knowledge of common and classic data structures, and a basic understanding of the principles involved in comparisons and analysis of algorithms.

In line with this philosophy, I do not feel obligated to present all the arcane details of the language (and C++ is a language *rich* in arcane details). My exposition will flow in a more narrative and less encyclopedic fashion, and I introduce features of the language as they are important to the problems at hand. By doing so, the reader will encounter repeatedly the most important and frequently used aspects of the language. In an encyclopedic approach, the reader is often hard pressed to distinguish what is important from what is incidental. On the other hand, it is frequently useful to convey at times additional information that does not easily fit into the narrative being developed. In these cases I have usually resorted to placing this information as boxed text. These boxes can almost always be ignored on first reading, and I would encourage students to do so. On subsequent readings, though, they will enrich and reinforce the students grasp of the material.

Thus, the goals of this book, in roughly decreasing order of importance, are:

▲ Introduce the reader to the classic data structures that are found in almost all computer programs.

▲ Instruct the reader in the use of analysis techniques with which to evaluate algorithms.

▲ Provide examples of modern software engineering principles and techniques, including object-oriented programming.

▲ Introduce the proper use of various features of the C++ programming language.

Outline of Presentation

This book is divided into three major parts, plus appendices. In Part 1 I explore basic material that is fundamental to the understanding of data structures. Instructors can move more slowly or quickly through this material, depending upon the student's background.

In Part 2 I explore the data structures that are provided as basic components in the standard template library. The instructor should note that although each chapter is obstensibly about a different data structure, many of the features of the C++ programming language are also introduced during the course of various discussions. These should be noted carefully to ensure no feature is omitted that will be needed later in the course.

Not all classic data structures are represented by the standard template library. So, in Part 3 I describe some of the more notable data structures that are not represented, but that can be easily constructed using the tools provided by the standard library.

Obtaining Source Code

Source code for the data structures and applications described in this book, as well as overhead slides and other associated material, can be obtained through the Internet. An FTP site is found at ftp://ftp.cs.orst.edu/pub/budd/. Items can also be accessed through my personal Web page at http://www.cs.orst.edu/~budd/. The author can be reached by electronic mail at budd@cs.orst.edu.

Acknowledgments

More people than I can possibly name or remember have in the past several years provided comments on my original data structures book. Many of their suggestions have found their way into the present work. Early versions of the manuscript for this book were read by Chris Nevison (Colgate University), Robert Cartwright (Rice University), Frederick Harris, Jr. (University of Nevada) and George Stockman (Michigan State University). Their reviews greatly improved the quality of the book. David Teague from Western Carolina University tested portions of the manuscript in his class, and provided many invaluable suggestions for improvement. Finally, invaluable advice, support, and direction have been provided by my editors at Addison-Wesley, Lynne Doran Cote and Debbie Lafferty.

ftp://ftp.cs.orst.edu/pub/budd/stl/sources

/ReadMe.html

CONTENTS

## Part I

FUNDAMENTAL TOOLS

## Chapter 1

Fundamentals

1.1 THE STUDY OF DATA STRUCTURES

Almost all nontrivial computer programs involve the manipulation of *collections* of quantities. A few techniques for the manipulation of collections have proven, over the years, to be so natural and powerful that they have come to be regarded as classic mechanisms. An appreciation of the variety and use of these containers is now considered to be fundamental to the understanding of computer programming. Examples of these classic containers include the linked list, the binary tree, and the hash table. The purpose of this book is to introduce these and other mechanisms to the student in the context of the programming language C++.

An example problem illustrates the need and the utility of these classic container abstractions. A common tool in the analysis of literary texts is the development of a *concordance*. A concordance is similar to an index, only instead of cross-referencing ideas, it categorizes the individual words that appear in a document. Each separate word is indexed, along with the line (or lines) on which the word appears. In this fashion researchers can, for example, document changes in the use of language within a single document, or compare the use of words in two different documents.

To build a concordance, the input text is scanned line by line. Each line is read as a single *string*–an array of characters. We will examine the `string` datatype in Chapter 7. The string is first processed to remove irrelevant characteristics, such as capital letters and punctuation. To find the individual elements, the string is broken into a *list* of words. The `list` data type, introduced in Chapter 9, is used when a collection of values is of indeterminate size and accessed sequentially.

To build the concordance database, we need a structure that is *indexed*. Indexed containers generally come in two varieties. If the index elements are integer values from zero to some upper limit, then a `vector` data type (Chapter 8) can be used. If, on the other hand, the index elements are some other data type, then a `map` (Chapter 16) is a more natural data representation. In the case of a concordance, the index value represents a word in the document, while the element being associated with the index represents the lines on which the word appears. Thus, the `map` is a natural choice for holding the concordance values.

Any particular word might appear on many lines. Indeed, discovering the lines on which a word appears is one of the primary reasons for creating a concordance. Thus, the value associated with any word (that is, any key) is itself a collection. The characteristics of this collection are that it is indeterminate in size (we cannot predict in advance how large the collection will be) and every element should be represented only once (we do not care if the same word appears multiple times on one line). These features are characteristic of the `set` data type, described in Chapter 12.

Thus, our analysis concludes that a concordance can best be implemented using a `map`, indexed by `string` values, that for each word holds a `set` of integer values that represent the lines on which the word appears.

1.1.1   The STL

In the past several years, the programming language C++ has undergone a significant transformation, as part of the process of producing a standard definition of the language. Part of this standardization process has been the creation of a standard library of data structures, commonly known as the *Standard Template Library*, or STL. Because the STL is defined as part of the C++ language definition, programs that use the STL should enjoy a high degree of portability, since any compiler that claims to support "standard C++" will have to provide an implementation of the STL.

The STL provides most of the classic data structures as basic abstractions, so the creation of even quite complex programs is relatively easy. An example is the concordance program just described, which is developed using the STL containers in Section 16.2.

1.2   LANGUAGE FUNDAMENTALS

In the remainder of this chapter we will review those features of the C++ programming language used in this text. Our discussion is not comprehensive, and should not be considered a complete introduction to the language. Rather, the intent is to simply remind readers of those portions of the language that they will encounter in subsequent example programs, and should already have seen in their earlier studies.

1.2.1   Comments

A *comment* is a section of text intended to document a portion of a program. Comments are ignored by the language processor, and hence are used purely as a documentation aid for the reader. A comment is formed by a pair of slash symbols. The comment extends to the end of the line on which the symbols appear. In order to improve readability, comments will be displayed in an italic font in this book.

// this is an example comment

An alternative style of comment is written as a matched set of beginning and ending symbols, /* ... */. The text between the symbols can be arbitrarily long, even spanning several lines:

```
/*
    this is a block of comment text
    that spans several lines
*/
```

Comments cannot be nested.

1.2.2   Constants

C++ supports several different types of constant values:

- ▲ *integer* constants: quantities such as 2, or -34573
- ▲ *octal* or *hexadecimal* constants: 07, 042, 0XFF, 0X42
- ▲ *character* constants: 'a', '\n'
- ▲ *floating-point* constants: 3.14159, $-2.4e17$
- ▲ *string literals*: "abc", "type your name:\n"

The suffixes U or L can be added to integer constants to indicate unsigned or long values, respectively. Integer values are interpreted as octal if they begin with a zero and the next character is a 1 through 7, and interpreted as hexadecimal if they begin with a zero and the following character is an X. The letters A through F are used for the hexadecimal "digits" 10 through 15.

Character constants represent single character values. Several "characters" that would otherwise be unprintable are represented by a backslash followed by an identifying character. The most common is the character '\n', which represents a newline character.

A string literal is actually a value of type "array of char," and is most often then implicitly converted into a character pointer (see Section 1.2.6). However, conversion operations also make it easy to convert a string literal into a value of type string (Chapter 7).

1.2.3   Basic Data Types and Declaration Statements

Fundamentally, programming in C++ involves the manipulation of *variables*. A variable is a quantity that has a *name*, a *type*, and a *value*. The name and the type are specified by the programmer, and are known when the program is compiled. The type specifies, among other things, the range of values the variable may hold.

Variables are defined using a *declaration statement*. This statement provides the type of the variable, followed by a list of names. A typical declaration statement is as follows:

```
int a, b, c; // declare three integer variables
```

Declarations can be combined with *initialization*, which provides the value the variable will hold when it is first created; it may subsequently be reassigned.

```
double pi = 3.1415926;
```

The fundamental data types are integers (`int`), floating-point values (`float` and `double`), and characters (`char`). Integers represent the signed natural numbers, such as 0, 1, or −3. On a computer these will always have a finite range. For example, on a 32-bit machine an integer can hold values between −2147483647 and 2147483648. Floating-point values represent an approximation to real numbers; again, on a computer these always have a fixed precision and range. Characters represent an abstraction of the printable characters, but are actually represented internally as small integer values. Most often characters are maintained as eight-bit quantities, but sixteen-bit character values have been proposed for inclusion in the C++ language, in order to represent both the Roman alphabet as well as non-Roman characters, such as Chinese.

The basic data types can be declared with modifiers. The most important modifiers are `signed`, `unsigned`, `long`, and `short`. An unsigned value (for example, `unsigned int`) is restricted to holding only non-negative values, while a signed value can hold both positive and negative quantities. A `long` or `short` value may have a different representation, depending upon the compiler and machine on which the program is executed. For example, on some machines an integer may represent a 32-bit quantity, while a `short int` may represent only a 16-bit quantity.

When modifiers are used without reference to a base type, the type `int` is assumed. That is, a declaration such as `unsigned short` is interpreted to mean `unsigned short int`.

Variables declared as `bool` maintain Boolean values, either true or false:

```
bool isSummer = false;
```

Enumerated values can be defined by providing an explicit range of constant values:

```
enum months {January, February, March, April, May, June, July,
    August, September, October, November, December};
```

Enumerated constants can be converted into integers, in which case the integer value will represent the position of the constant in the sequence. Subsequent declarations of variables need not repeat either the enum keyword nor the list of constant values, but only the name of the newly created enumerated type:

```
months workingMonth, vacationMonth;
months summerMonth = August;
```

Variables that are declared outside of any function are called *global*, and are accessible within all subsequent functions. Variables that are declared inside a function are termed *local*, and are available only within the bounds of the function (see Section 1.2.11). Variables can also be declared with even smaller scopes, such as being local to the body of a while loop (Section 1.2.8).

1.2.4   Expressions and Assignment Statements

The C++ language has a rich set of operators for forming expressions; some of these are described in Table 1.1. The most important classes of operators are the arithmetic operators (addition, multiplication, and the like), the relational operators (less than, greater than), and the logical operators (and, or). These can be used in conjunction with assignment statements in order to modify the value held by a variable.

```
double f, c; // Fahrenheit and Celsius temperature

c = 43;
f = (c * 9.0) / 5.0 + 32;
```

The bitwise operators work with integers, and operate bit by bit. Thus the bitwise *and* of 12 and 25 (binary 01100 and 11001, respectively) is 8 (binary 01000), while the bitwise *or* is 29 (binary 11101) and the bitwise *exclusive or* is 21 (binary 10101).

When used with integers, the operators << and >> represent left and right shifts, respectively. Thus, for example, $5 << 3$ is 40, because five is represented in binary as 0101, and this value when shifted left by 3 yields 0101000, or 40. We will see that the shift operators have an entirely different use for input and output.

Binary operators can be combined with assignment statements when the intended effect is simply to modify the target value. That is, a statement such as

```
i += 5;
```

Table 1.1   A few of the legal operators in C++

Unary operations	
Increment, decrement	`i++ ++i i-- --i`
Negation	`-i`
Arithmetic operations	
Addition, subtraction	`a + b a - b`
Multiplication, division	`a * b a / b`
Remainder after division	`a % b`
Bitwise operations	
And	`x & y`
Or	`x	y`
Exclusive-or	`x ^ y`
Bitwise negation	`~i`
Shift operations (also stream I/O)	
Left shift (also stream output)	`a << b`
Right shift (also stream input)	`a >> b`
Relational operations	
Less than	`a < b`
Less than or equal	`a <= b`
Equal	`a == b`
Not equal	`a != b`
Greater than or equal	`a >= b`
Greater than	`a > b`
Logical operations	
And	`x && y`
Or	`x || y`
Logical negation	`!i`
Pointer operations	
Dereference	`* p`
Dereference and access	`p->x`
Subscript	`p[i]`
Miscellaneous operations	
Function call	`f(a,b,c)`
Conditional expression	`c ? a : b`

has the same meaning as the statement

```
i = i + 5;
```

Other short-hand notations are also used in C++. The most common is the idiom

```
i++
```

which has the effect of incrementing the variable `i` by one.

1.2.5 Input and Output

The integer shift symbols $<<$ and $>>$ are given a different meaning when the left argument is a *stream* value; in this case the statements perform an input or an output operation. (When operators are provided with new meanings when used with certain argument types, we say the operators have been *overloaded*.) The most common stream is used to represent the standard output area, called the "console output." This global value is known as `cout`. Thus, output statements will often be written in the following form:

```
cout << "the Fahrenheit equivalent of " << c << " is " << f << endl;
```

A similar global variable, `cin`, is used to capture textual input values. An expression involving the $>>$ operator can be converted into a boolean, which is true if the input is successful, and false if end of input is reached or input does not match the correct type. As a side effect, the value of the right-hand argument is changed to the input value that was read. (A side effect is a change to variable or object by means other than explicit assignment. Because the modification may not be obvious to the unwary reader, side effects are a common source of programming difficulties.)

```
cin >> c; // get a new value of c
cout << "the Fahrenheit equivalent of " << c << " is " << f << endl;
```

The symbol `endl` stands for *end of line*. It is used to terminate a line of output, and results in a carrage return or a line feed. On many systems output is buffered, so that no text is actually printed until an end of line is processed.

1.2.6 Pointer Values

A *pointer* is simply a variable that maintains as value the address of another location in memory. Because memory addresses have a fixed limit, the amount of storage necessary to hold a pointer can be determined at compile time, even if the size or extent of the object to which it will point is not known.

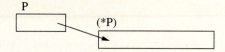

A *null pointer* is a pointer that does not refer to any object. A null pointer can be created by assigning the value zero to a pointer variable; however, the internal representation of a null pointer need not be the same as the integer constant zero.

Four principle mechanisms are used to access the values denoted by a pointer:

▲ A pointer variable can be subscripted. This is useful only if the pointer addresses an array of objects. The subscript index is used to determine the element accessed by the expression.

▲ A pointer can be explicitly *dereferenced* using the unary * operator. If p is a pointer to a value of some type, then *p is the value addressed by the pointer.

▲ A pointer to a structure, or class, can combine pointer dereferencing and member field extraction using the pointer operator. If p is a pointer to a value of a class type that contains a member field x, then p->x is the same as (*p).x.

▲ An addition operator can be used with a pointer as left argument and an integer value as right argument. It is assumed, as with subscripts, that the pointer is referencing an array of values. The expression p+i is the same as the address of the element p[i].

In this book, pointers are most commonly used to reference dynamically allocated memory, which is memory that is not tied to any particular function invocation. We will discuss this topic in more detail in the chapters on data structures.

1.2.7   Conditional Statements

Normally evaluation of a computer program proceeds in a sequential fashion, with each statement being executed after the preceding statement. This sequential order can be altered using if or switch statements. An if statement evaluates an expression, and executes the associated statement only if the expression is true. An optional else part can provide a statement that will be executed only if the expression is false.

```
month aMonth;
  .
  .
  .
if ((aMonth >= June) && (aMonth <= August))
    isSummer = true;
```

```
else
    isSummer = false;
```

Integer or pointer values can also be used as expressions in the conditional portion; an integer is considered true if it is nonzero, while a pointer is considered true if it is non-null.

A `switch` statement can be used to select one alternative out of many. The switch value must be either integer, character, or an enumerated value. Each case is followed by a sequence of statements, terminated by a `break` statement. If the break statement is omitted, control will pass on to the statements associated with the next case label. An optional `default` case can be used to match any value not otherwise matched. If no default clause is provided and the key does not match any case label, then no statements are performed, and execution continues with the next statement after the `switch`.

```
switch (aMonth) {
    case January:
        highTemp = 20;
        lowTemp = 0;
        break;
    case February:
        highTemp = 30;
        lowTemp = 10;
        break;
        .
        .
        .
    case July:
        highTemp = 120;
        lowTemp = 50;
        break;
    default:
        highTemp = 60;
        lowTemp = 20;
};
```

1.2.8   Loops

Loops are used to execute statements repeatedly until a condition is satisfied. The simplest looping statement is the `while` loop, which executes as long as the associated condition is true:

```
c = 0;
while (c <= 100) {
    cout << "Celsius " << c << " is Fahrenheit " <<
        ((9.0 * c) / 5.0 + 32) << endl;
c += 10;
}
```

As we have noted, the stream operator >> returns a value that can be converted into a boolean. This is often used as a test on a loop or conditional. The following loop, for example, will read integer values from the standard input until end-of-input is signaled, then print the sum of the values that were read:

```
int sum = 0;
int value;
while (cin >> value) {
    sum += value;
    }
cout << "sum is " << sum << endl;
```

Many loops are written as `for` statements. The `for` loop combines in one statement the tasks of initialization, test for termination, and update, thus making the loop easier to read:

```
for (c = 0; c <= 100; c += 10) {
    cout << "Celsius " << c << " is Fahrenheit " <<
        ((9.0 * c) / 5.0 + 32) << endl;
    }
```

When a new variable is needed for a loop, the declaration of the variable can be combined with the initialization portion of the `for` statement:

```
for (int i = 0; i < 12; i++) {
    cout << "i: " << i << " i squared " << i*i << endl;
}
```

Variables can also be declared within the body of a loop. Such variables are valid only while the loop is executing, and are not accessible once the loop has terminated:

```
for (int i = 0; i < 12; i++) {
    int isquare = i * i;
    cout << "i: " << i << " i squared " << isquare << endl;
}
```

1.2.9   Arrays

An *array* is a fixed-size collection of similarly typed values. Most commonly, the size of the array is specified when the value is declared. Individual elements of the array are accessed using a subscript operation. Legal subscript values range from zero to one less than the size of the array. However, the language does not check subscript index values to ensure they are legal, and out-of-range subscript expressions are a common source of programming errors.

```
    // declare an array of twelve integer variables
int Temperatures[12];
    // now assign them all values
Temperatures[0] = 0;
Temperatures[1] = 10;
Temperatures[2] = Temperatures[1] + 15;
    .
    .
    .
```

Arrays of higher dimension can be created when given an extent along each axis. The following declares a two-dimensional array of double precision values, with ten rows and twenty columns in each row:

```
double matrix[10][20];
```

A one-dimensional array is sometimes called a *vector*, although this term is usually reserved for the vector data abstraction in the standard library (Chapter 8). A two-dimensional array is often described as a *matrix*.

In C++ there is a close relationship between arrays and pointer values, and the two can often be used interchangeably. For example, as we noted in Section 1.2.6, array subscripts can be used with pointer values.

When used as global variables, arrays can also be initialized by specifying a set of values. (The datatype string will be introduced in Chapter 7.)

```
string MonthNames[12] = {"January", "February", "March",
    "April", "May", "June", "July", "August",
    "September", "October", "November", "December" };
```

Arrays can also be allocated dynamically, in which case the size of the array can be determined at run time, rather than at compile time:

```
char * buffer;
buffer = new char[maxSize];
```

When used as an argument value, an array need not declare a fixed size. For example, the following procedure takes as argument an array of integer values and an integer representing the number of elements held in the array, and computes the sum of the elements:

```
int arraySum (int values[ ], int n)
    // compute sum of array values[0] .. values[n-1]
{
    int result = 0;
    for (int i = 0; i < n; i++) {
        result += values[i]
        }
    return result;
    }
```

1.2.10   Structures

A *structure* is a collection of *fields*. Each field represents a data value, and the individual fields need not have the same type. A structure is therefore used to bring together individual data values that are associated with a common purpose.

```
struct person {
    string name;
    int age;
    enum {male, female} sex;
};
```

The individual fields of a structure are accessed using a field access dot. That is, if `employee` is a variable of type `person`, then the construct `employee.name` refers to the field `name` in the employee structure.

We will make little use of structures in this text, because most of what is accomplished using structures can be performed using the more general *class* mechanism, which will be described in detail in Chapter 2.

1.2.11   Functions

A *function* encapsulates a set of actions, so that later we can refer to the entire sequence by means of a single name. An example might be a function to convert a Celsius temperature into its Fahrenheit equivalent:

```
int Fahrenheit(int cTemp)
{
    return (cTemp * 9.0) / 5.0 + 32;
}
```

A *function header* has a return type, a name, and a list of arguments and types (possibly empty). The *function body* describes the sequence of statements that will be executed when the function is *invoked*. Within the body of a function, a `return` statement can be used to halt execution and return a value to the caller.

The return type for a function can be declared as `void`, which indicates the function does not return any value, and is executed merely for some other effect (such as printing a value). Such a function is often termed a *procedure*. A `return` statement inside a function declared as `void` need not provide a returning value. Indeed, `void` functions need not have any `return` statement whatsoever, as execution of the function will terminate when execution of the function body finishes the final statement.

Functions can be invoked from any location in which the function name is known. For example, the loop that produced a table of temperature equivalences could now be written as:

```
for (c = 0; c <= 100; c += 10) {
    cout << "Celsius " << c << " is Fahrenheit " <<
        Fahrenheit(c) << endl;
}
```

Functions help break complex sequences of actions into smaller parts, and are an invaluable aid in controlling the complexity of programs. We will make extensive use of functions throughout this book.

A function can be declared without providing a function body, using a function *prototype*. The prototype looks like a function header, but in addition to omitting the function body, a prototype need not specify the names of the argument values. The function must eventually be matched with a definition, but the definition may appear later in the program or even in a different file.

```
// prototype for Fahrenheit–definition occurs later
int Fahrenheit (int);
```

LOCAL VARIABLES

Variables declared within a function provide a local computing environment that is needed only for a short period of time while the function is executing. Such variables become active when the function first begins execution, and disappear when the function finishes execution. Function execution exhibits a strict *stack-like* behavior; if function A invokes function B, function B must terminate before function A can resume. This feature allows for a very efficient mechanism for handling local variables; each time a function begins execution a new section of memory is set aside on the *run-time stack*.

For example, suppose function A invokes function B, which in turn invokes function C. During the time C is executing, the run-time stack will appear as follows:

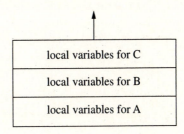

We will shortly encounter a type of function termed *recursive*. Recursive functions have the property that they will, in certain circumstances, invoke *themselves* in a function call. An important fact to remember regarding recursive functions is that each time the function is invoked, a *new* block of memory is set aside for local variables. For example, suppose procedure B has recursively called itself before invoking procedure C; the run-time stack would appear as follows:

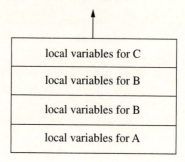

Note how there are two distinct sets of local variables for the procedure B. We will discuss recursive procedures again in more detail in a later chapter.

PARAMETER PASSING

Arguments to functions can be passed either by value or by reference. When an argument is passed by value, a copy of the argument is produced, and the associated parameter is essentially the same as a local variable for the procedure. That is, changes to the parameter variable will have no effect on the original argument value.

The alternative, pass by reference, is indicated by the presence of an ampersand in the argument list. When arguments are passed by reference, the parameter variable is essentially an *alias* for the argument value. Thus, changes in the parameter also alter the original argument.

```
void updater (int & x)
{
    // the following changes
    // both the local variable x
    // and the argument value as well

    x = x + 3;
}
```

Despite the seeming danger, pass by reference is frequently used when arguments are large structures, such as those we will encounter in the next chapter. In these cases, pass by reference is more efficient, because the alternative (pass by value) would duplicate the entire structure.

1.2.12   The Function main

A program must always include a function named main, the starting location for execution. The return type for main is an integer value, which describes the status of execution. By convention a return value of zero indicates successful completion, while a nonzero value can be used to indicate some sort of error during execution. How a nonzero status value is interpreted is inherently platform dependent, and will not be discussed further in this book.

```cpp
# include <iostream>

int main() {
    // program to write table of squares
    cout << "Table of Squares\n";

    for (int i = 0; i < 12; i++) {
        cout << "i: " << i << " i squared " << i*i << endl;
    }
    return 0;
}
```

1.2.13   Include Files

Many features used by C++ programs are not provided as part of the language, per se, but as part of the standard run-time library. These often require the programmer to provide an `include` directive, such as the one shown in the preceding section. Note that no semicolon appears after an include directive. Table 1.2 lists some of the more common include directives. (Some compilers may use slightly different names.) For example, an include statement for `iostream` must appear in any program that uses the stream I/O package. Earlier versions of the C++ language required include files to end with a `.h` extension. Although this requirement has now been removed, many such examples still persist.

1.2.14   Binding Times

The development of a working computer program, and the execution of the resulting program, is a process that extends over a considerable period of time. Within this larger process are several important events, or periods of time when specific actions take place. Some of the terms used to describe these different times, and the actions that occur, include:

- ▲ *Programming time.* This is the period when the programmer is thinking about how to go about solving the problem at hand, but has not yet written a complete solution. The programmer is free to experiment with many different approaches, alternative data structures, and so on. We say that very little has yet been *bound* during this period.

Table 1.2   Common include directives

Purpose	Name
Stream input/output	`iostream`
Assertion package	`assert.h`
Math functions	`math.h`
Complex numbers	`complex`
Boolean values	`bool.h`
Generic algorithms	`algorithm`
The `vector` abstraction	`vector`
The `list` abstraction	`list`
The `set` abstraction	`set`
The `map` abstraction	`map`

▲ *Compile time.* This occurs when the programmer has selected an approach, written the program, and submitted it to the compiler. By this time, features such as the use of different data structures have been bound, although the exact values those data structures will maintain have, of course, not yet been determined.

▲ *Link time.* This is an intermediate step that occurs after all the portions of a program have been compiled, but before they can be executed. During link time, the identities of functions named in function call statements are matched to the associated function bodies. Note that this is true only for ordinary functions; many method invocations (a topic discussed in more detail in Chapter 2) delay binding until run time.

▲ *Run time–initialization.* This is the time when a program is prepared for execution. Space for global variables is set aside, and global initializations are performed. The `main` procedure is then started.

▲ *Run time–procedure invocation.* Prior to beginning the execution of any procedure, space for local variables is created. This space will be released when the procedure exits.

▲ *Run time–statement execution.* As each statement is executed, it produces a change in the computing environment. The most obvious example is an assignment statement, which can modify the value of a variable. But all statements, even declaration statements, produce some change in either data values or flow of control.

A major reason for differentiating these different times is to better characterize when a name is tied to a specific characteristic (a type or a value).

These separate periods are often termed *binding times*. Thus, we say, for example, that an ordinary function name is bound to the function body at link time, while the execution of a member function (to be introduced in Chapter 2) delays binding to a function body until statement execution time.

One important difference between C++ and many other programming languages involves declaration statements. In C++, declaration statements are executed as a statement, and thus have their effect at statement execution time. In many languages the initialization of a declaration statement takes place at procedure invocation time.

1.3   CHAPTER SUMMARY

Key Concepts

- Comments
- Constants
- Basic data types
- Declaration statements
- Expressions and assignment
- Pointer values
- Conditional statements
- Loops
- Array values
- Functions
- Global and local variables
- Binding times
  - Programming time
  - Compile time
  - Link time
  - Run time

A comment is a section of text intended to document a portion of a program.

There are various different types of constants possible in C++ programs, including integers, octal integers, characters, floating-point values, and string literals.

Values in C++ programs are held in variables, which are created using declaration statements. The declaration statement provides the type associated with a variable, and optionally an initial value. The basic data types are `integer`, `char`, `double`, and `float`. These can be augmented using the modifiers `long`, `short`, `signed`, and `unsigned`. The `bool` data type holds a Boolean value. Enumerated values can be created for small collections of discrete elements.

A variable declared outside the scope of any function is termed global, and is available for use inside of any later function. Variables declared inside of functions are called local. Local variables come into existence when the function in which they are declared begins execution, and go out of existence when the function terminates.

Assignment statements are used to modify the value held by a variable. A rich set of unary and binary operators can be used to form expressions.

A pointer is a variable that stores the address of another location in memory.

Conditional statements, switch statements, and loops can be used to change the normally sequential flow of execution in a program.

An array is a fixed-size collection of values of the same type. Individual elements of an array are accessed using a subscripting operator.

Functions encapsulate a sequence of statements, providing them with a name and a list of argument values. Functions can then be invoked using a function call operator, which has the effect of transferring control to the associated function body. Functions execute in a strict stack-like fashion, with the most recently invoked function returning before earlier functions can complete.

Further Reading

C++ is an exceedingly rich language, and we have only described the most fundamental features. Any number of language reference manuals will explain the remaining elements of C++ in more detail; two of the best known are by Stroustrup [Stroustrup 91] (the developer of C++), and by Lippman [Lippman 91]. Because these are primarily intended as reference manuals, however, they are difficult to use as tools in learning the language. A more detailed reference manual by Stroustrup is known as the ARM (for *annotated reference manual*); this provides background explanations and motivation for many of the elements found in the language [Ellis 90]. A further history of the development of C++ has also been provided by the designer [Stroustrup 94].

A slightly more gentle introduction to C++ is provided by Eckel [Eckel 95]. An explanation of C++ for students already knowledgeable in Pascal can be found in either the book by Pohl [Pohl 91] or Horstmann [Horstmann 96]. Savitch [Savitch 96] provides a good introduction to problem solving in the context of the C++ language.

Study Questions & Exercises

Study Questions

1. Why is the study of data structures important?

2. What do the letters STL represent? What is the STL?

3. Write a comment in each of the two forms recognized by C++.

4. Write the value 42 as an integer constant, an octal constant, and a hexadecimal constant.

5. What is the difference between 'a' and "a" ?

6. What sort of values can be maintained in a variable of type unsigned short ?

7. What is a global variable? What is a local variable?

8. What is the effect of the binary $*=$ operator?

9. What is a null pointer?

10. What sort of values can be used as a key with a switch statement?

11. How many times will this loop execute?

```
for (int i = 0; i < 15; i++)
    :
    :
```

12. What are the valid subscript indices for an array declared in the following fashion?

```
int a[8];
```

13. In the following, identify the function header, the return type, the function name, the arguments, an argument name, an argument type, and the function body.

```
int min (int a, int b)
{
    if (a < b)
        return a;
    return b;
}
```

14. Assume function A has called function B, which in turn has called function C. Function C has then returned, and function B has subsequently called function D. Draw a picture of the run-time stack as it would appear when executing function D.

15. What is a binding time? What events occur at various binding times?

Exercises

1. What value is represented by the following octal or hexadecimal constants?
   a. 042
   b. 0X42
   c. 0XFF
   d. 0XCAB

2. Write a declaration statement for each of these:
   a. Three double precision floating-point variables
   b. An array of 7 character values
   c. An enumerated data type representing the days of the week
   d. Two variables that can hold values from the preceding enumerated data type

3. Write a statement that will convert a Fahrenheit value, held in the variable named f, into the corresponding Celsius value, and assign the result to the variable named c.

4. Write a function that will take three double precision values, and return their average.

5. What values will be printed by the statements shown below if the variable x is initially 1, initially 2, initially 3, or initially 4?

```
switch (x) {
    case 1:
        x++;
        break;
    case 2:
        x = 7;
    case 3:
        --x;
        break;
}
cout << "x is " << x << endl;
```

6. Describe how many times each of these loops will execute, and what values the loop variable will assume:
   a. `for (int i = 0; i < 15; i++)`

   b. `for (int i = 0; i < 15; i += 3)`

   c. `for (int i = 1; i < 15; i = i << 1)`

   d. `for (int i = 27; i > 0; i = i / 2)`

7. Write a function that will take as argument an array of double precision values, and an integer representing the length of the array, and return the average of the values.

8. For an array of n data values named d, the *variance* is defined to be the sum of the squares of the differences of each element from the average of d, divided by the quantity $n - 1$:

$$VARIANCE = \frac{\sum_{i=0}^{n-1} (d_i - \text{average}(d))^2}{n - 1}$$

Write a procedure that will take as argument an array of double precision values and an integer representing the size of the array, and return the variance.

9. Write a program that will output a table of n, n^2, and n^3, for values of n ranging from zero to 100.

Chapter

2

Classes and Object-Oriented Programming

Chapter Overview

The style of programming encouraged by the language C++, called *object-oriented* programming, proceeds by identifying categories of values and their associated behavior. The *class* is the primary mechanism for creating software components in C++. In this chapter we will introduce the basic features of the class mechanism, and illustrate object-oriented programming, by means of an extended example program.

Features of the C++ language that will be introduced during the development of the example program include constructors, overloaded function names, operators, stream input and output, member functions, prefix and postfix operators, inline function definitions, generic algorithms, message passing expressions, public and private features, pass by value and pass by reference, function objects, accessors, and mutator functions.

The chapter concludes by showing how structuring an application using classes can assist in maintainence and program modification. We do this by altering the developed application from a simulation of a card game into an interactive card game in which the user can take an active part.

Major topics discussed in this chapter include:

▲ The class construct

▲ Member functions, constructors, operators

▲ Making an interactive game

▲ Accessor and mutator functions

2.1   THE CARD GAME *WAR*

The game *WAR* is a simple card game for two players.[1] The 52 cards in a conventional deck are shuffled, and each player draws three cards. The remaining cards are placed in a pile face-down between the two players. Play then proceeds as a series of rounds. During each round both players select one of their three cards, and places it face up in front of them. If the ranks of both cards are the same, then both players retain their cards (setting them aside). Otherwise, the player with the highest ranking card keeps both cards (again, setting them aside). After playing their card, each player draws one card from the deck to replace the card just played. The game ends when the deck is exhausted, and the player with the most cards wins.

We can identify the elements of the game by searching for the nouns in the problem description, while the verbs serve to indicate the actions these elements are expected to perform. The first sentence, for example, describes cards, the deck, and players. Note that we are here interested in identifying the categories of objects, and not the actual objects themselves. There are two players, for example, and 52 cards, yet only one category for player or for card. For each of the three types of object we have identified, we will construct a class with the appropriate behavior.

2.2   THE CLASS CARD

Let us start with an individual card. A card is distinguished by two values, namely a rank and suit. (More sophisticated uses of card might require

---

1. The game presented here is not exactly the traditional version, but should be close enough to be recognizable.

further information; for example, a game in which card values were being displayed in a graphical fashion on an output device might also need to remember whether the card is face up or face down, and what the card looks like.) The only *behavior* we associate with the card in our description of the game is the ability to tell the rank and suit values of the card.

We can use integer values between 1 (Ace) and 13 (King) to represent the rank of a card. For the suit values, we can create an enumerated data type, as follows:

```
enum suits {diamond, club, heart, spade};
```

Using these, a definition for a `Card` class might be written as follows:

```
class Card {
public:
        // constructors
    Card ( );              // initialize a card with default values
    Card (suits, int);     // initialize a card with given values

        // data fields
    int   rank;            // hold rank of card
    suits suit;            // hold suit of card
};
```

Like a structure, a class can have data fields, which are often referred to as *data members* or *instance fields*. In this case, there are two data members, a rank and a suit. The difference between a class and a structure[2] is that a class can, in addition to data fields, have functions associated with the class. These are called *member functions*, or sometimes *methods*. In the case of the `Card` abstraction we have only one type of member function, which is called a *constructor* function.

A constructor is a special type of function that is invoked when an instance of the class is created, as it would be in a declaration statement. The constructor permits the data fields of the object to be initialized, thereby ensuring that all objects begin their existence in a proper state. Constructor functions always have the same name as the class in which they are declared. In the case of `Card` we have two constructor functions, distinguished by the number of arguments they take. The first requires no arguments, and is invoked when we create a simple instance of the class. The second function requires as argument a suit and rank value, and is invoked when the declaration specifically provides these starting values.

---

2. To be precise, this statement should read "the difference between a class in C++ and a structure in a more traditional language, such as C." In C++, both structures and classes can have member functions. The exact distinction between structures and classes in C++ is somewhat technical, and need not concern us here.

Like all functions, member functions must eventually be tied to a function *body*. The function body names both the function and the class in which it is found. The bodies for these two functions could be written as:

```
Card::Card ( )
        // initialize a new Card
        // default value is the ace of spades
{
        rank = 1;
        suit = spade;
}


Card::Card  (suits sv, int rv)
        // initialize a new Card using the argument values
{
        rank = rv;
        suit = sv;
}
```

Both function bodies simply initialize the data fields held by the playing

Constructors

When large structured objects are created, subtle errors may occur if they are not properly initialized. Both failing to initialize and initializing more than once can be a source of difficulty. The mechanism known as a *constructor* helps to eliminate these problems.

A constructor function will be implicitly invoked, without any explicit function call being written by the programmer, when an instance of the class in which the constructor appears is created. Most often this occurs as a result of a declaration statement, although in later chapters we will see how values can also be created using a mechanism called dynamic memory allocation.

As we noted in the section on binding times in the last chapter, this invocation occurs when a declaration statement is "executed." In many other programming languages declarations are all processed at procedure invocation time, while in C++ a declaration is simply another form of state-

ment, and is processed at statement execution time.

The sole purpose of a constructor is to ensure that the object being created is properly initialized. Often this is no more than simply assigning initial values to the instance data fields. However, the function is free to perform any actions that are necessary, and some constructors can become quite complex.

Constructors differ from other functions in a number of respects. The two ways seen in this example are that the constructor name must always match the name of the class in which it is defined, and that a constructor function does not specify a return type. In subsequent chapters we will encounter other unique features of constructors.

A constructor with no arguments is often termed a *default constructor*. Default constructors are used, for example, to initialize elements in an array of values. We will see an example of this in the Deck and Player abstractions.

card. The no-argument constructor initializes the values of the card to default values, in this case the ace of spades.

The `public` keyword identifies the portion of the class declaration containing the features that can be manipulated by other software components, outside the class itself. In the case of the `Card` abstraction, this is the entire interface. We will soon encounter classes for which the interface is more restrictive.

We can test our card abstraction by declaring a few values, and printing them out:

```
void main() {
    Card cardOne;
    Card cardTwo(diamond, 7);

    cout << "Card one\n";
    cout << cardOne.rank << endl;
    cout << "Card two\n";
    cout << cardTwo.rank << endl;
}
```

The result will verify the functionality of the `Card` abstraction, but is somewhat less than ideal. For example, aces, jacks, queens, and kings print out as rank 1, 11, 12, and 13, respectively. Worse, we cannot easily display the suit, because the output operator does not recognize enumerated data types. We can fix this problem by defining an output function for our card abstraction. You will recall from Chapter 1 that the left shift operator, <<, is used to output most C++ values, as in the previous example. Whenever we define a new data abstraction, such as our playing card example, we can give this operator a new meaning when used with our abstraction. We do this simply by defining a function to be associated with the left shift operator and our new data type, thereby overloading this operator with a new meaning. For our playing card abstraction, this could be done as follows:

Overloaded Function Names

A function name that has more than one different implementation, such as the constructor function defined for the `Card` class, is said to be *overloaded*. In C++ all function names can be overloaded. The only requirement imposed by the language is that the different implementations have unique and distinct sets of arguments. This is so the compiler can determine, for any particular function call expression, which function body to match to the function call. This determination is performed by simply finding the function body that matches the arguments being used with the call. In the case of the `Card` constructors, one function has no arguments at all, while the second has two arguments, a suit and an integer representing the rank of the card.

```
ostream & operator << (ostream & out, Card & aCard)
    // output a textual representation of a Card
{
    // first output rank
  switch (aCard.rank) {
      case 1:  out << "Ace";   break;
      case 11: out << "Jack";  break;
      case 12: out << "Queen"; break;
      case 13: out << "King";  break;
      default: // output number
         out << aCard.rank; break;
  }


    // then output suit
  switch (aCard.suit) {
      case diamond: out << " of Diamonds"; break;
      case spade:   out << " of Spades";   break;
      case heart:   out << " of Hearts";   break;
      case club:    out << " of Clubs";    break;
      }
  return out;
}
```

The keyword **operator** tells the compiler that we are providing a new meaning to the binary operator <<. The ampersands in the argument list and the return type indicate *pass-by-reference* parameter passing; this should be used when an argument is a large structure (such as a stream) that is being modified in the given procedure. The alternative, without the ampersand, is called *pass by value* and results in a *copy* of the argument being passed, rather than the original argument itself. Because, in this case, we do not want to create a copy of the output stream, we use pass by reference.

Having defined the output operator for a Card, we can execute a simple program to test the results:

```
void main() {
    Card cardOne;
    Card cardTwo(diamond, 7);

    cout << "Card One:" << cardOne << endl;
    cout << "Card Two:" << cardTwo << endl;
}
```

2.3   THE CLASS DECK

We move on to the abstraction that represents a deck of playing cards. For the deck abstraction we have slightly more interesting behavior, which we can describe as follows:

- ▲ A deck must maintain a collection of cards.
- ▲ The deck must be able to shuffle the cards it holds.
- ▲ The deck must be able to tell the user whether or not it is empty.
- ▲ The user of the deck must be able to draw a card (assuming the deck is nonempty).

These can be captured in a class description as follows:

```
class Deck {
public:
    // constructor
    Deck();                 // initialize a deck of 52 cards

    // operations on a deck
    void shuffle ();    // randomly change order of cards
    bool isEmpty ();    // return true if empty, false if not
    Card draw     ();   // return the next card

protected:
    Card cards[52];     // hold collection of cards
    int  topCard;       // hold index one larger than next available card
};
```

A deck maintains a data area that consists of an array of 52 cards and a single integer variable. By defining these in the `protected` portion of the class description, we ensure that they can be accessed only from within functions associated with the Deck object itself, not from outside the deck. This provides the developer of the deck abstraction with greater assurances concerning how these data values will be used. There are good reasons, in fact, that *all* data fields should be protected, and not public. Later in this chapter we will revisit our `Card` abstraction, and describe how we can make those data fields protected and the benefits of doing so.

You may have wondered why there were two constructors defined for the `Card` abstraction. The declaration of the array in the class `Deck` illustrates one part of the answer. The 52 elements of the array of cards will be initialized, but initialized using the constructor that takes no arguments (what we earlier labeled as the default constructor). Thus, all elements of the array will initially hold the ace of spades. In other situations, as we will see, it is useful to be able to explicitly specify the card value during the construction of a new card, and thus the second constructor form will be employed.

The Deck abstraction itself has a constructor. This constructor will replace the default values being held by the array with the actual playing card values from a normal card deck. The function body associated with the constructor is written as:

```
Deck::Deck ( )
    // initialize a deck by creating all 52 cards
{
    topCard = 0;
    for (int i = 1; i <= 13; i++) {
        Card c1(diamond, i), c2(spade, i), c3(heart, i), c4(club, i);
        cards[topCard++] = c1;
        cards[topCard++] = c2;
        cards[topCard++] = c3;
        cards[topCard++] = c4;
    }
}
```

There are several features to note concerning this function definition. Notice how the declaration of the local variable named i is combined with the loop. Variables declared in this fashion can be used only within the body of the loop, while a variable that is declared outside a loop would be valid throughout the procedure. Each iteration of the loop creates four new cards, a diamond, a spade, a heart, and a club. Because these variables are declared inside the body of the loop, they are local to the loop and a new set of values is created each iteration. On each iteration four different positions in the card array are assigned these new values.

Note the way in which the variable topCard is being used. As we described in the previous chapter, the idiom topCard++ has the effect of incrementing the value of the integer variable topCard by one. Not noted earlier was that the value of this expression is the value held in the variable *prior* to the increment. Using this value in the fashion shown combines the two tasks of specifying the subscript value to be used in the assignment, and incrementing the variable so as to be ready for the next subscript operation.

This idiom is exceedingly common in C and C++ subscript expressions, so readers should spend a few moments to make sure they understand everything that is happening here. The first time the loop is executed, the array elements 0, 1, 2, and 3 will be initialized with the four ace cards. On the second iteration, the elements 4, 5, 6, and 7 will be assigned the two of diamonds, two of spades, two of hearts, and two of clubs. The third iteration will fill the array positions 8, 9, 10, and 11, and so on throughout the entire deck.

We have identified three operations with the Deck abstraction. These are the ability to shuffle the deck, the ability to tell whether or not the deck is empty, and the ability to draw one card from the deck. We will describe the implementation of each of these in turn.

The `shuffle` method uses the first of many *generic algorithms* we will encounter in our later investigations of algorithms and data structures. This generic algorithm routine requires three arguments. The first two represent the beginning and the past-the-end bounds of the array being shuffled, while the third argument will be described shortly. The argument that represents the beginning of the range is simply the start of the array, which we indicate by giving the name of the array. The end of the array can be determined by using an addition operator with a array expression. (See Exercise 12 for an alternative approach that does not use the standard library.)

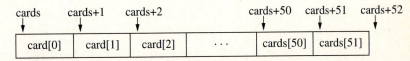

An expression such as `cards+52` is legal when the left argument to the addition is an array and the right argument is an integer. The integer is interpreted as the number of elements in the array to skip in locating the desired address. In this manner the expression, because the array has 52 elements, denotes the first address past the end of the array.

```
randomInteger randomizer; // create a global variable of type randomInteger

void Deck::shuffle ( )
    // randomly shuffle the cards array,
    // using the generic algorithm random_shuffle
{
    random_shuffle (cards, cards+52, randomizer);
}
```

Note the name of the function being defined here. A member function

---

Prefix and Postfix Operators

The operators ++ and −− are most often used, respectively, to increment or decrement an integer value. In addition, they can both be used in either a *prefix* or a *postfix* fashion. While both forms increment the associated integer argument, they differ in the resulting value produced when the expression is evaluated.

The ++ symbol after the integer variable, the *postfix* increment, means the increment is performed *after* the value of the expression is determined. Thus, the final value of this expression would be the original value of the integer variable, before the increment is performed.

In the *prefix* form, on the other hand, the symbol is written *before* the identifier, as in `++topCard`. In this case the increment is performed first, and the result is the value that has been already incremented. There are corresponding operators for decrementing values, which use the −− symbol. Soon we will see one example of the use of these.

is described using both the class name and the function name, in much the same fashion that people are identified using both a first name and a last name. This is required because the function name by itself may not be unique. We have a function named `draw`, for example, in both the class `Deck` and, as we will see shortly, in the class `Player`. The combination of class name and method name is often termed a *fully qualified name*.

The third argument is slightly more complicated. Many of the generic algorithms in the standard library require an object that acts like a function. In C++ the function call operator, the parenthesis operator, can be overloaded in the same manner as any other operator. Using this idea, we can define the following class:

```
class randomInteger {
    public:
        unsigned int operator () (unsigned int);
};
```

The implementation of the function call operator, the code that will actually be executed when this object is used in the fashion of a function, is as follows:

```
unsigned int randomInteger::operator () (unsigned int max)
{
    // rand return random integer
    // convert to unsigned to make positive
    // take remainder to put in range
    unsigned int rval = rand();
    return rval % max;
}
```

The code uses another library routine, `rand()`, which will return a random integer value. By converting this to unsigned we guarantee that the value is positive. By taking the remainder when divided by `max` we yield a value in the given range. An instance of a class, such as `randomInteger`, which defines the function call operator, is called a *function object*. One instance of this class has been defined and placed into a global variable. The shuffle routine passes this object to the generic algorithm. (We will subsequently use the same global variable in a few other methods).

Cards will be drawn from the end of the deck, one by one. We can do this by simply decrementing the value of the data field `topCard` and returning the card found at the corresponding location in the card array. The following function first tests to ensure the resulting subscript will be valid. This is good programming practice any time the validity of a subscript expression cannot be guaranteed from the immediately surrounding code.

```
Card Deck::draw ( )
    // return one card from the end of the deck
{
```

```
        if (! isEmpty())
            return cards[--topCard];
        else {    // otherwise return ace of spades
            Card spadeAce(spade, 1);
            return spadeAce;
        }
}
```

Because this function is a member function in class `Deck`, the call on the function `isEmpty()` will be automatically interpreted as an invocation of the member function of that name in the same class. In essence, what is being performed here is for the object responding to the `draw` function to ask if it itself is empty.

In this function we see one use of the prefix form of the decrement operator. The value being held by the variable `topCard` will be decremented by one, and *then* the result will be used as the subscript in determining which card to return.

The routine to determine if a deck is empty will simply test the value of the variable `topCard`:

```
bool Deck::isEmpty ( )
        // return true if the deck has no cards
{
        return topCard <= 0;
}
```

Defensive Programming

The call on the function `isEmpty` in the method `draw` in class `Deck` illustrates a use of *defensive programming*, a habit all good programmers should adopt.

The development of most realistic applications is not a task performed by a single individual working in isolation, but is commonly the result of a team of people working together. When object-oriented techniques are used, the class is often the separating interface between the work of one programmer and the work of another. That is, one programmer will be charged with developing a component, such as the card deck, while instances of this same component are being used by the code being written by a different programmer.

Therefore, the realistic programmer realizes that he or she may have very little control over how their component will be used, and must plan accordingly. Rather than *assume* that nobody will ever try to draw from an empty deck, the programmer checks the condition, and performs a suitable action if the assumption is not true.

Defensive programming is particularly important whenever arrays or pointers are involved in an algorithm, because the C++ language provides little low-level support for assuring that array subscripts are legal, or that pointers are guaranteed to be non-null.

2.3.1   In-Line Function Definitions

When function bodies are very short, as they are in two of the three functions associated with the Deck class, they are often combined with the class declaration, as in:

```
class Deck {
public:
        // constructor
    Deck ( );

        // operations
    void    shuffle ( )
      { random_shuffle (cards, cards+52, randomizer); }
    bool    isEmpty ( )
      { return topCard <= 0; }
    Card    draw ( );

protected:
    Card    cards[52];
    int     topCard;
};
```

Such a function body is said to be defined *in-line*. Note that the constructor and the function draw, both of which have longer definitions, have not been expanded in-line, and must still be defined in the manner presented earlier. In-line definitions should be reserved for functions that are very short, such as one or two statements in length.

2.4   THE CLASS PLAYER

The third class of object we will need for our game represents a player. Reading the description of the game, the most obvious function this class must provide is the ability to hold a hand of three cards, and randomly draw one of these three. However, it will simplify the game if each player is also charged with remembering his own score, and therefore we need functions to increment and return these values. Finally, each player must be given the ability to draw a new card from the deck. Adding a constructor to initialize the object, we arrive at the following class definition:

```
class Player {
public:
        // constructor
    Player (Deck &);
```

```
          // operations
     Card     draw ( );
     void     addPoints (int);
     int      score ();
     void     replaceCard (Deck &);

protected:
     Card     myCards[3];
     int      myScore;
     int      removedCard;
};
```

Each player will hold in his hand three cards, which we will again maintain in an array. An integer variable will represent the current score for the player. Another integer variable will be used to hold the location of the card played during the period between when a card is placed on the table and when it is replaced in the hand. These fields have been declared as `protected`, which means they are accessible only within the player abstraction.

The employment of the name myScore is a useful memory device. Protected data fields are accessible only to the member functions associated with the class, and are therefore not accessible outside the class object. Within the class methods we are referring to a specific player (one of the two players in the game). It is human nature to personify the things we create, such as computer programs, so we naturally think of a player object as something that executes its member functions in response to a request. The name myScore emphasizes that the score associated with the variable is the score associated with the object handling the message. Each of the two players will have his own object, and with it his own data fields. Within each of these two, when they execute one of the member functions, the data field they operate with will be their "own" data field.

Initialization of a `Player` object requires drawing an initial three cards from the deck (which is passed as an argument to the constructor), and setting the other two variables:

```
Player::Player (Deck & aDeck)
     // initialize the data fields for a player
{
     myScore = 0;
     for (int i = 0; i < 3; i++)
          myCards[i] = aDeck.draw();
     removedCard = 0;
}
```

We see here our first *message passing expression*. To invoke the method draw() from the class Deck we must first specify *which* deck we are taking about, then pass the message named `draw` to that deck. We can think of the action being performed as the current procedure *asking* the `deck` object to draw and return a card. In this case, the deck is being passed as argument. Note that the syntax used to describe the act of passing a message mirrors the syntax used to access a data field, in much the same way that the definition of a member function is similar to the definition of a data field in a structure.

Drawing a card involves selecting a random number between 0 and 2, then returning the selected card. We use the same random number generator constructed for the earlier shuffle operation. In addition, we remember the location of the card being returned by saving the index in the variable `removedCard`.

```
Card Player::draw ( )
      // return a random card from our hand
{
    removedCard = randomizer(3);
    return myCards[removedCard];
}
```

A pair of routines are used to increment and return the current score. The first of these illustrates the use of an assignment statement combined with a binary operator.

```
void Player::addPoints (int howMany)
      // add the given number of points to the current score
{
    myScore += howMany;
}
```

```
int   Player::score ( )
      // return the current score
{
    return myScore;
}
```

The last member function for our player abstraction simply replaces the last card played with a new card drawn from the deck. Once more the deck from which the card will be drawn is passed as an argument to the procedure.

```
void   Player::replaceCard (Deck & aDeck)
      // replace last card played with new card
{
    myCards[removedCard] = aDeck.draw();
}
```

2.5   THE GAME ITSELF

Having defined the behavior of the game components, the game itself is largely just a loop that initializes the various values, then draws cards for the players until the deck is exhausted. This can be written as:

```
void main() {
    Deck theDeck; // create and shuffle the deck
    theDeck.shuffle();

    Player player1(theDeck); // create the two
    Player player2(theDeck); // players

        // play until deck is empty
    while (! theDeck.isEmpty() ) {
        Card card1  = player1.draw();
        cout << "Player 1 plays " << card1 << endl;
        Card card2 = player2.draw();
        cout << "Player 2 plays " << card2 << endl;

        if (card1.rank == card2.rank) { // tie
            player1.addPoints(1);
            player2.addPoints(1);
            cout << "Players tie\n";
            }
        else if (card1.rank > card2.rank) {
            player1.addPoints(2);
            cout << "Player 1 wins round\n";
            }
        else {
            player2.addPoints(2);
            cout << "Player 2 wins round\n";
            }

            // now replace the cards drawn
        player1.replaceCard(theDeck);
        player2.replaceCard(theDeck);
    }
    cout << "Player 1 score " << player1.score() << endl;
    cout << "Player 2 score " << player2.score() << endl;
}
```

A program written in an object-oriented style is often very much like a simulation. The objects that compose the "universe" are initialized (the deck, the cards, the players) and then set in motion. The program stops when motion halts.

Note how the declarations of the two local variables that hold the cards appear within the loop, at the point where the cards are first used. Note as well the extensive use of message passing expressions, where we denote *which* player we are referring to using an expression such as:

```
Card card1 = player1.draw();
```

In this statement we declare a new variable of type card, then initialize the card using the value returned subsequent to passing the message `draw()` to the object `player1`. In a message passing expression, the value being manipulated is known as a *receiver*, and we say that the message draw is *being passed* to the receiver.

2.6   MAKING AN INTERACTIVE GAME

Watching the computer play itself is all well and good, but a much more interesting game can be constructed if we allow the human being running the program to act as one of the players in the game. Because of the way we have structured the program using independent components, this is not as difficult as one might at first suspect. We have already characterized the behavior of a player. For a human player, the only difference would be that the response to the `draw` command should display the cards currently being held in the hand, and allow the user to select which of the three cards to play. The interaction might go something like this:

```
  .
  .
  .
You currently hold in your hand:
a) Ace of spades
b) 3 of clubs
c) seven of diamonds
which one do you want to play? b
Human plays 3 of clubs
Computer plays 7 of spades
Computer wins round
You currently hold in your hand:
a) Ace of spades
b) 4 of diamonds
c) seven of diamonds
which one do you want to play?
  .
  .
  .
```

To do this, we simply create a new class abstraction that is identical to the earlier `Player` abstraction, but uses the following code to define the behavior for the `draw` command:

```
Card      HumanPlayer::draw ()
     // draw one card from the current hand
{
     cout << "You currently hold in your hand:" << endl;
     cout << "a) " << myCards[0] << endl;
     cout << "b) " << myCards[1] << endl;
     cout << "c) " << myCards[2] << endl;
     cout << "Which one do you want to play? ";
     char answer[80];
     removedCard = -1;
     while (removedCard == -1) {
         cin >> answer; // read response
         if (answer[0] == 'a')
             removedCard = 0;
         else if (answer[0] == 'b')
             removedCard = 1;
         else if (answer[0] == 'c')
             removedCard = 2;
         if (removedCard != -1)
             return myCards[removedCard];
         cout << "please specify a, b or c\n";
     }
}
```

Note how a loop is being used to repeatedly ask the user for his choice until a satisfactory answer is provided. The loop terminates from the middle, through the `return` statement, once a suitable response has been given. Otherwise, the user is once again prompted for a selection.

The remainder of the `HumanPlayer` class is exactly the same as the `Player` class we constructed earlier. To modify our game, all that is now necessary is to change the declarations of the first of the players from type `Player` to type `HumanPlayer`. In the exercises, we investigate various other variations and improvements that can be made in this game.

2.7   ACCESSOR AND MUTATOR FUNCTIONS

Earlier we noted that it is a useful design principle for all data fields held by an object to be declared `protected`. Doing so makes it easier to understand how the data fields are being manipulated, because only methods defined within the class can then access these values. For example, if methods only provide access to these data values, and not a means to modify them, then we know the data fields are constant, and cannot be changed (except through an assignment statement, which changes the entire value of the object). This is the situation with our playing card abstraction. We could rewrite this to use member functions instead of direct access to the data fields as follows:

```
class Card {
public:
        // constructors
    Card ( )
        { r = 0; s = spade; }
    Card (suits sv, int rv)
        { r = rv; s = sv; }

        // operations on Card
    int rank ( )
        { return r; }
    suits suit ( )
        { return s; }

protected:
        // data fields
    suits s;    // suit value
    int   r;    // rank value
};
```

All the member functions have been given in-line definitions. A member function that only returns the value of a data field is called an *accessor function*. A data field that is used to set or modify the value of a protected data field is called a *mutator*. We have seen an example mutator in the Player class, in the function addPoints, which modified the data field myScore.

2.8   CHAPTER SUMMARY

Key Concepts

- Class
- Data members
- Member functions
- Protected and public
- Constructors
- Default constructors
- Pass by reference
- Pass by value
- Function objects
- Message passing
- Receivers
- Accessor function
- Mutator

In an object-oriented application, programs are structured as a collection of interacting components. These components are defined using classes. A class is a general pattern, describing an encapsulated object that can maintain both data fields and perform actions by means of member functions. The public portion of a class describes the features that can be used by other components, while the protected portion describes characteristics (data fields and functions) that are used internally by the object. When instances of a class are created, such as with a declaration statement, a constructor function can be used to ensure the object is properly initialized. A default constructor is a constructor that requires no arguments, and is used (among other purposes) to initialize the elements of an array of objects.

Arguments to functions can be passed either by value or by reference. The default behavior is pass by value, in which a copy of the argument is produced and assigned to the corresponding parameter in the function. For large objects and objects for which the modification within the function should be reflected in changes in the argument value, the alternative of pass by reference should be used. This is indicated by placing an ampersand in the argument list.

To make an object perform one of its assigned methods, a message passing expression is employed. This is similar to the way a data field is designed in a structure. The receiver indicates the object that is being asked to perform the action. In the message passing expression the receiver is followed by a period, then by the name of the method being invoked, and finally by any arguments required by the corresponding member function.

A function object is an instance of a class that implements the function call operator (the parenthesis operator). Such an object can be used as if it were a function. Many of the generic algorithms in the standard library require function objects when they want an argument value that can perform as a function.

An accessor function is a member function whose primary responsibility is to provide access to a data field. A mutator is a member function designed to modify a data field.

Further Reading

An introduction to object-oriented programming in general, without reference to any particular language, is provided by [Budd 91]. Good introductions to computing from a pervasively object oriented point of view include [Mercer 95, Decker 95, Cohoon 97].

Readers knowledgeable about C++ will probably note, perhaps more than any thing else in this chapter, the vast number of concepts I have *not* discussed. My sole purpose in doing so has been to reduce the number of new ideas introduced. Among the most notable of the ideas omitted are:

▲ The use of the keyword const. This keyword can be used to declare data fields and arguments as constant, and such usage is considered by many to be good programming style.

▲ Copy constructors. We will soon encounter copy constructors, which are used to generate clones, or copies, of user-defined data items.

▲ Interface and implementation. The distinction between those portions of a class description that are found in an interface file and those that are found in an implementation file has not been presented.

▲ Assignment operators. C++ allows the programmer to provide new meaning to the assignment operator, in much the same way that we have overloaded the output operator. However, the desired meaning for the only assignment required by this example (namely, the assignment of class Card) matches the default behavior produced automatically by the compiler. In this instance, therefore, it is not necessary to introduce the concept.

▲ Inheritance. We could have simplified the development of the Human-Player abstraction by making it inherit from the existing Player class. But this would have necessitated introducing a host of other concepts, such as virtual functions. We will subsequently introduce inheritance in Chapter 9.

Study Questions & Exercises

Study Questions

1. What is the term used to describe the style of programming best supported by C++?

2. What is the name of the primary mechanism used to create software components in C++?

3. What is a data member?

4. What is a member function?

5. What is the purpose of a constructor function?

6. What is a default constructor? Name a situation in which a default constructor will be executed.

7. What is an overloaded name? How does the compiler distinguish between overloaded function names?

8. When the left argument is a stream, what purpose is served by the overloaded operator <<?

9. What functions are permitted to access data fields declared in the protected portion of a class?

10. What is the difference between the prefix ++ operator and the postfix ++ operator?

11. After a deck has been initialized, what value will be held by the variable topCard ?

12. What is a random number generator? What is the name of the random number generator provided by the C++ run-time library?

13. What is a fully qualified member function name?

14. How does the draw method in the class Deck illustrate defensive programming?

15. What is an in-line member function definition?

16. What is a message passing expression?

17. In what way is an object-oriented program like a simulation?

18. Why is a loop needed in the function HumanPlayer::draw?

19. What is an accessor function? What is a mutator? What is an advantage of using accessor functions instead of permitting direct access to data fields?

Exercises

1. What features of the program would need to be altered if, instead of holding three cards, each player held only two cards?

2. What features of the program would need to be altered if, instead of playing the game using one deck of cards, we wished to use two decks shuffled together?

3. Suppose we wanted to modify the game to play "aces-high"–that is, with aces counting higher than kings. What features of the program would need to be modified? Make your changes, and try the resulting program.

4. Identify all the message passing expressions in the main program given in Section 2.5.

5. Which of the member functions in class Player (Section 2.4) are candidates for being written in-line as part of the class description? Rewrite the class description as it would appear with these functions written in this form.

6. Consider the method replaceCard in class Player. What circumstances are required for this function to perform correctly? What happens if these conditions are not satisfied? What would a "defensive programming" approach look like to ensure that proper conditions are met before performing an action?

7. Modify the program to play a sequence of games, rather than just a single game. This involves a series of steps, as follows:

   a. First modify the Player abstraction so that it will maintain an additional new data value, which is the number of games won. Initialize this field in the constructor, and provide accessor and mutator functions to update the value.

b. Between the creation of the deck and the call on the shuffle routine, insert a loop that will execute for a fixed number of times, say five games. This loop will terminate near the end of the program.

c. At the end of each game, update and display the current game counts.

d. At the end of the series of games, display the final game counts.

8. Write a general-purpose Boolean routine that will take as argument a string, which represents a yes/no question, display the string, receive an answer from the user, and return true if the answer is yes and false if the answer is no. You can model this routine on the procedure HumanPlayer::draw described in Section 2.6.

9. Using the procedure you created in the previous question, modify the program you developed in Question 7 so that it will ask the user after each game whether or not to continue with another game.

10. What happens if, instead of changing the declaration for the first player from type Player to type HumanPlayer, we change the declaration for the second? How can this problem be overcome?

11. A bounded counter is a software device that maintains and updates a counter value. When the counter increments past a certain limiting value, set when the counter is first created, it wraps around back to zero. So, suppose we have a counter that is created with a limiting value of 17. A series of increments might take us through the values 14, 15, 16, 17, and then back to zero. Define a class that will implement a bounded counter. Give methods for increment, decrement, and accessing the current counter value.

12. We have not yet encountered all the C++ features used in the implementation of the generic algorithm random_shuffle, but we can construct a slightly simpler version. Write a function r_shuffle that takes as argument an array of integer values, an unsigned integer representing a number of values in the array, and a random number generator similar to the one used with random_shuffle. The heading for this function is:

```
void r_shuf (int data[ ], unsigned size,
unsigned rnd(unsigned))
{
    .
    .
    .
}
```

The body of the function should loop through each element of the array, swapping the value found at the corresponding location with another random selected value from the array. Execute your procedure to test it with several array values.

3

Algorithms: Descriptions of Behavior

Chapter Overview

Software components, regardless of how they are structured or defined, must perform actions in order to be useful. In the first two chapters we saw that such behavior is usually implemented by means of functions, member functions, or operators. In whatever form a sequence of statements is packaged, the heart of any behavior is a series of computer instructions to be executed under certain circumstances. Thus, fundamental to all of computer science is the creation and analysis of sequences of computer instructions. Such a sequence is known generically as an *algorithm*. In this chapter, and in Chapters 4 and 5 we will consider some of the properties of algorithms, and techniques that can be employed in the analysis of algorithms. These include:

▲ Properties of algorithms
▲ Recipes as algorithms
▲ Proving termination
▲ Recursive algorithms

3.1   PROPERTIES OF ALGORITHMS

An *algorithm* is a set of instructions used to solve a specific problem or, more commonly, employed to solve a general class of similar problems. Terms that have a similar meaning include *process, method, technique, procedure, routine, outline, pattern,* and even, as we will illustrate in a moment, *recipe.*

Once we have discovered an algorithm for a problem, the development of a solution is simply a matter of executing each instruction of the algorithm in turn. If this process is to be successful there are, in general, several properties an algorithm must possess. Among these are:

▲ *Accurate specification of the input.* The most common form of algorithm is a transformation that takes a set of input values and performs some manipulations to yield a set of output values. An algorithm must make clear the number and type of input values, and the essential initial conditions those input values must possess to achieve successful operation.

▲ *Precise specification of each instruction.* Each step of an algorithm must be precisely defined. There should be no ambiguity about the actions to be carried out at any point. As we will see shortly, algorithms presented in an informal descriptive form are sometimes ill-defined for exactly this reason, due to the ambiguities in English and other natural languages.

▲ *Correctness.* An algorithm is expected to solve a problem. For any putative algorithm, we must demonstrate that, in fact, the algorithm will solve the problem. Often this will take the form of an argument, mathematical or logical in nature, to the effect that *if* the input conditions are satisfied and the steps of the algorithm executed *then* the desired outcome will be produced.

▲ *Termination, time to execute.* It must be clear that for any particular input values the algorithm is guaranteed to terminate after a finite number of steps. We will postpone until later a more precise definition of the informal term "steps." It is usually not necessary to know the exact number of steps an algorithm will require, but it will be convenient to provide an upper bound and argue that the algorithm will always terminate in fewer steps than the upper bound. Usually this upper bound will be given as a function of some values in the input. For example, if the input consists of two integer values n and m, we might be able to say that a particular algorithm will always terminate in fewer than $n + m$ steps.

▲ *Description of the result or effect.* Finally, it must be clear exactly what the algorithm is intended to accomplish. Most often this can be expressed as the production of a result value having certain prop-

Lemon Soufflé

Ingredients / Input

1	Envelope unflavored gelatin
$\frac{1}{4}$	Cup cold water
6	Egg yolks
1	Cup sugar
$\frac{2}{3}$	Cup Lemon juice
1	Tablespoon grated Lemon rind
4	Egg whites
$1\frac{1}{2}$	Cup heavy cream

Actions

1. Soften the gelatin in water. Beat egg yokes and sugar until thick and light. Stir in lemon juice and cook over low heat, beating steadily with a whisk until thickened and hot but not boiling (10–15 minutes).

2. Pour mixture into large bowl, mix in gelatin until dissolved, and then add lemon rind. Stir occasionally until cool.

3. Beat egg whites until stiff but not dry. Fold into lemon mixture, then whip the cream and fold in. Pour into a two-quart soufflé dish (or large bowl) and refrigerate at least 12 hours.

Figure 3.1   A recipe for lemon soufflé

erties. Less frequently algorithms are executed for a *side effect*, such as printing a value on an output device. In either case, the expected outcome must be completely specified.

In the rest of this chapter and in Chapters 4 and 5, we will examine a number of different algorithms, and describe how we can evaluate each in terms of the properties given.

3.2   RECIPES AS ALGORITHMS

Probably the most common form of algorithm the reader is likely to have encountered previously is a recipe. A recipe is a structured set of instructions used to transform an input (the ingredients) into a finished product (the edible). Consider an example recipe, such as the recipe for Lemon Soufflé shown in Figure 3.1. Let us evaluate this recipe with respect to the properties of an algorithm described in the last section.

▲ *Input.* The recipe begins with a list of ingredients. These define the basic set of initial conditions required before the steps provided by the recipe can be undertaken. Note that input conditions consist of both a set of input objects (gelatin, water, eggs, sugar) and a set of conditions (the water must be cold, the cream heavy).

▲ *Result.* The primary result of the recipe is usually described by the name; in this case *Lemon Soufflé*. Incidental consequences of executing the recipe procedure (such as producing a messy kitchen) are usually of little interest and are left unstated.

▲ *Correctness.* It takes a talented cook to be able to simply look at a recipe and tell whether the outcome will be tasty or even edible if the recipe is correctly followed. For most people it is a matter of experimentation. As the saying goes, the proof of the pudding (or soufflé) is in the eating.

▲ *Time to execute.* It is somewhat difficult to guarantee from a mere examination of the steps involved in a recipe that the preparation can actually be carried out in a finite amount of time. In Step 1, are we guaranteed that when beating the egg yolks and sugar they will eventually become thick and light, or that when the result is cooked over a low heat it will always become thick and hot? What if it never becomes thick? Perhaps in realization of this possible problem, the author of the recipe has provided an estimated amount of time this operation should take. If the time estimate is greatly exceeded and the desired outcome has not yet been achieved, then the cook knows something is wrong.

▲ *Instruction precision.* It is in the area of definiteness, or instruction precision, that we see perhaps the greatest weakness of a recipe as an algorithm, and the significant differences between preparing a set of instructions for a human being to follow versus preparing instructions for a computer. What exactly is "thick and light" in Step 1? Does light refer to light in texture or light in color? How long should the mixture be whipped in Step 3? The success of the operation will depend upon answers to questions such as these, but the details are simply not found in the recipe itself. Instead, good cooks rely on experience and intuition to fill in missing information.

3.3   ANALYZING COMPUTER ALGORITHMS

In the next several sections we will analyze the features we have noted, and investigate how they are manifest in relation to computer algorithms. Two of the topics, the question of describing the amount of time it takes to execute a program, and the question of correctness for programs, are sufficiently complex, so we will devote the following two chapters to each of them.

3.3.1   Specification of the Input

An algorithm will, in general, only produce the desired outcome when it is used in a proper fashion. Restrictions may be placed not only on the input values manipulated by the algorithm, but on other conditions as well. In the case of computer algorithms, there are two general techniques used to specify these restrictions.

The first mechanism might be labeled simply as *type checking*. Input to an algorithm is usually provided in the form of parameters, global variables, or instance data fields (which are a more limited form of global variables). In each case, there is a *type* associated with the value, and the functioning of the algorithm is guaranteed only if the input values are drawn from the proper type. An algorithm for manipulating integer values, for example, the following algorithm, will not work correctly when the arguments are floating point quantities. Such errors, however, are usually easily caught by the compiler.

```
int min (int a, int b)
    // return smaller of two integer arguments
{

    int smallest;

    if (a < b)
        smallest = a;
    else
        smallest = b;
    return smallest;
}
```

Occasionally stronger input conditions are necessary, in addition to simply requiring that values have a certain type. A common form is a restriction on the range of values that can be processed. For example, the following procedure converts an integer into the corresponding character value, but is effective only for the integers between zero and nine:

```
# include <assert.h>    // include header file for assert mechanism

char digitChar (unsigned int val)
    // return the character equivalent for
    // the integer argument value
    // which must be between zero and nine
{
    // make sure value is in proper range
assert (val < 10);

switch (val) {
    case 0: return '0';
```

```
        case 1: return '1';
        case 2: return '2';
        case 3: return '3';
        case 4: return '4';
        case 5: return '5';
        case 6: return '6';
        case 7: return '7';
        case 8: return '8';
        case 9: return '9';
    }
}
```

Such conditions cannot be checked by the compiler, but they often can be validated at run-time. The assert mechanism, shown in the function digitChar, produces a run-time error and immediately halts execution if the condition is not satisfied.

A simplified version of this example program can be given, which makes use of the fact that the characters representing integer values are designed to be in sequence in the ASCII ordering, and that characters are treated as small integer values:

```
char digitChar (unsigned int val)
    // return the character equivalent for
    // the integer argument value
```

Algorithms Within Algorithms

How would one apply the analysis techniques described in this chapter to, for example, the card game application presented in the previous chapter? The answer is that the algorithms are analyzed in a recursive fashion, from the inside out.

First, each class is analyzed in isolation. Within each class, each member function can be considered a small algorithm all to itself. Many times the characterization of these is trivial, as in the case of accessor or mutator functions. For complicated methods, the analysis of algorithms may depend upon previous analysis of other methods. This is the case for the replace-Card method in class Player, for example, which depends upon the fact that a draw method has been previously performed. Attempting to provide a correctness argument for such methods will frequently reveal possibilities for defensive programming, when it becomes difficult to answer the question, "How do you know this property that you depend upon will be true at this point in execution?" Such situations should be documented, checked for, or removed entirely.

Once individual components (classes) have been analyzed in isolation, then the analysis of the program as a whole can begin. One can consider the main program described in Section 2.5 as an algorithm, for example, and argue about the running time or correctness of this algorithm based on previous analysis of the individual classes.

```
        // which must be between zero and nine
{
    assert (val < 10);
    return '0' + val;
}
```

There are other situations in which restrictions on input values are necessary, but such restrictions cannot be checked using `assert`. One example is an assumption that the input values are such that numeric overflow will not occur during the course of execution. This is illustrated in the following, which raises a floating point value to an integer exponent value. Where these conditions are important they should be documented, as comments, along with the code.

```
double power (double base, unsigned int n)
        // return the value yielded by raising the
        // double precision base to the integer exponent
        // assumes floating point overflow does not occur
{
        // initial result to base raised to zero
    double result = 1.0;

        // raise base to new powers
    for (unsigned int i = 1; i <= n; i++) {
        result *= base;
    }

    return result;
}
```

3.3.2   Description of the Result

Just as input conditions for computer programs are specified in a number of ways, the expected results of execution are also frequently documented in a variety of fashions.

The most obvious result is that yielded by a function. The name of the function identifies the result, while the return type indicates the form the value will take. If other characteristics are important they can be indicated in comments. An example is the min function, which was described in an earlier section:

```
int min (int a, int b)
        // return the smaller of two arguments
{
    .
    .
    .
}
```

Sometimes programs are executed not for their result, but for a *side effect* that occurs during the course of execution. Because this side effect may not be obvious from the procedure heading, it should be documented in a comment. An example is the recursive procedure `printUnsigned`, used to print the representation of a nonnegative integer value:[1]

```
void printUnsigned (unsigned int val)
    // print the character representation of
    // the unsigned argument value
{
    if (val < 10)
        printChar (digitChar(val));
    else {
            // print high order part
        printUnsigned (val / 10);
            // print last character
        printChar (digitChar(val % 10));
    }
}
```

Besides output, other frequent side effects include the modification of global variables or instance variables. These, too, should be documented with comments.

3.3.3   Instruction Precision

The computer is a true *idiot savant*. It is an extremely simple-minded device, notable only for its ability to perform simple instructions with almost unbelievable rapidity. For example, even relatively inexpensive computers can add several million integers in one second. This speed, however, is only possible when commands are precisely specified. Computer algorithms can have none of the ambiguity we find in English language descriptions. While English descriptions tend to describe more the objective being sought (the "what"), computer algorithms must specify in exacting detail the technique to be used in reaching those objectives (the "how").

For example, a reasonable request to another human being might be "go to the store and buy me something to make lunch." Here it is the objective that has been stated, and not the means. We rely on the person receiving the command to know from previous experience the steps necessary to achieve the goal (not only what elements are needed for a lunch, but how to operate a car, how to purchase the items, and so on). Not only is the

---

1. The algorithm `printUnsigned` has been written using a conventional name, rather than overloading the `<<` operator. This is designed to confuse the reader less, by omitting operator syntax.

process poorly specified, but even the objective is unclear. Is the request being conveyed that the second individual should purchase the items that together will constitute a lunch, or is the request that a "lunch-making" device be purchased (perhaps a personal robotic servant). To a computer, every step of the process necessary to achieve the goal must be outlined in detail.

3.3.4   Time to Execute

We will divide our discussion of execution time into two parts, often the course followed in practice. The first question to address with any algorithm is whether or not it terminates at all. Once we are satisfied that an algorithm *will* terminate for all legal input values, the next question is whether we can develop a more accurate characterization regarding the amount of time it will take to execute. In this section we address the first question; we will consider the second question in more detail in the next chapter.

A basic assumption is that all primitive operations in the language, with the exception of procedure calls and loops, will execute in some finite amount of time, and thus the question of termination for those procedures that consist only of such elements is trivially addressed. The majority of loops, as well, can be easily characterized as depending upon some input value, and thus termination is assured.

Only in rare cases must termination of an algorithm be explicitly addressed. Most often this occurs through the use of while loops, or through the use of recursion. By far the most common technique used to prove termination of an algorithm, when it is not immediately obvious, is to identify a property or value that possesses the following three characteristics:

1. The property or value can be placed in one-to-one correspondence with integer values. (Most commonly we simply use some integer quantity that appears in the problem; in other cases, it is necessary to construct a mapping from some quantity in the problem to the integers.)

2. The property or value is nonnegative.

3. The property or value decreases steadily as the algorithm executes. (Often we say that such a quantity is *monotonically decreasing*.)

If we can discover such a quantity, then the argument for finite termination can be expressed as follows: This quantity must begin with some value (even if we don't know precisely *what* that value might be). Over time the quantity is always decreasing. Because it can never be negative, the algorithm must necessarily terminate before the quantity is reduced below zero.

Loops that increment or decrement a value can frequently be characterized by identifying a formula involving the termination condition. The integer exponential algorithm, for example, will continually decrease the quantity $n - i$ as the variable i increases, so we can use this quantity to guarantee that the program will always terminate.

```
double power (double base, unsigned int n)
    // return the value yielded by raising the
    // double precision base to the integer exponent
    // assumes floating point overflow does not occur
{
        // initial result to base raised to zero
    double result = 1.0;

        // raise base to new powers
    for (unsigned int i = 0; i < n; i++) {
        result *= base;
        }
    return result;
}
```

Zeno's Paradox

The most nonintuitive of the three properties required for proving termination is the first: that the quantity or property being discussed can be placed into a one-to-one correspondence with a diminishing list of integers. To illustrate the necessity of this requirement, consider the following "proof" that it is possible to share a single candy bar with all your friends, no matter how many friends you may have. Take a candy bar and cut it in half, giving one half to your best friend. Take the remaining half and cut it in half once more, giving a portion to your second best friend. Assuming you have a sufficiently sharp knife, you can continue in this manner, at each step producing ever smaller pieces, for as long as you like. Thus, we have no guarantee of termination for this process. Certainly the sequence here ($\frac{1}{2}, \frac{1}{4}, \frac{1}{8}, \ldots$) consists of all nonnegative terms, and is decreasing. But a one-to-one correspondence with the integers would need to increase, not decrease.

In the 5th century B.C., the Greek philosopher Zeno used similar arguments to show that no matter how fast he runs, the famous hero

Achilles cannot overtake a Tortoise, if the Tortoise is given a head start. Suppose, for example, that the Tortoise and Achilles start as below at time A. When, at time B, Achilles reaches the point from which the Tortoise started, the Tortoise will have proceeded some distance ahead of this point. When Achilles reaches this further point at time C, the Tortoise will have proceeded yet further ahead. At each point when Achilles reaches a point from which the Tortoise began, the Tortoise will have proceeded at least some distance further. Thus, it was impossible for Achilles to ever overtake and pass the Tortoise.

Achilles   A $\longrightarrow$ B $\longrightarrow$ C $\longrightarrow$ D
Tortoise   A $\longrightarrow$ B $\longrightarrow$ C $\longrightarrow$ D

The paradox arises due to an infinite sequence of ever smaller quantities, and the nonintuitive possibility that an infinite sum can nevertheless result in a finite value. By restricting our arguments concerning termination to use only a decreasing set of *integer* values, we avoid problems such as those typified by Zeno's paradox.

An example in which termination may not be immediately obvious occurs in Euclid's Greatest Common Divisor algorithm, first developed in third century B.C. Greece.[2] Donald Knuth, the computer scientist who originated the term "analysis of algorithms" and who has done a great deal of research into the history of algorithms, has claimed that the sequence of operations presented by Euclid in Propositions 1 and 2 of Book 7 of the *Elements* is the earliest-known nontrivial completely specified mathematical algorithm. The algorithm is intended to compute, given two positive integer values n and m, the largest positive integer that exactly divides both values. The algorithm can be written as:

```
unsigned int gcd (unsigned int n, unsigned int m)
    // compute the greatest common divisor
    // of two positive integer values
{
    assert (n > 0 && m > 0);

    while (m != n) {
        if (n > m)
            n = n - m;
        else
            m = m - n;
    }

    return n;
}
```

Because we have no definite limit on the number of iterations for the while loop, termination may not seem assured. To prove termination, we must first observe that not only must n and m be initially nonzero, but they can never be assigned the values zero or less. (To see this, we must argue that the loop is only evaluated while m differs from n, and the subtractions can never produce a negative result). But even this observation does not directly give us a value we can use in our monotonically decreasing argument, because on each iteration one of n or m changes, but the other does not. To prove termination, we can consider the sum $n + m$, and note that this sum, although it does not occur anywhere in the algorithm, must nevertheless always decrease, as well as satisfy the other properties we require.

---

2. Readers not immediately convinced of the correctness, or even termination, of Euclid's algorithm must wait patiently until Chapter 5, when the topic of proving correctness will be addressed.

Recursive functions, functions that in certain circumstances invoke themselves, are another programming construct in which termination may not be immediately obvious. An example is the procedure printUnsigned, described earlier in Section 3.3.2. Here termination is assured once we note that the value being passed as argument in the recursive call is both positive and always strictly smaller than the original argument. Because for any input values there are only a finite number of times one can continue to find a quantity with these properties, termination must eventually occur.

3.3.5   Space Utilization

Most of the time, the amount of space required in the solution of a problem is determined by the problem itself, and the programmer will have little room for variation. Occasionally, however, variations in space utilization will be important, and we will point them out.

Many sorting algorithms, for example, operate by copying the input into an auxiliary structure, performing certain transformations, and then copying the results back into the original container. This doubles the amount of memory needed for this task. Other sorting algorithms are able to make their changes in place in the original vector, and thereby reduce this memory load.

In some cases it is possible to improve execution time (improve speed) by increasing the amount of memory devoted to a process, and vice versa. This is known as a *time/space tradeoff*. We will see examples of this later in the book. When time/space tradeoffs are present, deciding which of many alternatives make best use of limited resources (both time and space) may be subtle.

3.4   RECURSIVE ALGORITHMS

A procedure that under certain situations invokes itself is called *recursive*. The use of recursive procedures is a powerful programming technique, one we will employ frequently throughout the book.

A recursive procedure must always involve a conditional test that divides execution into two or more cases. At least one case must be handled without resort to the recursive call, because to do otherwise would result in an infinite sequence of procedure executions. These are often known as the *base cases*. In the printing procedure examined in Section 3.3.2, the base case occurs when the input value is less than ten.

For values larger than or equal to ten, the *recursive case* operates by dividing the number by ten, thereby producing a value with one fewer digit. The function then calls *itself* in order to print this smaller number, followed by another call to print the low-order character. Thus, to print the value 456, the procedure recursively calls itself to print the value 45,

which in turn recursively calls itself once more in order to print the value 4. With the argument 4, the base case is finally encountered, and execution starts to return. Once the 4 has been printed, we return to the procedure that was printing 45; this procedure then prints the low order digit (the 5). Returning from this procedure, we get back to the procedure printing the 456, which then prints its low order character (the 6). In this manner all three characters are finally produced.

In trying to understand how a recursive procedure can operate, it is important to remember that every time a procedure is invoked, new space is allocated for pass-by-value parameters and local variables (refer to Section 1.2.11 in Chapter 1). Each time the min procedure from Section 3.3.1 is executed, for example, new space is created for the parameters named a and b. This is true for recursive procedures as well. The only difference is that now there may be several parameters with the same name, but all copies are nonetheless distinct. In the case of printing the value 456, one copy of the parameter named val holds the value 456, while a second maintains the value 45, and a third is manipulating the value 4. This all happens automatically, with no instruction or assistance necessary on the part of the programmer.

We will illustrate the development of another recursive algorithm by considering a classic puzzle, the *Towers of Hanoi*. In this puzzle there are three poles, labeled A, B, and C. There are a number of disks of decreasing sizes, initially all on pole A.

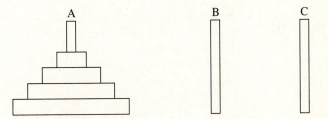

The goal of the puzzle is to move all disks from pole A to pole B, without ever moving a disk onto another disk with a smaller size. The third pole can be used as a temporary during this process. At any point, only the topmost disk from any pole may be moved.

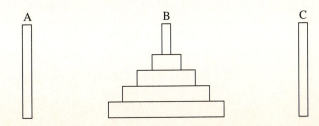

There are only two legal first steps, namely moving the smallest piece from pole A to pole B, or moving the same piece from pole A to pole C. However, there does not seem to be any good way to discover which of these alternatives is the correct choice without first solving the puzzle!

As is often the case with the development of recursive algorithms, a greater insight can be found by considering a point in the *middle* of execution. For example, consider in the picture above the point we must be one step *before* we move the largest disk. For this to be a legal move, we must have already moved all the disks except for the largest from pole A to pole C:

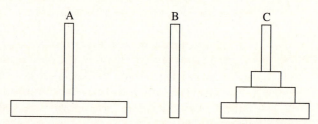

This observation gives us a hint as to how a solution can be developed. What we have discovered is that *if* we could move all but the largest disk from pole A to pole C, we could then move the largest disk from pole A to pole B. But then pole A would be empty, and so we could use it as a temporary. So, if we could *then* move all but the largest disks from their new location on pole C back to pole B, we would be finished.

It might not seem that we have accomplished very much, but indeed we have. This is because the new problem we have hypothesized is the same form as the original, but slightly smaller (in as much as it involves a stack of one fewer disks). If we could do this consistently, then we might have a solution. So our first stab at an algorithm for the Hanoi problem might be something like this:

```
void Hanoi (int n, char a, char b, char c)
    // move n disks from tower a to tower b, using tower c
{
        // first move all but last disk to tower c
    Hanoi (n-1, a, c, b);
        // then move one disk from a to b
    cout << "move disk from tower " << a << " to " << b << endl;
        // then move all disks from c back to b
    Hanoi (n-1, c, b, a);
}
```

If we try executing this program with a few simple values of *n*, we immediately see a problem. It never halts! It simply calls itself repeatedly forever. To avoid this problem, a recursive algorithm must always eventually reach a *base case*, which is handled directly. In the present problem, the obvious base case occurs when we have a pile with just one disk.[3] Moving one disk does not require first moving any disks stacked above, and hence can be performed directly. Adding the condition to test for this situation gives us the following revised program:

```
void Hanoi (int n, char a, char b, char c)
    // move n disks from tower a to tower b, using tower c
{
    if (n == 1) {
            // can move smallest disk directly
        cout << "move disk from tower " << a << " to " << b << endl;
    }
    else {
            // first move all but last disk to tower c
        Hanoi (n-1, a, c, b);
            // then move one disk from a to b
        cout << "move disk from tower " << a << " to " << b << endl;
        // then move all disks from c back to b
        Hanoi (n-1, c, b, a);
    }
}
```

If we simulate the execution of this algorithm for 3 disks, we get the following sequence of moves. The student can check that the moves satisfy the game rules, and result in the expected outcome:

```
move disk from tower A to tower B
move disk from tower A to tower C
move disk from tower B to tower C
move disk from tower A to tower B
move disk from tower C to tower A
move disk from tower C to tower B
move disk from tower A to tower B
```

---

3. A less obvious base case is the handling of a stack with *no* elements. Moving a stack of zero elements is even easier than moving a stack that has only one disk. Exercise 11 explores writing the algorithm that uses zero as the base case, instead of one.

3.5   CHAPTER SUMMARY

Key Concepts

- Properties of algorithms
- Specification of input conditions
- Definiteness of each instruction
- Correctness of the algorithm
- Termination of an algorithm
- Running time of an algorithm
- Result of execution
- Recursive procedures

An algorithm is a set of instructions used to solve a specific problem. To be useful, an algorithm must possess certain properties:

▲ The algorithm must accurately describe the input values.

▲ Each step of the algorithm must be completely specified.

▲ The algorithm must make the correct transformation of the inputs to the outputs.

▲ The algorithm must be guaranteed to terminate on all input values.

▲ The result, or effect, of the algorithm must be completely characterized.

An argument that an algorithm must terminate for all input values can be provided by finding an integer quantity that is nonnegative, and that decreases steadily as the algorithm executes.

A recursive algorithm is a procedure that calls itself during the course of execution. Recursive algorithms always consist of at least two parts:

▲ A base case that is handled in a conventional fashion. In the printing algorithm, the base case occurred in the printing of a number less than 10. In the Towers of Hanoi puzzle the base case involved moving a stack that contains only one disk.

▲ A recursive case that is solved directly in part, and in part by invoking the procedure on a problem of slightly smaller size. In the printing algorithm, the recursive case involved printing numbers greater than or equal to ten. The bottom-most digit was removed, and the algorithm involved recursively to print the resulting digit. After this task was performed, the final digit was printed. In the Towers of Hanoi, when the procedure was invoked to move a tower of n elements, it recursively invoked itself in order to move a tower of $n - 1$ elements.

Further Reading

The study of algorithms, as well as the term "analysis of algorithms", was popularized by Donald Knuth in his three-part series [Knuth 73, Knuth 81, Knuth 75]. The characteristics of algorithms described at the beginning of this chapter are adapted from Volume 1. A discussion of Euclid's GCD algorithm appears both in Volumes 1 and 2.

Since the 1970s, the study of algorithms has emerged as an important subdiscipline within computer science. More recent descriptions of the field can be found in the works by Sedgewick [Sedgewick 92], Cormen et al. [Cormen 90], and Harel [Harel 92].

I acquired the lemon soufflé recipe from a Belgian graduate student when I participated in an international dining club during the time of my dissertation studies at Yale University. Some would argue that no soufflé algorithm that uses gelatin can be considered correct, but the results are generally satisfactory.

Study Questions & Exercises

Study Questions

1. What is an algorithm?

2. What are two different techniques used to specify the input conditions for an algorithm?

3. What is an `assert` statement? What happens if the assertion being checked is not satisfied?

4. What are some ways used to describe the outcome, or result, of executing an algorithm?

5. Give an example of a procedure or function from the program in Chapter 2 that is executed for a side effect, and an example of a procedure or function that is executed in order to produce a result value.

6. What is a recursive procedure?

7. What quantity describes the number of times the procedure `printUnsigned` will recursively call itself for any given integer value?

8. Assume the recursive procedure `printUnsigned` has been invoked to print the value 456. Show the run-time activation stack at the point where the procedure is finally printing the character 4, and label the name and value of each local variable in the action stack sections.

9. In what way does the precision of instructions needed to convey an algorithm to another human being differ from that needed to convey an algorithm to a computer?

10. In considering the execution time of algorithms, what are the two general types of questions one can ask?

11. What are some situations in which termination of an algorithm would not be immediately obvious?

12. What are the three properties a value must possess in order to be used to prove termination of an algorithm?

13. What two sections must be part of every recursive procedure?

Exercises

1. Examine a recipe from your favorite cookbook. Evaluate the recipe with respect to each of the properties described at the beginning of this chapter.

2. Select an activity that you perform everyday. Examples might be getting ready for the day, studying for an exam, making a dinner, or driving to work. Describe this activity as an algorithm, being as precise as possible. Do you think somebody else would be able to replicate your actions by reading your algorithm?

3. Show that each of the three properties identified in Section 3.3.4 is necessary to assure termination of an algorithm. Do this by exhibiting three algorithms that each satisfy two of the three properties, but nevertheless do not terminate. Your descriptions need not be precise; they can just be informal directions.

4. In Section 1.2.9 a function that sums the values of an integer array was presented. Analyze this procedure with regard to each of the characteristics of algorithms described in this chapter.

5. What are some of the algorithms used in the program developed in Chapter 2?

6. How might we argue that the loop in the main program in the card game developed in Chapter 2 will always terminate? What quantity can be identified that satisfies the properties we require?

7. Write a recursive procedure to print out the hexadecimal representation of an integer value. Present an argument for termination of your algorithm. What quantity characterizes the number of times your procedure will invoke itself recursively?

8. Using the fact that the ASCII representation of characters places all the lowercase characters in sequence (between the values 0X61 and 0X7A) and similarly all the uppercase characters in sequence, write a procedure `islower` that takes

a single character argument and returns true if the character is a lowercase value, and false otherwise. Write a similar procedure `isupper` for uppercase values.

9. Write a procedure `tolower` that takes a single-character value, and if uppercase returns the corresponding lowercase letter, and if not upper case returns the argument value unchanged. (Hint: If c is known to be an uppercase value, then the expression $c - $ `'A'` will return the index of the character in the alphabet.)

10. List the sequence of moves the Towers of Hanoi problem would make in moving a tower of five disks from the source pole to the destination pole.

11. Rewrite the Towers of Hanoi problem so that the base case corresponds to moving a stack of size zero. Is the resulting program smaller or larger than the one given in the text? Is it easier to understand?

4

Analyzing
Execution Time

Chapter Overview

It might appear, at first, that describing the execution time of a computer program should be easy. One merely runs the program with a stopwatch in hand (or any number of technological variations of a similar theme) and records the results. And indeed, such a value, called a *benchmark*, is occasionally useful. We will examine benchmarks later in this chapter.

Most of the time, however, a benchmark is not a good characterization of a computer algorithm. A benchmark only describes the actual performance of a program on a given machine. Different processors can have dramatically different performances (computer manufacturers go to great lengths to remind users of this fact in hopes of enticing them to purchase faster, and more costly, machines). Even working on a single machine, there may be a selection of many alternative compilers for the same programming language. These compilers will produce slightly different machine code instructions for the same source language, and thus have varying execution times. Finally, execution timings for multiprocessing computers (computers that can perform many tasks simultaneously) will be altered by the other tasks being performed at the same time.

In this chapter we introduce the concept of *algorithmic analysis* (or *analysis of algorithms*), a technique used to characterize the execution behavior of algorithms in a manner independent of a particular platform, compiler, or language. Many of the standard library containers described in the second part of this book provide similar functionality, but different execution times for various operations. Thus, selecting the appropriate type of container for any particular problem involves not only an understanding of a container's capabilities, but an understanding of how execution times are determined and contrasted as well.

The topics discussed in this chapter include the following:

▲ Algorithmic analysis
▲ Big-Oh notation
▲ Benchmarks

4.1   ALGORITHMIC ANALYSIS AND BIG-OH NOTATION

We would like a way to abstract away small variations, and describe the performance of programs in a more idealized, processor-independent fashion. It is clear that alternative algorithms for the same problem can have dramatically different execution times. Ask yourself, for example, why dictionaries list words in alphabetical order. The reason, we know, is that doing so permits the reader to discover a word by repeatedly moving back and forth over increasingly smaller sections of the book (a process we will label *binary search* in Section 4.2.4). If words were not so ordered, then to discover whether a particular word appeared in the dictionary the reader would have to examine the volume in sequence from one end to the other, comparing the test word against each entry in turn; obviously this process would be considerably slower than the former.

The technique we use to capture this more-or-less intuitive notion of complexity is an idea called *algorithmic analysis*. In algorithmic analysis (sometimes termed *asymptotic analysis*) we gain power by, ironically, losing precision. By systematically ignoring constant amounts, and instead concentrating on an abstract characterization of the *size* of a problem, we can make more intelligent comparisons.

Determining whether a word appears in an unorganized list of n alternatives requires, for example, comparing each word against the target, and therefore uses approximately n comparisons. We assume each of these comparisons can be performed in a constant amount of time (the particular constant is unimportant, being greater or smaller depending upon the machine being used). In total, the running time of the process is therefore $c \times n$ for some unknown constant c. If the list is ordered, on the other hand, we will see (later in this chapter) that the search can be performed using only $\log n$ comparisons. Thus the real running time is some function $d \times \log n$ for some unknown value d.

Because the actual constants involved are unknown and, largely, irrelevant, we can eliminate them from our description. We introduce a notation, called "big-Oh" notation, which captures this intuitive idea. We say that searching an unorganized list uses $O(n)$ steps (read "big-Oh of n steps"), whereas searching a sorted and randomly accessible list can be performed in $O(\log n)$ steps (read "big-Oh of log n steps").

The formal definition of big-Oh states that if $f(n)$ is a function that represents the *actual* execution time of an algorithm, then the algorithm is $O(g(n))$ if, for all values n larger than some fixed constant n_0, there exists some constant c, such that $f(n)$ is always bounded by (smaller than or equal to) the quantity $c \times g(n)$. Although this formal definition may be of critical importance to theoreticians, it is the opinion of the author that an intuitive feeling for algorithmic execution is of more practical importance, and thus the remainder of the first section of this chapter will be devoted to providing this understanding. (For those readers who insist on a more formal approach, several of the exercises at the end of the chapter are designed to place the concept of algorithmic analysis on a firm foundation.)

4.2   EXECUTION TIME OF PROGRAMMING CONSTRUCTS

In the following sections we will discuss the most common programming constructs and illustrate the analysis of the running times using several algorithms. In some cases, the fact that these algorithms are correct may not be immediately obvious to the reader. We will return to these examples as illustrations in Chapter 5 when we discuss techniques useful in software validation.

4.2.1   Constant Time

The bare C++ language provides a number of primitive data types, such as integers and floating-point numbers. We begin by assuming that operations on such values (such as addition and subtraction) can be performed within a constant amount of time. Assignment of a primitive value to a variable also requires only constant time. A fixed sequence of constant time operations, such as the following sequence of assignments, still requires only constant time.

```
Card::Card  (suits sv, int rv)
    // initialize a new Card using the argument values
{
    rank = rv;
    suit = sv;
}
```

The maximum time it takes to perform a conditional if statement is the sum of the times it takes to perform a test, and the maximum time required by either alternative. If all three can be performed in constant time, then the time to execute the `if` statement can still be bounded by some constant value:

```
int min (int a, int b)
    // return the smaller of two arguments
{
    int smallest;

    if (a < b)
        smallest = a;
    else
        smallest = b;
    return smallest;
}
```

Even when procedures are quite lengthy, if they do not include loops or procedure calls, then the total execution time must remain constant. For example, consider the procedure `digitChar` described in Section 3.3.1. Like the conditional `if` statement, the algorithmic execution time of the `switch` statement is the maximum execution time of any case. In this situation all cases have a constant execution time, and therefore the total algorithmic execution time is still constant.

4.2.2   Simple Loops

A loop that performs a constant number of iterations is still considered to be executing in constant time. An example was given earlier in the constructor for the `Deck` abstraction, described in Chapter 2:

```
Deck::Deck ( )
    // initialize a deck by creating all 52 cards
{
    topCard = 0;
    for (int i = 1; i <= 13; i++) {
        Card c1(diamond, i), c2(spade, i), c3(heart, i), c4(club, i);
        cards[topCard++] = c1;
        cards[topCard++] = c2;
        cards[topCard++] = c3;
        cards[topCard++] = c4;
    }
}
```

Such loops, however, are relatively rare in comparison to loops in general. More commonly, the number of iterations a loop will perform is determined in some fashion by the input values. To describe the running time of a loop we need to characterize how many iterations the loop will perform, and then multiply this value by the running time of the body of the loop. The simplest case occurs when the limits of the loop are fixed by the input value, and the body of the loop uses constant time. An example in which this occurs is a procedure that takes as arguments a vector of values and an integer representing the number of elements in the vector, and returns the smallest value in the vector:

```
double minimum (double values [ ], unsigned int n)
    // return the minimum value found
    // in the vector of double precision values
{
    // make sure there is at least one element
    assert(n > 1);
    double minValue = values [0];

    for (unsigned int i = 0; i < n; i++) {
            // if current value
            // is less than minimum so far
        if (values[i] < minValue)
                // then save it
            minValue = values[i];
    }
    return minValue;
}
```

Here the loop will clearly execute *n* times. Because at each iteration we are performing at most one comparison and one assignment, the execution time for the body of the loop is constant. The total running time for the procedure is therefore $O(n)$.

Loops need not always have a simple terminating condition, and therefore a careful analysis of the algorithm may be necessary in order to characterize the number of iterations a loop will perform. A good example of this is a procedure to determine if an unsigned integer value represents a prime number. To do this we need only test integers that are smaller than the square root of the value, because if a value has any factors it must have at least one factor smaller than this amount. This can be accomplished by the following procedure, which returns a true value if the integer argument is prime, and false otherwise:

```
bool isPrime (unsigned int n)
    // return true if the argument value is prime
    // and false otherwise
{
    for (unsigned int i = 2; i * i <= n; i++) {
            // if i is a factor, then not prime
        if (0 == n % i)
            return false;
    }
```

```
        // if we end loop without finding factor
        // then n must be prime
    return true;
}
```

In this case, the loop terminates when the value of the loop variable exceeds the square root of the original value. Thus, the number of iterations is approximately $\sqrt{n}$. Because each iteration of the loop is performing only a constant amount of work, the entire algorithm is said to be $O(\sqrt{n})$. Notice in this case that the loop could very well terminate early (it will almost always do so, unless the number is prime). The algorithmic execution time represents a bound on the *worst case* execution time.

4.2.3   Nested Loops

As noted earlier, the execution time of a loop statement is the number of iterations of the loop multiplied by the execution time for the body of the loop. This becomes slightly more complex for nested loops.

The simplest case occurs when the limits of the loops are independent of one other. In this situation, the execution time is the product of the values representing the number of times each loop will iterate multiplied by the execution time of the body. An example of this is the classic algorithm for multiplying two *n* by *n* matrices, to produce a new *n* by *n* matrix product.[1]

```
const int n = 10;

void matprod (double a[n][n], double b[n][n], double c[n][n])
    // multiply the matrix a by b, yielding new matrix c
{
    for (unsigned int i = 0; i < n; i++) {
        for (unsigned int j = 0; j < n; j++) {
            c [i][j] = 0.0;
            for (unsigned int k = 0; k < n; k++) {
                c[i][j] += a[i][k] * b[k][j];
            }

        }
    }
}
```

---

1. The obvious syntax for declaring multiple dimension array arguments only works for arrays with fixed bounds, hence the defined constant. In Chapter 18 we will introduce an alternative technique for dealing with more general matrices.

The number of iterations in each loop is n. The body of the innermost loop, which performs only a multiplication, an addition, and an assignment, is constant time. Therefore the total running time is $O(n^3)$.

A slightly more complex analysis is required when the limits of iteration for the inner loops are linked to an outer loop. An example of this behavior is found in the procedure bubbleSort, which places the values of a vector into sorted order. An outer loop provides the index for the value to be placed. An inner loop then compares elements against each other, "bubbling" larger elements to the top of the array. By the end of each iteration of the inner loop the largest remaining value will have been moved into position.

```
void bubbleSort (double v[ ], unsigned int n)
    // exchange the values in the vector v
    // so they appear in ascending order
{
        // find the largest remaining value
        // and place into v[i]
    for (unsigned int i = n - 1; i > 0; i--) {

        // move large values to the top
    for (unsigned int j = 0; j < i; j++) {

            // if out of order
        if (v[j] > v[j+1]) {
            // then swap
            double temp = v[j];
            v[j] = v[j + 1];
            v[j + 1] = temp;
            }
        }
    }
}
```

To determine the running time of this procedure we can simulate execution on a few values. The pattern that quickly becomes apparent is that on the first iteration of the outermost loop, the inner loop will execute $n - 1$ times. On the second iteration of the outermost loop, the inner loop will execute $n - 2$ times, and so on until on the final iteration the inner loop executes 1 time. The number of iterations is therefore the sum of $(n - 1) + (n - 2) + \cdots + 1$.

MATHEMATICAL INDUCTION

In order to determine the size of the sum $(n - 1) + (n - 2) + \cdots + 1$, we introduce a powerful technique, called *mathematical induction*. We will encounter mathematical induction (or induction, for short) in many different places and guises in our investigations of data structures, and thus it is useful to be well versed in the technique.

To apply mathematical induction one first forms a *hypothesis*, a statement of the result you think will hold. In this case, our hypothesis will be that the sum of the values from 1 to n is given by the formula $\frac{n(n+1)}{2}$. Discovering a hypothesis is sometimes the most difficult part of a mathematical induction proof. Sometimes the hypothesis will be provided for you naturally in the problem statement; other times it can only be discovered by, for example, looking for patterns in several different cases.

The next step is to verify this formula for one or more *base cases*. If we select 1 for n, for example, we have 1 for the sum, and $\frac{2}{2}$ for the fraction, so the result holds. If we select 2 for n, we have 3 for the sum, and $\frac{2 \times 3}{2}$ for the fraction, so the result again holds.

The final step is to verify the formula for all remaining integers. We do this by *assuming* the hypothesis holds for some indeterminate value n, then proving it must therefore hold for the value $n + 1$. Doing so generally requires understanding how the hypotheses for n and $n + 1$ are linked, and *reducing* the $n + 1$ case to the size n situation.[2]

For example, in our present problem we assume that the summation of values from 1 to n is $\frac{n(n+1)}{2}$. We then inquire as to the sum of the values from 1 to $n + 1$. But this can be written as $(1 + 2 + \cdots + n) + (n + 1)$. Our *induction hypothesis* tells us that we can substitute $\frac{n(n+1)}{2}$ for the first term. The resulting expression is $\frac{n(n+1)}{2} + (n + 1)$, or $\frac{n(n+1)}{2} + \frac{2(n+1)}{2}$, which simplifies to $\frac{(n+1)(n+2)}{2}$. Because this matches our induction hypothesis for $n + 1$, we are done.

From this analysis, we can deduce that the number of iterations of the body of the loop in the bubble sort algorithm is $\frac{(n-1)n}{2}$. This is $\frac{n^2+n}{2}$. As we will see when we discuss the addition of terms in algorithmic analysis, this therefore shows that the running time of this algorithm is $O(n^2)$.

MATHEMATICAL INDUCTION AND RECURSION

There is a close relationship between the technique of mathematical induction and the use of recursion as a programming technique.

▲ Both begin by identifying one or more *base cases* that are handled using some other means.

▲ Both proceed by showing how a large problem can be *reduced* to a slightly smaller problem *of the same form*.

▲ The analysis then proceeds by showing first that the base cases are correct, and then a conditional argument of the form that *if* the

---

2. Sometimes it is easier to *assume* the hypothesis holds for $n - 1$, and then *prove* it must therefore hold for n.

induction formula (or recursive function call) is correct, *then* the larger expression must be correct.

We will see more of both mathematical induction and recursive algorithms in later chapters.

4.2.4   While Loops

The analysis of while loops is similar to that of for loops. The key is to determine the number of iterations the loop will perform. If the while loop is doing a linear traversal over some range, this may be straightforward. An example is the insertion sort algorithm, given as follows:

```
void insertionSort (double v [ ], unsigned int n)
    // exchange the values in the vector v
    // so they appear in ascending order
{
    for (unsigned int i = 1; i < n; i++) {

        // move element v[i] into place
        double element = v[i];
        int j = i - 1;
        while (j >= 0 && element < v[j]) {
            // slide old value up
          v[j+1] = v[j];
            // decrement j
          j = j - 1;
          }
        // place element into position
        v[j+1] = element;
      }
}
```

Unlike the bubble sort algorithm, the insertion sort algorithm places the lower portion of the array into sequence first. Each new value is inserted into place, sliding elements over until the proper location for each new value is established.

The outer loop clearly executes n steps. The inner loop *may* terminate early, but in the worst case must shift over elements all the way to the bottom. (This worst case occurs if the input is initially sorted backwards, and thus each value in turn is swapped until it reaches the zeroth element). We see, therefore, that in the worst case the number of iterations of the inner loop follows the pattern $1 + 2 + 3 + 4 + \cdots + (n - 1)$. As we have seen, the sum of this series is $\frac{(n-1)n}{2}$, and thus the algorithm is $O(n^2)$. (An optimist might argue that this worst case performance is rare, citing that in the best case the inner loop only executes one step, and therefore in this situation the insertion sort algorithm is $O(n)$. Unfortunately, though the mathematics are more complicated than we can present here, it is possible to show that the average case behavior of insertion sort is still $O(n^2)$.)

More complicated uses of the while loop occur when the variables involved are not simply tracing out an arithmetic progression. An example in which this occurred was Euclid's greatest common divisor algorithm, introduced in Chapter 3. In the analysis given there, we noted that the sum $n + m$ was an upper bound on the number of times the while loop could iterate (because on each iteration either n or m was decremented, and neither was permitted to reach zero). We indicate this by saying the algorithm is $O(n + m)$.

Another classic example of a nontrivial while loop occurs in the binary search algorithm. Here we assume that the input vector is an already ordered collection of values. The task is to determine if a particular value occurs in the list and, if not, the position immediately prior to the location where the element would be placed.

```
unsigned int binarySearch (double v [ ], unsigned int n, double value)
    // search for value in ordered array of data
    // return index of value, or index of
    // next smaller value if not in collection
{
    unsigned int low = 0;
    unsigned int high = n;


        // repeatedly reduce the area of search
        // until it is just one value
    while (low < high) {
        unsigned mid = (low + high) / 2;
        if (v[mid] < value)
            low = mid + 1;
        else
            high = mid;
    }

        // return the lower value
    return low;
}
```

The program works by repeatedly dividing in half the range of values being searched.[3] Because there were originally n values, we know the

---

3. Again, we note that if the correctness of this, or any other, procedure is not obvious, the patient reader should wait until the following chapter, when we will investigate techniques used in increasing confidence in the validity of algorithms.

number of times the collection can be subdivided is no larger than roughly log n (see nearby box on logarithms). This is sufficient to tell us that the entire procedure is $O(\log n)$.

4.2.5 Function Calls

When function or procedure calls occur, the running time of the call is taken to be the running time of the associated procedure. For example, suppose we wished to print the values of all prime numbers less than n. We could use an algorithm such as the following:

```
void printPrimes (unsigned int n)
    // print numbers between 1 and n
    // indicating which are prime
{
    for (unsigned int i = 2; i <= n; i++) {
        if (isPrime (i))
            cout << i << " is prime\n";
        else
            cout << i << " is not prime\n";
    }
}
```

We know the execution time of the `isPrime` routine is $O(\sqrt{n})$. (In fact, we can make the even stronger statement that it is $O(\sqrt{i})$, but doing so results in a summation that is difficult to analyze, so we will bound each call by the larger limit.) Because we are making roughly n calls, the total running time of the procedure is no greater than $O(n\sqrt{n})$.

Logarithms

To the mathematician, a *log* is generally envisioned as the inverse of the exponential function, or perhaps it is associated with the integral calculus (that is, $\log_e a = \int_1^a \frac{1}{x}dx$). To a computer scientist, the intuition concerning the log function should be something very different.

The log (base n) of a positive value x is *approximately* equal to the number of times that x can be divided by n.

Most often the log function will arise when quantities are repeatedly split in half. This is why logarithms in computer science are, almost invariably, used with a base value two.

The log (base 2) of a positive value x is *approximately* equal to the number of times that x can be divided in half.

The word "approximately" is used, because the log function yields a fractional value, and the exact figure can be as much as one larger than the integer ceiling of the log. But, as we have already noted, integer constants can be safely ignored when discussing upper bounds.

4.2.6   Recursive Calls

As we noted in Chapter 3, a procedure that, during execution, invokes itself with slightly different arguments is said to be recursive. Recursive functions or procedures add another dimension to our analysis, because the total running time is determined by the number of levels of recursion (that is, the number of times the function calls itself). Just as characterizing loops required describing the number of iterations in terms of the input values, characterizing recursive procedures requires the determination of the number of recursive calls, and multiplying this value by the amount of work performed at each level.

In the previous chapter we introduced the following example recursive procedure that was used to print the value of an unsigned integer in decimal format:

```
void printUnsigned (unsigned int val)
    // print the decimal character representation of
{   // the unsigned argument value
    if (val < 10)
       printChar (digitChar(val));
    else {
         // print high order part
       printUnsigned (val / 10);
         // print last character
       printChar (digitChar(val % 10));
    }
}
```

Recursion and Induction

There are close connections between the programming technique of recursion and the analysis tool of mathematical induction. In both situations, a key insight is to find a way to reduce a problem of large "size" into a problem of slightly smaller size, and so do repeatedly until eventually a base case is encountered.

In printing integer values, for example, numbers of four digits in length are printed by dividing the problem into two parts–printing a number of three digits in length and printing a single digit. Similarly, printing a number of three digits in length is performed by splitting the task into printing a two digit number, and printing a single digit. The base case is finally reached when a number consisting of only a single digit is printed.

$$
\begin{array}{lll}
\text{print } 456 & & 456 \\
\downarrow & & \uparrow \\
\text{print } 45,\text{ then print } 6 & & 45 \\
\downarrow & & \uparrow \\
\text{print } 4,\text{ then print } 5 \longrightarrow & & 4
\end{array}
$$

Because of this close connection, mathematical induction is often used in the analysis of recursive algorithms. This is true both to discover a running time and, as we will see in Chapter 5, to argue that an algorithm will correctly perform its intended task.

Because at each level of recursion we are dividing the argument value by 10, the number of recursive calls is the log (base 10) of the original argument value (see earlier box on logarithms). If we exclude the recursive call the remaining work performed at each level of recursion is constant, so the total running time of the procedure is $O(\log_{10} n)$, where n represents the value of the original argument. Because logarithms of different bases differ in magnitude by only a constant factor, this is usually written as $O(\log n)$.

Another interesting recursive algorithm is an improved approach to raising a double precision value to an integer exponent. Consider the following two observations:

$$x^{2n} = (x^2)^n$$
$$x^{2n+1} = (x^2)^n x$$

We can use these observations as basis for a new algorithm, which follows. The algorithm is recursive, with one special base case, namely the exponent zero. For positive non-zero values the base is squared while the exponent is halved prior to a recursive call. To compute x^{53}, for example, the following sequence of multiplications takes place. $x^{53} = x * (x^2)^{26}$, $x^{26} = (x^2)^{13}$, $x^{13} = x * (x^2)^6$, $x^6 = (x^2)^3$, $x^3 = x * (x^2)^1$, $x^1 = x * (x^2)^0$. Because at each recursive step of the algorithm the exponent is halved, the number of recursive calls is at most $\log n$, thereby showing that the algorithm is $O(\log n)$.

```
double power (double base, unsigned int n)
    // return the value base
    // raised to the integer n value
{
    if (n == 0)
        return 1.0;
    else if (even(n))
        return power (base * base, n / 2);
    else
        return power (base * base, n / 2) * base;
}
```

This $O(\log n)$ algorithm is a considerable improvement over the $O(n)$ algorithm presented earlier, a fact we will return to when we discuss benchmarking.

The exponent program illustrates how thinking recursively can yield a very fast algorithm. (However, the analysis that lies at the back of this algorithm is not limited only to recursive procedures. Exercise 20 at the end of this chapter explores the development of a fast iterative algorithm for the same task.) Not all recursive algorithms are fast. We can illustrate this by considering the Towers of Hanoi puzzle presented in the previous chapter. Using the algorithm presented there, to move a tower of size 1 required only constant work (which we will label c). To move a tower of size 2 required two recursive calls, each of which required a constant amount of work, so the total is $2 \times c$. To move a tower of size 3 required two recursive calls, each of which was moving a tower of size 2, so the total work is $2 \times 2 \times c$. To move a tower of size 4 required two recursive calls, each of which was moving a tower of size 3, so the total work is $2 \times 2 \times 2 \times c$. In general, the pattern is that to move a tower of size n requires 2^{n-1} recursive calls.

We therefore can say that the Towers of Hanoi algorithm we developed is $O(2^n)$, making it a very costly algorithm indeed. For example, the original citation for the puzzle described 64 golden disks, and claimed that the world would end when they were all moved from one pole to the next. The value 2^{63} is roughly 3.7×10^{19}. If we assume that one disk can be moved every minute, the total operation would still require about 7×10^{13} years!

4.3   SUMMING ALGORITHMIC EXECUTION TIMES

Consider the following procedure for initializing an n by n matrix as an identity matrix.

```
void makeIdentityMatrix ( double & m [n][n], unsigned int n)
    // initialize m as an identity matrix
{
        // first make matrix of all zeros
    for (unsigned int i = 0; i < n; i++) {
        for (unsigned int j = 0; j < n; j++) {
            m [i, j] = 0.0;
            }
        }

        // then place ones along diagonal
    for (i = 0; i < n; i++) {
        m [i, i] = 1.0;
        }
}
```

Clearly the first set of loops has an $O(n^2)$ execution time, and just as clearly the latter loop has $O(n)$ behavior. One might be tempted to assert that the entire process therefore has $O(n^2 + n)$ performance. Instead, in this section we will argue for a simpler rule, namely, *when adding algorithmic complexities, the larger value dominates.* Therefore, the entire algorithm just shown is $O(n^2)$.

To know what functions will dominate others, we must have some sort of ranking. The following table gives one such ordering, with the fastest growing functions listed near the top, and the slower growing functions listed below. Formally, we say that a function $f(n)$ dominates a function $g(n)$ if there exists a constant value n_0 such that for all values $n > n_0$, it is the case that $g(n) < f(n)$.

Function	Common name
$n!$	Factorial
2^n	Exponential
$n^d, d > 3$	Polynomial
n^3	Cubic
n^2	Quadratic
$n\sqrt{n}$	
$n \log n$	
n	Linear
$\sqrt{n}$	Root–n
$\log n$	Logarithmetic
1	Constant

Also shown in this table is the common name used to describe the algorithmic behavior. We use such names when we say, for example, that the matrix multiplication algorithm given in Section 4.2.3 is cubic, or the algorithm to raise a value to an integer exponent shown in Section 4.2.6 is logarithmic.

In the following discussion we will motivate this rule in a variety of fashions. The first is intended merely as an intuitive illustration. The reader has probably had the experience of sitting in a car during a rainstorm, and may have noted that small raindrops will stay fixed on the angled front window, even if the car remains at rest. If more water collects in the drop, however, it eventually falls off. There is a certain limit in size beyond which drops seemingly cannot remain fixed on the window.

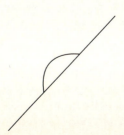

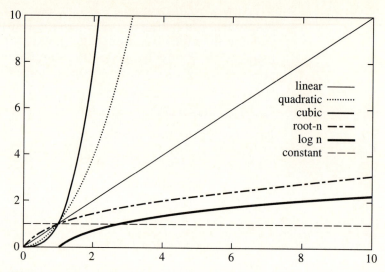

Figure 4.1   Characteristic curves for various functions

The force pulling the drop down is gravity, while the force permitting the drop to remain on the windscreen is friction, or the surface tension between the drop and the glass. We can idealize the situation slightly and consider the drop to be a perfect hemisphere. If r represents the radius of the drop, the surface area between the drop and the plane is πr^2. Gravity, on the other hand, operates on the entire volume of the drop, which is proportional to r^3. Thus, the force of gravity can be described by $c \times r^3$, for some unknown constant c, and the force of surface tension is similarly described by $d \times r^2$, making use of some unknown constant d.

The observed phenomenon is that small drops will remain on the surface. This is the situation when the force of the surface tension is greater than that of gravity. As the drop becomes larger, its radius increases. Eventually, no matter what the constants may be, a cubic (r^3) function will always become larger than a quadratic (r^2) function. Thus, we would predict that large drops must always fall off the surface, because gravity prevails over surface tension. This, of course, matches what we observe.

We can see this behavior in a graphical fashion by noting the curves given by various functions. All functions possess a certain characteristic curve. Figure 4.1 illustrates these curves for various functions. An n^3 function will always grow faster than, and thus always eventually surpass, an n^2 function, regardless of the constant values involved either as coefficient on the function or as an additive amount. This is shown in Figure 4.2, where the function $\frac{n^2}{4}$ is compared against the amount $200 + n \times \log n$. Although the latter is initially much larger, the n^2 function must always eventually dominate.

When two functions of different orders of magnitude are combined, the

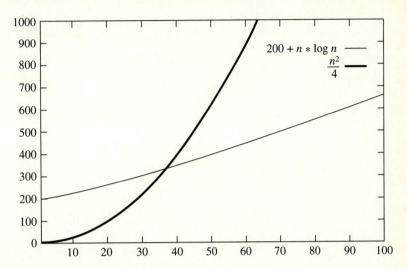

Figure 4.2 Comparing $n \log n$ and n^2 growth

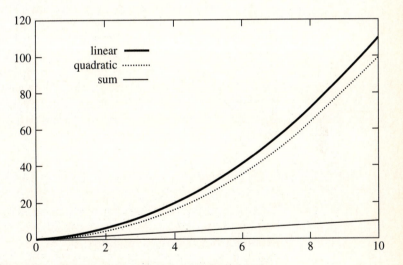

Figure 4.3 Addition of a linear and a quadratic function

larger function will dominate the smaller one, so that the characteristic shape of the result matches the larger, and not the smaller. This is shown in Figure 4.3, which compares the functions n, n^2, and the combination $n^2 + n$.

Another way to understand this is to consider a few actual values for the various functions. Assume, for example, that we can perform one operation every microsecond (that is, 10^6 operations per second), and we have some task that requires input of size 10^5. The figures in Table 4.1 illustrate how

Table 4.1   Execution times for a task using $n = 10^5$ input values, assuming 10^6 operations can be performed per second

function	Running time
2^n	More than a century
n^3	31.7 years
n^2	2.8 hours
$n\sqrt{n}$	31.6 seconds
$n \log n$	1.2 seconds
n	0.1 seconds
$\sqrt{n}$	3.2×10^{-4} seconds
$\log n$	1.2×10^{-5} seconds

long it would take to perform this task, assuming various different running times. The multiplication of the dominant function by a constant will, of course, change the running time, but only by a constant factor. Consider a task that requires $n^2 + n \log n$ steps. The n^2 part will mean the task will require several hours to complete, while the $n \log n$ component will add an insignificant few additional seconds to the execution time. Taking all of these arguments into consideration, it seems intuitive that when we add algorithmic execution times, it is safe to ignore all terms except the dominant function. (For those who have a natural dislike for intuitive arguments, some of the exercises at the end of the chapter will place this assertion on a more formal grounding.)

4.4   BENCHMARKING ACTUAL EXECUTION TIMES

There are situations where an overemphasis on the algorithmic execution bounds of a proposed algorithm, ignoring other factors, can lead one astray. Examples of such cases include:

1. A program may be composed on several algorithms, but the actual execution time dominated by only a few. Analysis of algorithms that have little impact on overall execution time is not important.

2. If a program is to be executed only a few times and then discarded, the cost of writing and debugging will likely dominate the cost of executing. Simple algorithms that can be easily validated are preferable in this situation to complex, but potentially more efficient, algorithms.

3. If the inputs are always small, then the asymptotic behavior is not a good predictor for execution time. For example, theoreticians know of an integer multiplication algorithm that is asymptotically faster than the more conventional algorithm, yet it is never used in practice

because the leading constants are so large that the improvement in execution behavior would not be significant for any realistically sized values. In choosing between the two algorithms shown in Figure 4.2, for example, the quadratic algorithm might be preferable if the value n were never larger than 20.

4. A complicated algorithm may be undesirable if it cannot be easily explained or documented. Software is almost always eventually examined and modified by individuals other than the original author. It is important that the working of a software system be easily understood from a simple examination of the code.

5. Often faster algorithms achieve their speedup at the expense of using additional memory. This is sometimes called a *time/space tradeoff*. If the memory requirements are prohibitive, then no matter how fast the algorithm promises to execute, it cannot be used.

6. The algorithmic analysis may fail to consider factors that will eventually dominate execution time. An example factor easily overlooked is excessive memory usage, causing extensive and repeated swapping of a program from main memory to disk.

7. Finally, in many numerical algorithms, issues such as accuracy and stability under perturbation may be just as important as algorithmic efficiency. Nobody really cares how fast you can compute the wrong answer.

An alternative to characterizing algorithms by their algorithmic complexity is to compare algorithms by their actual running times on some machine. Usually this is employed to compare algorithms of the same complexity. Comparing algorithms that are performing the same task but have differing complexities will usually simply reinforce our knowledge that an asymptotically faster algorithm will most often also be faster in practice. For example, Table 4.2 shows the running times for computing integer powers of a double precision base, using both the linear algorithm given in Section 4.2.2 and the logarithmic algorithm described in Section 4.2.6. As we would expect, the logarithmic algorithm is faster for almost all values.

Consider a comparison of two sorting algorithms. In Section 4.2.3 we described bubble sort, and in Section 4.2.4 we introduced insertion sort. Both algorithms are $O(n^2)$. Because algorithmic complexity provides no basis for comparing the two algorithms, we must resort to comparing actual running times if we wish to form some opinion as to the relative performance of the two techniques.

A comparison of running times is a technique fraught with uncertainty. Not only must we select a specific compiler and machine for our measurements, but it is possible to examine only a small number of input values as test cases. The running time for many algorithms is often tied in a very subtle fashion to the particular input values used. We can see this in the

Table 4.2 Comparison of running times for integer power algorithms

n	Execution time Linear alg	Execution time Log alg	Multiplications Log alg
10	3.2	3.2	6
20	5.8	3.8	7
30	8.5	4.0	9
40	11.1	4.5	8
50	13.7	4.6	9
60	16.4	4.6	10
70	19.0	5.2	10
80	21.6	5.1	9
90	24.2	5.3	11

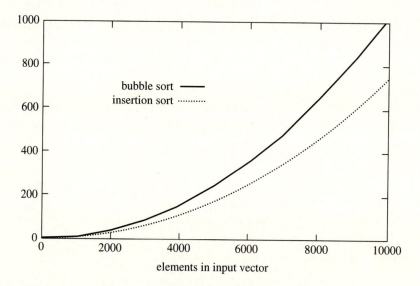

Figure 4.4 Execution timing for bubble sort and insertion sort

insertion sort algorithm, where a "good" input vector (one that is sorted or almost sorted already) will produce very fast behavior, while a "bad" input vector (one that is sorted in reverse, or very nearly so) will produce dramatically different results. Using a random number generator for input may give us some idea of an "average" test case, but it is an approximation at best.

Figure 4.4 shows the results of executing bubble sort and insertion sort on vectors of random values of various sizes. The results show the characteristic n^2 form, and suggest, but not prove, that in almost all cases, insertion sort is the faster algorithm. (However, we will eventually encounter algorithms that are even faster then either of these.)

4.5 CHAPTER SUMMARY

Key Concepts

- Algorithmic complexity
- Big-Oh notation
- Recursion
- Mathematical induction
- Benchmarks

On a coarse level, algorithms can be compared by their algorithmic growth. The algorithmic characterization of an algorithm is usually given by a "big-Oh" expression. This expression characterizes the behavior of the algorithm as input values grow ever larger. However, even with relatively small inputs, an algorithm with a smaller algorithmic complexity will usually execute more quickly than one with a larger algorithmic complexity.

Mathematical induction is a powerful analysis technique used in proving properties of general formulas. In computer science, mathematical induction is used in the analysis of program fragments that are executed repeatedly, either as loops or as recursive algorithms. Mathematical induction is used in proving termination, analyzing execution time, and proving correctness.

Mathematical induction and the development of recursive algorithms are very similar. Some of the common features of both include:

▲ The discovery of base cases that can be handled by other mechanisms, and to which all larger problems will ultimately be reduced.

▲ The discovery of how a larger problem can be reduced to a slightly smaller problem of the same form.

In comparing two algorithms with the same algorithmic complexity, actual running times, or benchmarks, may be employed. While a benchmark can provide an accurate time estimate for a particular machine and particular input conditions, it is sometimes difficult to extrapolate such a number to new machines or different input values.

Further Reading

The basic concepts of computational complexity were originally developed by Juris Hartmanis and Richard E. Stearns [Hartmanis 65], for which they were awarded the ACM Turing award in 1993. As we noted in Chapter 3, the study of algorithms was popularized by Donald Knuth in his three-part series [Knuth 73, Knuth 81, Knuth 75]. A discussion of Euclid's GCD algorithm appears both in Volumes 1 and 2.

Study Questions & Exercises

Study Questions

1. Why is a benchmark not generally a good characterization of the running time of an algorithm?

2. What does it mean to say that an algorithm is $O(f(n))$ for some function $f(n)$?

3. What is the formula that describes the algorithmic execution time of a conditional (if) statement? How about a switch statement?

4. What is the algorithmic running time of the constructor for the class Player, described in Section 2.4?

5. What is the algorithmic running time of the procedure named power, used to raise a double precision value to an integer exponent, that we earlier described in Section 3.3.1?

6. What are the parts of an argument that uses mathematical induction?

7. What is the best and worst case algorithmic running time of the insertion sort algorithm?

8. To a computer scientist, what should be the intuitive meaning of the log function?

9. What are the two pieces of information needed to characterize the algorithmic running time of a recursive procedure?

10. What rule is used in adding two algorithmic complexity formulas?

11. Assume a person could move one disk in the Towers of Hanoi puzzle every second. What is the largest number of disks that could be solved as a puzzle in one hour?

12. What are some situations where a benchmark provides more useful information than an algorithmic complexity characterization?

Exercises

1. The following three exercises are intended to place the concept of algorithmic analysis on a slightly more firm theoretical foundation. In particular, these exercises will help support the idea that (a) additive constants can be ignored, (b) constant coefficients can be ignored, and (c) when adding two algorithmic complexities, only the dominant function need be considered.

   Recall that the definition of big-Oh notation said that a function $f(n)$ is $O(g(n))$ if there exist constants n_0 and c such that for all values $n > n_0$, $f(n) < c \times g(n)$.

   For the first problem, assume that $f(n)$ is $O(g(n))$, where $f(n)$ and $g(n)$ are both functions of n, $g(n) > 1$ for all n. Demonstrate that $f(n) + c$, for any constant c, is still $O(g(n))$. Hint: Show that there exists some new constant c_2, which bounds $f(n) + c$.

2. Constant coefficients can be ignored. Assume that $f(n)$ is $O(g(n))$. Demonstrate that $c \times f(n)$, for any constant c, is still $O(g(n))$.

3. Addition of big-Oh terms. Assume $f_1(n) < f_2(n)$ for all values larger than some n_0, and that $f_2(n)$ is $O(g(n))$. Show that $f_1(n) + f_2(n)$ is $O(g(n))$.

4. Prove that the function ax^i is $O(x^{i+j})$ for any value $j >= 0$.

5. Using the proof from the previous question, prove that any polynomial $a + bx + cx^2 + \cdots + hx^i$ is $O(x^i)$, that is, that the largest polynomial term will dominate.

6. Prove that the function $\log_a n$ is $O(\log_2 n)$ for any constant value a (hence, we need not state the base of a log when using big-Oh notation).

7. Prove, using mathematical induction, that a common multiplier can be factored out of a summation. That is, for any constant c and nonnegative integer n:

$$\sum_{i=1}^{n} c \times f(i) = c \times \sum_{i=1}^{n} f(i)$$

8. Prove, by mathematical induction, that the sum of powers of 2 is one less than the next higher power. That is, for any nonnegative integer n:

$$\sum_{i=0}^{n} 2^i = 2^{n+1} - 1$$

9. What is wrong with the following induction proof that for all positive numbers a and integers n, it must be true that a^{n-1} is 1. For the base case we have that for $n = 1$, a^{n-1} is a^0 which is 1. For the induction case let us assume it is true for 1, 2, 3, ... n. To verify the condition for $n + 1$ we have

$$a^{(n+1)-1} = a^n = \frac{a^{n-1} \times a^{n-1}}{a^{n-2}} = \frac{1 \times 1}{1} = 1$$

So the conjecture must hold for $n + 1$ as well.

10. Critique the following argument that purports to show that all horses gathered in a single corral are the same color. Suppose there exists a horse. Let us consider a corral that contains this horse. Thus, we have a base case, because for n equal to one (this one horse) all horses in the corral are the same color. Let us assume this color is black. Now let us consider the induction step by adding a new horse, of unknown color, to the corral. The corral still contains the black horse, so let us remove it. We now have a corral containing n horses and by our induction assumption they must all be black. But the horse we removed is also black, therefore when we return it to the corral we will have $n + 1$ black horses. We can continue in a similar manner adding horses one by one, and thus no matter how many horses we add to the corral they must all be black.

11. Suppose by careful measurement we have discovered a function that describes the precise running time of some algorithm. For each of the following such functions, describe the algorithmic running time in big-Oh notation.
    a. $3n^2 + 3n + 7$
    b. $(5 * n) * (3 + \log n)$
    c. $\frac{5n+4}{6}$
    d. $1 + 2 + 3 + 4 + \cdots + n$
    e. $n + \log n^2$
    f. $\frac{(n+1)\log n}{2}$

12. For each of the following program skeletons, describe the algorithmic execution time as a function of n. You can assume the remaining portions of the loops require only constant execution time.

    a.

    ```
    for (int i = 0; i < n; i++) {
        ...
    }
    for (int j = n; j >= 0; j--) {
        ...
    }
    ```

    b.

    ```
    for (int i = 0; i < n; i++) {
      for (int j = 0; j < n; j++) {
        ...
      }
    }
    ```

    c.

    ```
    for (int i = 0; i < n; i++) {
      for (int j = 0; j < i; j++) {
        ...
      }
    }
    ```

    d.

    ```
    for (int i = n; i > 0; i = i / 2) {
        ...
    }
    ```

    e.

    ```
    for (int i = 0; i < n; i++) {
      for (int j = 0; j * j < n; j++) {
        ...
      }
    }
    ```

    f.

    ```
    for (int i = n; i > 0; i = i >> 1) {
      for (int j = 0; j < n; j++) {
        ...
      }
    }
    ```

13. Suppose we have an n^2 algorithm that for $n = 80$ runs slightly longer than one hour. One day we discover an alternative algorithm that runs in time $n \log n$. If we assume the constants of proportionality are about the same, about how long would we expect the new program to run?

14. Simulate the execution of bubble sort (Section 4.2.3) on the array of value 7 2 3 9 4. Show the state of the array at the end of each iteration of the outermost loop.

15. Simulate the execution of insertion sort (Section 4.2.4) on the array of value 7 2 3 9 4. Show the state of the array at the end of each iteration of the outermost loop.

16. The recursive version of the power algorithm (Section 4.2.6) required the use of a procedure even, used to determine if an integer value is even or odd. Give an algorithm for this procedure. What is the algorithmic running time of your algorithm?

17. How are we guaranteed that the isPrime procedure (Section 4.2.2) will terminate? Find a quantity for this algorithm that satisfies the

properties described in Section 3.3.4 of the previous chapter.

18. How are we guaranteed that the bubbleSort procedure (Section 4.2.3) will terminate? Find a quantity for this algorithm that satisfies the properties described in Section 3.3.4 of the previous chapter.

19. How are we guaranteed that the binarySearch procedure (Section 4.2.4) will terminate? Find a quantity for this algorithm that satisfies the properties described in Section 3.3.4 of the previous chapter.

20. In Section 4.2.6 we introduced a recursive algorithm to compute integer exponents in logarithmic time. It is possible to create an iterative (nonrecursive) algorithm that also has logarithmic running time. To do so, we introduce a third value, which we will label A. Let A initially hold the value 1. We can therefore say that instead of wanting to compute x^n, we are computing $A \times x^n$. We can then make the following observations:

  - If n is even, then $A \times x^n$ is the same as $A \times (x^2)^{(n/2)}$. So if x is replaced by x^2, and n by $n/2$, the value of the expression $A \times x^n$ will be the same as the original.

  - If n is odd, then $A \times x^n$ is the same as $(A \times x) \times (x^2)^{((n-1)/2)}$. So if A is replaced by $A \times x$, x is replaced by x^2, and n by $(n-1)/2$, the value of the expression $A \times x^n$ will be the same as the original.

To create an algorithm, the values of A, x, and n are all repeatedly modified until n has the value zero. When n is zero, the result will be held by variable A (since x^0 is 1). Create the algorithm that is based on these observations.

21. Empirically test the assertion that bubbleSort is an $O(n^2)$ algorithm. To do this, execute the algorithm using vectors of different size (say, multiples of 100 between 0 and 10000), and record the resulting execution times. If the algorithm is indeed $O(n^2)$, it would mean that there exists a constant c so that $c \times n^2$ is the observed running time. Since you know the running time and can compute n^2, you can work backwards and compute the value c for each of your trial executions. If the values of c you compute are roughly equal, then the algorithm is indeed $O(n^2)$.

22. Using the value of c you computed in Exercise 21, estimate how long it would take to sort a vector of 100,000 elements.

23. Do the same analysis as in Exercise 21 for the insertionSort algorithm.

## Chapter 5

Increasing Confidence in Correctness

Chapter Overview

In this chapter we will investigate techniques that are used to increase confidence in the likelihood that a program will execute correctly. There are two primary approaches to this task. One is the mechanism of *program testing*, where a function or procedure is executed with actual test values. The second is a process that is often termed *proving program correctness*. However, the phrase is somewhat misleading. The arguments developed using the techniques described here are not "proofs" in the strict mathematical sense. Rather than providing absolute assurances, proofs of programs should be considered to be confidence building measures.

Techniques used in developing arguments for the correctness of programs include *assertions* and *invariants*. After introducing techniques used in program proving, this chapter concludes with a discussion of program testing techniques and objectives. Major topics include:

▲ Program proofs
▲ Assertions
▲ Invariants
▲ Program testing

5.1   PROGRAM PROOFS

Proofs of programs are techniques used by programmers to increase their own confidence in the correctness of their algorithms, and to discover and highlight those places where such confidence is misplaced (that is, find errors).[1] To properly understand the role of program proofs the reader should remember that, in the large, programming is a social activity pursued by a team of individuals working cooperatively on a given task. A program proof is not for the benefit of the computer; indeed, the greater portion of the proof is documented by comments in the program text, which are not processed by the computer at all. Similarly, a proof is only partially intended for the benefit of the original programmer. Most often, programmers examine each others code in a structured setting, called a *code walk-through*. In such a walk-through, a programmer traces the execution of an algorithm, and presents arguments to justify the contention that the particular section of code under scrutiny will perform as expected. Proofs of program correctness are an essential part of this process.

While the role of the programmer is to argue for the correctness of the program, the role of the other members participating in a code walk-through is to try to anticipate ways in which failure can occur, and highlight potential weakness. Although it is not our place here to discuss in detail principles of software engineering, we note in passing that great care must be taken during code walk-through to ensure that the atmosphere remains one of cooperation, and that programmers are not permitted to have the feeling that they are defending their code against "attacks" by other programmers.

5.1.1   Invariants

The major tool employed in formulating an argument that can be used to justify belief in the correctness of an algorithm is the *invariant*. An invariant is nothing more than a comment, but it is a comment that describes the state of the computation at the point the comment would be encountered during the course of execution. The art of using invariants lies in finding statements that are most meaningful to a human audience. To do so, an invariant should describe the processing being performed in the high-level language of the problem domain, and not necessarily in the low-level language of the actual calculation being performed.

---

1. There have been attempts to develop systems whereby formal proofs of algorithms can be presented, but such techniques tend to be tedious to employ, do not scale well to large problems, and generally provide no more practical benefits than the much less formal techniques we will describe here. The references cited at the end of the chapter should be consulted for further information.

Here is a program that contains an error. Let us see how the use of invariants could be used to uncover the bug. The program purports to characterize three sides of a triangle, returning 1 if the triangle is equilateral (all sides equal), 2 if isosceles (two sides equal), and 3 if scalene (no sides equal).

```
int triangle (int a, int b, int c)
    // characterize the triangle with sides a, b, and c
{
    if (a == b) {
        if (b == c) {
            // inv: a equals b, b equals c,
            // so a equals c and all are equal
            return 1;
        }
        else {
            // inv: a equals b, but b does not equal c
            // so only two sides are equal
            return 2;
        }
    }
    else {
        if (b == c) {
            // inv: a not equal to b, but b equals c,
            // so two sides are equal
            return 2;
        }
        else {
            // inv: so no sides are equal
            return 3;
        }
    }
}
```

To form an argument to justify belief in the correctness of an algorithm, we trace execution from beginning to end, following all possible paths, and demonstrate that the invariant must be true when execution reaches the point where the invariant is placed, and furthermore that the invariant establishes the correct result.

If we imagine a test case that fails the first if statement and also the second, we can see the error in the program. At the point of the invariant immediately prior to returning the value 3, the information we have is that a is not equal to b, and that b is not equal to c (since both these conditions have failed). But we do not therefore know that all sides are unequal, since it is possible for a to be equal to c. Thus, the invariant that we have written (which, if it were true, would justify the following statement) cannot be

supported by an argument. (This illustrates that invariants should not be
assumed to be true until proven by argument.)

Invariants become more useful, but also more complicated, when programs contain loops. In a program with loops we cannot simply execute
all possible paths. However, the concept of an invariant remains the same.
That is, an invariant simply describes the state of execution at the point
the invariant appears. In Chapter 4 we described an algorithm that could
be used to find the minimum value from a vector of *n* floating-point quantities. This function could be augmented with invariants in the following
fashion:

```
double minimum (double values [ ], unsigned int n)
    // return the minimum value found
    // in the vector of double precision values
{
    // make sure there is at least one element
    assert(n > 0);
    double minValue = values [0];
        // inv 1: minValue is the minimum value found in
        // the range 0 .. 0
    for (unsigned int i = 1; i < n; i++) {
        // inv 2: minValue is the minimum value found in
        // the range 0 .. i-1
        if (values[i] < minValue)
            minValue = values[i];
        // inv 3: minValue is the minimum value found in
        // the range 0 .. i
        }
    // inv 4: minValue is the minimum value found in
    // the range 0 .. n-1
    return minValue;
}
```

In the next section we will describe how invariants are used in formulating an argument to increase confidence in the correct functioning of an
algorithm.

5.1.2   Analyzing Loops

To create an argument that can be used to increase confidence in an algorithm, the programmer traces all possible execution paths through a
program that leads from one invariant to the next. In each case, the programmer creates an argument which asserts that *if* the first invariant is
true, and *if* the intervening statements are executed, *then* the second invariant must be true. We will illustrate this process with the function given
in the previous section.

The first step is to verify the initial invariant. The assertion is necessary to ensure that there is at least one value. Having determined this, the assignment statement is used to initialize the variable `minValue` to this value. The variable, therefore, holds the minimum value of the vector in the range 0 to 0 (indeed, it holds the only value in this range).

```
        ⋮
double minValue = values [0];
        // inv 1: minValue is the minimum value found in
        // the range 0 .. 0
for (unsigned int i = 1; i < n; i++) {
        // inv 2: minValue is the minimum value found in
        // the range 0 .. i-1
        ⋮
```

We next argue from invariant 1 to invariant 2. Just as we did with induction, we are now making the *assumption* that invariant 1 is true, and arguing that if this is the case, then invariant 2 must be true when execution reaches the point at which it has been placed. Between these two points, the only value that is changed is the variable i, which is assigned the value 1, and has been tested to ensure it is less than n. But i − 1 is therefore 0, and if invariant 1 were previously true, then invariant 2 must now be true, because it is asserting the same fact.

```
        ⋮
        // inv 2: minValue is the minimum value found in
        // the range 0 .. i-1
        if (values[i] < minValue)
            minValue = values[i];
```

Loop Invariants and Mathematical Induction

The validity of the use of loop invariants can be demonstrated by turning a proof based on invariants into a proof using mathematical induction. To do so, we simply let the *number of times execution has passed through the loop* be the induction value.

Consider how invariants are used in the analysis of the minimum value function considered in Section 5.1.2. Cases in which the loop is executed zero times and in which the loop is executed one time are handled as base cases. For the induction case, we assume the loop has been executed n times, and will loop at least $n + 1$ times (that is, at least one more time). The argument presented in the text then demonstrates that if invariant 3 is true during the nth iteration, then invariant 2 must be true on the $n + 1$ iteration.

This shows that no matter how many times the loop iterates, invariant 3 will always be true when it is encountered. A separate argument then traces the flow from invariant 3 to invariant 4, and we are finished.

```
//  inv 3: minValue is the minimum value found in
//  the range 0 .. i
```
.
.
.

Next, we consider the flow of execution between invariant 2 and invariant 3. This time, instead of assuming we are on the first iteration (as we did between invariant 1 and invariant 2), we now assume we are on some indefinite iteration. We therefore have no specific information concerning the value i, other than it must have a value between 1 and n (the limits of the loop). Invariant 2 tells us that the variable `minValue` holds the minimum value in the vector for indices in the range 0 to i - 1. If we examine the code between invariants 2 and 3, we see that we can divide our argument into two cases. Either the value held by the vector at index position i is smaller than this minimum, or it is not. In the former case the variable `minValue` is updated to hold this new value. Therefore, in either case, by the time we reach invariant 3 we can argue that the value held by `min-Value` is now the smallest element in the range of data values indexed by 0 through the position i.

Note that invariant 2 and invariant 3 are very similar. We often say that invariant 2 has been *strengthened* in order to reach invariant 3. In this case, strengthening means that we have extended the range of values under consideration from $(0 .. i - 1)$ to $(0 .. i)$.

From invariant 3 there are two possible directions that execution could flow. Both must be investigated. In both cases, the variable i will be incremented. The new value of i then either is or is not greater than or equal to the limit value n. If it is not, then the loop will iterate once more, and invariant 2 will once again be reached. In this circumstance we are assuming that invariant 3 is true, and arguing that invariant 2 must now be true. But invariant 3 is asserting the same condition as invariant 2, under the condition that variable i has been incremented.

The second possibility is that the loop terminates, and execution flows from invariant 3 to the final invariant 4. But this will only occur if the updated value of i (which is monotonically increasing) is now n. Therefore invariant 3 is transformed into invariant 4 with the substitution of n - 1 for i. (We must subtract one to "undo" the fact that i was incremented prior to the test.)

.
.
.

```
//  inv 1: minValue is the minimum value found in
//  the range 0 .. 0
```

```
for (unsigned int i = 1; i < n; i++) {
```
.
.
.

```
// inv 3: minValue is the minimum value found in
// the range 0 .. i
}
```

```
// inv 4: minValue is the minimum value found in
// the range 0 .. n-1
```

The last flow of control is the easiest to forget. It is possible to move directly from invariant 1 to invariant 4 without encountering any other invariants. This will occur only when the size of the vector is exactly one, and therefore the condition controlling the loop is false when it is first encountered. But in this circumstance the value n must be 1, and therefore invariant 4 is asserting the same condition as invariant 1.

5.1.3 Asserting the Outcome is Correct

The final invariant in any procedure should always assert the conditions corresponding to the desired outcome. These, however, may only be indirectly addressed by the actions of the program. For example, the invariants in the isPrime procedure deal with finding factors of the input value. Only if no factors are found is the number known to be prime. Note that, as in the minimum number procedure, the invariant at the end of the loop is a simple conjunction of the invariant at the start of the loop and the negation of the looping condition.

```
bool isPrime (unsigned int n)
    // return true if the argument value is prime
    // and false otherwise
{
    for (unsigned int i = 2; i * i <= n; i++) {
            // inv 1: n has no factors between 2 and i-1

        if (0 == n % i) {
                // inv 2: i divides n
                // therefore n is not prime
            return false;
            }

                // inv 3: n has no factors between 2 and i
        }

            // inv 4: n has no factors between 2 and
            // ceiling(sqrt(n)), therefore number must
            // be prime
    return true;

}
```

5.1.4   Progress Toward an Objective

Invariants inside a loop describe an intermediate stage within a calculation. In such situations, only partial progress has been made toward an ultimate objective. To describe such invariants, it is necessary to understand not only the ultimate objective, but also how the intermediate stage relates to the intended outcome.

For example, in the binary search procedure we initially know only that the target value, if it appears at all, appears in positions indexed between 0 and $n - 1$ (that is, the entire vector). By repeatedly examining the middle value in a range, we divide in half the region in which the value can potentially be found. This continues until the region is reduced to a single element.

```
unsigned int binarySearch (double v [ ], unsigned int n, double value)
        // search for value in ordered array of data
        // return index of value, or index of
        // next smaller value if not in collection
{
        unsigned int low = 0;
        unsigned int high = n;

        while (low < high) {

                // inv: data[0 .. low-1] less than value
                // data[high .. max] greater than or equal to value

        unsigned mid = (low + high) / 2;
        if (data[mid] < value)
                low = mid + 1;
        else
                high = mid;

        }

        // inv: data[0..low-1] less than value
        // and value less than or equal to data[low+1]

        return low;

}
```

When loops are nested, each loop may be pursuing its own objective, and each may therefore have a different set of invariants. In the bubble sort procedure, for example, the outer loop is placing elements into position, starting from the top. The inner loop is designed to ensure that the largest remaining value is moved into the topmost position. This is accomplished by moving the loop variable j upward through all possibilities, and maintaining the condition that the largest value seen so far is kept at position j+1. We could augment this procedure with invariants as follows:

```
void bubbleSort (double v[ ], unsigned int n)
        // exchange the values in the vector v
        // so they appear in ascending order
{
        for (unsigned int i = n - 1; i > 0; i--) {
                // inv: elements indexed i+1 to n-1 are correctly ordered

                for (unsigned int j = 0; j < i; j++) {
                        // inv: v[j] holds largest value from range (0..j)

                                // if out of order
                        if (v[j+1] < v[j]) {
                                // then swap
                                double temp = v[j];
                                v[j] = v[j + 1];
                                v[j + 1] = temp;
                        }

                // inv: v[j+1] holds largest value from range (0..j+1)
                }

                // inv: v[i] holds largest value from range (0..i)
                // inv: therefore, elements i to n-1 are correctly ordered
        }

        // inv: elements indexed 0 to n-1 are correctly ordered
}
```

5.1.5   Manipulating Unnamed Quantities

When using invariants, the need to discuss quantities that are not explicitly named in the program commonly arises. An example occurs in the greatest common divisor program from Chapter 3. To argue that this procedure is correct we require the observation that if d is a divisor for both n and m, and n is larger than m, then d must also be a divisor for $n - m$. (To see this, note that $\frac{n}{d}$ must be integer, as must $\frac{m}{d}$, and therefore $\frac{n}{d} - \frac{m}{d}$ must be integer, but this is the same as $\frac{n-m}{d}$). The invariants for the loop must therefore assert that while we have changed n and m, the GCD of the original values, which is not a quantity that has been given a name by the program, has not been altered.[2]

```
unsigned int gcd (unsigned int n, unsigned int m)
     // compute the greatest common divisor
     // of two positive integer values
{
     assert (n > 0 && m > 0);

     while (m != n) {
         if (n > m)
             n = n - m;
             // inv: gcd of n and m
             // has not been altered
         else
             m = m - n;
             // inv: gcd of n and m
             // has not been altered
     }

         // n equal to m,
         // so n is divisor of both
     return n;
}
```

5.1.6   Function Calls

When a procedure invokes another procedure, the argument concerning the correctness of the first procedure is always expressed conditionally, based on the assumption that the invoked procedure is performing in the correct manner. Although it is not necessary to repeat the argument for the correctness of the called procedure, it *is* necessary to address the question of whether the arguments that are being passed to the underlying procedure are valid; that is, within the range of elements the procedure is prepared to handle.

For example, the `printPrimes` procedures can be shown to be correct, based on the assumption that the `isPrime` procedure operates correctly. The `isPrime` procedure executes correctly for values larger than 2, and this condition is clearly satisfied.

---

2. To be precise, all we have demonstrated by this argument is that the result will be *a* divisor of the original *n* and *m* values. To assert that the result is the largest possible divisor requires a more subtle mathematical argument, which is not relevant to our discussion here.

```
void printPrimes (unsigned int n)
    // print numbers between 2 and n
    // indicating which are prime
{
    for (unsigned int i = 2; i <= n; i++) {
        if (isPrime (i))
            cout << i << " is prime\n";
        else
            cout << i << " is not prime\n";
    }
}
```

5.1.7   Recursive Algorithms

The analysis of recursive algorithms is simply an extension of the technique used for ordinary procedure calls. As we noted in Chapter 4, the execution of recursive procedures is always divided into two cases. One or more *base cases* can be handled without recursive invocation. The *recursive* (or *inductive*) cases are handled by the procedure calling itself.

The base cases are analyzed as any other procedure, using invariants if necessary. To handle the recursive case, we simply *assume* that the recursive invocation will perform correctly, and argue the remainder of the procedure accordingly. For example, consider the procedure from the previous chapter to print an unsigned integer value:

```
void printUnsigned (unsigned int val)
    // print the character representation of
    // the unsigned argument value
{
    if (val < 10)
        printChar (digitChar(val));
    else {  // print all but final character
        printUnsigned (val / 10);
            // print final character
        printChar (digitChar(val % 10));
    }
}
```

If the argument is less than ten, it is easy to see that the procedure performs as expected (assuming that the two procedures digitChar and printChar operate properly). The recursive case is hardly any more complex; we assume the recursive call will work, and the remainder is simply another set of calls on printChar and digitChar.

Once again, to place this technique on firm formal footing requires relating the analysis to mathematical induction. One argues that in situations where no recursive calls are invoked the correct results are produced. One then assumes that the correct result is produced in all situations where n recursive calls are necessary. Based on this, one then formulates an argument that if $n + 1$ recursive calls are necessary the correct result will be produced, because this reduces to a case where n calls are necessary.

In both proving mathematical formulas using induction and in the analysis of recursive algorithms, the following steps must be performed:

1. Identify the base cases, and establish that the formula or algorithm works for these cases.

2. Argue that, in all situations, the reduction being performed must eventually reach one of the base cases.

3. Provide a conditional argument which asserts that *if* the recursive call produces the correct outcome, *then* the remainder of the program must produce the correct result.

The recursive version of the integer exponential algorithm illustrates once more that invariants are related more to the problem domain than to the mechanics of execution. In this case, the only invariant necessary is used to assert that although the recursive calculation being performed is different, the resulting value is the same as the original request.

```
double power (double base, unsigned int n)
    // return the value base
    // raised to the integer n value
{
    if (n == 0)
        return 1.0;
    else if (even(n))
            // base ˆ n is same as
            // (base ˆ 2) ˆ (n / 2) for even n
        return power (base * base, n / 2);
    else
            // base ˆ n is same as
            // base * (base ˆ 2) ˆ (n / 2) for odd n
        return power (base * base, n / 2) * base;
}
```

The Towers of Hanoi puzzle gives us an even more dramatic example of how the analysis of recursive algorithms is performed by conditionally assuming the correct functioning of the recursive case. This algorithm could be augmented with invariants as follows:

```
void Hanoi (int n, char a, char b, char c)
    // move n disks from tower a to tower b, using tower c
{
    if (n == 1) {
```

```
            cout << "move disk from tower " << a << " to " << b << endl;
                // inv: have moved stack of size 1
                // from tower a to tower b
        }
    else {
        Hanoi (n-1, a, c, b);
                // inv: have moved stack of size n-1 from
                // stack a to stack c

        cout << "move disk from tower " << a << " to " << b << endl;
                // inv: move moved largest disk from stack a
                // to stack b

        Hanoi (n-1, c, b, a);
                // inv: have moved stack of size n-1 from
                // stack c back to stack b, on top of
                // disk previously moved,
                // therefore now have stack of size n
                // on stack b

    }
}
```

We *assume* the recursive call will perform the task we describe. Based on that assumption, we then prove that the current task is correctly executed. The base cases are handled by a separate argument. If all of these arguments are correct, then the entire algorithm must be correct, regardless of the input values.

5.2   PROGRAM TESTING

Testing is the process of executing computer code on actual values, and verifying the resulting output for correctness. As a side effect, programming errors are often uncovered when the expected output is not produced. Testing should always be an intrinsic part of any software development effort.

Testing can, and should, be performed at all levels:

▲ Individual functions or methods can be tested as they are written.

▲ A class can be tested in isolation from the remainder of a program.

▲ Finally, a complete program can be tested as an application.

In the first two cases we are testing small portions of a program, independent of the remainder of the application. To do this it is often necessary to write short-term, temporary code to "harness" the software being tested. This harness code can be divided into two categories:

▲ *Driver* code acts as the calling procedure. This code sets up the argument values, global variables, or whatever input is necessary for the code under test; then it invokes the procedure, and finally validates the result (or prints the result, leaving it to the programmer to perform the validation).

▲ *Stub* code simulates the actions of any procedures that may be called by the algorithm under test. While stub code simulates the actions that will be found in the resulting application, they need not perform exactly the same process. For example, a stub might merely print the argument values, then prompt the programmer to supply the result that will be returned.

In Chapter 2 we illustrated some of this testing process, showing how simple main programs could be written to test, for example, the `Card` class in isolation without reference to the rest of the application. Once the `Card` component was satisfactorily tested, the `Deck` class could similarly be exercised. Having completed the analysis of the `Deck`, the final program could then be evaluated.

Functions should always be tested using a number of different input values. The following guidelines can be considered in creating good test values:

▲ Make sure every statement in the function is exercised by at least one test value.

▲ Make sure to use test data that exercises both the true and false alternatives for every `if` and `while` expression. Test each legal label of a `switch` statement.

▲ If there is a minimal legal input value, such as an empty array or a smallest integer value, use this as one of your test cases.

▲ If the function (or program) has both legal and illegal inputs, a set of test cases should include both clearly legal values and clearly illegal values, as well as values that are "barely" legal and "barely" not legal.

▲ If the program involves loops that can exercise a variable number of iterations, try to develop a test case in which the loop executes zero times.

Several more specific guidelines have also been suggested. The readings cited at the end of the chapter can be examined for further details.

5.3   CHAPTER SUMMARY

Key Concepts

- Program proofs
- Invariants
- Using invariants in tracing execution flow
- Relationship between recursion and mathematical induction
- Software testing

An invariant is a statement that describes the state of computation when execution reaches a particular point in a program. By tracing the flow of execution from invariant to invariant, invariants can be used to structure arguments used to increase confidence in the validity of an algorithm or function.

Even when a proof of correctness has been presented, software testing should be employed as an alternative technique to increase the confidence in the correct performance of a function or application.

Further Reading

The argument that programming (and, indeed, mathematics) is a social activity was given forceful exposition in a classic paper by Richard De-Millo, Richard Lipton and the late Alan Perlis [DeMillo 79].

The notion of program invariants was developed by Robert Floyd. For this contribution (among others) he was presented with the 1979 Alan Turing award by the Association for Computing Machinery, a major computer science professional organization.

Many researchers have tried to raise the level of program proofs to a formal mathematical process. Such proofs tend to be many times more complex than the arguments we develop in this book. A good introduction to program proving can be found in the book by David Gries [Gries 81]. Another prominent advocate of program proving is Edsger Dijkstra [Dijkstra 76].

A good description of the art of software testing is [Beizer 90].

Study Questions & Exercises

Study Questions

1. What are the two primary mechanisms for increasing confidence in the correctness of programs?

2. For whom is a program proof created? That is, who will read a program proof?

3. What is a code walk-through?

4. What is an invariant?

5. Explain the steps used in proving a program correct using invariants.

6. Assume an algorithm consists of a single loop, such as the minimum algorithm presented in Section 5.1.1. Assume that within the loop there are invariants at both the beginning and end of the loop body, as well as invariants prior to and after the loop. How many different arguments must be given that move from invariant to invariant?

7. What is the objective toward which "progress" is being made in the binary search algorithm?

8. What is the unnamed quantity that is referred to by the invariants for the GCD algorithm?

9. What are the steps involved in proving the correctness of a recursive algorithm?

10. What is the unnamed quantity that is referred to by the invariants for the power procedure described in Section 5.1.7?

11. At what point in the development process should testing be performed?

12. What is a testing harness? A driver? A stub?

13. What are some basic guidelines for developing good test cases?

Exercises

1. Complete the task of arguing the correctness of the isPrime procedure described in Section 5.1.3. That is, give arguments to move from each invariant to each possible succeeding invariant.

2. Complete the task of arguing the correctness of the binarySearch procedure described in Section 5.1.4. That is, give arguments to move from each invariant to each possible succeeding invariant.

3. Provide invariants for the linear time power procedure from Chapter 4.

```
double power (double base, unsigned int n)
{
    double result = 1.0;
        // inv 1:

    for (unsigned int i = 1; i <= n; i++) {
        // inv 2:
    result *= base;
        // inv 3:
    }

        // inv 4:
    return result;
}
```

4. Using the invariants you developed in the previous question, give arguments that support the validity of the invariants by tracing possible execution flows.

5. Complete the loop invariants for the following procedure that sums the values of an array.

```
//
```

```
//    sum the elements of a double array
//
```

```
double sumArray(double data[ ], unsigned
int size)
{
    double sum = 0.0;
    // inv:
    for (int i = 0; i < size; i++) {
        // inv:
    sum += data[i];
        // inv:
    }
    // inv:
    return sum;
}
```

6. Using the invariants you developed in the previous question, give arguments that support the validity of the invariants by tracing possible execution flows.

7. Complete the loop invariants for the following procedure that computes the factorial function for an unsigned integer argument.

```
//
// compute the factorial of an integer value
//
```

```
double factorial(unsigned int val)
{
    double result = 1.0;
    // inv:
    for (int i = 1; i <= val;  i++) {
        // inv:
        result *= i;
        // inv:
    }
    // inv:
    return result;
}
```

8. Using the invariants you developed in the previous question, give arguments that support the validity of the invariants by tracing possible execution flows.

9. Provide a set of invariants for the insertion sort algorithm described in Section 4.2.4. Using

these invariants as a base, give arguments that support the validity of the invariants by tracing possible execution flows.

10. What are some test cases one might use to exercise the function `minimum` described in Section 5.1.1?

11. What are some test cases one might use to exercise the function `isPrime` described in Section 5.1.3?

12. What are some test cases one might use to exercise the function `binarySearch` described in Section 5.1.4?

13. Augment the main program in the application developed in Chapter 2 with invariants, and with these provide an informal proof of correctness.

Part **II**

THE STANDARD
CONTAINERS

Chapter

6

The Standard Library Container Classes

Chapter Overview

It is likely that the most widely used data structures are those employed for the purpose of holding quantities of similar objects. Data abstractions designed for such purposes are almost always built using variations on a few simple techniques. We will call these classic forms of data structure *container classes*, because instances of these classes are objects that store (or contain) other objects. In this chapter we will briefly characterize various types of containers, and note the type of problem each is designed to help solve. In subsequent chapters we will then examine each form of collection in greater detail.

In Part II of this book we examine the container classes that are provided by the C++ standard library. This is a rich set of components for maintaining collections of values, and includes most of the classic data structures that are found as part of almost all nontrivial computer programs. However, not every useful container is represented by the elements of the standard library. In Part III we will examine some of the more notable container types that are not found directly in the standard library, but that can easily be implemented by making use of some of the standard library features.

The last section of this chapter introduces the concept of an *iterator*. An iterator allows access to the elements being held by a container, without exposing, or requiring, detailed knowledge of the internal container structure. Iterators are key to the effective use of the standard library, and will be employed extensively throughout the remainder of the book.

Major topics discussed in this chapter include the following:

▲ Container classes

▲ Selecting a container

▲ Iterators

6.1   CONTAINER CLASSES

Table 6.1 summarizes several operations on the container classes provided by the standard library, as well as some of their other properties. In subsequent chapters we will explore these data structures in more detail, describing not only how the standard library classes can be used, but also how they are implemented.

6.1.1   Vectors

A *vector* is a fixed-length group of elements of uniform type, indexed by integer keys. Vectors can be considered to be a generalization of the built-in C++ *array* type; however, vectors have several other notable features not associated with the basic array. Vectors are useful when the number of items to be maintained by a collection is at least approximately known in advance. Vectors are also important when the ability to rapidly access arbitrary elements is important, because, as with an array, individual elements in a vector can be directly indexed. The elements in a vector are assumed to be unsequenced; however, the operation of *sorting* can be used to place the elements of a vector into order. We have seen two sorting algorithms already (bubble sort and insertion sort, in Chapter 4) and we will see several similar algorithms in later chapters.

v [0]	v [1]	v [2]	...	v [n–2]	v [n–1]

Access to an element of a vector, either for assignment or to read the associated value, can be performed in constant (that is, $O(1)$) time. If the collection is unordered, determining whether or not a specific element occurs in a vector can be accomplished only by examining each value in

Table 6.1   Summary of asymptotic time for operations

Structure	Addition of new element	Removal of first element	Removal of middle element	Inclusion test
Vector	$O(1)$ or $O(n)$ [a]	$O(n)$	$O(1)$ or $O(n)$ [a]	$O(n)$ or $O(\log n)$ [b]
Indexed, random access to elements, bounded size				
List	$O(1)$	$O(1)$	$O(1)$	$O(n)$
Sequential access to elements, rapid insertion and removal				
Deque	$O(1)$	$O(1)$	$O(n)$	$O(n)$ or $O(\log n)$ [b]
Random access, rapid insertion to front and back				
Stack	$O(1)$	$O(1)$	NA	NA
Insertion and removal only from front				
Queue	$O(1)$	$O(1)$	NA	NA
Insertion only from front, removal only from back				
Priority Queue	$O(\log n)$	$O(1)$ or $O(\log n)$ [c]	NA	NA
Rapid removal of largest element				
Set	$O(\log n)$	$O(\log n)$	$O(\log n)$	$O(\log n)$
Ordered collection; unique values; rapid insertion, removal and test				
A `multiset` allows repeated elements				
Map	$O(\log n)$	$O(\log n)$	$O(\log n)$	$O(\log n)$
Collection of key-value pairs				
A `multimap` allows multiple elements with same key				

a. Constant if accessing existing position, linear if inserting/removing
b. Logarithmic if ordered, linear if not ordered
c. Constant access time, logarithmic removal

turn, and is thus an $O(n)$ task, where n represents the number of values being maintained in the collection. If the elements of a vector are held in sorted order, the *binary search* operation, introduced in Chapter 4, can be used to reduce this to an $O(\log n)$ task.

A notable operation on the `vector` data type, not possible with arrays, is that the size of the vector can be dynamically increased or decreased. However, such operations may, in the worst case, require time proportional to the size of the collection (that is, $O(n)$).

6.1.2   Strings

A *string* can be considered to be a vector of character values. Just as the subscript operator is used to obtain individual elements within a vector, in the same manner the subscript operator is used to access individual characters within a string. In addition, there are many high level operations specific to the `string` data type. We will explore the `string` class in Chapter 7.

```
string aName = "Benjamin Franklin";
```

6.1.3   Lists

A *list* is a data structure of choice when the number of elements in a collection cannot be bounded, or varies widely during the course of execution. Like a vector, a list maintains values of uniform type. Unlike a vector, a list can hold any number of values. Lists are not indexed. Instead, elements must be examined one by one in sequence. For this reason, the amount of time required to access an element in a list depends upon the position the element holds in the list; accessing the first or final values of a list (called the *head* or the *tail* element) can be performed in constant time, whereas accessing values near the middle requires a sequential traversal through the list (and is thus $O(n)$ in the worst case).

Using an iterator to denote a given location, insertion into or deletion from a list can be performed in constant time. (Finding the appropriate location to perform an insertion may be a more costly operation.) As with a vector, to determine whether or not a specific value occurs in a list requires a sequential search, and is therefore an $O(n)$ operation. While a list can be ordered, it is not possible to perform binary search on a list, and therefore the sequential search time is generally the best that can be achieved. We will examine the `list` data type in Chapter 9.

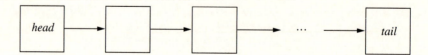

6.1.4   Double-Ended Queues

An unusual data structure provided by the standard library is a *deque*, or *double-ended queue*. Like a list, a deque has an arbitrary size, growing or shrinking as elements are added or removed. The deque is optimized for insertion or removal of elements from either end. This operation can be performed in constant time. Insertions or removals of interior values is possible, but may in the worst case require time proportional to the size of the collection.

Like a vector, a deque is an indexed data structure, allowing rapid (constant time) access to any element. As values are inserted into the front of the structure, the index positions by which an element is accessed will constantly change to reflect the inclusion of the new values. Deques can be ordered and use binary search to determine if a value is present in the collection, otherwise a linear search is necessary and requires $O(n)$ steps. We will examine the deque data type in Chapter 11.

6.1.5 Stacks and Queues

Stacks and *queues* can be thought of as specialized forms of a deque. Elements in a stack obey the last-in, first-out, or *LIFO* protocol. Elements can be added and removed only from the front of a stack. Thus, an element removed from a stack is the element that has been held for the least amount of time. A queue, on the other hand, maintains the first-in, first-out protocol, or *FIFO*. Elements are inserted in the back of the queue, and removed from the front. Thus, an element removed from a queue is the element that has been held by the queue for the longest amount of time. Stacks and queues are important data structures when elements in a problem need to be examined in a specific order that matches either the LIFO or FIFO properties. We will investigate stacks and queues in Chapter 10.

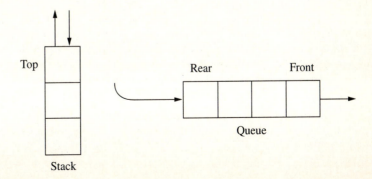

6.1.6   Sets

A *set* is a simple collection of unique values. Although the abstract concept of a set does not require ordering, the `set` data structure in the standard library maintains values in an ordered representation. This permits rapid insertion, removal, and testing for inclusion of a specific element. All can be performed in $O(\log n)$ time. In addition, operations are provided for forming the intersection and union of two sets.

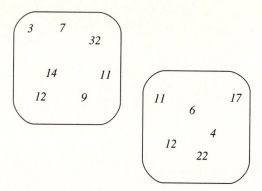

A `multiset` (sometimes called a *bag*) is similar to a set; however, a multiset is allowed to contain multiple copies of the same element, whereas each element in a set must be unique. The `set` and `multiset` data types will be introduced in Chapter 12.

6.1.7   Priority Queues

A *priority queue* is optimized for insertion of arbitrary new elements, and for removal of the largest element; both operations can be performed in $O(\log n)$ time. A priority queue can be visualized as a funnel, in which the largest element in the collection is always available for immediate access, whereas the other elements of the collection are largely unordered. We will discuss uses of the `priority_queue` data type in Chapter 15.

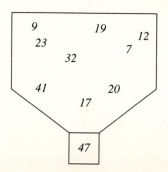

6.1.8   Maps (Dictionaries)

A *map* (sometimes called a *dictionary* or a *table*) is, like a vector, an indexed collection. However, unlike a vector, the index values need not be integer, but can be any ordered data values. A map can therefore be thought of as a collection of *associations* of key and value pairs. An example map-like structure in the real world is a dictionary, where the keys represent words, and the values represent definitions. A multimap is similar to a map, only it permits multiple entries to be accessed using the same key value. We will describe the map and multimap data types in Chapter 16.

$$key_1 \rightarrow value_1$$
$$key_2 \rightarrow value_2$$
$$key_3 \rightarrow value_3$$
$$...$$
$$key_n \rightarrow value_n$$

6.2   SELECTING A CONTAINER

The following series of questions can help in determining which type of container is best suited for solving a particular problem.

▲ *How are values going to be accessed?*

If random access is important, than a vector or a deque should be used. If the values are going to be accessed in order, then a set (which is always implicitly ordered) should be used. If sequential access is sufficient, then one of the other structures may be suitable.

▲ *Is the order in which values are maintained in the collection important?*

There are a number of different ways in which values can be sequenced. If a strict ordering is important throughout the life of the container, then the set data structure is an obvious choice, because insertions into a set are automatically placed in order. On the other hand, if this ordering is important only at one point (for example, at the end of a long series of insertions), then it might be easier to place the values into a list or vector, and sort the resulting structure at the appropriate time. If the order that values are held in the structure is related to the order of insertion, then a stack, queue, or list may be the best choice.

▲ *Will the size of the structure vary widely over the course of execution?*

If true, then a list or set might be the best choice. Either lists or sets use memory only to hold the values currently being stored in the collection, while a vector or deque will continue to maintain a large buffer even after elements have been removed from the collection. Conversely, if the size of the collection remains relatively fixed, then a vector or deque will use less memory than a list or set holding the same number of elements.

▲ *Is it possible to estimate the size of the collection?*

The vector data structure provides a way to preallocate a block of memory of a given size (using the reserve() member function). This ability is not provided by the other containers.

▲ *Is testing to see whether a value is contained in the collection a frequent operation?*

If so, then the set or map containers would be a good choice. Testing to see whether a value is contained in a set or map can be performed in a very small number of steps, whereas testing to see if a value is contained in one of the other types of collections might require comparing the value against every element being stored by the container.

▲ *Is the collection indexed? That is, can the collection be viewed as a series of key/value pairs?*

If the keys are integers between 0 and some upper limit, then a vector or deque should be employed. If, on the other hand, the key values are some other ordered data type (such as characters, strings, or a user defined type), then the map container can be used.

▲ *Can values be related to each other?*

All values stored in any container provided by the standard library must be able to test for equality against another similar value, but not all need to recognize the relational less-than operator. However, if values cannot be ordered using the relational less-than operator, then they cannot be stored in a set or a map.

▲ *Is finding and removing the largest value from the collection a frequent operation?*

If this is true, the priority queue is the best data structure to use.

▲ *At what positions are values inserted into or removed from the structure?*

If values are inserted into or removed from the middle, then a list is the best choice. If values are inserted only at the beginning, then a deque or a list is the preferred choice. If values are inserted or removed only at the end, then a stack or queue may be a logical choice.

▲ *Is a frequent operation the merging of two or more sequences into one?*

If true, then a set or a list would seem to be the best choice, depending upon whether or not the collection is maintained in order.

Merging two sets is a very efficient operation. If the collections are not ordered, the efficient `splice()` member function from class `list` can be used.

In many situations any number of different containers may be applicable to a given problem. In such situations, one possibility is to compare actual execution timings using different containers to determine which alternative is best.

6.3   ITERATORS

For many types of container, one of the most common operations is to cycle through and examine the values being maintained by the collection. The inherent difficulty in this task is to find a way to permit the programmer to easily construct such loops, without exposing the often complex internal structure of the collection class. The solution used by the standard library is a mechanism known as an *iterator*.

Abstractly, an iterator is simply a pointer-like object used to cycle through all the elements stored in a container. Because different algorithms need to traverse containers in a variety of fashions, there are different forms of iterators. Each container class in the standard library provides a corresponding iterator with functionality appropriate to the storage technique used in implementing the container. The category of iterators required as arguments chiefly distinguishes which generic algorithms in the standard library can be used with which container classes.

The easiest way to understand iterators is by analogy to simple pointers. Just as pointers can be used in a variety of ways in traditional programming, iterators are also used for a number of different purposes. An iterator can be used to denote a specific value, just as a pointer can be used to reference a specific memory location. On the other hand, a *pair* of iterators can be used to describe a *range* of values, in a manner analogous to the way in which two pointers can be used to describe a contiguous region of memory.

Recall, for example, the use of the generic algorithm `random_shuffle` in Chapter 2. Two pointer values were used to denote the beginning and ending of the array of card values:

The values `cards` and `cards+52` were passed as arguments to the generic function `random_shuffle`. These two arguments described the beginning and end of the array. In the case of iterators, however, the values being described are not necessarily physically in sequence; rather they are logically in sequence, because they are derived from the same container, and the second follows the first in the order that elements are maintained by the collection.

The convention used by the container classes in the standard library is to return, in response to the member function named begin(), an iterator that accesses the first element in the collection. An iterator denoting the end of the collection is yielded by the member function end(). Thus, for example, if aVector is an instance of the vector class, and we wanted to shuffle the elements in the vector, we could execute this statement:

```
random_shuffle(aVector.begin(), aVector.end(), randomizer);
```

Conventional pointers can sometimes be *null*, that is, they point at nothing. Iterators, as well, can fail to denote any specific value. Just as it is a logical error to dereference and use a null pointer, it is an error to dereference and use an iterator that is not denoting a value.

When two pointers that describe a region in memory are used in a C++ program, it is conventional that the ending pointer is *not* considered to be part of the region. We see this in the picture of the cards array, where the array is described as extending from cards to cards+52, even though the element at cards+52 is not part of the array. Instead, the pointer value cards+52 is the *past-the-end value*—the element that is the next value *after* the end of the range being described. Iterators are used to describe a range in the same manner. The second value is not considered to be part of the range being denoted. Instead, the second value is a *past-the-end element*, describing the next value in sequence after the final value of the range. Sometimes, as with pointers to memory, this will be an actual value in the container. Other times it may be a special value, specifically constructed for the purpose. The value returned by the member function end() is usually of the latter type, being a special value that does not refer to any element in the collection. In either case, it is never legal to try to dereference an iterator that is being used to specify the end of a range. (An iterator that does not denote a location, such as an end-of-range iterator, is often called a *null iterator*.)

An examination of a typical generic algorithm will help illustrate how iterators are used. The generic function named find() can be used to determine whether or not a value occurs in a collection. It is implemented as shown:[1]

```
iterator find (iterator first, iterator last, T & value)
{
    while (first != last && *first != value)
```

---

1. This version of the find() algorithm has been simplified to omit detail. For example, binding the types for the iterators and the argument value returns involves the use of the template feature, which we will not encounter until Chapter 8.

```
      ++first;
  return first;
}
```

The following shows how we could use this algorithm to search for a value being held by a conventional C++ array:

```
int data[100];
    .
    .
    .
int * where = find(data, data+100, 7);
```

Alternatively, the following declares a new variable, then searches for the value 7 in a `list` of integers, assigning the resulting iterator to the variable:

```
list<int>::iterator where = find(aList.begin(), aList.end(), 7);
```

The resulting value is either the end-of-list iterator (equal to the value returned by the function `end()`) or it represents the location of the first 7 in the list.

As with conventional pointers, the fundamental operation used to modify an iterator is the increment operator (operator ++). When the increment operator is applied to an iterator that denotes the final value in a sequence, it will be changed to the "past the end" value. An iterator j is said to be *reachable* from an iterator i if, after a finite sequence of applications of the expression ++i, the iterator i becomes equal to j.

Ranges can be used to describe the entire contents of a container by constructing an iterator to the initial element and a special "ending" iterator. Ranges can also be used to describe subsequences within a single container by employing two iterators to specific values. Whenever two iterators are used to describe a range it is assumed, but not verified, that the second iterator is reachable from the first. Errors can occur if this expectation is not satisfied.

The `find()` algorithm illustrates three requirements for an iterator:

1. An iterator can be compared for equality to another iterator. They are equal when they point to the same position, and are otherwise not equal.

2. An iterator can be dereferenced using the * operator, to obtain the value being denoted by the iterator. Depending upon the type of iterator and variety of underlying container, this value can also sometimes be used as the target of an assignment in order to change the value being held by the container.

3. An iterator can be incremented, so that it refers to the next element in sequence, using the operator ++.

Iterators are possible due to the fact that these characteristics can all be provided with new meanings in a C++ program, because the behavior of the given functions can all be modified by *overloading* the appropriate operators. An example is the list iterator, shown in Figure 9.1. Because of this overloading, iterators are possible. Each of the various container classes comes equipped with an associated iterator class. Member functions attached to this iterator class will then provide new overloaded meanings for the iterator operations.

For example, in Chapter 9 we will discuss the list class. A characteristic of the linked list data abstraction is that the actual elements are stored in different places in memory, not necessarily adjacent to each other. The following diagram illustrates how one could imagine a linked list occupying positions in memory:

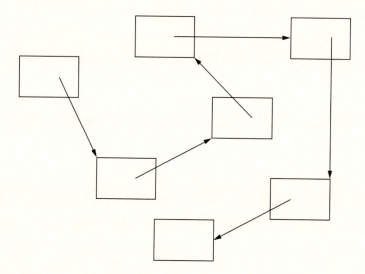

An iterator for a linked list will maintain a pointer to the "current" element. The * operator applied to this iterator will yield the value of the current element, while two iterators will compare equal if they point to the same element. The ++ operator is redefined so that instead of meaning "advance to the next element physically in memory" (as it does with pointer values), it instead means "advance to the next element along the linked list chain." With these interpretations, the exact same algorithm for the find function we described earlier will now work for list values. By means of iterators, the same generic algorithms can be adapted to work with a wide variety of different containers.

There are two major categories of iterator constructed by the containers in the standard library. The types list, set, and map produce *bidirectional iterators*. These iterators recognize the increment and decrement operators (the latter moving the iterator *backwards* one element), but cannot be randomly accessed. The types vector, string, and deque, on the other hand, generate *random-access iterators,* which permit the subscript operator and the addition of integer values to an iterator (analogous to adding an integer value to a pointer, as with the expression `cards+52`). Some of the generic algorithms, such as `random_shuffle`, depend upon this subscripting ability, and therefore cannot be used with lists or sets.

There are other varieties of iterator, and other mechanisms for constructing iterators of various forms. However, these will be introduced as they are needed in our discussions of various containers.

Further Reading

As with the introduction of the C++ language in Chapter 1, our discussion of the standard library classes in this book is not intended to be comprehensive, but simply used as a vehicle for introducing the classic data structures and associated algorithms. Readers interested in a more complete description of the data structures portion of the standard library are referred to the book by Musser and Saini [Musser 96], or similar books [Glass 96, Ladd 96].

Some of the material in this and subsequent chapters has been adapted from a tutorial I wrote for Rogue Wave Software, Inc., to be used in conjunction with their proprietary version of the standard library.

6.4 CHAPTER SUMMARY

Key Concepts

- Container class
- Vector
- String
- List
- Stack
- Queue
- Priority queue
- Set
- Map
- Iterator

In this chapter we have introduced the various container classes provided by the C++ standard library, briefly characterizing the features of each. We also introduced the concept of an iterator, a mechanism for providing access to the elements held by a collection without exposing the implementation details of the holding container.

Study Questions & Exercises

Study Questions

1. What is a container class?

2. What features characterize each of the following containers: vector, string, list, stack, queue, deque, priority queue, set, and map?

3. What problem is being solved by introducing the iterator mechanism?

4. What is a null iterator?

5. What does it mean to say that a terminating iterator is a *past-the-end* value?

6. What does it mean to say that one iterator is *reachable* from another?

7. How does a bi-directional iterator differ from a random access iterator?

Exercises

1. Suppose a program is designed to manage a collection of student records for a university. The appropriate data structure to use to hold the actual records might depend upon what tasks needed to be performed. For each of the following, describe briefly what data structures you think might be appropriate:

   a. Adding and deleting students from different classes, eventually producing printed lists of students in each class.

   b. Same as the first, but printing the students in alphabetical order.

   c. Merging class lists together; for example, merging lists of students in different sections of the same class into one master list.

   d. Associating grade reports with students by name; that is, an on-line system whereby an instructor could enter the student's name and see a report on the grades the student received in previous courses.

2. Using the iterator operations described in this chapter, sketch in pseudocode an implementation of the `random_shuffle` generic algorithm. As in Exercise 12 of Chapter 2, the body of the function should loop through each element of the array, swapping the value found at the corresponding location with another randomly selected value from the container.

The string Data Type

Chapter Overview

Next to numbers, individual characters and strings of characters are perhaps the most common data values used in programming. After reviewing some of the features of characters and character literals in the C++ language, in this chapter we go on to consider the string data abstraction as provided by the standard library. In a pattern to be followed throughout the remaining chapters, we will first illustrate how string values are used in the solution of several small problems. This will then be followed by a summary of the valid operations for the data type. Finally, we will examine some of the problems involved, and techniques employed, in the implementation of this abstraction.

Although the primary purpose of this chapter is the discussion of the string data type, along the way we encounter a number of features of the C++ language that we have not examined yet. These include the use of pointers, functions as arguments, copy constructors, dynamic memory allocation, destructors, the distinction between member functions and ordinary functions, and the return of references as function results.

Major topics discussed in this chapter include the following:

▲ The string data abstraction
▲ Primitive (C-style) strings

▲ The string data type in the standard library

▲ An example implementation

7.1   THE STRING DATA ABSTRACTION

Almost any application that must send textual information to a human reader, or process input received from a user interface, will employ character values. Yet the basic C++ language does not provide a string type as a primitive, instead it builds rudimentary strings out of pointers and arrays of characters, in a fashion C++ inherited from its parent language, C. For this reason, a string class is a logical candidate for development as a library class.

In one sense, a string is basically just an indexable sequence of characters. If fact, nearly all the operations associated with arrays or vectors can be applied equally well to strings. However, a string is also a much more abstract entity; in addition to simple vector operators, the string datatype provides a number of useful and powerful high-level operations.

7.1.1   Include Files

One confusing aspect of the string facility is the presence of two different include files. The statement:

```
# include <string.h>
```

includes a file that declares a number of small utility routines useful in conjunction with older, C-style character values. We will shortly describe some of these routines. To use the string data type, the programmer must include the string file (without the .h extension).

```
# include <string>
```

7.1.2   Primitive (C-style) Strings

In C++ a character is treated simply as a type of integer value. Integer operations can be used to manipulate character quantities. We have seen this already in the function digitChar (Section 3.3.1), used to convert an integer value into a character equivalent. Relational tests are also useful with character values. The following function, for example, returns true if a character argument represents an uppercase (capital) letter:

```
int isupper(char c)
{ // return true if c is an upper case letter
    return (c >= 'A') && (c <= 'Z');
}
```

Even more obscure is the following expression, used to convert an uppercase letter into lowercase:

```
c = (c - 'A') + 'a';
```

In the basic C++ language, the closest concept that corresponds to the intuitive notion of a character string is a pointer to the first value in a sequence of characters. String literals, sequences of characters surrounded by double quote marks, are treated by the compiler as though they represented an array of character values. The address of this array is then implicitly converted into a character pointer. Thus, in a pair of statements such as:

```
char * p;
p = "hello world!";
```

it is a mistake to think that any assignment of characters is being performed. Instead, the *address* of the unnamed array of characters that holds the text "hello world!" is being assigned to the pointer p. The value of the literal is the address in memory where the characters are maintained.

As we noted in Chapter 1, pointers in C++ can be subscripted. The expression p[0] yields the character 'h', and p[6] returns the character 'w'. A subscripted pointer is a legal target for an assignment. Consider the following statements:

```
p[0] = 'y';
p[5] = p[6];
p[6] = ' ';
p[8] = 'i';
p[10] = '?';
```

The effect of this sequence of modifications will be to change the text array into "yellow oil?!". C++ provides no checks on the validity of subscripts applied to pointers. Thus, it is possible (but rarely useful) to subscript a pointer with a negative value, or a value larger than the size of the array of characters being referenced. In our case, doing so will yield unpredictable values.

By convention, strings are terminated by a null character, a character with value zero. Thus, the unnamed string representing the text "hello world!" actually contains 13 characters, the last character being the null character indicating the end of a string.

Pointer values can be assigned to pointer variables. This can result in two pointers referring to the same data area. For example, the following sequence results in the modification of the value referred to as q[2], which is the same value referred to by p[2]:

```
char * q;
q = p;
q[2] = 'x';
```

If a buffer to hold string values is desired, it is declared simply as an array of characters. Such a buffer can be initialized with a string literal, which must have a length smaller than the number of elements declared in the buffer, as:

```
char hellobuffer[20] = "hello world!";
```

Although the declared size of the array is 20 characters (meaning it can hold a maximum of 19 characters and the null character), only the first 13 positions are initialized. The values of the remaining 7 positions are undefined.

Pointers on Pointers

A *pointer* is simply a variable that maintains as value the address of another location in memory. Because memory addresses have a fixed limit, the amount of storage necessary to hold a pointer can be determined at compile time, even if the size or extent of the object to which it will point is not known.

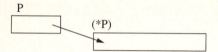

A *null pointer* is a value that does not reference any other memory location, and should not be considered to point to any valid object. A pointer can always be assigned the value zero in order to make it null, although the actual internal value used to represent the null pointer can differ from one platform to another. A pointer can also be tested for equality to the value zero, in order to determine whether or not it represents a null pointer. A pointer that is not equivalent to a null pointer on such a test is said to be non-null.

There are four principle mechanisms used to access the values denoted by a pointer:

1. A pointer variable can be subscripted. This is useful only if the pointer addresses an array of objects, as in the string data structure. The subscript index is used to determine the element accessed by the expression.

2. A pointer can be explicitly *dereferenced* using the unary * operator. If p is a pointer to a value of some type, then *p is the value addressed by the pointer.

3. An integer value can be added to or subtracted from a pointer in order to yield a new pointer. It is assumed (but not verified) that the pointer references an array of values.

4. A pointer to a structure, or class, can combine pointer dereferencing and member field extraction using the pointer operator. If p is a pointer to a value of a class type that contains a member field x, then p->x is the same as (*p).x.

A pointer should be distinguished from a *reference*, such as is generated using the pass-by-reference parameter passing mechanism. While internally they are implemented in much the same manner, they differ in three important regards:

1. A reference can never be null; it must always refer to a legitimate object.

2. Once established, a reference can never be changed to make it point to a different object.

3. A reference does not require any explicit mechanism to dereference the memory address and access the actual data value.

The manipulation of pointers can be tricky, and is one of the most common sources of programming errors. For this reason we will encapsulate, for the most part, manipulation of pointer values within a class, and use few explicit pointer values in our example programs.

There are a number of library routines that manipulate literal strings, represented as pointers to a sequence of characters terminated by a null character. The two most common are the functions `strlen`, which returns the number of non-null characters in a string, and the function `strcpy`, which copies one such string into another. In Section 7.4 we will subsequently use both of these in the implementation of the higher level `string` abstraction. A third function, `strcmp`, will also be used in the implementation of the relational comparison operators.

```
cout << strlen(hellobuffer) << endl;
strcpy (hellobuffer, "goodby C");
```

7.2 PROBLEM SOLVING WITH STRINGS

There are a number of ways in which the `string` data abstraction provided by the standard library is an improvement upon the representation of strings as simple pointers to character arrays. Among the most important are:

▲ The `string` abstraction provides high level operations, such as append, catenate, insert, and replace.

▲ Assignment of string values results in copies, not sharing of the memory referenced by pointer values.

▲ Comparisons between string values can be performed using relational operators, such as $<=$ and $>$, and these result in the comparison of the string values, not a comparison of their pointer addresses.

In this section we will describe two typical problems that can be solved using the `string` data abstraction.

7.2.1 Palindrome Testing

A *palindrome* is a word that reads the same forwards and backwards, such as "civic," or "rotator," or a phrase with the same property, such as "able was I ere I saw elba," or a string of words that can be made into a palindrome if we remove certain punctuation and spaces, such as the phrase "a Man, a Plan, a Canal, Panama!". We will create a series of functions to test a string for the palindrome property, using each as a vehicle to illustrate different operations that are available using the `string` data type.

What we will term a "type 1" palindrome is simply a word that reads the same backwards and forwards, such as "civic." To test for this property, we create a function that takes a string as argument, duplicates the string, reverses the duplicate, and finally tests to see if the original string is equal to the duplicate. This could be written as:

```
bool isPalindrome_type1 (string & aString)
    // test to see if aString is an exact word palindrome
{

    string temp;       // declare temporary
    temp = aString;    // duplicate argument
    reverse (temp.begin(), temp.end());   // reverse duplicate
    return temp == aString;   // test for equality
}
```

Note first that the argument is being passed by reference. Recall from Chapter 5 that any nontrivial argument can be more efficiently passed in this fashion.

Within the body of the function, a local variable named temp is created. This variable is assigned the argument string, in effect duplicating the value of the argument.

The generic algorithm reverse creates an in-place reversal of its argument, which is specified by a pair of bi-directional iterators. Following this operation, the temporary variable will hold the reversal of the argument string. To determine if the argument is a palindrome, the original argument is simply compared against the temporary.

Notice that the comparison operators == and ! =, as well as the relational operators <, <=, > and >=, compare the *contents* of the two string arguments, not their addresses in memory, as is the case with character pointers.

While this palindrome test is simple, it will not recognize text in which the characters represent a palindrome, but differ in case. An example is the phrase, "Rats Live on No Evil Star," which reverses as "ratS livE oN no eviL staR." We can call such a text a "type 2" palindrome, and recognize it with the following:

```
bool isPalindrome_type2 (string & aString)
    // test to see if aString is a case insensitive palindrome
{

    string allLow (aString);
    transform (aString.begin(), aString.end(), allLow.begin(), tolower);
    return isPalindrome_type1 (allLow);
}
```

This algorithm illustrates an alternative mechanism for duplicating a string variable. A *copy constructor* is simply a constructor that requires, as argument, another instance of the same class in which the constructor is defined. In this case, we are using a constructor for class string, which takes as argument another string value. This time, the duplicate is then converted, element by element, using the generic algorithm named transform(). This algorithm has an argument list that requires three iterators, two representing the original text, and the third representing the target for the updated text, and a final argument that must be a unary function. The unary function is applied to each element of the collection, and the resulting value assigned to the new location. A simplified version of this algorithm could be described as:

```
void transform (iterator start, iterator stop, iterator to, char fun(char))
{
    while (start != stop)
        *to++ = fun(*start++);
}
```

In the isPalindrome_type2 function, the transformation being applied is the unary function `tolower`, which converts its argument to a lowercase letter if uppercase, leaving the argument unchanged if not uppercase. (This function was discussed in Exercise 9 in Chapter 3; it is also available in the standard library in the include file `ctype.h`). The result following the transformation will be a text that is entirely lowercase. The function `isPalindrome_type1()` can then be used to determine if it is a palindrome.

Even this function, however, will not work for text such as "I Love Me, Vol. I." Here we must first eliminate the spaces and punctuation before testing to see if the result is a palindrome. We will do this by first writing a general purpose function to remove certain specified character values from a given string. To tell if a string represents a "type 3" palindrome, we simply first remove all punctuation characters, then see if the resulting text is a type 2 palindrome. This can be accomplished as follows:

```
bool isPalindrome_type3 (string & aString)
    // see if text is a punctuation insenstive palindrome
{
        // remove all punctuation and space characters
    string punctChars = " ,.!?";
    string temp = remove_all (aString, punctChars);
        // then test resulting string
    return isPalindrome_type2 (temp);
}
```

The development of the `remove_all` function illustrates again the use of many of the high-level operations provided by the `string` data type:

```
string remove_all (string & text, string & spaces)
    // remove all instances of characters from spaces
{
    string result;
    int textLen = text.length();
    int spacesLen = spaces.length();

    for (int i = 0; i < textLen; i++) {
```

```
        string aChar = text.substr(i, 1);
        int location = spaces.find(aChar, 0);
        if ((location < 0) || (location >= spacesLen))
            result += aChar;  // not found
    }
    return result;
}
```

The two argument values for this routine represent the original text, and a string containing all the "space" characters, that is, the characters to be eliminated. The function will produce the answer by building up the result string, one character at a time. The local variable named `result` will hold the resulting value; this variable is declared without arguments, and will thus initially be assigned an empty string. Two integer variables are created to hold the maximum lengths of the two argument strings, which are quantities that can be determined using the `length()` member functions. A loop then cycles over each position in the test string.

The member function `substr` will, in this case, generate a string of length 1 containing just the character being tested. This value is held by the local variable named aChar. The member function `find` seeks to locate this text in the string representing the spaces. If successful, the `find()` method returns the position of the match, returning an illegal index if the text is not located. Most implementations of the standard library will return a large value, one greater than the last legal index value, but this behavior is not guaranteed by the standard. Hence testing the result both against zero and against the length of the string is necessary to determine whether or not the search was successful. However, it is only if the search was not successful that we want to append the argument string to the result. This *append* operation is performed using the $+=$ version of assignment.

We can simplify the testing of our palindrome procedures by writing a single test function, as follows:

```
void pal_test (string & aString)
    // test the argument string to see if it is a palindrome
{
    cout << "string:" << aString;
    if (isPalindrome_type1(aString))
        cout << "is a type 1 palindrome\n";
    else if (isPalindrome_type2(aString))
        cout << "is a type 2 palindrome\n";
    else if (isPalindrome_type3(aString))
        cout << "is a type 3 palindrome\n";
    else
        cout << "is not a palindrome\n";
}
```

7.2.2   Split a Line into Words

Our second example of the use of operators on strings will be a generalization of the function `remove_all` described in the previous section. This function will take a string as argument, and split the string into individual words, where a "word" is defined by a string of separator characters, also passed as argument. We will make use of the `list` data type, to be discussed in Chapter 9.

```
void split (string & text, string & separators, list<string> & words)
        // split a string into a list of words
        // text and separators are input,
        // list of words is output
{
        int textLen = text.length();

            // find first non-separator character
        int start = text.find_first_not_of(separators, 0);
            // loop as long as we have a non-separator character
        while ((start >= 0) && (start < textLen)) {
                // find end of current word
        int stop = text.find_first_of(separators, start);
        if ((stop < 0) || (stop > textLen)) stop = textLen;
            // add word to list of words
        words.push_back (text.substr(start, stop - start));
            // find start of next word
        start = text.find_first_not_of (separators, stop+1);
        }
}
```

The procedure begins by finding the first character that is not a separator, using the member function `find_first_not_of`. This function returns the index of the first position that holds a character not found in the list of separators, returning an illegal index value if no such character can be found. The loop therefore cycles as long as the result of the search remains in bounds as a legal index value.

Starting at the given position, the member function `find_first_of` is then used to find the first character that *is* from the list of separator values. A special case must be recognized for the situation where no such character can be found, that is, where the final word ends the original text string. We are only guaranteed that if no such value is found, the result will be an illegal index, so the `if` statement is used to ensure this value is changed to the size of the text array should no such character be located.

The `substr` member function, which we have already encountered in the previous section, is then used to extract the word between the two boundaries. As we will see later in Chapter 9, the function `push_back` is used to append this value to the end of the list of words. Following this, a search is then performed for the start of the next word, and the loop continues.

To illustrate a use of this function, imagine we have a text and wish to find the lexicographically largest and smallest words in the text. This could be accomplished by this program:

```
void main() {
    string text = "it was the best of times, it was the worst of times.";
    string smallest = "middle";
    string largest = "middle";

    list<string> words;
    split(text, " .,!?:", words);

    list<string>::iterator current;
    list<string>::iterator stop = words.end();
    for (current = words.begin(); current != stop; ++current) {
        if (*current < smallest)
            smallest = *current;
        if (*current > largest)
            largest = *current;
    }
    cout << "smallest word " << smallest << endl;
    cout << "largest word " << largest << endl;
}
```

The result would indicate that the smallest word was best, and the largest word was worst.

We will make use of this function in a case study in Chapter 16.

7.3   STRING OPERATIONS

In this section we will quickly review operations that can be used with the string data type from the standard library. Table 7.1 summarizes these operations.[1] The following sections will explain each in more detail.

To use the string data type it is first necessary to include the string header file.

```
# include <string>
```

---

1. As will be true of all the standard library containers we discuss, our presentation here is intended to be representative, but not comprehensive. Not all the available operations on the string data type will be presented. Readers interested in more complete information should consult the reference manuals for their particular platform, or examine some of the references cited at the end of Chapter 6.

Note that there is no `.h` following this name. On most systems the include file `string.h` will contain descriptions of older C-style string manipulation functions.

7.3.1   Declaring String Variables

The simplest forms of declaration for a string simply names a new variable, or names a variable along with the initial value for the string. As we noted in Chapter 5, a declaration and initialization can be written using one of two alternative forms:

```
string s1;
string s2 ("a string");
string s3 = "initial value";
```

A *copy constructor* is a constructor used to copy, or clone, a value from another value of the same type. A copy constructor for the string abstraction, for example, will initialize a newly created string with the value being held by another string.

```
string s4 (s3); // initialize s4 with value of s3
```

7.3.2   Character Access

An individual character from a string can be accessed or assigned using the subscript operator.

```
cout << s4[2] << endl;
s4[2] = 'x';
```

The member function `substr()` returns a string that represents a portion of the current string. The range is specified by a position and a length. We have encountered this function already in the examples presented earlier in the chapter.

```
cout << s4.substr(3, 2) << endl;
```

The member function `c_str()` returns a C-style character pointer. This is most often used when a string value must be passed to a function that expects an older style character array.

```
File * fin = fopen(fileName.c_str(), "w");
```

As we will later see when we describe the string implementation, the underlying character buffer will often be moved when insertions or catenations are made to a string variable. For this reason, the value returned by the `c_str()` function is not guaranteed to remain valid following any subsequent string operations.

Table 7.1   Operations for the string data type

Constructors

`string s;`	Default constructor
`string s ("text");`	Initialized with literal string
`string s (aString);`	Copy constructor

Character Access

`s[i]`	Subscript access
`s.substr(pos, len)`	Return substring starting at position of given length
`s.c_str()`	Return a C-style character pointer

Length

`s.length()`	Number of characters in string
`s.resize(int, char)`	Change size of string, padding with char
`s.empty()`	True if string has no characters

Assignment and Catenation

`s = s2;`	Assignment of string
`s += s2;`	Append second string to end of first
`s + s2`	New string containing s followed by s2

Iterators

`string::iterator t`	Declaration of new iterator
`s.begin()`	Starting iterator
`s.end()`	Past-the-end iterator

Insertion, Removal, Replacement

`s.insert(pos, str)`	Insert string after given position
`s.remove(start, length)`	Remove length characters after start
`s.replace(start, length, str)`	Insert string, replacing indicated characters

Comparisons

`s = s2  s != s2`	Comparisons for equality/inequality
`s < s2  s >= s2`	Comparisons for relation
`s <= s2  s >= s2`	

Searching Operations

`s.find(str)`	Find start of argument string in receiver string
`s.find(str, pos)`	Find with explicit starting position

Table 7.1   Operations for the string data type

`s.find_first_of(str, pos)`	First position of first character from argument
`s.find_first_not_of(str, pos)`	First character not from argument

Input / Output Operations

`stream << str`	Output string on stream
`stream >> str`	Read word from stream
`getline(stream, str, char)`	Read line of input from stream

7.3.3   Extent of String

The member function `length()` returns an integer value that describes the number of characters currently being held by a string. The member function `resize()` changes the size of a string, either truncating characters from the end or inserting new characters. The optional second argument for `resize()` can be used to specify the character inserted into the positions of a newly enlarged string value.

```
s7.resize(15, '\t'); // add tab characters at end
cout << s7.length() << endl; // write new length
```

The member function `empty()` returns `true` if the string contains no characters, and is usually faster than testing the length against a zero constant.

```
if (s7.empty())
    cout << "string is empty" << endl;
```

7.3.4   Assignment and Append

A string variable can be assigned the value of either another string, a literal C-style character array, or an individual character.

```
s1 = s2;
s2 = "a new value";
s3 = 'x';
```

The operator `+=` can also be used with any of these three forms of argument, and specifies that the value on the right hand side should be *appended* to the end of the current string value.

```
s3 += "yz"; // s3 is now xyz
```

The addition operator + is used to form the catenation of two strings.

The + operator creates a copy of the left argument, then appends the right argument to this value.

```
cout << s2 + s3 << endl;
```

7.3.5   Iterators

The member functions begin() and end() return beginning and ending random-access iterators for the string. The values denoted by the iterators will be individual characters. The qualified name string::iterator can be used to declare a variable that can hold an iterator for a string value.

```
string::iterator itr = aString.begin();
for ( ; itr != aString.end() ; ++itr)
      .
      .
      .
```

Note that the contents of an iterator are not guaranteed to be valid after any operation that might force a reallocation of the internal string buffer, such as an append or an insertion.

7.3.6   Insertion, Removal, and Replacement

The insert() member function takes as argument a position and a string, and inserts the string into the given position. The remove() function takes two integer arguments, a position and a length, and removes the characters specified. The replace() function takes two similar integer arguments as well as a string, and replaces the indicated range with the string.

```
s3.insert (3, "abc"); // insert at position 3
s3.remove (4, 2); // remove positions 4 and 5
s3.replace (4, 2, "pqr"); // replace position 4 and 5 with "pqr"
```

7.3.7   String Comparisons

The two comparison operators for equality and inequality (== and ! =) can be used with strings, and they compare the two argument strings character by character. The relational operators (<, <=, >=, >) are similarly defined, and compare the two values in lexicographic, or "dictionary" order.

7.3.8   Searching Operations

The member function find() determines the first occurrence of the argument string in the current string. An optional integer argument allows the programmer to specify the starting position for the search. (Remember that string index positions begin at zero.) If the function can locate such a match, it returns the starting index of the match in the current string. Otherwise, it returns an illegal index value. Depending upon the implementation, this value can either be larger than the set of legal indices, or negative.

```
//    012345678901234567890123456789012345678901234567890 1
s1 = "It was the best of times, it was the worst of times.";

cout << s1.find("times") << endl;      // returns 19
cout << s1.find("times", 20) << endl;  // returns 46
```

The functions `find_first_of()` and `find_first_not_of()` treat the argument string as a set of characters. As with many of the other functions, one or two optional integer arguments can be used to specify a subsequence of the current string. These functions find the first character that is either present (or absent) from the argument set. The position of the given character, if located, is returned. If no such character exists, then an illegal index value is returned. We saw a use for these member functions in the word split algorithm presented in Section 7.2.2.

```
i = s2.find_first_of ("aeiou"); // find first vowel
j = s2.find_first_not_of ("aeiou", i); // next non-vowel
```

7.3.9 Useful Generic Algorithms

Table 7.2 identifies a few of the generic algorithms that are frequently employed with string arguments. Some of these, such as `reverse`, and `transform`, we have encountered already in the example programs presented in Section 7.2.

To illustrate the use of some of these algorithms, assume we have written the following unary function that takes a character argument and returns true if the value is a vowel:

```
bool isVowel (char c)
{
    return c == 'a' || c == 'e' || c == 'i' || c == 'o' || c == 'u';
}
```

The generic algorithms `count` and `count_if` count the number of values that match a given argument value, or that satisfy a function that is passed as argument. The following, for example, would first count the number of e characters in a word, then the number of vowels. Note that this function modifies an integer argument that is passed as reference, instead of returning the count as the function result.

Table 7.2 Generic algorithms useful with strings

```
reverse (iterator start, iterator stop)
```
Reverse text in the given portion of string

```
count (iterator start, iterator stop, target value, int & counter)
```
Count elements that match target value, incrementing counter

```
count_if (iterator start, iterator stop, unary fun, int & counter)
```
Count elements that satisfy function, incrementing counter

```
transform (iterator start, iterator stop, iterator dest, unary fun)
```
Transform text using unary function from source, placing into destination

```
find (iterator start, iterator stop, value)
```
Find value in string, returning iterator for location

```
find_if (iterator start, iterator stop, unary fun)
```
Find value for which function is true, returning iterator for location

```
replace (iterator start, iterator stop, target value, replacement value)
```
Replace target character with replacement character

```
replace_if (iterator start, iterator stop, unary fun, replacement value)
```
Replace characters for which function is true with replacement character

```
sort(iterator start, iterator stop)
```
Places characters into ascending order

```
int ecount = 0; // number of e's
int vcount = 0; // number of vowels

count (aString.begin(), aString.end(), 'e', ecount);
count_if (aString.begin(), aString.end(), isVowel, vcount);
```

The `replace` algorithms will overwrite characters in their argument string. The characters must either match a target value (for the function `replace`) or satisfy a unary function passed as argument (for the function `replace_if`). The first of the following two routines replaces all e characters with an x, while the second replaces all remaining vowels with a y.

```
replace (aString.begin(), aString.end(), 'e', 'x');
replace_if (aString.begin(), aString.end(), isVowel, 'y');
```

7.3.10   Input/Output Routines

The left and right shift operators are overloaded to create input and output stream operators. The output operator writes the entire string to the associated stream. The input operator reads a "word" into the string, where a word is any sequence of characters separated by white space (spaces, tab characters, or newline characters). The input operator is frequently used as the conditional in a loop, because the value it returns can be converted into a Boolean that will become true when the end of input is encountered.

```
string aString = "Find Average Word Length\n";
cout << aString;
string aWord;
int count = 0;
     // make size double so division is real
double size = 0;
while (cin >> aWord) {
     size += aWord.length();
     count++;
     }
cout << "Average word length:" << (size / count) << endl;
```

The procedure `getline` can be used to read an entire line of input. The three arguments to this procedure are an input stream, a string, and the terminating character for the line of input (usually the newline character). As with the input operator, $>>$, this operation is often used as a condition in a loop.

```
string aLine;
while (getline(cin, aLine, '\n'))
     .
     .
     .
```

7.4   THE IMPLEMENTATION OF STRINGS

In a pattern to be continued throughout the remainder of this book, we will not describe here the exact implementation techniques used by the `string` data abstraction in the standard library. The full library versions are usually exceedingly complex, often differ from platform to platform, and in many cases represent proprietary code. Instead, we will explore a simplified version of the data structure, but one that nevertheless accurately represents the salient characteristics of the abstraction.

A class description for our simplified `string` abstraction is shown in Figure 7.1. Note that this class description includes some features that have not yet been introduced, but will be explained shortly.

The most challenging problem for the string abstraction is that the number of characters to be maintained is not known at compile time, and sometimes is not even fixed when a `string` variable is declared. Instead, the quantity can grow or shrink dynamically as operations such as `insert` and `remove` are performed.

To accommodate this, we must make use of *dynamic memory allocation* to separate the process of creating memory for values from the process

```
class string {
public:
    typedef char * iterator; // define iterator type

    string  ();  // constructors
    string  (char *);
    string  (string &);
    ~ string  (); // destructor

        // member functions
    iterator    begin   ();
    bool        empty   ();
    iterator    end     ();
    int         find    (string &, int);
    int         find_first_of    (string &, unsigned int);
    int         find_first_not_of (string &, unsigned int);
    void        insert  (unsigned int, string &);
    int         length  ();
    string      substr  (unsigned int, unsigned int);
    void        remove  (unsigned int, unsigned int);
    void        replace (unsigned int, unsigned int, string &);
    void        resize  (unsigned int, char)

        // operators
    char &      operator [ ]  (unsigned int);
    void        operator =    (string &);
    void        operator +=   (string &);

        // friends
    friend bool operator == (string &, string &);
    friend bool operator != (string &, string &);
    friend bool operator <  (string &, string &);
    friend bool operator <= (string &, string &);
    friend bool operator >  (string &, string &);
    friend bool operator >= (string &, string &);

protected:     // data areas
    char *              buffer;     // pointer to dynamic buffer
    unsigned short int  bufferLength;     // length of dynamic buffer
};
```

Figure 7.1   Description of a simplified string class

of procedure entry and exit. As we saw in Chapter 1, the operator `new` can be used to allocate such memory values.

Our `string` class therefore maintains two data fields. These represent a *pointer* to a dynamically allocated buffer, and an integer that represents the size of this data field. A string variable stored in an activation record therefore *does* have a fixed size; namely, it requires the amount of storage necessary to hold a pointer and an integer. However, the area referenced by the pointer is allowed to grow and shrink during the course of execution.

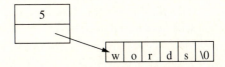

The management of this dynamic memory area will be largely hidden from the individual who simply uses the string abstraction; indeed, the fact that details such as this *can* be hidden by an appropriately constructed class definition is a major advantage of programming using the `class` mechanism.

In the following sections we will describe the major features involved in the implementation of the different parts of the string class.

7.4.1   Constructors, Assignment

The implementation of the constructors for the `string` class illustrate one of the most important principles of software development:

> Wherever possible, seek out repeated or common operations, and factor the code performing these operations into their own routines.

In the case of the string abstraction, one common operation is allocating a buffer of a given size, and initializing this buffer with character values. But we have already identified this (in Section 7.3.3) as a task that is performed by the member function named `resize()`. Making use of this routine greatly simplifies the implementation of the constructor functions.

```
string::string ()
      // default constructor, length zero
{
      buffer = 0;
      resize (0, ' ');     // allocate buffer of length zero
}

string::string (char * cp)
      // initialize string from literal C-style string
{
```

```
    buffer = 0;
    resize (strlen(cp), ' ');     // allocate buffer of correct size
    strcpy (buffer, cp);     // then fill with values
}
```

As we noted earlier, a copy constructor is simply a constructor that initializes a value using data from another instance of the same class, in effect cloning the argument value. For the `string` abstraction this simply means creating a new string with the same size as the argument string, then copying the values into the new buffer. Note that, although the buffer data field is declared as protected, other instances of the `string` class are still permitted access. Thus, the copy constructor can directly refer to the `buffer` data field of the argument value.

```
string::string (string & str)
    // initialize string from argument string
{
    buffer = 0;
    resize (str.length(), ' ');   // allocate buffer of correct size
    strcpy (buffer, str.buffer); //   then fill with values
}
```

In terms of actions, assignment is not so very different from initialization. So it is probably not surprising that the code performed by the assignment operator looks very similar to that performed by the constructors. Note that in implementing this operation, the assignment operator is being defined as a member function; it is a "message" passed to the receiver, with the right-hand size as argument. This is one of two ways in

---

Operators: Functions or Methods

A few operators, such as the various forms of assignment, are required to be defined as member functions. For most operators, however, the programmer has the choice of defining the operator either as an ordinary function, or as a member function.

To decide which option is preferable, there are basically two points to keep in mind:

▲ An ordinary function is normally not permitted access to the protected portions of the class, whereas a member function is allowed such access. (The phrase "normally" is used, because in Section 7.4.8 we will describe a mechanism, friend functions, to circumvent this restriction in a controlled manner.)

▲ Implicit conversions, say from integer to float, will be performed for both right and left argument if the operator is defined in functional form, but only for the right argument if the operator is defined as a member function.

Thus, the member function form is preferable if the left argument is modified, as in assignment. The functional form is preferable if the left argument is not modified, or if conversions are permitted on both arguments.

which binary (that is, two argument) operators can be overloaded. In Chapter 5 we saw the alternative, where the left shift operator was overloaded to mean output. Note in that situation there were two arguments defined for the binary operator, while in this situation there is only one.

```
void string::operator = (string & str)
    //   reassign string to the argument value
{

    resize (str.length(), ' ');
    strcpy (buffer, str.buffer);
}
```

7.4.2   Destructor and Delete

Because dynamically allocated memory is not freed automatically by the system, it must be freed by the programmer. Once freed, memory is "recycled" by the run-time system for use in subsequent allocations. Removal of memory is accomplished using the operator `delete`.

There are two forms of the delete operator. The form shown in the `string` data structure is used when deleting an entire array. If only a single value is being deleted, the square brackets are omitted.

To facilitate actions that must be performed when variables are released, such as dynamic memory management, C++ provides a feature called a *destructor*. A destructor is, in a sense, the opposite of a constructor. It is called implicitly by the system whenever a variable is about to be deleted, either automatically when the procedure containing the variable declaration is being exited, or as a result of an explicit operation by the programmer. A destructor is written as the class name preceded by a tilde. A destructor for our string abstraction could be defined as follows:

Implicit Function Calls

Many function calls are performed in C++ "behind the scenes," that is, without any explicit function call appearing in a program. Constructors are one example of this, although the syntax used for passing arguments to constructors make them look like function calls. But destructors are almost never explicitly invoked by the programmer; rather, they are almost always implicitly executed.

Another general category of implicit function calls deals with conversions. It is possible to implicitly convert a value from an integer to float, or from a pointer-to-char into a `string`. Thus, in a function invocation that expects a `string` argument, but that instead is provided with a pointer to char, a temporary will be created and initialized using the constructor for the class `string` that uses a pointer-to-char as an argument. This temporary is then destroyed (in the process calling the destructor) when the function returns.

```
string::~string()
        // called implicitly when a string is about to be deleted
        // free the memory associated with the buffer
{
        delete [ ] buffer;
}
```

Destructors are almost never directly invoked by the user; instead, they are implicitly called by the run-time system. Note that this destructor is invoked when the `string` is to be deleted. Dynamic memory is only freed using the `delete` operator. Without the destructor the dynamic memory allocated to the buffer would still be considered "in use" by the run-time system. Repeated operations on strings would then eventually result in a failure when memory becomes exhausted.

7.4.3   Resize Internal Buffer

As we have seen, the `resize` method is central to the creation of new string values; it is also a member function that can be directly invoked by users of the `string` abstraction. For these reasons, it is important to give it careful attention.

Who Cleans Up?

Destructors are used primarily for housekeeping tasks, such as the release of dynamically allocated memory. Care must be taken, however, in assuring that the memory being released is not being used by some other value. As we noted earlier, the implementation of strings in simple C++ allows two character pointers to denote the same buffer, as in this diagram:

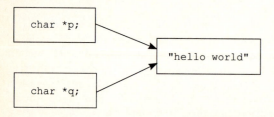

The diagram is symmetric. Which value "owns" the memory area, and thus should be in charge of deleting it? There are twin problems to be avoided here; both not deleting the memory and deleting it more than once will likely lead to eventual error.

In our string abstraction we will avoid this problem by adhering to the principle that every string maintains its own protected data area that is not shared, and every string is responsible for deleting its own data area. When one string is assigned to another, the assignment will copy the contents of the old string into the new one, rather than sharing a common buffer.

In more complex situations sharing is an important part of memory usage. In these cases, deciding how to perform memory management can be a complicated problem. In basic terms this usually comes down to the simple question, "Who is in charge of cleaning up?" Some of the books cited in the References section present more information on this issue.

```
void string::resize (unsigned int newLength, char pad)
{
        // if no current buffer, length is zero
    if (buffer == 0)
        bufferLength = 0;
        // case 1, getting smaller
    if (newLength < bufferLength) {
            // just add new null character
        buffer[newLength] = '\0';
        }
    else {    // case 2, getting larger
            // allocate new buffer, allow space for null character
        int i;
        char * newbuffer = new char[newLength + 1];
        assert (newbuffer != 0);
            // first copy existing characters
        for (i = 0; i < bufferLength && buffer[i] != '\0'; i++)
            newbuffer[i] = buffer[i];
                // then add pad characters
        for ( ; i < newLength; i++)
            newbuffer[i] = pad;
                // add terminating null character
        newbuffer[i] = '\0';
            // free up old area, assign new
        if (buffer != 0)
            delete [ ] buffer;
        buffer = newbuffer;
        bufferLength = newLength;
    }
}
```

The version of resize we present here will only allocate a new buffer when the size increases, not when the buffer size is made smaller. The resize method allocates a new buffer area, using the new operator to create the dynamic memory. An assertion is used to verify that the memory allocation was successful.[2] It then copies the values from the current buffer into the new area, either truncating or padding depending upon whether the new length is smaller than or larger than the current length. Finally, it frees the current buffer, returning the space to the run-time system so that

---

2. This may or may not be necessary, depending upon the version of C++ on which the code is executed. Some systems will return a null pointer when memory becomes exhausted, while others will generate a run-time error. In any case, it does no harm to check the result of the allocation.

it can be recycled in future memory requests, then changes the values of the data fields that maintain the pointer to the buffer and the buffer length.

7.4.4   Computing Length

In computing the length of the current string, one possibility would be to simply use the `strlen` function, as we did in the constructor. But this assumes the null character has not been (perhaps inadvertently) overridden. A safer alternative is to explicitly loop until either the null character is found or the end of buffer is encountered:

```
int string::length ()
    // return number of characters in string
{
    for (int i = 0; i < bufferLength; i++)
        if (buffer[i] == '\0')
            return i;
    return bufferLength;
}
```

The `empty` member function need only examine the first location of the buffer to determine whether or not the string is empty:

```
bool string::empty ()
    // see if string is empty
{
    return buffer[0] == '\0';
}
```

Declaring Local Variables

In most of the programs presented in the book, the declaration of a loop index variable is combined with the initialization portion of a loop, as in this example:
```
for (int i = 0; i < 10; i++)
    .
    .
    .
```

In the method `string::resize`, the declaration is instead moved several lines earlier:
```
int i;
    .
    .
    .
```

```
for (i = 0; i < bufferLength &
        buffer[i] != '\0'; i++)
    .
    .
    .
```

This is because a variable that is declared in the initialization portion of the loop is valid only inside the loop, and cannot be accessed once the loop has finished execution. In this case, however, we need to access the final value of the variable i after the loop halts. Thus, it must be declared *outside* the loop.

7.4.5   Character Access

The requirements for the standard library do not specify whether index values for the string subscript operator are checked for validity; although our version does this, the version of the `string` abstraction supplied by other vendors may or may not do it. Our version will check, using `assert`, that the index values are legal.

By declaring the argument to the subscript operator as `unsigned` we can ensure that it will be positive. It is therefore only necessary to check that it is smaller than the current buffer length:

```
char & string::operator [ ] (unsigned int index)
    // return reference to character at location
{

    assert (index <= bufferLength);   // not required by standard
    return buffer[index];
}
```

Note that this function is returning a *reference* to the given character, and not the *value* of the character. A reference can be considered to be a form of pointer, yet one that is always valid and that does not require dereferencing to access. Because this function returns a reference, the result can be used as the target of an assignment statement:

```
aString[3] = 'd';
```

In addition, note that the index value is checked to determine whether it is less than *or equal to* the length; this allows the subscript operator to return the terminating null character that should be found on the end of all strings. This is necessary because many loops are written to test for this condition:

```
for (int i = 0; aString[i] != '\0'; i++)

    .
    .
```

Because it is possible both to assign to a string position and to return the terminating null character in a string, it is possible, although unwise, for the programmer to erase the terminating null character at the end of a string. In Exercise 15 at the end of this chapter, we will explore one way that this problem could be overcome.

The second form of access is the substring operator. This is similar to a constructor, in that a new value is being created and initialized. A string is declared and, using `resize`, set to the correct size. The appropriate characters are then copied into the new string, and the value is returned.

```
string string::substr (unsigned int start, unsigned int len)
    // return a subportion of string
{
```

```
        assert (start + len <= length());
        string sub;      // create new value
        sub.resize (len, ' ');      // resize appropriately
        for (int i = 0; i < len; i++)
            sub[i] = buffer[start + i];      // copy characters
        return sub;
}
```

7.4.6   Iterators

As we noted in Chapter 6, ordinary pointers satisfy all the properties required of iterators. We can therefore use ordinary character pointers into the underlying buffer as iterator values. Note that this implementation satisfies the requirements of the language definition, but is not the only possible technique. Other implementations of the standard library may use more sophisticated mechanisms.

A `typedef` statement appears in the class definition, defining the name `iterator` as a synonym for a pointer to an array of `char` values. This allows variables to be declared using the `iterator` keyword in a fully qualified name, without requiring the programmer to know how such iterators are implemented:

Returning References

The subscript operator returns a *reference*, while the substring operator returns a *value*. It is useful to consider the differences in these actions, and the circumstances under which each should be used.

A reference can only be returned if the object being referenced will continue to exist even after the procedure has exited. In the case of the subscript operator, the reference is to a position in the buffer array, which was neither created nor deleted by the subscript operator, and thus should continue to exist until some other string operation is performed.

The substring operator, on the other hand, creates a new value within the body of the function. The local variable sub will go out of existence when the function returns, but by returning the value of this expression as the function result, a *copy* of the variable (formed using the copy con-

structor) will be created and returned, to be used in whatever subsequent expression the substring operator appeared.

By returning a reference, the subscript operator permits the result value to be used as a target for an assignment statement. A substring could be used in this fashion, but would not have the effect that was probably intended. A statement such as:

        str.substr(2, 4) = "abc";

would create a temporary variable holding the substring, as well as a temporary variable for the string literal abc. The first temporary would then be reassigned the value of the second. Both temporary variables would then immediately be destroyed, because they can appear in no further computation. The effect the programmer probably intended in this case can be produced using the member function `replace`.

```
string::iterator start = aString.begin();
string::iterator stop = aString.end();

for ( ; start != stop; ++start)
        .
        .
        .
```

The begin and end member functions merely return a pointer to the beginning and end of the buffer, respectifully:

```
char * string::begin ()
        // return starting iterator, just use pointer to buffer
{
        return buffer;
}


char * string::end ()
        // return past-the-end iterator
{
        return buffer + length();
}
```

7.4.7   Insertion, Removal, Replacement, and Append

Removing characters from a string can be performed without reallocating a new buffer; it is only necessary to move the values to the left, overwriting the deleted characters. Be sure to remember to keep the terminating null character in the correct place. An additional clause checks to ensure we do not exceed the buffer length. This is a small price to pay just in case the terminating null character is somehow overwritten.

```
void string::remove (unsigned int start, unsigned int len)
        // remove len characters from given location
{
            // compute end of deleted run
        int stop = start + len;
            // move characters into place
        while ((stop < bufferLength) && (buffer[stop] != '\0'))
            buffer[start++] = buffer[stop++];
        buffer[start] = '\0';
}
```

An insert is slightly more tricky. It is necessary to make sure the buffer is large enough to support the new characters, then move the existing characters to the right in order to make room for the new values, finally copying the new characters into place. Note that opening up the space for the new characters must be performed right to left, not left to right.

```
void string::insert (unsigned int position, string & newText)
    // insert text, starting at position
{
    int len = length();     // current length
    int ntLen = newText.length();     // additional length
    int newLen = len + ntLen;     // new length

        // if necessary, resize buffer
    resize(newLen, '\0');

        // move existing characters over
    for (int i = len; i > position; i--)
        buffer[i + ntLen] = buffer[i];

        // insert new characters
    for (int i = 0; i < ntLen; i++)
        buffer[position + i] = newText[i];
}
```

Having defined removal and insertion, replacement is then just a combination, while the append operator is simply an insertion to the end of
the string. These two functions illustrate the use of the principle that,
wherever possible, more complex functions should be implemented using
simpler functions.

```
void string::replace (unsigned start, unsigned len, string & newText)
    // replace start to start + len with new text
{
    remove (start, len);
    insert (start, newText);
}


void string::operator += (string & right)
    // append argument string to end of current string
{
    insert (length(), right);
}
```

As yet another illustration of this principle, the catenation operator can
be constructed as a combination of a copy constructor and append. Note
that this operator is defined as an ordinary function, not as a member
function:

```
string operator + (string & left, string & right)
    // catenate two string values, forming a new string
{
    string clone(left);     // copy left argument
```

```
    clone += right;        // append right argument
    return clone;          // return result
}
```

There are important reasons for trying to find and exploit common operations. Not only is the code shorter both textually and in machine instructions when operations are defined in terms of other operations, but reliability is increased. If errors are made in the implementation of one of the more basic routines, they are much more likely to be uncovered, because the code repeatedly is being exercised in a variety of ways. Fixing such an error reaps double rewards. If essentially the same code is duplicated two or more times, it is quite likely that an error, should one occur, would be found and repaired in only one location.

7.4.8   Comparison Operators

The six relational operators (<=, <, !=, ==, >, and >=) are, like the catenation operator described in the last section, implemented as true operators, not as member functions. The primary advantage is that, because of this, the compiler will perform automatic conversions on either the left or right argument. If sue is a string variable, then both of these expressions are legal:

```
sue > "sammy"
"allan" <= sue
```

Because the six relational operators are so similar, it is useful to factor out the common task into one operation. This is a slightly different illustration of our principle of finding repeated work. Each of the six individual operations will then be implemented as a call on this common function.

The common operation is actually provided by a primitive string routine, named strcmp. This routine has this rather cryptic definition:

```
int strcmp (char * p, char * q)
{
    while ((*p != '\0') && (*p == *q)) { p++; q++; }
    return *p - *q;
}
```

The compare function loops over the characters in the two strings, using a pair of pointer values. As long as both pointers yield non-empty characters, the characters are compared. If they are unequal, then the comparison can halt. The loop exits either when an unequal pair of characters is encountered, or when either character pointer encounters a null character. If both strings terminate simultaneously, both pointers will point to a null value and zero will be returned. If only the first string terminates, a negative result will be generated because the null value is zero, indicating the second string is larger. Conversely, if only the second string terminates, a positive value will be generated, indicating the first string is larger.

Having defined `compare`, the six relational operators can be easily constructed. The following illustrates the declaration of the "less than" operator. The other operators are similar.

```
int operator < (string & left, string & right)
    // test if left string is lexicographically less than right string
{
    return strcmp(left.buffer, right.buffer) < 0;
}
```

The only difficulty is that the `buffer` data field is not part of the public interface for our `string` abstraction, and is therefore not normally accessible to functions that are not part of the class definition. This problem is circumvented by the class declaring the six relational operators as *friends*. A friend function is, unlike other functions, permitted access to the protected fields of a class. Note that friendship is something that is explicitly given away by the `string` class, and no other functions are permitted access to `protected` data fields or member functions.

7.4.9   Substring Matching

The final function we will present is the member function `find`, which tries to match a target string to a substring of the receiver. The target string and the starting position for the match are passed as arguments.

```
int string::find (string & target, unsigned int start)
    // search for target string as a substring
{
    int targetLength = target.length();
        // stop is last possible starting position
    int stop = length() - targetLength;

    for (int i = start; i <= stop; i++)
        if (substr(i, targetLength) == target)
            return i;

        // no match found, return out of bound index
    return bufferLength;
}
```

The algorithm used by this member function forms a substring at each possible test location, then compares this substring to the target string. If they are equal, then a match has been found, and the starting position of the substring is returned. If the loop completes without finding any match, then an out-of-bounds index value is returned.

The functions `find_first_of` and `find_not_first_of` are left as exercises.

Further Reading

The `string` class library is a relatively recent addition to the C++ language, so many older C++ books may not discuss the topic. A few references that do discuss it include [Musser 96, Ladd 96].

7.5   CHAPTER SUMMARY

Key Concepts

- Pointers and references
- Copy constructor
- Distinction between function and method
- The `string` abstraction
- Friend functions

Study Questions & Exercises

Study Questions

1. What is the type associated with a literal string value?

2. What is the distinction between a pointer and a reference?

3. What are some ways in which the `string` data type differs from the array of characters representation of strings?

4. What is a copy constructor, and what is its purpose?

5. What actions are produced by the generic algorithm named `transform`?

6. What is the meaning of the + = assignment operator when used with two string values?

7. If `str` is a string containing ten characters, explain the effect of the following commands:
   a. `str.insert(3, "abc");`
   b. `str.remove(3, 4);`
   c. `str.replace(3, 2, "pqr");`

8. What is a dynamically allocated memory value? How is it created? How is it released?

9. What are the two ways in which an overloaded binary operator can be redefined in C++?

10. What is a destructor, and what is its purpose?

11. Under what conditions is it legal to return a reference to a variable as the result of a function invocation?

12. What does it mean when a function is listed as a `friend` in a class definition?

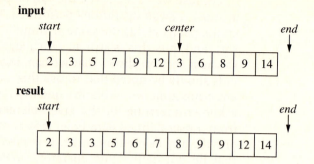

To build a sorting algorithm out of these routines, we must first discover a way of producing ordered lists that can be merged to produce the desired result. The approach used by the merge sort algorithm is to break the original input vector into two roughly equal-sized parts. Each of these parts is then similarly broken in half. This continues until the portions consist of only a single element.

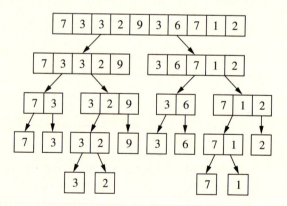

But a collection that consists of only one element is, indeed, ordered. So, to produce a completely ordered sequence, all that is necessary is to merge the subportions into ever larger sequences as we return through the collection of calls. When we reach the original vector, the entire collection has been ordered.

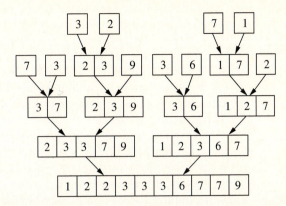

The heart of the program that realizes these ideas is the following recursive procedure. The input is specified by an iterator, and two integer values that represent the start and the past-the-end value for the range to be sorted.

```
template <class Itr>
void m_sort(Itr start, unsigned int low, unsigned int high)
     // internal merge source routine
{
     if (low + 1 < high) {
          unsigned int center = (high + low) / 2;
          m_sort (start, low, center);
          m_sort (start, center, high);
          inplace_merge (start + low, start + center, start + high);
          }
}
```

If the size of the range being specified by the two integer arguments is larger than a single value, then a new integer is created that will hold the value mid-way between the two arguments. The portions of the vector between the lower index and the center, and between the center and the upper index are then separately sorted. The call on `inplace_merge` then combines these two sorted collections, moving the values back into the original locations.

A wrapper procedure named `mergeSort` simply begins the sequence of recursive calls, using the values zero and the size of the vector as the limiting values:

```
template <class T>
void mergeSort(vector<T> & s)
     // sort vector into ascending order using merge sort algorithm
{
     m_sort(s.begin(), 0, s.size());
}
```

Recall from Chapter 4 that to determine the algorithmic complexity of a recursive procedure, we must determine the amount of work performed at each level of call, as well as the depth of the recursive call stack. Because the `inplace_merge` is a linear operation, it is relatively easy to see that at each level of call we are doing $O(n)$ work. To bound the recursive call depth, note that at each step we are dividing the size of the input in half. Therefore, $\log n$ is an approximation to the depth of recursion (see sidebar on logarithms in Section 4.2.4).

We aren't quite finished, because *two* recursive calls are made at each level, before the merge is used to combine the values back into one vector. What saves the running time of this algorithm is that each of these two recursive calls are given a vector that is only half the size of the original. Thus, adding together the linear execution times of the merge operations on the immediately next lower level results in an execution time that is still no larger than $O(n)$.

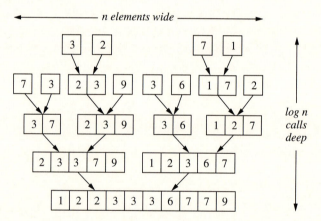

Putting everything together then yields a $O(\log n)$ depth of recursive function calls, each one of which is performing $O(n)$ work. The result is an $O(n \log n)$ sorting algorithm. This is, in practice, a great improvement over the $O(n^2)$ algorithms we have seen earlier. However, `mergeSort` has the unfortunate property of using $O(n)$ temporary storage (here hidden in the `inplace_merge` operation). We will eventually encounter $O(n \log n)$ algorithms that perform equally well in practice and do not require this additional space.

8.3.4   Silly Sentence Generation*

An interesting feature of the `vector` abstraction that is not true of simple arrays is that the size of a vector can change dynamically. Not

---

* Section headings followed by an asterisk indicate optional material.

only can vectors be resized, in the same fashion as the strings discussed in the last section, but single elements can be added or removed from the back of an array. These last operations are performed using the member functions push_back and pop_back. We will illustrate the effect of these operations with a simple program that generates a series of silly sentences. The sentences will all have the form subject–verb–object.

To start, we create three vectors. The vectors are declared as maintaining string values, but are not given a size:

```
vector<string> subject, verb, object;
```

Values are added to these vectors by pushing them on to the end. As each new value is added, the size of the vector is extended to accommodate the new element:

```
// add subjects
subject.push_back("alice and fred");
subject.push_back("cats");
subject.push_back("people");
subject.push_back("teachers");

// add verbs
verb.push_back("love");
verb.push_back("hate");
verb.push_back("eat");
verb.push_back("hassle");

// add objects
object.push_back("dogs");
object.push_back("cats");
object.push_back("people");
object.push_back("donuts");
```

Memory management of vectors is efficient. Like the string class, the vector will hold a buffer of values. There are two quantities that characterize this buffer: the "logical" size and the "physical" size.[2] Popping elements from the vector, or reducing the size, does not necessarily result in a new buffer being allocated; it merely results in the logical size being decremented. Similarly, increasing the size need not require a new allocation, as long as the new logical size does not exceed the current physical size.

To generate a sequence of sentences, we simply loop some number of times, selecting a random value from each of the three vectors. To obtain a

---

2. This was true of the string abstraction as well, but not as obvious. The explicit size maintained by the string was the physical buffer size, while the terminating null character in the string denoted the logical string size.

random subscript, we first use the `size` member function to determine the number of elements in the array, then use the `randomInteger` class from Chapter 4 to generate a random number between 0 and this value.

```
randomInteger randomizer;
    .
    .
    .
for (int i = 0; i < 10; i++) {
    cout << subject[randomizer(subject.size())] << " "
         << verb[randomizer(verb.size())] << " "
         << object[randomizer(object.size())] << endl;
    }
```

Example output from the program might be something like:

alice and fred hate dogs
teachers hassle cats
alice and fred love cats
people hassle donuts
people hate dogs

8.3.5   Matrices*

In Chapter 18 we will describe in detail several different implementation techniques for matrices, that is, two (or more) dimensional arrays. One of these techniques will involve a vector whose elements are themselves vectors. Such an object might be declared as follows:

```
vector< vector<int> > mat(5);
```

Recall that elements of a vector are initialized using the default constructor for the element type. In this case, the default constructor generates a vector of zero elements. So the result of the previous declaration is to produce a vector of five values, each of which is itself a vector of zero elements.

To produce a more useful matrix, each of these inner vectors must be resized to a larger quantity. This is accomplished using the member function `resize()`. The following, for example, would resize each element to be a vector of size 6:

```
for (int i = 0; i < 5; i++)
    mat[i].resize(6);
```

The result can be thought of as a five by six matrix. Individual elements of this matrix can be accessed using a pair of subscript operators, as in the following:

---

* Section headings followed by an asterisk indicate optional material.

> > versus >>

Be careful with spaces in a declaration such as that shown for the variable mat. The space between the two right angle braces is very important. Without it, the compiler will interpret the text as one symbol, the right shift operator. With	most compilers the resulting error messages are very confusing.
	
	`vector< vector<int> > mat(5); // correct`
	`vector<vector<int>> mat(5); // NOT correct !`

```
mat[3][2] = 42;
cout << "value 3,2 is " << mat[3][2] << endl;
```

8.4 SUMMARY OF VECTOR OPERATIONS

To use the vector data type, the programmer must first include the vector interface file:

```
# include <vector>
```

Table 8.1 summarizes the set of legal operations that can be used with the vector data type.[3] The following sections then explain each in more detail.

8.4.1 Declaration and Initialization of Vectors

Because it is a template class, the declaration of a vector must include a designation of the component type. This can be a primitive language type (such as integer or double), a pointer type, or a user-defined type. In the latter case, the user-defined type *must* implement a default constructor (a constructor with no arguments), because this constructor is used to initialize newly created elements.

Like an array, a vector is most commonly declared with an integer argument that describes the number of elements the vector will hold:

```
vector<int> vec_one(10);
```

---

3. As was true of the string abstraction, here we will not describe all the functions that are provided as part of the standard library class, merely the most useful. Similarly, the implementation we will present in Section 8.5 is a simplified form of the standard class implementation.

Table 8.1   Operations for the `vector` **data type**

Constructors		
`vector<T> v;`	Default constructor	$O(1)$
`vector<T> v (int);`	Initialized with explicit size	$O(n)$
`vector<T> v (int, T);`	Size and initial value	$O(n)$
`vector<T> v (aVector);`	Copy constructor	$O(n)$
Element Access		
`v[i]`	Subscript access, can be assignment target	$O(1)$
`v.front ()`	First value in collection	$O(1)$
`v.back ()`	Last value in collection	$O(1)$
Insertion		
`v.push_back (T)`	Push element on to back of vector	$O(1)$ [a]
`v.insert(iterator, T)`	Insert new element after iterator	$O(n)$
`v.swap(vector<T>)`	Swap values with another vector	$O(n)$
Removal		
`v.pop_back ()`	Pop element from back of vector	$O(1)$
`v.erase(iterator)`	Remove single element	$O(n)$
`v.erase(iterator, iterator)`	Remove range of values	$O(n)$
Size		
`v.capacity ()`	Maximum elements buffer can hold	$O(1)$
`v.size ()`	Number of elements currently held	$O(1)$
`v.resize (unsigned, T)`	Change to size, padding with value	$O(n)$
`v.reserve (unsigned)`	Set physical buffer size	$O(n)$
`v.empty ()`	True if vector is empty	$O(1)$
Iterators		
`vector<T>::iterator itr`	Declare a new iterator	$O(1)$
`v.begin ()`	Starting iterator	$O(1)$
`v.end ()`	Ending iterator	$O(1)$

a. push_back can be $O(n)$ if reallocation of the internal buffer is necessary, otherwise it is $O(1)$.

There are a variety of other forms of constructor that can also be used to create vectors. In addition to a size, the constructor can provide a constant value that will be used to initialize each new vector location. If no size is provided, the vector initially contains no elements, and increases in size automatically as elements are added. The copy constructor creates a clone of a vector from another vector.

```
vector<int> vec_two(5, 3); // five elements, initial value 3
vector<int> vec_three;  // no elements in vector
vector<int> vec_four(vec_two); // copy of vector two
```

8.4.2   Subscripting a Vector

The value being maintained by a vector under a specific index can be accessed or modified using the subscript operator, just like a `string` or an ordinary array. And, like arrays, the definition of the standard library does not insist that any attempt be made to verify the validity of the index values, although some implementations elect to do so. Attempts to index a vector outside the range of legal values will generate unpredictable and spurious results:

```
cout << vec_five[1] << endl;
vec_five[1] = 17;
```

The member function `front()` returns the first element in the vector, while the member function `back()` yields the last.

```
cout << vec_five.front() << " ... " << vec_five.back() << endl;
```

8.4.3   Element Insertion

The member function `push_back()` takes a new value as argument, and inserts the element at the end of the vector, increasing the size of the vector by one. The more general function `insert()` takes as arguments an iterator and a value, and inserts the new element preceding the position specified by the iterator. Again, the size of the vector is increased by one.

The member function `swap()` takes as argument another vector that holds the same type of elements. The values of the two vectors are then exchanged; after the operation all values from the argument will be held by the receiver vector, and all elements in the current vector will be held by the argument. This swapping is efficiently performed in constant time, regardless of the size of the two vectors.

8.4.4   Element Removal

The member function `pop_back()` removes the last element of the vector, reducing the size of the vector by one. The more general function `erase` has two forms. In the easier form a single location is specified using an iterator, and the value denoted by the iterator is removed from the vector. Again, the size of the vector is then reduced by one. Note that eliminating a value can be $O(n)$ in the worst case, as all successive elements may need to be moved over by one position.

The more general form of `erase()` takes two iterator arguments, which specify a range of values within the vector. All elements within this range are removed. Regardless of the number of elements being removed, this operation is $O(n)$ in the worst case.

8.4.5   Extent and Size-Changing Operations

There are, in general, two different "sizes" associated with any vector. The first is the number of elements currently being held by the vector. The second is the maximum size to which the vector can be expanded without requiring that new storage be allocated. The following illustrates these values. Here, a buffer with maximum capacity six is being used to store only four elements.

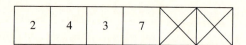

The two sizes are yielded by the member functions `capacity()` and `size()`, respectively.

```
cout << "size: " << vec_five.size() << endl;
cout << "capacity: " << vec_five.capacity() << endl;
```

As we noted earlier, elements can be added to or removed from a vector in a variety of ways. When elements are removed from a vector, the memory for the vector is generally not reallocated, and thus the size is decreased but the capacity remains the same. A subsequent insertion does not force a reallocation of new memory if the original capacity is not exceeded.

An insertion that causes the size to exceed the capacity generally results in a new block of memory being allocated to hold the vector elements. Values are then copied into this new memory using the assignment operator appropriate to the element type, and the old memory is deleted. Because this can be a potentially costly operation, the `vector` data type provides a means for the programmer to specify a value for the capacity of a vector. The member function `reserve()` is a directive to the vector, indicating that the vector is expected to grow to at least the given size. If the argument used with `reserve()` is larger than the current capacity, then a reallocation occurs and the argument value becomes the new capacity. (It may subsequently grow even larger; the value given as argument need not be a bound, just a guess.) If the capacity is already in excess of the argument, then no reallocation takes place. Invoking `reserve()` does not change the size of the vector, nor the element values themselves (except that they may potentially be moved should reallocation take place).

```
vec_five.reserve(20);
```

A reallocation invalidates all references, pointers, and iterators denoting elements being held by a vector.

The member function `empty()` returns true if the vector currently has a size of zero (regardless of the capacity of the vector). Using this function is generally more efficient than comparing the result returned by `size()` to zero.

8.4.6   Iterators

As with the `string` class, the `vector` class contains a type definition for the name `iterator`. This permits an iterator to be easily declared for any particular type of vector value:

```
vector<double>::iterator itr;
for (itr = aVec.begin(); itr != aVec.end(); ++itr)
    :
    :
```

The member functions `begin()` and `end()` yield random access iterators for the vector. Again, note that the iterators yielded by these operations can become invalidated after insertions or removals of elements.

8.4.7   Generic Algorithms

As with the `string` abstraction, a lot of the useful functionality associated with the `vector` data type comes not from member functions, but from generic algorithms that are common to many different data structures. ~~Figure~~ Table 8.2 summarizes some of these. Many we have encountered already in earlier chapters. The following will describe some of the others.

A `vector` does not directly provide any method that can be used to determine if a specific value is contained in the collection. However, the generic algorithms `find()` or `count()` can be used for this purpose. The following, for example, illustrates two ways in which one could test to see whether or not an integer vector contained the element 17:

Table 8.2 Generic algorithms useful with vectors

```
fill (iterator start, iterator stop, value)
```
Fill vector with a given initial value

```
copy (iterator start, iterator stop, iterator destination)
```
Copy one sequence into another

```
max_element(iterator start, iterator stop)
```
Find largest value in collection

```
min_element(iterator start, iterator stop)
```
Find smallest value in collection

```
reverse (iterator start, iterator stop)
```
Reverse elements in the collection

```
count (iterator start, iterator stop, target value, counter)
```
Count elements that match target value, incrementing counter

```
count_if (iterator start, iterator stop, unary fun, counter)
```
Count elements that satisfy function, incrementing counter

```
transform (iterator start, iterator stop, iterator destination, unary)
```
Transform elements using unary function from source, placing into destination

```
find (iterator start, iterator stop, value)
```
Find value in collection, returning iterator for location

```
find_if (iterator start, iterator stop, unary function)
```
Find value for which function is true, returning iterator for location

```
replace (iterator start, iterator stop, target value, replacement value)
```
Replace target element with replacement value

```
replace_if (iterator start, iterator stop, unary fun, replacement value)
```
Replace elements for which fun is true with replacement value

```
sort (iterator start, iterator stop)
```
Places elements into ascending order   *the < operator must be defined on data type*

```
for_each (iterator start, iterator stop, function)
```
Execute function on each element of vector

```
iter_swap (iterator, iterator)
```
Swap the values specified by two iterators

```
vector<int>::iterator start = aVec.begin();
vector<int>::iterator stop = aVec.end();

if (find(start, stop, 17) != stop)
    ... // element has been found

int counter = 0;
```

```
count (start, stop, 17, counter);
if (counter != 0)
... // element is in collection
```

Note that the `count()` member function does not return its result as the function return value, but instead modifies the value of an integer variable that is passed by reference as an argument.

The function `max_element` can be used to discover the largest value in a collection. This function returns an iterator that describes the given position.

```
vector<int>::iterator maxValue = max_element (start, stop);
cout << "Largest value is " << *maxValue << endl;
```

We can use `max_element` to create a short (but not necessarily efficient) version of the selection sort algorithm. This time the input to the algorithm is specified as a pair of iterators, and thus this algorithm will work for vectors, deques, as well as strings and conventional C++ arrays.

```
template <class Itr>
void maximum_sort (Itr bottom, Itr top)
{
    while (bottom != top) {
        Itr max = max_element (bottom, top);
        iter_swap (max, --top);
    }
}
```

8.4.8   Sorting and Sorted Vector Operations

A vector does not automatically maintain its values in sequence. However, a vector can be placed in order using the generic algorithm `sort()`, or one of the other sorting algorithms we have presented. The simplest form of the generic algorithm uses for its comparisons the less-than operator for the element type. An alternative version permits the programmer to specify the comparison operator as a function object. This can be used, for example, to place the elements in descending rather than ascending order:

```
    // sort ascending
sort (aVec.begin(), aVec.end());

    .
    .
    .

class greaterInt {
public:
    operator () (int a, int b) {return a > b; }
};
```

Table 8.3 Generic Algorithms useful with Sorted Vectors

```
merge(iterator s1, iterator e1, iterator s2, iterator e2, iterator dest)
```
Merge two sorted collections into a third

```
inplace_merge(iterator start, iterator center, iterator stop)
```
Merge two adjacent sorted sequences into one

```
binary_search (iterator start, iterator stop, value)
```
Search for element within collection, returns a boolean

```
lower_bound (iterator start, iterator stop, value)
```
Find first location larger than or equal to value, returns an iterator

```
upper_bound (iterator start, iterator stop, value)
```
Find first element strictly larger than value, returns an iterator

```
        :
        :
    // sort descending, by specifying the ordering algorithm explicitly
    greaterInt compareFun;
    sort (aVec.begin(), aVec.end(), compareFun );
```

A number of operations can be applied to a vector holding an ordered collection. For example, two vectors can be merged using the generic algorithm `merge()`:

```
    // merge two vectors, placing output in third
    vector<int> result(vecOne.size() + vecTwo.size());
    merge (vecOne.begin(), vecOne.end(),
        vecTwo.begin(), vecTwo.end(), result.begin());
```

Sorting a vector also lets us use more efficient binary search algorithms, instead of a linear traversal algorithm such as `find()`. Table 8.3 describes some of the generic algorithms that can be used with sorted vectors.

8.5   THE IMPLEMENTATION OF VECTOR

In Figure 8.2 we repeated the class definition of the `vector` data type, this time including the implementation of a number of member functions as in-line definitions. We will discuss the implementation of the various operations in the sections that follow.

8.5.1   Constructors

As with all constructors, the major task for the constructors associated with the vector class is to ensure the data fields are properly initialized. In

```
template <class T> class vector {
public:
    typedef T * iterator;
    typedef T   value_type;

        // constructors
    vector  () { buffer = 0; resize(0); }
    vector  (unsigned int size) { buffer = 0; resize(size); }
    vector  (unsigned int size, T initial);
    vector  (vector & v);
    vector  () { delete [ ] buffer; }

        // member functions
    T        back () { return buffer[mySize - 1];}
    iterator begin () { return buffer; }
    int      capacity () { return myCapacity; }
    bool     empty () { return mySize == 0; }
    iterator end () { return begin() + mySize; }
    T        front () { return buffer[0]; }
    void     pop_back () { mySize--; }
    void     push_back (T value);
    void     reserve (unsigned int newCapacity);
    void     resize (unsigned int newSize)
                { reserve(newSize); mySize = newSize; }
    int      size () { return mySize; }

        // operators
    T & operator [ ] (unsigned int index)
        { return buffer[index]; }
protected:
    unsigned int mySize;
    unsigned int myCapacity;
    T * buffer;
};
```

Figure 8.2 The class vector with in-line definitions

a fashion similar to the handling of string, the member function resize() will be used to create a buffer of the appropriate size. The differences between the various constructors is in the manner in which they initialize this buffer.

The default constructor and the constructor that provides only the size of the initial buffer simply call resize(). These two forms were shown in the in-line definition in Figure 8.2. The constructor that provides an initial value for each element of the vector uses a generic algorithm called `fill()`, which sets each value of the iterator range to a value that is provided as an argument:

```
template <class T> vector<T>::vector (unsigned int size, T initial)
    // create vector with given size,
    // initialize each element with value
{
    buffer = 0;
    resize(size);
        // use fill algorithm to initialize each location
    fill (begin(), end(), initial);
}
```

The copy constructor uses a different generic algorithm, `copy()`, to initialize the new area. The `copy()` algorithm takes three iterator arguments: the first two identify the source, while the third marks the beginning of the target destination. It is assumed (but not verified) that the destination has at least as much space as the source.

```
template <class T> vector<T>::vector (vector & v)
    // create vector with given size,
    // initialize elements by copying from argument
{
    buffer = 0;
    resize(v.length());
        // use copy algorithm to initialize locations
    copy (v.begin(), v.end(), begin());
}
```

The destructor simply releases storage for the dynamically allocated buffer. This is coded as an in-line function definition.

Implicit and Explicit Member Function Invocation

The copy constructor for class `vector` illustrates both the implicit and explicit invocation of member functions. There are two different objects receiving the `begin()` message in the code shown. One is the argument named v, and in this case the receiver of the message is explicitly written. In the other call on `begin()`, no receiver is written. Whenever a member function is invoked and the receiver is not explicitly mentioned, it is implicitly assumed that the current object is the receiver.

In the rare cases when it is required to explicitly name the current receiver (for example, when it is needed as an argument in a function), the pseudo-variable `this` is used. The variable `this` represents a *pointer* to the current receiver for a method. Thus, the call on `begin()` could alternatively have been written as `this->begin()`.

8.5.2 Reserve and Resize

Both the capacity and the size are stored as integer data fields. The values of these fields can be accessed using the member functions `size()` and `capacity()`. The functions `resize()` and `reserve()` are used to set the values of these two fields. The first, `resize()`, merely calls `reserve()` to ensure the capacity is at least as large as the new size, then sets the size field. This function was given an in-line definition in Figure 8.2. The `reserve()` member function is more complex, and is defined as follows:

```
template <class T> void vector<T>::reserve (unsigned int newCapacity)
    // reserve capacity at least as large as argument value
{
    if (buffer == 0) { // no buffer, zero size
        mySize = 0;
        myCapacity = 0;
        }
        // don't do anything if already large enough
    if (newCapacity <= myCapacity)
        return;
            // allocate new buffer, make sure successful
    T * newBuffer = new T [newCapacity];
    assert (newBuffer);
            // copy values into buffer
    copy (buffer, buffer + mySize, newBuffer);
            // reset data field
    myCapacity = newCapacity;
            // change buffer pointer
    delete [ ] buffer;
    buffer = newBuffer;
}
```

If the current capacity is already larger than the requested capacity, then no additional action is necessary. Otherwise, a new buffer is allocated and the copy generic algorithm (the same algorithm used by the copy constructor) is used to copy the values from the old buffer into the new one. Afterwards, the old buffer is deleted and the data fields changed to point to the new area.

8.5.3 Access to Data Values

Access to data fields is provided through the subscript operator and the member functions `front()` and `back()`, all of which are short enough to be defined as in-line functions (Figure 8.2). Note that the subscript operator shown in this class definition does not check to ensure the index is legal.

This is something a programmer should always verify before using a C++ subscript.

The functions front() and back() return the first and last element of the vector. It is an error to invoke these functions on a vector that has no elements.

The function pop_back() reduces the size of the vector by one, thereby removing the final value from the collection. The corresponding function push_back(T) must first check to see if there is sufficient room. Rather than simply increasing the capacity by one, if the capacity is exceeded the vector is enlarged by five elements. (The value 5 is arbitrarily chosen, and is unique to this implementation. Other implementations may elect to perform different actions in this situation.)

```
template <class T> void vector<T>::push_back (T value)
    // push value on to end of vector
{
        // grow buffer if necessary
    if (mySize >= myCapacity)
        reserve(myCapacity + 5);
    buffer [mySize++] = value;
}
```

8.6   IMPLEMENTING GENERIC ALGORITHMS

The template feature is also key to the implementation of generic algorithms. Thus far we have only been able to discuss in pseudocode the implementation of these functions. With the introduction of templates, we can now illustrate the real implementation.

For example, the fill() algorithm used in the implementation of one of the constructors (Section 8.5.1) has the following definition. Note that there are two template arguments. One is used as the type for the iterators, while the other is used as the type for the initial value. Both types are determined individually for each use of the fill() function.

```
template <class ItrType, class T>
    void fill (ItrType current, ItrType stop, T value)
{
    while (current != stop) {
        *current = value;
        current++;
        }
}
```

The copy() generic algorithm uses a similar loop, but requires two different iterator types as template arguments.

```
template <class SourceItrType, class DestItrType>
    void copy (SourceItrType current, SourceItrType stop,
        DestItrType dest)
{
    while (current != stop)     *dest++ = *current++;
}
```

Note that for generic algorithms, unlike template classes, the types used for the template arguments are determined automatically, based on the argument types used with the call. The user need not explicitly indicate the template argument values.

The `merge()` generic algorithms, introduced in Section 8.3.3, are some of the more complex algorithms we have encountered. As we have noted, the inplace merge operation uses a temporary buffer, merging the two sequences into this temporary, then copying the values back into the original. It could be described as follows:[4]

```
template <class Itr, class T>
void inplace_merge (Itr start, Itr center, Itr stop)
{
    int distance = stop - start;
    vector<T> temp(distance);
    merge(start, center, center, stop, temp.begin());
    copy (temp.begin(), temp.end(), start);
}
```

instantiates "copy" template

The general `merge()` operation uses one loop to merge values as long as both sequences are producing. When either the first or second sequence ends, a loop is used to copy the remaining values to the destination:

```
template <class Itr1, class Itr2, class Itr3>
void merge (Itr1 start1, Itr1 stop1, Itr2 start2, Itr2 stop2, Itr3 dest)
{
    while ((start1 != stop1) && (start2 != stop2))
        if (*start1 < *start2)
            *dest++ = *start1++;
        else
            *dest++ = *start2++;

    // copy remainder.  Note only one of the following loops will
    // actually execute, but we can't predict which one
    while (start1 != stop1) *dest++ = *start1++;
    while (start2 != stop2) *dest++ = *start2++;
}
```

---

4. Most commercial implementations of `inplace_merge` will be more complex, using a variety of techniques to avoid whenever possible the dynamic allocation of memory.

8.7   CHAPTER SUMMARY

Key Concepts

- Vector
- Class templates
- Function templates
- Merge sort
- Generic algorithms

A vector is an indexed collection of similarly typed values. Vectors permit random and rapid access to all elements. In creating a vector data abstraction, the `template` mechanism allows the data type to be parameterized, thereby permitting vectors of many different sorts of value. The template mechanism can also be applied to functions, thereby permitting the creation of generic functions that can work with a variety of different data types.

In this chapter we have investigated the vector data type, and a number of different uses for this data structure. These include the merge sort algorithm, which is the first $O(n \log n)$ sorting algorithm we have encountered in this book.

We concluded this chapter by describing an implementation of the vector data type, similar to (but simpler than) the implementation used by the standard C++ library.

Study Questions & Exercises

Study Questions

1. What are some reasons that motivate the creation of the `vector` as an abstract data type?

2. What does it mean to say that a vector is a parameterized data type?

3. What is the purpose of the sieve of Erastosthenes?

4. How does the selection sort algorithm differ from the bubble sort algorithm?

5. For a vector of size n, how many levels of recursive calls will be performed by the merge sort algorithm?

6. What is the algorithmic complexity of the merge sort algorithm?

7. Explain the difference between the logical size and the physical size of a vector.

8. Explain the difference between the functions `reserve` and `resize`.

Exercises

1. Write and test a template version of the `abs` function, which produces the absolute value of a numeric quantity.

2. Write the function `join`, with prototype definition:

```
string join(vector<string>& values,
            string & separator)
```

The `join` function takes a vector of string values and concatenates them together to form a single string value, using the separator between successive values.

3. We did not define output operations for our vector data type. What should such an operation do? Modify the vector class to include a stream output operation.

4. Another operation we did not define was the equality comparison between two vectors. What is a reasonable interpretation for this operator? What does it mean to say that two vectors are equal?

5. What is a rough upper bound on the algorithmic complexity of the sieve algorithm given in Section 8.3.1? To make the bound easier to discover, you can assume the increment value in the innermost loop is 1, rather than i. (Certainly this gives us an upper bound, as i is always at least as large as 1.)

6. Rewrite the bubble sort and the insertion sort algorithms from Chapter 4 using the template mechanism, the `vector` data type, and the `swap` procedure.

7. Assume a vector has the following initial configuration:

15	88	36	9	2	95	5

Simulate the execution of all three sorting algorithms, bubble sort, selection sort, and insertion sort. For each algorithm, show the state of the vector at the end of the inner loop.

8. The following algorithm tries to combine features of bubble sort and insertion sort.

```
template <class T>
void bubbleInsertionSort(vector<T> & data)
{
    int max = data.size();
    int i = 1;

    while (i < max) {
        // inv: data[0 .. i-1] is sorted
      if ((i > 0) && (data[i] < data[i-1])) {
            swap(data[i], data[i-1]);
            i--;
            }
    else
            i++;
        // inv: data[0 .. i-1] is sorted
        }
    // inv: data[0..max-1] is properly ordered
}
```

a. Give an argument for correctness of this algorithm.

b. Give an argument to show that the algorithm will always terminate.

c. What is the worst case performance for this algorithm? What type of input data will cause this worst case behavior?

d. What is the best case performance for this algorithm? What type of input data will cause this best case behavior?

9. A sorting algorithm is said to be *stable* if two values that compare equally are in the same relative ordering following the sort that they had prior to the sort. Which of the sorting algorithms that we studied in this chapter are stable? Hint: Simulate the sort on a small vector that contains repeated values, such as:

15_a	88_a	15_b	9	88_b	15_c	2

10. Using the technique described in Exercise 19 of Chapter 4, empirically test the assertion that selection sort is an $O(n^2)$ algorithm.

11. Using the technique described in Exercise 19 of Chapter 4, show that merge sort is *not* an $O(n^2)$ algorithm, but is instead an $O(n \log n)$ algorithm.

12. Using the value of c you computed in Exercise 11, estimate how long it would take to sort a vector of 100,000 elements using the merge sort algorithm.

13. Rewrite the transform() generic algorithm, introduced in Section 7.2.1, to use templates.

14. One of the operations in the standard library version of vector that we have not implemented in our simplified class is the erase member function. This function has two forms. The first takes a single iterator value and removes the element stored at the associated position, reducing the size of the vector by one and sliding the remaining elements from locations with higher index values over one position. The second form of erase() uses a range defined by two iterator values and removes all the elements described by the range. Extend the implementation of the simplified vector class to include both of these operations.

15. Another operation in the standard library version of the vector class is swap. This member function takes as argument another vector of the same element type and swaps the values held by the two vectors. Describe an implementation of this operation. What is the algorithmic complexity of the operation when using your implementation technique?

16. Another operation in the standard library version of the vector class is insert. This member function takes two arguments, an iterator and a value of the same type as the elements in the vector. The new value is inserted at the position immediately preceding the iterator. What is the worst case algorithmic complexity of an insertion?

17. Fill in the algorithmic complexities in the
following chart for the vector implementation
described in Section 8.5:

Operation	Asymptotic Complexity
Constructors Let n represent argument integer	
`vector<T> v (int);` `vector<T> v (int, T);`	
Copy Constructor Let n represent number of elements in argument vector	
`vector<T> v (aVector);`	
Operations Let n represent number of elements in vector	

`v[i]`
`v.front ()`
`v.back ()`
`v.push_back (T)`
`v.pop_back ()`
`v.capacity ()`
`v.size ()`
`v.resize (unsigned, T)`
`v.reserve (unsigned)`
`v.empty ()`
`v.begin ()`
`v.end ()`	

## Chapter 9

Lists: A Dynamic Data Structure

Chapter Overview

The vector data type is not well suited to problems in which the number of elements increases or decreases over a wide range during the course of execution, or when the number of elements cannot be estimated in advance. For these situations, the linked list data abstraction is a preferable alternative.

In this chapter we discuss the concept of a linked list, and introduce the list data type from the standard library. While discussing this data type, we also introduce a number of programming techniques that greatly extend the power of the tools provided by the STL. These techniques include adaptors, insert iterators, function objects, and inheritance. Because elements of a list are not immediately adjacent to each other in memory, the list data structure is the first data type we describe that requires an explicit iterator class.

Major topics discussed in this chapter include the following:

▲ The linked list data abstraction
▲ Example programs
▲ An example implementation
▲ List iterators
▲ Variations on lists

▲ Programming tools
  • Adaptors
  • Insert iterators
  • Function objects
  • Inheritance

9.1   THE LIST DATA ABSTRACTION

The concept of a linked list is a natural data abstraction that arises in problems in which a data structure must maintain a collection of elements, but the number of elements is not known in advance, or varies over a wide range. Basically, the idea of a linked list is to maintain the elements of the collection in a chain, with each dynamically allocated link holding a single value and a pointer to the next link. The pointer either contains the address of the next link or a null value if the link is the last element in the list. The list data structure itself is simply a placeholder, in its simplest form maintaining only a pointer to the first link.

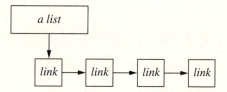

There are many variations on the concept of a linked list. By maintaining a pointer to both the first and the last link, for example, a list can allow for efficient (constant time) insertions to both the front and the rear of a list.

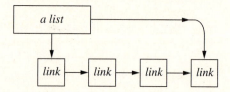

Another common technique is for each link to maintain two pointers, one pointing to the next element in the sequence and the second to the previous element. This allows sequential traversal of the list elements in both directions, rather than simply in a forward direction. A list using this technique is said to be *doubly-linked*.

9

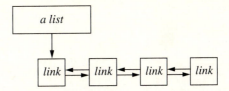

The `list` abstraction provided by the standard library combines both of these variations. The head and tail pointers permit efficient insertion and removal from either end of the list, while the double links permit traversal (via iterators) in either a forward or backwards direction.

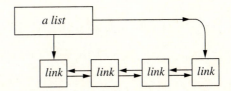

9.2 SUMMARY OF LIST OPERATIONS

Table 9.1 provides a summary of the operations provided by the `list` data type in the standard library. As with the `vector` data type, the utility of the `list` type is greatly extended by combining `list` member functions with the generic algorithms provided in the standard library.

Whenever you use a list, you must include the `list` header file:

```
# include <list>
```

To declare a new list, the programmer uses a template argument to specify the type of value the list will maintain. This can be a primitive language type (such as integer or double), a pointer type, or a user-defined type. In the latter case, the user-defined type *must* implement a default constructor (a constructor with no arguments), as this constructor is used to initialize newly created elements. A collection declared in this fashion will initially not contain any elements.

```
list <int> list_one;
list <Widget *> list_two; // list of pointers to widgets
list <Widget> list_three; // list of widgets
```

A *copy constructor* can be used to initialize a list with values drawn from another list. The assignment operator performs the same actions. In both cases the assignment operator for the element type is used to copy each new value.

```
list <int> list_four (list_one);
list <Widget> list_five;
list_five = list_three;
```

Table 9.1   Summary of list operations

Constructors and Assignment		
`list<T> v;`	Default constructor	$O(1)$
`list<T> v (aList);`	Copy constructor	$O(n)$
`l = aList`	Assignment	$O(n)$
`l.swap (aList)`	Swap values with another list	$O(1)$
Element Access		
`l.front ()`	First element in list	$O(1)$
`l.back ()`	Last element in list	$O(1)$
Insertion and Removal		
`l.push_front (value)`	Add value to front of list	$O(1)$
`l.push_back (value)`	Add value to end of list	$O(1)$
`l.insert (iterator, value)`	Insert value at specified location	$O(1)$
`l.pop_front ()`	Remove value from front of list	$O(1)$
`l.pop_back ()`	Remove value from end of list	$O(1)$
`l.erase (iterator)`	Remove referenced element	$O(1)$
`l.erase (iterator,iterator)`	Remove range of elements	$O(1)$ [a]
`l.remove (value)`	Remove all occurrences of value	$O(n)$
`l.remove_if (predicate)`	Removal all values that match condition	$O(n)$
Size		
`l.empty ()`	True if collection is empty	$O(1)$
`l.size ()`	Return number of elements in collection	$O(n)$ [b]
Iterators		
`list<T>::iterator itr`	Declare a new iterator	$O(1)$
`l.begin ()`	Starting iterator	$O(1)$
`l.end ()`	Ending iterator	$O(1)$
`l.rbegin ()`	Starting backwards moving iterator	$O(1)$
`l.rend ()`	Ending backwards moving iterator	$O(1)$
Miscellaneous		
`l.reverse ()`	Reverse order of elements	$O(n)$
`l.sort ()`	Place elements into ascending order	$O(n \log n)$
`l.sort (comparison)`	Order using comparison function	$O(n \log n)$
`l.merge (list)`	Merge with another ordered list	$O(n)$

a. Freeing the memory used by erased cells will require time proportional to the number of elements deleted.

b. Some implementations keep track of the number of elements in a list, and thus can determine the size in $O(1)$.

Two lists can exchange their entire contents by means of the operation swap(). The argument container will take on the values of the receiver, while the receiver will assume those of the argument. A swap is very efficient, and should be used, where appropriate, in preference to an explicit element-by-element transfer.

```
list_one.swap (list_four); // exchange values in lists one and four
```

The member functions front() and back() return, but do not remove, the first and last items in the container, respectively. For a list, access to other elements is possible only by removing elements (until the desired element becomes the front or back) or through the use of iterators. In particular, note that the subscript operator is not implemented by the list data type.

Values can be inserted into a list in a variety of ways. Elements are most commonly added to the front or back of a list. These tasks are performed by the push_front() and push_back() operations, respectively. These operations are efficient, having guaranteed constant time performance.

```
list_one.push_front (12);
list_three.push_back (Widget(6));
```

There is also a member function, named insert(), that allows values to be inserted into the middle of a list. The insert member function takes two arguments, an iterator and a value. The value is inserted at the point just *prior* to the element referenced by the iterator. The insert() operation itself returns an iterator denoting the location of the inserted value. This value is often, as in the following example, ignored by the programmer.

```
    // insert widget 8 at end of list
list_three.insert (list_three.end(), Widget(8));
```

The generic algorithm find can be used to find a specific value in a list. This value can then be used with the insert member function. If the find does not find a value, the ending iterator will be returned, and the insertion will be made at the end of the list.

```
    //   find the location of the first 5 value in list
list<int>::iterator location =
        find (list_one.begin(), list_one.end(), 5);
    // and insert an 11 immediately before it
location = list_one.insert (location, 11);
```

Just as there are a number of different ways to insert an element into a list, there are a variety of ways to remove values from a list. The most common operations used to remove a value are pop_front() or pop_back(), which delete the single element from the front or the back of the list, respectively. These member functions simply remove the given element, and do not themselves return any useful result. To look at the values before deletion, use the member functions `front()` or `back()`.

The `erase()` operation can be used to remove a value denoted by an iterator. For a list, the argument iterator, and any other iterators that denote the same location, become invalid after the removal, but iterators denoting other locations are unaffected. We can also use `erase()` to remove an entire subsequence, denoted by a pair of iterators. The values beginning at the initial iterator and up to, but not including, the final iterator are removed from the list. Erasing elements from the middle of a list is an efficient operation, requiring only constant time.

```
list_nine.erase (location);
```

```
                // erase all values between the first 5 and the following 7
list<int>::iterator start = find (list_nine.begin(), list_nine.end(), 5);
list<int>::iterator stop = find (start, list_nine.end(), 7);
list_nine.erase (start, stop);
        // start and stop are no longer valid iterators
```

The `remove()` member function removes *all* occurrences of a given value from a list. A variation, `remove_if()`, removes all values that satisfy a given predicate.[1] These operations are more efficient than using the generic algorithms of the same name.

```
list_nine.remove (4); // remove all fours
list_nine.remove_if (divisableByThree); //   remove elements divisible by 3
```

The member function `size()` will return the number of elements being held by a container. The function `empty()` will return true if the container is empty, and is more efficient than comparing the size against the value zero.

```
cout << "Number of elements: " << list_nine.size () << endl;
if ( list_nine.empty () )
    cout << "list is empty " << endl;
else
    cout << "list is not empty " << endl;
```

The `list` data structure definition includes a number of type definitions. The two most frequently used definitions are `iterator`, which defines an iterator appropriate for use with lists, and `value_type`, which simply renames the declaration of the template argument. The most common use for these is in declaration statements. For example, an iterator for a list of integers can be declared in the following fashion:

```
list<int>::iterator l_itr;
```

---

1. The `remove_if` operation is not supported by all vendors' implementations of the STL.

There are two types of iterators that can be constructed for lists. The member functions `begin()` and `end()` construct iterators that traverse the list in forward order. The alternative functions `rbegin()` and `rend()` construct iterators that traverse in reverse order, moving from the end of the list to the front.

The `list` data type does not directly provide any method that can be used to determine if a specific value is contained in the collection. However, either the generic algorithms `find()` or `count()` can be used for this purpose. The following statements, for example, test to see whether an integer list contains the element 17.

```
int num = 0;
count (list_five.begin(), list_five.end(), 17, num);
if (num > 0)
    cout << "contains a 17" << endl;
else
    cout << "does not contain a 17" << endl;
```

The member function `sort()` places elements into ascending order, using an efficient $O(n \log n)$ algorithm. If a comparison operator other than < is desired, it can be supplied as an argument.

```
list_ten.sort ( ); // place elements into sequence
list_twelve.sort (widgetCompare); // sort using the widget compare function
```

The member function `reverse()` reverses the order of elements in the list.

```
list_ten.reverse(); // elements are now reversed
```

The `merge` member function merges two ordered lists. It is similar to, but more efficient than, the generic algorithm discussed in Chapter 8.

9.2.1 Insert Iterators

Assignment to an iterator normally overwrites the contents of the corresponding element. Generic algorithms that loop over an entire container can use this property to overwrite an entire sequence. For example, if `list_one` holds the elements 1, 2, and 3, while `list_two` holds the values 7, 8, 9, and 10, the statement:

```
copy (list_one.begin(), list_one.end(), list_two.begin());
```

will completely erase the first three values in `list_two`, resulting in the list holding the values 1, 2, 3, and 10.

However, when used with a `list` (and with later data structures, such as the `set` and `multiset`), these overwriting semantics are often not the desired actions. Instead, it would be useful if the iterator operations could instead perform an *insertion*, adding the new elements to the container, rather than overwriting existing values.

In the standard library, this effect can be achieved by constructing an *insert iterator*. An insert iterator performs the same operations as an iterator, but instead of performing an overwrite when the assignment operator is invoked, it performs an insertion. We could use the copy generic algorithm to append one list to the end of another in this manner:

```
copy (list_one.begin(), list_one.end(), back_inserter(list_two));
```

If the two lists had their original values as described above, the result after executing this statement would be that `list_two` would have the values 7, 8, 9, 10, 1, 2, and 3.

There are three forms of insert iterators. In addition to the `back_inserter`, just described, there is a `front_inserter` that inserts elements at the front of a collection. The adaptor `back_inserter` uses push_back to add values to the collection, while `front_inserter` uses push_front. Thus, `back_inserter` can be used with both vectors and lists, while `front_inserter` can be used only with lists. A third form, `inserter`, takes two arguments. The first is the container into which the elements are to be inserted, and the second is an iterator into the container. This form copies elements into the location specified by the iterator.

The following simple program illustrates the use of all three forms of insert iterators. First, the values 3, 2, and 1 are inserted into the front of an initially empty list. Note that as they are inserted, each value becomes the

---

Adaptors

An *adaptor* is a class that is constructed simply to change, or adapt, an interface from one form to another. Technically, an insert iterator is a form of adaptor. The adaptor itself does little or no work, but relies on an underlying component to perform the given behavior.

In this case, the adaptor is using the list itself for the underlying software component. The purpose of the adaptor is to create a device that looks like an iterator, but performs differently behind the scenes. In the copy algorithm, the destination iterator is used as follows:

```
iterator copy (iterator start,
    iterator stop, iterator dest)
{
    while (start != stop)
        *dest++ = *start++;
```

```
    return dest;
}
```

A programmer could copy the values from, for example, a vector into a list with an expression such as:

```
copy (aVector.begin(), aVector.end(),
    front_inserter(aList));
```

The inserter changes the meaning of the assignment statement in the copy algorithm. Rather than overwriting an existing container, the assignment instead inserts the right-hand side into the container. The "increment" operator is overloaded to do nothing, and the assignment operator is overloaded to perform an insertion.

In later chapters we will encounter a variety of different forms of adaptor.

Initialization Clauses

The class Widget illustrates the use of a constructor syntax we have not seen up to this point. An initialization section on a constructor indicates how the value being produced should be initialized. In this instance, the function

```
Widget (int a) : id(a) { }
```

is equivalent to

```
Widget (int a) { id = a; }
```

That is, the initialization clause is simply a short-hand for an assignment. There are some forms of initialization, such as initialization of a value of type reference, that can only be performed with an initialization clause, and not a statement. It is useful to become accustomed to writing initializations in constructors using initialization clauses.

---

new front, so that the resultant list is ordered 1, 2, 3. Next, the values 7, 8, and 9 are inserted into the end of the list. Finally, the find() operation is used to locate an iterator that denotes the 7 value, and the numbers 4, 5, and 6 are inserted immediately prior. The result is the list of numbers from 1 to 9 in order.

```
// create three arrays of numbers
int threeToOne [ ] = {3, 2, 1};
int fourToSix [ ] = {4, 5, 6};
int sevenToNine [ ] = {7, 8, 9};

list<int> aList;

copy (threeToOne, threeToOne+3, front_inserter (aList));
copy (sevenToNine, sevenToNine+3, back_inserter (aList));

list<int>::iterator seven = find (aList.begin(), aList.end(), 7);
copy (fourToSix, fourToSix+3, inserter(aList, seven));
```

9.3 EXAMPLE PROGRAMS

9.3.1 An Inventory System

We will use a simple inventory management system to illustrate the use of several list operations. Assume a business, named WorldWideWidget-Works, requires a software system to manage their supply of widgets. Widgets are simple devices, distinguished by different identification numbers:

```
class Widget {
public:
        // constructors
        Widget () : id_number (0) { }
        Widget (int a) : id_number (a) { }
```

```
                    // operations
            int id () { return id_number; }
            void operator =  (Widget & rhs)
                { id_number = rhs.id_number; }
            bool operator == (Widget & rhs)
                { return id_number == rhs.id_number; }
            bool operator <  (Widget & rhs)
                { return id_number < rhs.id_number; }

protected:
            int id_number; // widget identification number
};


ostream & operator << (ostream & out, Widget & w)
        // output printable representation of widget
{
            return out << "Widget " << w.id();
}
```

The state of the inventory is represented by two lists. One list represents the stock of widgets on hand, while the second represents the type of widgets that customers have backordered. The first is a list of widgets, while the second is a list of widget identification types. To handle our inventory, we have two commands: the first, order(), processes orders; the second, receive(), processes the shipment of a new widget.

```
//
// class inventory
//   manage inventory control

class inventory {
public:
        void order (int wid); // process order for widget type wid
        void receive (Widget wid); // receive widget of type wid in shipment

protected:
        list <Widget> on_hand;
        list <int> on_order;
};
```

When a new widget arrives in shipment, we compare the widget identification number with the list of widget types on back order. We use find() to search the back order list, immediately shipping the widget if necessary. Otherwise, it is added to the stock on hand.

```
void inventory::receive (Widget wid)
        // process a widget received in shipment
```

```
{
      cout << "Received shipment of widget " << wid << endl;
      list<int>::iterator we_need =
            find (on_order.begin(), on_order.end(), wid.id());
      if (we_need != on_order.end()) {
            cout << "Ship " << wid << " to fill back order" << endl;
            on_order.erase(we_need);
            }
      else
            on_hand.push_front(wid);
}
```

When a customer orders a new widget, we scan the list of widgets in stock to determine if the order can be processed immediately. We can use the function find_if() to search the list. To use this function, we need a unary predicate that takes as argument a widget, and determines whether the widget matches the type requested. There is just one small problem; no such function exists, and furthermore, the value representing the target widget type is being held by a local variable.

The solution is an idiom that is commonly encountered when using the standard library, one that the user should learn and know how to apply. A small class is created with the sole purpose of defining the function call operator, in effect allowing an instance of the class to be used as a function. The constructor for the class sets the test value, which is then used by the function call operator.

Functions and Function Objects

In C++ the parentheses that indicate a function is being invoked are simply yet another operator, just like the addition operator or the subscript operator. As with all operators, the user can provide a new meaning by defining the operator as a member function in a class definition. Doing so allows the user to create objects that act like functions. Such an object is called a *function object*. A function object can be created and passed as argument to those generic algorithms that expect to receive a function as argument.

The most common reason for using function objects is the situation illustrated by the widget example. In this situation, the generic algorithm expects to manipulate a one-argument function, yet the task to be performed (comparing a widget id against a fixed value) requires two items. The solution is to pass one of the values as an argument to the constructor when the function object is created.

Two templated function objects provided in the standard library are often used when a comparison function is needed. The object less<T> encapsulates the less-than relational test for objects of type T, while the function greater<T> encapsulates the greater-than test.

Function objects are an extremely powerful device, and one that will be used in many subsequent example programs.

```
class WidgetTester {
public:
    WidgetTester (int id) { test_id = id; }
    int test_id;

        // define the function call operator
    bool operator () (Widget & wid)
        { return wid.id() == test_id; }
};
```

An instance of this class is then created and passed as argument to the generic algorithm `find_if`. This is illustrated in the following function:

```
void inventory::order (int wid)
    // process an order for a widget with given id number
{
    cout << "Received order for widget type " << wid << endl;
    WidgetTester wtest(wid); // create the tester object
    list<Widget>::iterator we_have =
        find_if(on_hand.begin(), on_hand.end(), wtest);
    if (we_have != on_hand.end()) {
        cout << "Ship " << *wehave << endl;
        on_hand.erase(we_have);
        }
    else {
        cout << "Back order widget of type "  << wid  << endl;
        on_order.push_front(wid);
        }
}
```

9.3.2   A Course Registration System

Our second example program will be a simple registration system, such as one that might be used when assigning students to classes.

Assume we have two input files. The first is a list of course names and the maximum number of students permitted in each course:

```
        .
        .
        .
ART101 60
HIS213 75
MTH412 35
        .
        .
        .
```

The second file holds a list of students and the courses they have requested. To simplify matters, we will write the student name as a contiguous string, and have separate records for each student/course pair:

```
        .
        .
        .
Smith,Amy ART101
Smith,Amy MTH412
Jones,Randy HIS213
        .
        .
        .
```

The task is to assign students to classes, not exceeding the given class size, and producing reports both for the student (the classes they have been assigned) and the instructor (the students in their class). Classes are filled on a first-come, first-served basis, so that when a class becomes full, subsequent requests will be denied.

We start by creating a global variable that represents the list of classes. Each course will be represented by a class structure such as:

```
//
//   class course
//        information about one individual course

class course {
public:
      course (string n, int s) : name(n), size(s) { }

          // operations
      bool full () { return students.size() >= max; }
      void addStudent (student * s) { students.push_back(s); }
      void generateClassList ();


      protected: // data fields
        string name;
        int max;
        list <student *> students;
}
```

The course will hold a name, a size, and a list of students. The operation addStudent adds a new student to the course, while the operation full indicates whether or not the course is full. Because the same student data structure may appear as an element in many different course lists, we must store a *pointer* to the student record in the course list, rather than the student record itself.

A global variable all_courses will hold the list of all courses. This is created from the first data file, using this procedure:

```
list <course *> all_courses;

void readCourses (istream & infile)
    // read the list of courses from the given input stream
{
    string name;
    int max;

    while (infile >> name >> max) {
        course * newCourse = new course (name, max);
        all_courses.push_back (newCourse);
        }
}
```

Each student will be represented by a different class structure, as follows:

```
//
//    class student
//        information about a single student

class student {
    // provide a shorter name for course iterators
    typedef list <course *>::iterator citerator;

public:
        // constructor
 student (string n):nameText(n) { }

        // operations
    string name() { return nameText; }
    void addCourse (course * c) { courses.push_back(c); }
    citerator firstCourse () { return courses.begin(); }
    citerator lastCourse () { return courses.end(); }
    void removeCourse (citerator & citr) { courses.erase(citr); }

protected:
    string nameText;
    list <course *> courses;
};
```

Student values are maintained on a different global variable, named `all_students`. This value is initialized by the procedure that follows. Note that the courses section of each student record initially holds the list of classes the student has requested. Classes that the student is unable to get into will eventually be removed from this list, until finally the list will hold only those classes for which the student is registered.

```
list <student *> all_students;

void readStudents (istream & infile)
        // read the list of student records from the given input stream
{
        string name;
        string course;

        while (infile >> name >> course) {
                student * theStudent = findStudent (name);
                course * theCourse = findCourse (course);
                if (theCourse != 0)
                        theStudent->addCourse (theCourse);
                else
                        cout << "student " << name <<
                                " requested invalid course " << course << endl;
        }
}
```

The two utility routines `findStudent` and `findCourse` find a record that corresponds to the given entry. The first creates a new student record if no corresponding element is found, while the second returns a null pointer. We show only the first:

```
student * findStudent (string & searchName)
        // find (or make) a student record for the given name
{
```

Pointer Dereferencing

Remember that the right arrow syntax is equivalent to a combination of pointer dereferencing and field access. That is, the statement
`theStudent->addCourse (theCourse);`
is equivalent to
`(*theStudent).addCourse (theCourse);`

This can be confusing when iterators are used on structures that hold pointers. A pointer dereference is used to get hold of the value the iterator references, which is itself then a pointer. The statement
`if ((*start)->name() == searchName)`

is equivalent to
`if ((**start).name() == searchName)`
One star operator dereferences the iterator, while the second dereferences the pointer value.

Finally, note that many iterator definitions omit any definition of the pointer operator. Thus, while we have described iterators as being equivalent to pointers, nevertheless field access with these iterators must be performed using the combination of `*` and the field access dot, and not using the pointer arrow.

```
        list <student *>::iterator start, stop;
        start = all_students.begin();
        stop = all_students.end();
        for ( ; start != stop; ++start)
            if ((*start)->name() == searchName)
                return *start;


            // not found, make one now
        student * newStudent = new student(searchName);
        all_students.push_back (newStudent);
        return newStudent;
}
```

Note that we cannot use the `find` generic algorithm here, because the values held by the list are pointers, and the comparison we wish to make is between the values denoted by the pointers, not the pointers themselves. We could have used `find_if`, but that would have required writing a function object.

Having initialized the two global variables, the first task is to assign as many students as possible to their requested classes. This is accomplished by iterating through the list of students and testing each requested course against the maximum enrollment. If the course is not full, the student is assigned to the course. Otherwise, the course is removed from the list of student courses.

```
void fillCourses ()
    // fill as many students as possible in each course
    // priority given by input order (first come, first served)
{
    list<student *>::iterator s_start, s_end;
    s_start = all_students.begin();
    s_end = all_students.end();

    for ( ; s_start != s_end; ++s_start) {
        list<course *>::iterator c_start, c_end, c_next;
        c_start = (*s_start)->firstCourse();
        c_end = (*s_start)->lastCourse();
        for ( ; c_start != c_end; c_start = c_next) {
            c_next = c_start; ++c_next;
                // if not full, add student
            if (! (*c_start)->full())
                (*c_start)->addStudent (*s_start);
            else
                (*s_start)->removeCourse(c_start);
        }
    }
}
```

It is useful to study carefully the inner loop used in the heart of this algorithm, because it is typical of situations that occur when iteration is combined with the removal of values from a list. The cardinal principle is that once a list element has been eliminated using an erase, it can never again be referenced.

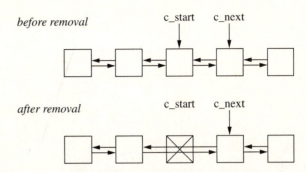

Because the removeCourse function can potentially remove the value referenced by the iterator c_start, the increment portion of the loop cannot count on the variable having a valid reference. Hence, the *next* iterator element is calculated and stored in c_next *before* c_start is possibly eliminated. Incrementing the loop corresponds to changing c_start by assigning it the value held in c_next. In this manner, any invalid references to c_start are avoided.

At this point, each course structure has the name of every student in the class. We can produce a report for the instructor containing this information. To better help the instructor, we will first sort the list of names. To do this, we need a comparison function that takes two pointer values, and returns the comparison of the values referenced by the pointer. (Because the lists contain pointers, if we used the default < operator when comparing values, we would be ordering items by their memory addresses, not their values). We can write such a function as:

```
bool studentCompare (student * a, student * b)
     // compare the names of two students
{
     return a->name() < b->name();
}
```

The course report generating function then loops over the list of courses, and calls the generateClassList function on each. The generate-ClassList member function sorts each list of students according to the function we provided, then prints the list.

```
void generateCourseReports ()
     // generate class lists for each course
{
     list<course *>::iterator start, stop;
```

```
        start = all_courses.begin();
        stop = all_courses.end();
        for ( ; start != stop; ++start)
            (*start)->generateClassList();
}


void course::generateClassList ()
    // print the class list of all students
{
        // first sort the list
    students.sort (studentCompare);

        // then print it out
    cout << "Class list for " << name << endl;
    list<student *>::iterator start, stop;
    start = students.begin();
    stop = students.end();
    for ( ; start != stop; ++start)
        cout << (*start)->name() << endl;
}
```

Finally, students must be told what classes they have been registered for, because they may have tried registering for courses that they were not assigned. We iterate over the list of students, and for each generate a list of courses:

```
void generateStudentReports ()
    // generate class lists for students
{
    list <student *> s_start, s_stop;
    list <course *> c_start, c_stop;
    s_start = all_students.begin();
    s_stop = all_students.end();

        // generate the list for each student
    for ( ; s_start != s_end; ++s_start) {
        cout << "Class list for " << (*s_start)->name() << endl;
        c_start = (*s_start)->firstCourse();
        c_stop = (*s_start)->lastCourse();
        for ( ; c_start != c_stop; ++c_start)
            cout << (*c_start)->name() << endl;
    }
}
```

```
template <class T>
class list {
public:
            // type definitions
        typedef T value_type;
        typedef listIterator<T> iterator;

            // constructor and destructor
        list () firstLink(0), lastLink(0) { }
        ~ list ();

            // operations
        bool empty () { return firstLink == 0; }
        int size();
        T & back () { return lastLink->value; }
        T & front () { return firstLink->value; }
        void push_front(T &);
        void push_back(T &);
        void pop_front ();
        void pop_back ();
        iterator begin () { return iterator (this, firstLink); }
        iterator end () { return iterator (this, 0); }
        void sort ();
        iterator insert (iterator, value);
        void erase (iterator & itr) { erase (itr, itr); }
        void erase (iterator &, iterator &);

protected:
        link <T> * firstLink;
        link <T> * lastLink;
};
```

Figure 9.1 A Simple implementation of class `list`

9.4 AN EXAMPLE IMPLEMENTATION

As we did with the `vector` abstraction studied in the last chapter, we will analyze an implementation of the `list` class that is legal, but slightly simpler than the actual standard library class. Our purpose in presenting an implementation is not to be comprehensive, but to illustrate some of the difficulties that must be overcome by the software developer.

The class definition for our `list` abstraction is shown in Figure 9.1, which also provides in-line definitions for many of the simpler member functions. The class holds two data fields, which are pointers to instances of class `link`. The class `link` is a *facilitator class*, a class that operates behind the scene but is not observable as part of the interface for the `list` class. Instances of class `link` are used only to store values. A definition of the class `link` can be given as follows:

```
template <class T> class link {
private:
    link (T & v):value(v), nextLink(0), prevLink(0) { }
    T value;
    link<T> * nextLink;
    link<T> * prevLink;
        // allow lists to see element values
    friend class list<T>;
    friend class listIterator<T>;
};
```

Because lists and list iterators are declared as *friends*, they are allowed to access the otherwise hidden data fields in instances of class `link`.

Among the member functions that are given direct in-line definitions are those that access the first or last element, and that test whether or not the collection is empty. Some of the remaining operations are only slightly more complex. Counting the number of items in a list, for example, requires only a simple loop:

```
template <class T> int list<T>::size ()
    // count number of elements in collection
{
    int counter = 0;
    for (link<T> * ptr = firstLink; ptr != 0; ptr = ptr->nextLink)
        counter++;
    return counter;
}
```

Notice that this `for` loop is allowed to access the `link` fields, because it is *internal* to the `list` implementation. We do not, however, want *users* of the list to write loops in this form, because they need not even know that the `link` class exists. Instead, users will use iterators to access the values of the list.

Adding a new element to the front of a list requires adding a new `link`, then making sure the pointer values are properly updated. Adding an element to an empty list must be handled as a special case, because in this case the field `lastLink` must also be updated.

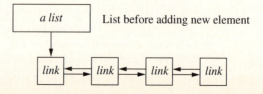

a list   List before adding new element

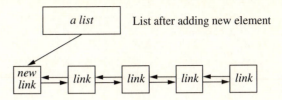

List after adding new element

The code to perform this is as follows:

```
template <class T> void list<T>::push_front (T & newValue)
     // add a new value to the front of a list
{
     link<T> * newLink = new link<T> (newValue);
     if (empty())
          firstLink = lastLink = newLink;
     else {
          firstLink->prevLink = newLink;
          newLink->nextLink = firstLink;
          firstLink = newLink;
          }
}
```

The removal of the first element from a list is conceptually simply the inverse of the addition operation.

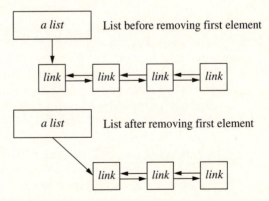

List before removing first element

List after removing first element

The operation is complicated by the need to update the pointer values, the need to delete the node value that is no longer required, and the need to check for empty lists.

```
template <class T> void list<T>::pop_front()
     // remove first element from linked list
{
     link <T> * save = firstLink;
     firstLink = firstLink->nextLink;
```

```
        if (firstLink != 0)
            firstLink->prevLink = 0;
        else
            lastLink = 0;
        delete save;
}
```

The destructor simply runs through the elements, removing each in turn. Notice that we must read and store the value of the `nextLink` field prior to deleting the current element. It is never legal to try to read a data field from a value that has been deleted.

```
template <class T> list<T>::~list ()
        // remove each element from the list
{
        link <T> * first = firstlink;
        while (first != 0) {
            link <T> * next  = first->nextLink;
            delete first;
            first = next;
            }
}
```

9.4.1   List Iterators

Because the elements of a linked list are not adjacent to each other contiguously in memory, we cannot simply use pointers for iterators, as we did with the `vector` abstraction. Instead, list iterators must redefine the iterator protocol. The easiest scheme is to have instances of the class `listIterator` maintain two internal pointer values, one a pointer to the original list, and the second a pointer to the current link. A class definition that illustrates this is shown in Figure 9.2.

Almost all of the iterator operations have trivial implementations that can be given in-line as part of the class description. For example, the dereference operator simply returns the value held by the current link. Two iterators are equal if they reference the same element, and so on.

The increment and decrement operators are slightly more difficult, and deserve some explanation. There are two forms of these operators. When used in a prefix fashion, the member function with no arguments is invoked. In this case, the value of the current link is updated, and a reference to the current value (available through the pseudovariable `this`) is returned. However, when used in a postfix fashion, the semantics are more complex. To match the semantics of the postfix increment operator on pointers, the iterator must be updated to the next value, but the current

```
template <class T> class listIterator {
    typedef listIterator<T> iterator;
public:
        // constructor
    listIterator (list<T> * tl, link<T> * cl)
        : theList(tl), currentLink(cl) { }


        // iterator protocol
    T & operator * ()
        { return currentLink->value; }
    void operator = (iterator & rhs)
        { theList = rhs.theList; currentLink = rhs.currentLink; }
    bool operator == (iterator & rhs)
        { return currentLink == rhs.currentLink; }
    iterator & operator ++ (int)
        { currentLink = currentLink->nextLink; return this; }
    iterator operator ++ ();
    iterator & operator -- (int)
        { currentLink = currentLink->prevLink; return this; }
    iterator operator -- ();


protected:
    list <T> * theList;
    link <T> * currentLink;
};
```

Figure 9.2 The list iterator class

value *prior* to the update must be returned as the function result. This effect is most easily achieved in a three-step process. First, a clone (or copy) of the current iterator is created. This clone preserves the current state. Next, the current iterator is updated, moving it to the next element. Finally, the clone, which continues to point to the original value, is returned as the result of the operation.

```
template <class T> listIterator<T> listIterator<T>::operator ++ (int)
    // postfix form of increment
{
        // clone, then increment, return clone
    listIterator<T> clone (theList, currentLink);
    currentLink = currentLink->nextLink;
    return clone;
}
```

Note that the postfix form of the increment is considerably more complex than the prefix form. For this reason the prefix form should always be used when the user has the option of selecting either version, as occurs in a typical iterator loop. Also note how the preorder version can return a reference to itself, as the receiver will continue to exist even after the function terminates, while the postorder version must return a value, because the local variable clone will be erased once execution of the procedure ceases.

Having provided the implementation of the list iterator class, we can now return and describe the implementation of the list member functions that make use of iterators. An insertion, for example, uses the iterator to describe a specific value, and must make sure the pointers surrounding that value are properly updated.

```
template <class T> void list<T>::insert (listIterator<T> & itr, T & value)
    // insert a new element into the middle of a linked list
{
    link<T> * newLink = new link(value);
    link<T> * current = itr->currentLink;

    newLink->nextLink = current;
    newLink->prevLink = current->prevLink;
    current->prevLink = newLink;
    current = newLink->prevLink;
    if (current != 0)
        current->nextLink = newLink;
}
```

Erasing a range of values simply involves tying the two ends together. Special cases must check for the first value being the beginning of the list, or the final value being the end-of-range iterator for the list. Note that once again care must be exercised in the loop that deletes the values being removed, because it is not legal to access the fields in a value that has been deleted.

```
template <class T>
void list<T>::erase (listIterator<T> & start, listIterator<T> & stop)
    // remove values from the range of elements
{
    link<T> * first = start->currentLink;
    link<T> * prev = first->prevLink;
    link<T> * last = stop->currentLink;
    if (prev == 0) {  // removing initial portion of list
        firstLink = last;
        if (last == 0)
            lastLink = 0;
```

```
                else
                    last->prevLink = 0;
            }
        else {
            prev->nextLink = last;
            if (last == 0)
                lastLink = prev;
            else
                last->prevLink = prev;

        }
        // now delete the values
    while (start != stop) {
        link<T> * next = start;
        ++next;
        delete start;
        start = next;
        }
}
```

9.5   VARIATION THROUGH INHERITANCE

Often a data structure required in the solution of a specific problem can be described as a simple variation of an existing structure. In this section we will describe a powerful facility provided by object-oriented languages for constructing such values, and illustrate this with two examples.

Inheritance is a mechanism that can be used in the description of a new class. When inheritance is used, the new class is described in relation to an older existing class. The older class is often called the *parent class*, while the new class is termed the *child class*, or sometimes the *derived class*. The use of inheritance implies that all public and protected information known about the parent class is also applicable to the child class. Thus, all data fields and all member functions that are defined in the parent class can be used by instances of the child class, without needing to rewrite any new lines of code. The child class can, of course, also add new data fields or new member functions.

9.5.1   Ordered Lists

We can illustrate the use of inheritance by developing an *ordered list class*. An ordered list maintains values in sequence, rather than in the order of insertion. To do this, we can simply add a single new member function, a method to add a new value to the list.

```
template <class T>
class orderedList : public list<T> {
public:
    void add (T & newValue);
};
```

The colon following the class name indicates that inheritance will be used. The `public list<T>` part names the parent class. Through the use of inheritance, all the other member functions associated with the `list` class become available immediately to the new data abstraction. Thus, we can form iterators for ordered lists, remove values from ordered lists, and perform generic algorithms on ordered lists.

To implement the `add` operation for ordered lists, we form an iterator loop. The loop searches for the first value larger than the element being inserted. The loop halts either when it reaches the end of the list or when such a value is found. Because an `insert` prior to the end of list indicator is treated as an insertion at the end of the list, we can simply perform an `insert` at the resulting location, regardless of which condition terminated the loop.

```
template <class T>
void orderedList<T>::add (T & newValue)
    // add a new element to an ordered list
{
    list<T>::iterator start, stop;
    start = begin();
    stop = end();
    while ((start != stop) && (*start < newValue))
        ++start;
    insert (start, newValue);
}
```

Unfortunately, to find the appropriate location for the new element may require examining the entire list. Thus, adding a new element to an ordered list may require, in the worst case, $O(n)$ steps.

APPLICATION: LIST INSERTION SORT

We can illustrate an application of an ordered list by creating yet another sorting algorithm, this one with a particularly simple structure. The input values are merely copied into an ordered list, then copied back to their original container.

```
template <class T>
void listInsertionSort (vector<T> & v)
    // place a vector into order, using an ordered list
{
    orderedList<T> sorter;
```

```
        // first copy vector to list
    vector<T>::iterator start = v.begin();
    vector<T>::iterator stop = v.end();
    for ( ; start != stop; ++start)
        sorter.add(*start);

        // then copy list back to vector
    list<T>::iterator itr = sorter.begin();
    for (start = v.begin(); start != stop; ++start)
        *start = *itr++;
}
```

Unfortunately, the n insertions, each of which is itself $O(n)$, imply that this algorithm is in the worst case $O(n^2)$. However, in practice it is nevertheless often faster than other $O(n^2)$ algorithms, such as bubble sort.

9.5.2 Self-Organizing Lists

Many problems using lists have the characteristic that tests to determine if a value is present in a list occur much more frequently than insertions or deletions. Furthermore, it is also often the case that once such a test has been performed, the likelihood is increased that the same element will be subsequently requested. In such situations, the rather poor $O(n)$ behavior of the find generic algorithm can be improved by always moving an element to the front of the list on a successful search. A data structure that tries to improve *future* performance based on current usage is said to be *self-organizing*.

To create a self-organizing list, we need only define a member function for testing to determine whether a value occurs in the list. If the element is not found, the function returns false. If the element is found, it is removed from the list, and inserted once more on the front of the list. In this position, a subsequent search will find the element very quickly.

```
template <class T>
class selfOrganizingList<T> : public list<T> {
public:
    bool include (T & value);
};

template <class T>
bool selfOrganizingList<T>::include (T & value)
        // see if argument value occurs in list
{
        // first find element in list
    list<T>::iterator stop = end();
    list<T>::iterator where = find(begin(), stop, value);
```

```
            // if not found, return false
    if (where == stop)
        return false;
            // else remove from list, and move to front
    if (where != begin()) {
        erase (where);
        push_front (value);
        }
    return true;
}
```

To illustrate the effectiveness of the self-organizing concept, consider a list containing the numbers 1 to 9, initially in order. Assume that a sequence of requests is performed as shown in Table 9.2. Here we have constructed the request sequence so that requests for the values 4 and 7 are more frequently performed than requests for the other values. The table indicates the position of the request in the current list, which is thus the number of comparisons performed to find the given element. The table also shows the self-organized list following each search. After thirty searches, the self-organizing list will have performed only 129 comparisons, while the non-self-organizing list would have required 154 comparisons.

9.5.3   Private and Protected

When inheritance is used, the idea of encapsulating data fields within the class structure becomes slightly more complicated. Three different levels of protection can be distinguished by access specifier keywords:

▲ Data fields and member functions that are declared as public are accessible by anybody, both inside and outside the class.

▲ Data fields and member functions that are declared as protected are accessible only inside a class or derived class. Such fields can only be manipulated by member functions declared as part of the class, or by friends.

▲ A new category, private, indicates fields that are even more limited than protected fields. A data value or member function that is declared as private is accessible only within the class in which the attribute is declared. Such values are not even accessible to derived classes.

Table 9.2 Example execution of a self-organizing list

Request	Position	New list
7	7	7 1 2 3 4 5 6 8 9
4	5	4 7 1 2 3 5 6 8 9
4	1	4 7 1 2 3 5 6 8 9
7	2	7 4 1 2 3 5 6 8 9
3	5	3 7 4 1 2 5 6 8 9
7	2	7 3 4 1 2 5 6 8 9
8	8	8 7 3 4 1 2 5 6 9
6	8	6 8 7 3 4 1 2 5 9
4	5	4 6 8 7 3 1 2 5 9
3	5	3 4 6 8 7 1 2 5 9
4	2	4 3 6 8 7 1 2 5 9
3	2	3 4 6 8 7 1 2 5 9
5	8	5 3 4 6 8 7 1 2 9
9	9	9 5 3 4 6 8 7 1 2
5	2	5 9 3 4 6 8 7 1 2
4	4	4 5 9 3 6 8 7 1 2
2	9	2 4 5 9 3 6 8 7 1
4	2	4 2 5 9 3 6 8 7 1
5	3	5 4 2 9 3 6 8 7 1
7	8	7 5 4 2 9 3 6 8 1
6	7	6 7 5 4 2 9 3 8 1
6	1	6 7 5 4 2 9 3 8 1
7	2	7 6 5 4 2 9 3 8 1
4	4	4 7 6 5 2 9 3 8 1
2	5	2 4 7 6 5 9 3 8 1
4	2	4 2 7 6 5 9 3 8 1
7	3	7 4 2 6 5 9 3 8 1
4	2	4 7 2 6 5 9 3 8 1
7	2	7 4 2 6 5 9 3 8 1
6	4	6 7 4 2 5 9 3 8 1
154	129	Total number of comparisons

9.6   CHAPTER SUMMARY

Key Concepts

- List
- Links
- Adaptors
- Initialization clauses for constructors
- Function objects
- Inheritance
- Ordered lists
- Self-organizing lists
- Access specifier keywords: public, protected, and private

In this chapter we have examined the concept of a linked list. A list is an unordered collection of values. Unlike a vector, a list has no fixed size, but instead grows or shrinks as elements are added or removed from the structure. In the basic list structure, elements can be added or removed only from the front or back of the list. By means of iterators, elements can be added or removed from the middle of a list.

An adaptor is a class that wraps around another class, changing the interface while providing minimal functionality itself.

A function object is a class that implements the parenthesis operator. Instances of this class can therefore be used in situations where a function is required.

Inheritance is a powerful programming technique that can be used whenever a new class can be described as a variation on an existing class. The facilities of the older class are made available to the new abstraction without the need to write new code. We have illustrated the use of inheritance by describing two variations on lists, an ordered list and a self-organizing list.

The level of access of a data field or member function can be specified by means of an access specifier. Values can be declared as either public (accessible everywhere), private (accessible only within the class in which the value is declared), or protected (accessible within the original class or within derived classes).

Further Reading

As with almost all data structures we will consider, the classic description of algorithms on linked lists is provided by Knuth in Volume 1 of his series "The Art of Computer Programming" [Knuth 73]. A number of algorithms for memory allocation are discussed by Knuth in Volume 1, as well as in the book by Aho, Hopcroft, and Ullman [Aho 83]. A good analysis of self-organizing lists is presented by Gonnet and Baeza-Yates [Gonnet 91].

A recent change to the C++ language permits the nesting of class definitions one within another. By use of this mechanism, facilitator classes, such as our class link, can be entirely and effectively hidden from users of the list abstraction. Such a style is advocated by Coplien [Coplien 92], as well as others. Here, I have avoided the use of nested classes for two reasons. First, the explanation of this feature would be yet one more little bit of syntax, an unnecessary addition in a book already brimming with explanations of syntax. Second, because this is a relatively new change to C++, not all compilers can be expected to support this feature.

Study Questions & Exercises

Study Questions

1. When should a linked list be used as a container, as opposed to when a vector should be used?

2. What is the advantage of keeping a pointer to both the first and last element in a linked list?

3. What is a doubly linked list?

4. If a list holds elements of a user-defined type, what operations must the user-defined type provide?

5. What functions are used to access the first and last elements of a linked list? How can these values be removed from the list?

6. What are insert iterators? Why are they needed in order to use the generic algorithms with the list data type?

7. What is an adaptor?

8. What is a function object?

9. What must you be careful about when removing elements from a linked list in the middle of a loop?

10. What data values are maintained by the class `list`? What data values by the class `link`? What data values by the class `listIterator`?

11. How is the prefix form of the list iterator increment operator different from the postfix form?

12. What task does inheritance perform?

13. What is a parent class? What is a child class?

14. How does an instance of class `orderedList` differ from an instance of the class `list`?

15. What is the asymptotic execution time for list insertion sort?

16. What is a self-organizing data structure?

17. What operation does the class `selfOrganizingList` try to optimize?

18. What is the difference between a field declared as `private` and one declared as `protected`?

Exercises

1. Write a copy constructor for our sample `list` class.

2. Write the methods `push_back()` and `pop_back()` for our sample `list` class.

3. Write the method `remove()` for our list class. Remember this method must remove *all* occurrences of the given value.

4. Write a method for the class `list` that, given an integer value n, returns the nth item in the list. What is the execution time of your operation? How does this compare to the execution time for the corresponding operation on a vector?

5. Write a reverse iterator that could be used to implement the operations `rbegin()` and `rend()`.

6. Write the member function `reverse()` that reverses the elements in a list.

7. Write a function that takes a list as an argument and returns a new list in which the order of the elements is the exact reversal of the argument list. (Hint: This is easier than it seems.)

8. Write a procedure named append that takes as arguments two lists and returns a new list containing elements from both arguments, in which all the elements of the second list appear after all the elements from the first list. Would it be easier to write as a method?

9. Suppose for a certain application it was important to always know the number of elements in a list. To discover this value we could use the method `size`. But as defined, this method employs a loop, and thus has $O(n)$ execution time. Using inheritance, write a new template class named `countedList` that maintains an explicit count on the number of values held in the list, and can thus respond to the `size` method in constant time. For this problem you can ignore insertions and deletions performed using iterators.

10. Rewrite the `findStudent` function to use the `find_if` generic algorithm by writing a function object to perform the correct comparison test.

11. Using the techniques described in the problem in Section 4.3 of Chapter 4, test the hypothesis that list insertion sort is an $O(n^2)$ algorithm. Using the value of c that you compute, estimate for the list insertion algorithm how long it would take to sort a vector of 100,000 elements.

12. Imagine you have two ordered lists, L_1 and L_2. Write a procedure to efficiently yield a new ordered list that is the union of the two lists (you can assume values in either list are

unique). Write a procedure to efficiently yield the intersection of the two lists. Write the same procedures for unordered lists, and compare the efficiency of your two approaches.

13. Another technique for making lists self-organizing is the transpose method. Using this technique, whenever a search is successful in finding a value, the element is swapped with the value that immediately precedes it in the list (provided, of course, it is not already at the front of the list). Describe the `includes` method for a self-organizing list using this approach.

10

Stacks and Queues

Chapter Overview

In this chapter we first explore the concepts of a *stack* and a *queue* as an abstract data type, and then discuss the realization of these concepts in the standard library. The stack and queue data types in the STL are interesting because they are not provided as true stand-alone data types, but rather are constructed as *adaptors* placed on top of other containers. We illustrate the use of these abstractions in the solution of several programming problems.

Major topics discussed in this chapter include the following:

▲ The stack and queue data abstractions

▲ Adaptors

▲ Reverse polish notation calculators

▲ Queues in simulation

▲ Ring buffer queues

10.1 THE STACK AND QUEUE DATA ABSTRACTIONS

Most people have a good intuitive understanding of the stack and queue data abstractions, based on experience with everyday objects. An excellent example of a stack is a pile of papers on a desk, or a stack of dishes in a cupboard. In both cases, the important characteristic is that the item on the top is most easily accessed. New items are similarly most easily added to the collection by placing them above all the current items in the stack. In this manner, an item removed from a stack is the element that has been most recently inserted into a stack.

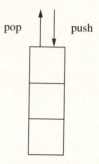

An everyday example of a queue, on the other hand, is a line of people waiting to enter a theater. Here, new additions are made to the back of the queue as new people enter the line, while items are removed from the front of the structure as patrons enter the theater. The removal order for a queue is the opposite of that for the stack. In a queue, an item removed is the element that has been present in the queue for the longest period of time.

A stack is sometimes referred to as a *LIFO* structure, and a queue called a *FIFO* structure. The abbreviation LIFO stands for *Last In, First Out*. This means the first entry removed from a stack is the last entry that was inserted. The term FIFO, on the other hand, is short for *First In, First Out*. This means the first element removed from a queue is the first element that was inserted into the queue.

Stacks are used at the heart of the most common implementation technique for programming languages. Space for parameters and local variables is created internally within the computer using a stack. Using for our example the playing card abstraction developed in Chapter 2, recall the steps used to print instances of the class Card on an output stream. The stream output (<<) operator for class Card calls the stream output operator for the integer numerator. The integer stream output operator invokes the stream output method for unsigned integers, which recursively calls itself once for each digit in the number. (We saw a simplified version of this algorithm in Section 4.2.6.) Finally, each digit value is printed by calling the stream output function with a character argument.

For each function call, a memory stack is incremented to create space for the parameters and local variables associated with the function. This space for local variables and parameters is known as the *activation record* for the function call. The use of a stack to perform memory allocation has many beneficial advantages. It allows recursive procedures, such as the recursive routine to print unsigned integers, to possess in each iteration a unique data area for local variables. The release of memory simply means decrementing the stack, and invoking destructors for any values that define destructors. This can be performed very rapidly. Finally, no more memory is required for the stack than is necessary for the local variables and parameters in use at any one time.

```
top  →    local variables
          and parameters for
          ostream << char
          ───────────────────
          local variables
          and parameters for
          ostream << unsigned
          ───────────────────
          local variables
          and parameters for
          ostream << unsigned
          ───────────────────
          local variables
          and parameters for
          ostream << integer
          ───────────────────
          local variables
          and parameters for
          ostream << Card
```

An interesting use of stacks occurs in the input stream mechanism. There is a method, `putback`, that can be used with input streams. The `putback` method "returns" a character to an input stream. A subsequent character read operation will first yield the pushed-back character, before continuing with the remainder of input from the file.

The stream data structure maintains two data areas. It must hold a pointer to the file from which the raw characters are obtained. It also maintains a stack of characters that have been pushed back into the input. Suppose, for example, the stream is returning the text of this chapter. Imagine the words "Most people have a good" have been read, and subsequently the four characters of the word "good" are pushed back into the input. We could visualize this as follows:

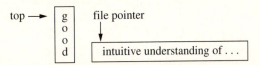

A two-step process is used to read a character from a stream. First the stack of pushed-back characters is examined. If it is not empty, the topmost character from the stack is popped and returned. Only if the pushback stack is empty is the next character read from an input file.

Queues are also extensively used in the internal functioning of computer systems. When output is submitted to a printer, for example, it is typically placed in a queue with several other tasks. This permits the printer system to receive output requests even when the printer is busy responding to a previous job. Because a queue is used to hold pending tasks, rather than a stack, output will be produced in the order the requests are received.

10.2   ADAPTORS

In the standard library, both the data types stack and queue are *adaptors*. This means they do not directly implement the structures that hold the data values, but are instead built on top of other containers. They "adapt" the interface to these containers, providing names for the operations that make sense in the context of their use as a stack or queue, rather than as a different container.

Recall that in Section 9.2.1 we described a different form of adaptor, the list inserter adaptor that changed the iterator protocol into insert operations. In subsequent chapters we will encounter yet more types of adaptor. In each case, the important property is that the adaptor does little work itself, but principally is used to change the interface from one form to another.

10.3   STACKS

The class description for the stack adaptor is shown in Figure 10.1. The underlying container used to hold the data values is a template argument.[1] An instance of this type is created as a local variable internal to the stack. All the stack operations are implemented in terms of operations on the underlying container type.

Any container that defines the internal type named value_type, and that implements the operations empty(), size(), back(), push_back(), and pop_back(), can be used as a container for a stack. Both vector and list support these operations, as well as the data type deque we will describe in the next chapter. Thus, any of the three can be used to create a stack:

---

1. Currently, some implementations of the standard library also require the element type as a second argument, but this is nonstandard.

```
template <class Container>
class stack {
public:
    typedef Container::value_type value_type;

        // operations
    bool       empty () { return c.empty(); }
    int        size ()  { return c.size(); }
    value_type & top ()    { return c.back(); }
    void       push (value_type & x) { c.push_back(x); }
    void       pop ()    { c.pop_back(); }

protected:
    Container c;
};
```

Figure 10.1 The stack adaptor

```
stack < vector<int> > stack_one;
stack < list<double> > stack_two;
stack < deque<string> > stack_three;
```

Recall that space for a vector grows dynamically, but seldom shrinks. On the other hand, space for a list both grows and shrinks as elements are added and removed from the collection. However, for a given size collection, a vector will use less overall memory space than will a list. Thus, a vector or deque is a good candidate container if the size of the collection being maintained by a stack will remain relatively stable in size, while a list is a more appropriate choice if the collection will vary widely in size during the course of execution.

These differences can be more easily appreciated if we consider the actions on the underlying container in response to the stack operations. Consider the use of a vector as the container. A snapshot of the vector at some point during execution might reveal the following. The capacity of the vector is given by the largest number of elements it has been asked to hold up to the current point, whereas the size represents the number of elements the vector currently holds. A push will simply increase the size, unless the size reaches the capacity, in which case a memory reallocation will be performed to create a larger buffer.

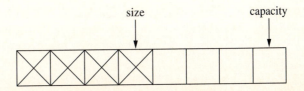

In the `list` implementation, on the other hand, only the elements currently in the collection are maintained. Each value added to the list causes a new memory allocation, and each element freed releases a list node.

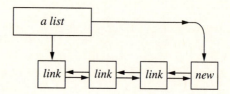

10.3.1   Application: RPN Calculator

One application of a stack is the simulation of a calculator. Operands, such as integer constants, are pushed on a stack of values. As operators are encountered, the appropriate number of operands are popped off the stack, the operation is performed, and the result is pushed back on the stack.

We can divide the development of our calculator simulation into two parts. A calculator engine is concerned with the actual work involved in the simulation, but does not perform and direct input or output operations. The name is intended to suggest an analogy to a car engine or a computer processor—a mechanism that performs the actual work but with which the user does not normally directly interact. Wrapped around this, the calculator simulator will interact with the user, passing appropriate instructions to the calculator engine. By dividing responsibilities in this manner, our design can offer greater flexibility than would be possible if the two tasks were combined; for example, the calculator engine component will not change even if we make changes to the user interface.

A class definition for the calculator engine can be given as follows. Inside the class declaration we define an enumerated list of values to represent each of the possible operators the calculator is prepared to accept. We have made two simplifying assumptions: All operands will be integer values, and we will only handle binary operators.

```
//
//     class calculatorEngine
//          simulate the behavior of a simple integer calculator
//

class calculatorEngine {
public:
    enum  binaryOperator {plus, minus, multiply, divide};

    int   currentMemory   () { return data.top (); }
```

```
    void  pushOperand      (int value) { data.push (value); }
    void  doOperator       (binaryOperator theOp);

protected:
    stack < list<int> > data;
};
```

An integer stack is used to hold the actual data values. To push an operand into the calculator memory the value is simply pushed onto the data stack. To view the current memory value for the calculator we simply return the topmost element in the stack. To perform an operation the arguments are popped from the stack (notice the right argument is on top of the left argument), the appropriate operation is executed, and the result is pushed back on the stack.

```
void calculatorEngine::doOperator(binaryOperator theOp)
    // perform a binary operation on stack values
{
    int right = data.top();
    data.pop();
    int left = data.top();
    data.pop();
    int result;
    switch(theOp) { // do the operation
        case plus:
            result = left + right;
            break;
        case minus:
            result = left - right;
            break;
        case multiply:
            result = left * right;
            break;
        case divide:
            result = left / right;
            break;
    }

    // push the result back on the stack
    data.push(result);
}
```

In developing the second component in our simulation, we will again make a simplifying assumption. We will assume the input is presented in *postfix Polish notation* (sometimes called *reverse Polish notation*, or RPN). Polish notation was named for its inventor, the logician Jan Lukasiewicz, who lived in the early part of the twentieth century.[2] The major virtue of the form is that it can be processed one symbol at a time reading left to right, and does not require parentheses. For example, an expression such as $(17 + 23 * 42) + 55$ would be written in postfix Polish notation as $17\ 23\ 42\ *\ +\ 55\ +$. Input is composed either of operators (such as $+$ or $-$) or operands (only integers in our simple example). Operands are pushed on a stack as they are encountered. By the time an operator is encountered, all operands will have been seen already and pushed on the stack. The appropriate number of operands for the operator are popped from the stack, the operation performed, and the result pushed back on the stack.

The procedure that follows is our reverse Polish calculator program. In addition to the arithmetic operators, the letters p and q are used as operators. The letter p prints, but does not remove, the current top of stack. The letter q is used to halt the program. Notice the handling of digits. A digit character may represent the first character in a multicharacter number, such as 132. The character is pushed back into the input, making use of the stack of characters used by the stream I/O package, and the entire number reread using the stream operator with an integer argument. Notice also the use of a disambiguation prefix used to clearly indicate the value of the binary operator enumerated values declared in the calculator engine class.

```
void calculator()
{    int intval;
     calculatorEngine calc;
     char c;

     while (cin >> c) {
        switch(c) {
            case '0': case '1': case '2': case '3': case '4':
            case '5': case '6': case '7': case '8': case '9':
               cin.putback(c);
               cin >> intval;
               calc.pushOperand(intval);
               break;

            case '+':
               calc.doOperator(calculatorEngine::plus);
               break;

            case '-':
               calc.doOperator(calculatorEngine::minus);
```

---

2. Then why isn't Polish notation referred to as Lukasiewicz notation?

```
                                      break;

                          case '*':
                              calc.doOperator(calculatorEngine::multiply);
                              break;

                          case '/':
                              calc.doOperator(calculatorEngine::divide);
                              break;

                          case 'p':
                              cout << calc.currentMemory() << '\n';
                              break;

                          case 'q':
                              return; // quit calculator
                      }
                  }
              }
```

10.3.2 Application: Conversion of Infix to Postfix*

Another classic application for a stack is the conversion of standard, or *infix*, expressions into postfix form. Factors that complicate infix notation are parentheses and the different precedence of operators. An expression written in infix format as:

$$5 * (27 + 3 * 7) + 22$$

would be translated into postfix as:

$$5 \ 27 \ 3 \ 7 \ * \ + \ * \ 22 \ +$$

When an operand (such as a constant) is read, it is immediately appended to the output. Operators, such as + and *, cannot be output until both their arguments have been processed. Thus, they must be saved on a stack. If an operator being pushed on a stack has a lower precedence than the current top of stack, then the top of stack is popped and output. This occurs, for example, in the expression $4 * 6 + 5$. When the + is encountered the output contains the symbols 4 and 6, and the top of stack holds the * operator. Because the precedence of multiplication is higher than that of addition, the multiplication symbol is output and the addition symbol placed on the stack.

The opposite, on the other hand, would occur had the input been $4 + 6 * 5$. In this case, the 4 would have been left on the stack until after the program processed the multiplication of the 6 and the 5, when finally the addition of the 4 and the resulting value would be handled.

A left parenthesis is immediately pushed on the stack, regardless of the precedence of the current top of stack. Left parenthesis will be considered to have "precedence" lower than any other symbol, and thus will never be popped off the stack by the rule described in the preceding paragraph. Instead, right parenthesis will cause the stack to be popped and output until the corresponding left parenthesis is found. The left parenthesis is popped, but not output. Finally, when the end of input is encountered the stack is popped until empty, appending symbols to the output.

We need a way to encode the precedence of operators. An easy way to do this is to use the ordering of an enumerated datatype, listing operators from lowest precedence to highest:

```
// operators listed in precedence order
enum operators { leftparen, plus, minus, multiply, divide };
```

To display a visual representation of the operators, we need a way to convert from their enumerated type to a string. An easy way to do this is to write a function, as follows:

```
string opString (operators theOp)
    // return a textual representation of an operator
{
    switch (theOp) {
        case plus:    return " + ";
        case minus:   return " - ";
        case multiply:  return " * ";
        case divide: return " / ";
    }
}
```

The procedure to implement the infix to prefix converter is shown in Figure 10.2. As with the calculator application, a main loop reads new tokens. Constants are immediately appended to the result string. The processing of parentheses is as described earlier. Operators must test their precedence value against the current stack contents. This is accomplished using this short routine:

```
void processOp
    (operators theOp, stack<list<operators> > & opStack, string & result)
{
    // pop stack while operators have higher precedence
    while ((! opStack.empty()) && (theOp < opStack.top())) {
        result += opString(opStack.top());
        opStack.pop();
        }
    // then push current operator
    opStack.push(theOp);
}
```

```
string infixToPⱥefix(string infixStr)
{     stack < list<operators> > opStack;
      string result("");
      int i = 0;

      while (infixStr[i] != '\0') {
          if (isdigit(infixStr[i])) { // process constants
              while (isdigit(infixStr[i]))
                  result += infixStr[i++];
              result += " "; // add separator
              }
          else
              switch(infixStr[i++]) { // process other characters
                  case '(':
                      opStack.push(leftparen);
                      break;
                  case ')':
                      while (opStack.top() != leftparen) {
                          result += opString(opStack.top());
                          opStack.pop();
                          }
                      opStack.pop(); // pop off left paren
                      break;
                  case '+': processOp(plus, opStack, result);
                      break;
                  case '-': processOp(minus, opStack, result);
                      break;
                  case '*': processOp(multiply, opStack, result);
                      break;
                  case '/': processOp(divide, opStack, result);
                      break;
                  }
              }
      while (! opStack.empty()) { // empty the stack on end of input
          result += opString(opStack.top());
          opStack.pop();
          }

      return result; // return result string
}
```

Figure 10.2   Infix to postfix conversion program

```
template <class Container>
class queue {
public:
    typedef Container::value_type value_type;

        // operations
    bool        empty () { return c.empty(); }
    int         size  () { return c.size(); }
    value_type & front () { return c.front(); }
    value_type & back  () { return c.back(); }
    void        push  (value_type & x) { c.push_back(x); }
    void        pop   () { c.pop_front(); }

protected:
    Container c;
};
```

Figure 10.3   The queue adaptor class

An important property to note is that the infix to postfix conversion requires only one pass through the input.

10.4   QUEUES

The queue data type, like the stack, is implemented as an adaptor that wraps around an underlying container. The queue adaptor is shown in Figure 10.3. As with the stack, the queue adaptor does not actually provide any new functionality, but simply modifies the interface. Operations are provided with their conventional queue-like names, but are actually performed using operations on the underlying containers. Containers in the standard library that implement the necessary operations for the queue adaptor include the list, and the deque data structure that we will introduce in the next chapter. (Vectors cannot be used, as they do not provide the pop_front operation.)

Note that the queue class in the standard library provides the ability to access both the front *and* the back elements of the queue, while the conventional description of the queue data abstraction only permits access to the front.

10.4.1   Example Program: Bank Teller Simulation

Queues are often found in businesses, such as supermarkets or banks. Suppose you are the manager of a bank, and you need to determine how many tellers to have working during certain hours. You decide to create a computer simulation, basing your simulation on certain observed behavior. For example, you note that during peak hours there is a 90 percent chance that a customer will arrive every minute.

We create a simulation by first defining objects to represent both customers and tellers. For customers, the information we wish to know is the average amount of time they spend waiting in line. Thus, customer objects simply maintain two integer data fields: the time they arrive in line and the time they will spend at the counter. The latter is a value randomly selected between 2 and 8. (See Chapter 2 for a discussion of the random-Integer class.)

```
//
//      class Customer
//          a single customer waiting in the bank teller line

randomInteger randomizer;

class Customer {
public:
        // constructors
        Customer (int at) : arrivalTime(at),
            processTime(2 + randomizer(6)) {}
        Customer () : arrivalTime(0) processTime(0) { }

        // operations
        bool done    () { return --processTime < 0; }
        int  arrival () { return arrivalTime; }

        operator < (Customer & c) // order by arrival time
            { return arrivalTime < c.arrivalTime; }

        operator == (Customer & c) // no two customers are alike
            { return false; }

protected:
        unsigned int arrivalTime;
        unsigned int processTime;
};
```

Because objects can only be stored in standard library containers if they can be compared for equality and ordering, it is necessary to define the < and == operators for customers. Customers can also determine when they are done with their transactions.

Tellers are either busy servicing customers or they are free. Thus, each teller value holds two data fields: a customer and a Boolean flag. Tellers define a member function to answer whether they are free or not, as well as a member function that is invoked when they start servicing a customer.

```
//
//    class Teller
//         a teller servicing customers in a bank teller line

class Teller {
public:
     Teller() { free = true; }

     bool isFree() // see if teller is free to work
     {
         if (free) return true;
         if (customer.done())
                free = true;
             return free;
     }

     void addCustomer(Customer & c) // start servicing customer
     {
         customer = c;
         free = false;
     }

protected:
     bool free;
     Customer customer;
};
```

The main program is a large loop, cycling once each simulated minute. Each minute a new customer is, with probability 0.9, entered into the queue of waiting customers. Note that the customer value is *copied* into the list, so even if the local variable newCustomer is destroyed following the conditional statement, the list will continue to hold a copy with the same data fields. Each teller is polled, and if any are free they take the next customer from the queue. Counts are maintained of the number of customers serviced and the total time they spent in queue. From these two values we can determine, following the simulation, the average time a customer spent waiting in the line.

```
void main() {
     int numberOfTellers = 5;
     int numberOfMinutes = 60;
     double totalWait = 0;
     int numberOfCustomers = 0;
```

```
vector < Teller > teller(numberOfTellers);
queue < list< Customer > > line;

for (int time = 0; time < numberOfMinutes; time++) {
    if (randomizer(10) < 9) {
        Customer newCustomer(time);
        line.push(newCustomer);
        }
    for (int i = 0; i < numberOfTellers; i++) {
        if (teller[i].isFree() & ! line.empty()) {
            Customer frontCustomer = line.front();
            numberOfCustomers++;
            totalWait += (time - frontCustomer.arrival());
            teller[i].addCustomer(frontCustomer);
            line.pop();
            }
        }
    }
cout << "average wait:" <<   (totalWait / numberOfCustomers) << endl;
}
```

By executing the program several times, using various values for the number of tellers, the manager can determine the smallest number of tellers that can service the customers while maintaining the average waiting time at an acceptable amount.

10.4.2   Ring Buffer Queues

A variation of the idea of a queue is a *ring buffer*. While not found as part of the standard C++ library, this data structure is nevertheless commonly encountered as a solution to many problems.

Just as the queue can be built on top of a linked list, a ring buffer is constructed on top of a circular list. As with the linked list implementation, the elements in our ring buffer will be maintained in instances of class link. However, unlike the list implementation, these will not be dynamically allocated and released when elements are added or removed from the queue. Instead, a collection of links is simply allocated when the data structure is created. These links are reused over and over again, thus saving the expense of dynamic memory management.

A pair of pointers are maintained into the dynamically allocated data area. These are similar to the pointers used by the vector data structure. The lastFilled pointer references the element that was last filled by an enqueue operation, while the lastFree pointer refers to the last position in the free section of the list (see Figure 10.4).

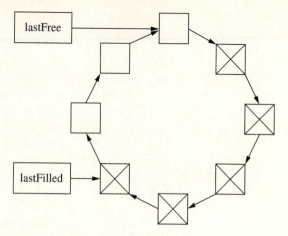

Figure 10.4 Snapshot of a ring buffer queue

To remove an element from the queue, we simply advance the last free pointer to the next position, which must be the first filled position.

```
template <class T> T queueRingBuffer<T>::dequeue()
{       // remove element from front of queue
        // cannot dequeue from empty queue
        assert(! empty());
        // advance last free position
        lastFree = lastFree->nextLink;
        // return value stored in last free position
        return lastFree->value;
}
```

The `front` method returns the next element following the `lastFree` pointer, without advancing the last free pointer.

The enqueue method advances the last filled pointer. However, when the queue becomes full, rather than issuing an error message, a new link will be created and inserted into the structure. Queue overflow conditions can never occur with this structure.

```
template <class T> void queueRingBuffer<T>::enqueue(T val)
{       // add new element to end of queue buffer
        // first check for potential overflow
        if (lastFilled->nextLink == lastFree) {
            link<T> * newLink = new link<T>(val);
            newLink->prevLink = lastFilled;
            newLink->nextLink = lastFilled->nextLink;
            lastFilled->nextLink->prevLink = newLink;
            lastFilled->nextLink = newLink;
            }
        else {
```

```
        // simply advance the last filled pointer
        lastFilled = lastFilled->nextLink;
        lastFilled->value = val;
        }
}
```

Because the ring buffer can dynamically grow as new elements are needed, it is not necessary to have a fixed size known in advance of execution. On the other hand, because dynamic memory allocation occurs only at the beginning, and when queue overflow occurs, the efficiency penalty of the simple list implementation is minimized.

The constructor for the class queueRingBuffer takes a count of the number of elements to initially allocate in the ring buffer.

```
queueRingBuffer<T>::queueRingBuffer(unsigned int max)
{       // constructor for queues based on ring buffers
        // create the first link
        T initialvalue;
        lastFree = new link<T>(initialvalue);
        lastFilled = lastFree;
        // make value point to itself
        lastFilled->nextLink = lastFilled;
        lastFilled->prevLink = lastFilled;
        // now add the remainder of the elements
        while (max-- > 0) {
            link<T> * newLink = new link<T>(initialvalue);
            newLink->prevLink = lastFilled;
            newLink->nextLink = lastFilled->nextLink;
            lastFilled->nextLink->prevLink = newLink;
            lastFilled->nextLink = newLink;
            }
}
```

The destructor must cycle around the buffer and delete all links.

```
template <class T> queueRingBuffer<T>::~queueRingBuffer()
{   // delete all memory associated with ring buffer
    link<T> * p = lastFree;
    link<T> * next;

    // walk around the circle deleting nodes
    while (p->nextLink != lastFree) {
        next = p->nextLink;
        delete p;
        p = next;
        }
}
```

Ring buffers are used, for example, by an operating system in the processing of character input typed at a keyboard. When a character is typed at the keyboard, an interrupt routine must process the character very quickly, before the user has time to hit another key. The value of the character is read and placed into a ring buffer. Application programs that are reading from the standard input respond at a much slower rate. When a sufficiently large number of characters have been read, an entire line of text is removed from the ring buffer, and handed over to the application program.

10.5   CHAPTER SUMMARY

Key Concepts

- Stack and queue operations
- LIFO and FIFO
- Vector implementation
- List implementation
- Ring buffer implementation

In this chapter we have introduced the abstract concepts of a stack and a queue. Both structures maintain collections of values in a linear sequence. In a stack, items are inserted and removed from one end:

In a queue, on the other hand, values are inserted at one end and removed from the other:

Both stacks and queues can be built on top of list structures. A stack can also be built on top of a vector, and both can be constructed out of deques (to be discussed in the next chapter). Generally the advantage of a vector or deque implementation is improved performance, while the advantage of a list implementation is greater flexibility, because the number of elements need not be known in advance. In addition to the vector and list implementation techniques for a queue, we have described a third implementation approach using a ring buffer. The ring buffer provides both speed and flexibility.

To illustrate the use of the stack data type, we have described a program to simulate a reverse Polish calculator, and a program to convert infix expressions into reverse Polish (postfix) notation. To illustrate the use of

the queue data type, we have described a program to simulate the servicing of customers in a bank teller line.

Further Reading

Stacks and queues are discussed extensively by Knuth [Knuth 73]. The terms LIFO and FIFO were first used by accountants. The following hypothetical example illustrates the use of the terms in the accounting field. Suppose in March Mr. Jones purchases ten shares of stock at $70, and in April purchases twenty more shares at $90. Now imagine that in July Mr. Jones sells ten shares of stock at $80. Should the shares be considered to be those purchased in March (first in, first out), or should they be considered to be the ones purchased in April (last in, first out)? Under the one assumption the investment will have shown a profit, while under the other the investment will have lost money.

Because Polish notation simplifies so many notation problems, it is actually surprising that it was not discovered before 1929. The original source is [Lukasiewicz 29].

Study Questions & Exercises

Study Questions

1. What are the defining characteristics of a stack and of a queue? Give an everyday example of each.

2. What do the terms LIFO and FIFO mean?

3. Give an example that shows how a stack is used by a computer system. Give a similar example for a queue.

4. What is an adaptor?

5. What types of containers can be used to hold the values in a stack? What considerations would help you decide which type of container to use?

6. Why is Polish notation called "Polish"?

7. What types of containers can be used to hold the values in a queue?

8. Why can't a vector be used as the underlying container for a queue?

9. What is a ring buffer?

Exercises

1. What type of structure might be described by the term LILO (last in, last out)?

2. What is the Polish notation representation of the following expression?
$$(a * (b + c)) + (b/d) * a$$

3. Add the following instructions to the reverse Polish notation calculator.

Letter	Meaning
c	Clear all values from stack
d	Double top value on stack

4. The reverse Polish notation calculator produces an assertion error and halts if an operation is attempted with too few values; for example, in the input "23 − +". Change the program so as to produce a more helpful error message, and to one which will recover gracefully from such errors.

5. How does the infix to prefix conversion routine described in Figure 10.2 handle runs of operators of the same precedence, such as $a + b + c$? For some operators, the normal rules associate to the left, so $a + b + c$ is properly interpreted as $(a + b) + c$, while other operators associate to the right. Describe how the conversion algorithm must be modified to be able to handle both situations.

6. Write a program to check for balanced curly braces { } in a file of characters.

7. Expand upon the program for the last exercise so that it will check for properly nested parenthesis, curly braces, and square brackets. (Hint: Use a stack to store the most recent unmatched left symbol.)

8. Explain how it is possible to implement two stacks using one array. Your stacks should not generate an overflow condition unless the sum of the number of elements held in the stacks exceeds the size of the array.

9. Write a class description for the ring buffer queue.

10. Add the following methods to the ring buffer queue.
    a. `size()`–return the number of elements in the queue
    b. `empty()`–return true if the queue has no elements

11. A *deque* (pronounced either "deck" or "DQ") is a data structure that maintains a linear collection of values and supports addition or removal from either end. Thus, deque can logically be considered a combination of a stack and queue. Write an adaptor that can construct a deque, using a linked list as the underlying container.

Chapter 11

Deques: Double-Ended Data Structures

Chapter Overview

In this chapter we will introduce the deque data structure from the standard template library, and then use the data type to illustrate two important general search techniques, depth- and breadth-first search. Next, we will revisit the topic of inheritance, introduced in Chapter 9, showing how inheritance can be used to construct *frameworks*, which are skeleton applications used as the basis for solving similar problems. Finally, we conclude the chapter by presenting a simplified deque implementation, similar to the standard library data structure.

Major topics discussed in this chapter include the following:

▲ The deque abstraction
▲ Depth- and breadth-first searching
▲ Frameworks
▲ A simplified implementation

237

11.1   THE DEQUE ABSTRACTION

The deque data type (pronounced either "deck" or "DQ") is one of the most interesting data structures in the standard template library. Of all the STL containers, the deque is the least conventional. It represents a data type that is seldom considered to be one of the "classic" data abstractions, as are vectors, lists, sets, or trees. Nevertheless, the deque is a powerful and versatile abstraction.

The operations provided by the deque data type, shown in Table 11.1, are a combination of those provided by the classes vector and list. Like a vector, the deque is a randomly accessible structure. This means that instances of the class deque can be used in most situations in which a vector might be employed. Like a list, elements can be inserted into the middle of a deque, although such insertions are not as efficient as they are with a list.

The term deque is short for double-ended queue, and describes the structure well. The deque is a combination of stack and queue, allowing elements to be inserted at either end. Whereas a vector only allows efficient insertion at one end, the deque can perform insertion in constant time at either the front or the end of the container. Like a vector, a deque is a very space-efficient structure, using far less memory for a given size collection than will, for example, a list. However, again like a vector, insertions into the middle of the structure are permitted, but are not efficient. An insertion into a deque may require the movement of every element in the collection, and is thus $O(n)$ worst case.

One of the most common uses for a deque is as an underlying container for either a stack or a queue. The deque is a preferable container for such employment if the size of the collection remains relatively stable during the course of execution, although if the size varies widely a list or vector is preferable. In many cases, the decision concerning which structure is most appropriate can only be made by performing direct measurement of program size or execution time.

Because the meaning of the operations on a deque is similar to the operations of a vector or a list, we will not describe them in detail. Instead, we will proceed to an example program that makes use of the features provided by a deque.

Table 11.1   Summary of deque operations

Constructors and Assignment

`deque<T> d;`	Default constructor
`deque<T> d (anInt);`	Construct with initial size
`deque<T> d (anInt, a_T_value);`	Construct with initial size and initial value
`deque<T> d (aDeque);`	Copy constructor
`d = aDeque;`	Assignment of deque from another deque
`d.swap (aDeque);`	Swap contents with another deque

Element Access and Insertion

`d[i]`	Subscript access, can be assignment target
`d.front ()`	First value in collection
`d.back ()`	Final value in collection
`d.insert (iterator, value)`	Insert value before iterator
`d.push_front (value)`	Insert value at front of container
`d.push_back (value)`	Insert value at back of container

Removal

`d.pop_front ()`	Remove element from front of vector
`d.pop_back ()`	Remove element from back of vector
`d.erase (iterator)`	Remove single element
`d.erase (iterator,iterator)`	Remove range of elements

Size

`d.size ()`	Number of elements currently held
`d.empty ()`	True if vector is empty

Iterators

`deque<T>::iterator itr`	Declare a new iterator
`d.begin ()`	Starting iterator
`d.end ()`	Stopping iterator
`d.rbegin ()`	Starting iterator for reverse access
`d.rend ()`	Stopping iterator for reverse access

11.2   APPLICATION: DEPTH- AND BREADTH-FIRST SEARCH

In this section we will examine a program that will discover a path through a maze, such as the one that follows. We will assume that the starting point for the search is always in the lower right corner of the maze, and the goal is the upper left corner.

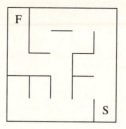

Our purpose in presenting this example is not only to contrast two different types of search techniques, but also to demonstrate the operations of the deque data type, and finally to show how a deque can be used either in a stacklike or queuelike fashion. These two broad approaches to searching are known as *depth-first search* and *breadth-first search*.

We want the maze searching program to be general, able to solve any two-dimensional maze, and not simply the example maze just shown. We therefore design a scheme so that the description of the maze can be read from an input file. Different files can be used to test the program on a variety of different mazes. To see how to do this, note that a maze can be described as a sequence of squares, or *cells*. The example maze just shown, for example, is a five-by-five square of 25 cells. Each cell can be characterized by a number, which describes the surrounding walls. Sixteen numbers are sufficient. In this fashion, we have this vocabulary for describing cells:

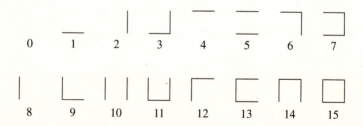

The pattern of the numeric values becomes apparent if one considers the number not as a decimal value, but as a binary pattern. The 1's position indicates the presence or absence of a south wall, the 2's position the east wall, the 4's position the north wall, and the 8's position the west wall. A value such as 13 is written in binary as 1101. This indicates there are walls to the north, west, and south, but not the east.

Using this scheme, the example maze could be described by 25 integer values. In the following, we have superimposed these values on the maze to better illustrate their relationship to the original structure.

14	12	5	4	6
10	9	4	3	10
9	5	2	13	2
14	14	10	12	2
9	1	1	3	11

This *external* representation of the maze must be mapped on to an *internal* representation. The internal representation need not match the external representation, as long as there is a means of conversion between the two. The internal representation will again be a sequence of cells. Each cell is an instance of the class `cell`. Instances of class `cell` maintain three data fields:

1. A number. This is an integer value used to identify the cell. Cells are numbered consecutively from left to right and top to bottom.

2. A `list` of neighboring cells. Each cell will have an entry in this list for all other neighbor cells that can be reached.

3. A Boolean value, named `visited`, that will be used to mark a cell once it has been visited. Traversing a maze often results in dead ends, and the need to back up and start again. Marking visited cells avoids repeating effort and potentially walking around in circles.

A class description for `cell` follows. The member function `addNeighbor` simply inserts a value into the list of neighbors. The member function `visit` will encode the searching algorithm. We will describe this after we have outlined the rest of the program.

```
class cell {
public:
        // constructor
        cell (int n) : number(n), visited(false) { }

        // operations
        void addNeighbor (cell * n) { neighbors.push_back(n); }
        void visit (deque<cell *> &);

protected:
    int number;
    bool visited;
    list <cell *> neighbors;
};
```

The class that represents the entire maze structure is called `maze`, and has the following structure:

```
class maze {
public:
     maze (istream &);
     void solveMaze ();

protected:
     cell * start;
     bool finished;
     deque <cell *> path;
};
```

The class `maze` maintains three data fields. The first is a pointer to the starting cell. The second is a Boolean flag that is set to true once the goal cell has been reached. The third data field is a deque, used to hold the path (or paths) currently being traversed.

The constructor for the class `maze`, shown in Figure 11.1, reads the maze description from an input file (passed as argument), converting from the external representation to the internal representation. The first two integer values in the file represent the number of rows and columns of the maze. In order to set the links properly, a `vector` is maintained that represents the cells in the row *previous* to the row currently being read from the input file. (This is the row to the immediate north of the current.) Recall that the two-argument form used in the constructor for this vector initializes each entry to the second argument value, in this case a null pointer value. After each new cell has been processed, the entry in this vector for the corresponding column has changed. The following picture illustrates the use of this vector. Here the first two rows have been processed, as well as the first two columns in the third row. The boxed elements indicate the current value of the vector. Note that the value of the vector with the same column number as the present element is the neighbor to the north, while the value with the index one smaller than the current column is the neighbor to the west.

$$
\begin{array}{ccccc}
14 & 12 & 5 & 4 & 6 \\
10 & 9 & \boxed{4} & \boxed{3} & \boxed{10} \\
\boxed{9} & \boxed{5} & 2 & &
\end{array}
$$

As each new value is read, it is determined whether it has a link to the north (to the previous row) or to the west (to the most recently processed cell). If so, then links are established. Notice that links cannot be created to the east and south, because these cells have not yet been created. However, note that a link to the south or east corresponds to a link from the north or west in the adjoining cells, so by making both sets of connections at once it is only necessary to recognize north and west connections. After the cell

```
maze::maze (istream & infile)
    // initialize maze by reading from file
{
    int numRows, numColumns;
    int counter = 1;
    cell * current = 0;

        // read number of rows and columns
    infile >> numRows >> numColumns;

        // create vector for previous row
    vector <cell *> previousRow (numRows, 0);

        // now read data values
    for (int i = 0; i < numRows; i++)
        for (int j = 0; j < numColumns; j++) {
            current = new cell(counter++);
            int walls;
            infile >> walls;
                // make north connections
            if ((i > 0) && ((walls & 0x04) == 0)) {
                current->addNeighbor (previousRow[j]);
                previousRow[j]->addNeighbor (current);
                }
                // make west connections
            if ((j > 0) && ((walls & 0x08) == 0)) {
                current->addNeighbor (previousRow[j-1]);
                previousRow[j-1]->addNeighbor (current);
                }
            previousRow[j] = current;
            }
        // most recently created cell is start of maze
    start = current;
    finished = false;
}
```

Figure 11.1   Constructor for class maze

has been completely processed, it is assigned to the corresponding position in the vector, and the next element is read.

14	12	5	4	6
10	9	4	3	10
9	5	2	13	

This process continues until all the maze description values have been read. Having entered the maze data, we can now describe the algorithm used to solve the maze. The fundamental problem occurs when there is a choice of several directions to pursue. In our example maze, this occurs immediately after the first step, when there are possible moves both north and west. One or the other paths must be selected. However, because a selection may ultimately be wrong (resulting in a dead end), it is important to keep track of the alternative possibilities. We do so using a deque. At each step, the deque will hold pointers to cells that are known to be reachable, but have not yet been visited.

Describing the first few steps in the process will clarify the approach. There is only one cell reachable from the starting position, and thus initially the deque contains only one element. The following also repeats the maze, with the cells showing their given number.

the deque

front | 20 | back

1	2	3	4	5
6	7	8	9	10
11	12	13	14	15
16	17	18	19	20
21	22	23	24	25

This value is pulled from the deque, and the neighbors of the cell are inserted back into the deque. This time there are two neighbors, so the deque will have two entries:

front | 19 | 15 | back

Only one value can be explored at any time, so the first element is removed from the deque, its neighbors inserted, and so on. Two steps later we again have a choice, and both neighbors are inserted into the deque. At this point, the deque has the following contents:

front | 22 | 18 | 15 | back

The next cell to be explored will be 22, but cells 18 and 15 are also known to be reachable, and are waiting to be considered should the current path not prove to be a solution. This, in fact, occurs when we reach cell 16, at which point the deque looks like this:

front | 16 | 17 | 18 | 15 | back

Because cell 16 adds no new values to the deque (having no unvisited neighbors), the next entry is automatically popped from the deque. In this fashion we start pursuing the path from 17, which also immediately dead-ends. Finally, the entry 18 is popped from the deque, and the search continues. The solution is ultimately found in fifteen steps. The following shows the path to the solution, with the cells numbered in the order in which they were considered.

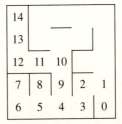

The code to perform this search is found in two methods. The overall control is the function solveMaze in class maze. This function pulls cells from the deque as long as the deque remains nonempty and the solution has not yet been found.

```
void maze::solveMaze ()
    // solve the maze puzzle
{
    start->visit (path);
    while ((! finished) && (! path.empty ())) {
        cell * current = path.front ();
        path.pop_front ();
        finished = current->visit (path);
        }
    if (! finished)
        cout << "no solution found\n";
}
```

When each cell is visited, it places all unvisited neighbors into the deque.

```
bool cell::visit (deque<cell *> & path)
    // visit cell, place neighbors into queue
    // return true if solution is found
{
    if (visited) // already been here
        return false;
    visited = true; // mark as visited
    cout << "visiting cell " << number << endl;
    if (number == 1) {
        cout << "puzzle solved\n";
```

```
        return true;
        }


        // put neighbors into deque
    list <cell *>::iterator start, stop;
    start = neighbors.begin ();
    stop = neighbors.end ();
    for ( ; start != stop; ++start)
        if (! (*start)->visited)
            path.push_front (*start);
    return false;
}
```

The strategy embodied in this code doggedly pursues a single path until it either reaches a dead end or until the solution is found. When a dead end is encountered, the most recent alternative path is reactivated, and the search continues. This approach is called a *depth-first search*, because it moves deeply into the structure before examining alternatives. A depth-first search is the type of search a single individual might perform in walking through a maze.

Suppose, on the other hand, that there is a group of people walking through the maze. When a choice of alternative directions is encountered, the group may decide to split itself into two smaller groups, and pursue each path simultaneously. When another choice is reached the group again splits, and so on. In this manner all potential paths are investigated at the same time. Such a strategy is known as a *breadth-first search*.

What is intriguing about the maze searching algorithm is that the code for a breadth-first search is almost identical to the code for depth-first search. In fact, all that is necessary is to change the command `path.push_front` in the `visited` member function to instead perform a `path.push_back`.

```
bool cell::visit (deque<cell *> & path)
{
    .
    .
    .
    for ( ; start != stop; ++start)
        if (! (*start)->visited)
            path.push_back (*start); // i-note change
    return false;
}
```

In doing so, we change our use of the deque from being stacklike, to being queuelike. This can be illustrated by once more describing the state of the deque at various points during execution. For example, after the first step, the deque has the following values. Note how the elements are in the opposite order from the order they held in the depth-first searching algorithm.

front | 15 | 19 | back

The element 15 is pulled from the deque, but its neighbors, the cells 10 and 14, are placed on the *back* of the queue. The next node to be investigated will, therefore, not be one of the immediate neighbors of the most recent node, but an entirely different path altogether.

front | 15 | 10 | 14 | back

A few steps later the search has been split several times, and the deque contains these values:

front | 17 | 21 | 2 | 8 | 8 | 12 | back

As one might expect, a breadth-first search is more thorough, but may require more time than a depth-first search. Recall that the depth-first search was able to discover the solution in 15 steps. The depth-first search is still looking after 20 steps. The following describes the search at this point.

```
17  12   9   7
    18  13   4
19  14   5   2
    15  10   3   1
16  11   8   6   0
```

Trace carefully the sequence of the last few cells that were visited. Note how the search has jumped around all over the maze, exploring a number of different alternatives at the same time. Another way to imagine a breadth-first search is that it describes what would happen if ink was poured into the maze at the starting location, as the ink slowly permeates every path until the solution is reached.

Depth-first and breadth-first searches are both valuable techniques in a variety of searching problems, and arise in a number of different forms and contexts. These differences exist between breadth-first and depth-first searching:

▲ Because all paths of length one are investigated before examining paths of length two, and all paths of length two before examining paths of length three, a breadth-first search is guaranteed to always discover a path from start to goal containing the fewest steps, whenever such a path exists.

▲ Because one path is investigated before any alternatives are examined, a depth-first search *may*, if it is lucky, discover a solution more quickly than the equivalent breadth-first algorithm. Notice this occurs here, where the goal is encountered after examining only 15 locations in the depth-first algorithm, while the goal is only reached after 25 iterations in the breadth-first algorithm. But this benefit is not certain, and a bad selection of alternatives to pursue can lead to many dead-end searches before the proper path to the goal is revealed.

▲ In particular, suppose for a particular problem that some but not all paths are infinite, and at least one path exists from start to goal that is finite. A breadth-first search is guaranteed to find a shortest solution. A depth-first search may have the unfortunate luck to pursue a never-ending path, and can hence fail to find a solution.

11.3   APPLICATION: A FRAMEWORK FOR BACKTRACKING

If we generalize the approach used in the depth-first search solution of the maze, we discover a technique termed *backtracking*. To use backtracking, a problem must have the characteristic that a solution is discovered as a sequence of steps. At some of these steps there may be multiple alternative choices for the next step, and insufficient information to decide which alternative will ultimately be the correct choice. A stack is used to record the state of the computation at the point of choice, permitting the program to subsequently "restart" the calculation from that point and pursue a different alternative.

To illustrate the idea of backtracking, we will analyze a classic puzzle involving the knight chess piece. In chess, a knight can legally move in an "L" shaped pattern, either one forward or backward and two left or right, or two forward or backward and one left or right. Figure 11.2 illustrates the legal moves for a knight starting in the given position on a conventional eight-square chess board. A piece may not move off the board, so near the edges of the board the number of legal moves may be less than eight.

A *knights tour* is a sequence of 64 moves in which a knight visits, using only legal moves, each and every square on the board once. The classic knights-tour problem is to discover a knights tour starting from a specific location. For example, the following table shows the steps in a complete knights tour starting from the upper left corner.

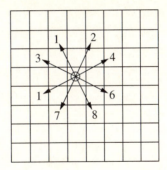

Figure 11.2 Legal knight moves

1	10	31	64	33	26	53	62
12	7	28	25	30	63	34	51
9	2	11	32	27	52	61	54
6	13	8	29	24	35	50	41
3	18	5	36	49	40	55	60
14	21	16	23	46	57	42	39
17	4	19	48	37	44	59	56
20	15	22	45	58	47	38	43

As an illustration of backtracking, consider the following state in which our program finds itself rather early in the search for a solution after having successfully performed 57 moves. There is no legal unvisited location to which the piece at move 57 can advance. The program will "back up" to move 56, and try a different alternative. But, in fact, there is no other alternative possible at move 56, so the program will back up to move 55, and then to 54, 53, and 52. Only at move 52 will a new untried legal alternative be discovered, namely to move to the bottom left corner. This move is tried, but then immediately abandoned because there is no successor. No further alternative is possible for move 52, nor for move 51, or 50. We must backtrack all the way to move 49 before we can find another possibility, which is to make the new move 50 be the now vacant location of the previous move 52.

1	10	31		33	26	57	42
12	7	28	25	30	43	50	
9	2	11	32	27	34	41	56
6	13	8	29	24	49	44	51
3	18	5	38	35	40	55	
14	21	16	23	48	37	52	45
17	4	19	36	39	46		54
20	15	22	47		53		

Nonrecursive programs that solve a problem using backtracking generally have a very similar structure. We can use this observation to develop a generic *framework* for such problems. A framework is a class (or, in more complicated situations, a set of classes and functions) that provides the skeleton outline for the solution to some problem, but does not provide any specific details. The most common frameworks are associated with graphical user interfaces, but many other types of frameworks are possible. To generate a solution to a specific problem, the programmer specializes the framework, generally using inheritance.

11.3.1   Specialization Using Inheritance

As we noted in Chapter 9, *inheritance* is a powerful mechanism for quickly and easily creating new data abstractions that are variations or extensions of existing software. To use inheritance, the programmer writes the name of the existing class (called the *parent* class) following the name of the new class. By doing so, the new class (called the *child* class, or sometimes the *derived* class) is then treated as an extension of the older class. All data fields, all member functions of the existing structure are therefore immediately accessible in the new structure. In addition, the programmer can add new data fields and new functions.

We will illustrate the use of inheritance in the development of our framework for backtracking problems. The solution to a generic backtracking problem can be described like this:

```
template <class T> bool backtrackFramework<T>::run ()
{
    // initialize the problem
    initialize ();
    done = false;

    // do the main loop
    while ((! done) && (! theStack.empty ())) {
        // if we can't advance from current state
```

```
    // then pop the stack
    if (! advance(theStack.top ()))
        theStack.pop ();
}

    // return true if stack is not empty
    return ! theStack.empty ();
}
```

A procedure `initialize` is used to establish whatever conditions need to be set to start the problem, including pushing the first state on the stack. A Boolean variable `done` indicates when the problem is finished. This variable may be set by the application-specific code to terminate the loop early if, for example, a solution is found. The heart of the algorithm is a simple loop. At each step, a procedure known as `advance` is called, passing as argument the current state. If it is possible to advance to a new state, then execution continues, otherwise the topmost state is popped off the stack, and execution backtracks to a previous point.

The method just given is from a class called `backtrackFramework`. The template parameter is the class used to encode state information. The complete class description is as follows:

```
//
//    class backtrackFramework
//        general framework for solving problems
//        involving backtracking
//

template <class T> class backtrackFramework {
public:
    // protocol for backtrack problems
    virtual void    initialize    ();
    virtual bool    advance       (T newstate);
    virtual bool    run           ();

protected:
    stack < deque <T> >  theStack;
    bool            done;
};
```

Note that the general purpose class has no information specific to the knights-tour problem. In order to specialize this general approach to make a solution to the knights-tour problem, we first need to describe how we record information concerning the current position.

The encapsulation for the "state" of the search at any point will be an instance of a class we will call `Position`. A `Position` corresponds to a location on the chess board. A position will maintain a pair of x and y values corresponding to coordinates on the board, a variable moveNumber that will record the sequence of moves in the solution, and a fourth integer variable, named visited, that will indicate what subsequent moves have been attempted. To encode this last value, we will simply try, at each step, the moves in order and numbered as in Figure 11.2. A zero stored in the visited variable indicates the position has not yet been used on the knights tour, while a nonzero value indicates the position has been used on the knights tour and, furthermore, the type of move that was used to generate the next step.

The following is the class description for Position. The output operator is used to print the final result.

```
//
//      class Position
//          record a position in the knights move tour
//

class Position {      // position in chessboard
public:
     void          init          (int, int);
     Position *  nextPosition ();

protected:
     // data fields
     // x and y are coordinate positions
     int     x, y;
     // moveNumber records the sequence of steps
     int     moveNumber;
     // visited is a bit vector marking what positions have been visited
     int     visited;

     // internal method used to find the next move
     Position * findMove(int visitedPosition);

     // friends
     friend class knightsTour;
     friend ostream & operator << (ostream & out, Position & v);
};
```

The chessboard itself will simply be declared a two-dimensional matrix of positions, named board. Because the array constructor does not permit the initialization of each position individually, initialization of each element is performed with a loop that simply invokes the init method for each value. We will see this shortly in the initialization portion of the program.

A hallmark of object-oriented programming and the responsibility-driven design technique outlined in Chapter 2 is the concept of making data structures responsible for their own operation. The Position data structure illustrates this idea. Each position is responsible for finding the next potential move in the solution. The process of finding the solution is performed by the method nextPosition. This method returns a pointer to a position, returning a null pointer if no legal alternative exists. In order to discover a position, the method increments the value held in the variable visited, using the facilitator method findMove to perform the encoding of the number into a position value. If the incremented value of the visited variable denotes a position that is legal and not yet visited, it is returned; otherwise the loop continues. If all eight possible moves have been examined, then no alternative exists and a null value is returned. Before returning in this case we zero the variable visited, so that the position can be revisited along a different path. We saw this in the earlier example of backtracking, where position 52 was first abandoned but later reached from a different direction.

```
Position * Position::nextPosition()
{
    while (++visited < 9) {
        Position * next = findMove(visited);
        // if there is a neighbor not visited then return it
        if ((next != 0) && (next->visited == 0))
            return next;
    }
    // can't move to any neighbor, report failure
    visited = 0;
    return 0;
}
```

The method findMove simply translates a value between 1 and 8 into a position, filtering out moves that are not on the board.

```
Position * Position::findMove(int typ)
{   int nx, ny;

    switch(typ) {
        case 1: nx = x - 1; ny = y - 2; break;
        case 2: nx = x + 1; ny = y - 2; break;
        case 3: nx = x - 2; ny = y - 1; break;
        case 4: nx = x + 2; ny = y - 1; break;
        case 5: nx = x - 2; ny = y + 1; break;
        case 6: nx = x + 2; ny = y + 1; break;
        case 7: nx = x - 1; ny = y + 2; break;
        case 8: nx = x + 1; ny = y + 2; break;
    }
```

```
        //   return null value on illegal positions
        if ((nx < 0) || (ny < 0))
            return 0;
        if ((nx >= boardSize) || (ny >= boardSize))
            return 0;

        //   return address of new position
        return & board[nx][ny];
}
```

We are finally in a position to show how to use inheritance to specialize the general purpose backtracking solution we created earlier in order to create a solution to the knights-tour problem. To create a solution to the knights-tour problem, we need to tie the `Position` data structure into our backtracking framework. By saying that the new class `knightsTour` inherits from `backtrackFramework` (a process termed *derivation*), all the data fields and methods of the parent class are made available to the new class. In addition, those methods that were labeled `virtual` in the parent class can be *overridden*, and provided with new meanings. In this fashion the `initialize` and the `advance` methods can be made specific to the current problem. The complete class description is:

```
//
//      class knightsTour
//          solve the n by n knights-tour problem
//

class knightsTour : public backtrackFramework<Position *> {
public:
            // redefine the backtracking protocol
    virtual void    initialize      ();
    virtual bool    advance         (Position *);

        // new method
    void            solve           ();
};
```

The initialization method loops over each board position to establish the initial conditions for each value. It then pushes the starting location, board position 0:0, on to the stack. This board position is our initial state.

```
const int boardSize = 8;
Position board[boardSize][boardSize];

void knightsTour::initialize ()
{
```

```
// initialize the parent class
backtrackFramework<Position *>::initialize ();

// initialize chessboard
for (int i = 0; i < 8; i++)
    for (int j = 0; j < 8; j++)
        board[i][j].init(i, j);

// set move number on first position
board[0][0].moveNumber = 1;

// push initial position
theStack.push(& board[0][0]);
}
```

To complete the framework we need only describe how to discover the next move from any given position. This is performed by the method advance. The advance method is given, in the argument, the current state. It asks a position to try to find a next position in sequence. It does this by invoking the nextMove method described earlier. The advance function returns a true value if advancement is possible from the current position, and a false value if no advancement can be made. An additional responsibility is to test to see if the solution to the problem has been found. If so, then the done flag must be set.

```
bool knightsTour::advance(Position * currentPosition)
    // try to advance from a given position
{
    Position * newPosition = currentPosition->nextPosition ();
    if (newPosition) {
        // move forward
        newPosition->moveNumber = currentPosition->moveNumber + 1;
        theStack.push(newPosition);
        // if we have filled all squares we are done
        if (newPosition->moveNumber ==  boardSize * boardSize)
                done = true;
        // return success
        return true;
        }
    else
        return false; // can't move forward
}
```

The final method to describe is the one new method added by class knightsTour to the framework protocol. This method simply starts the

---

Overriding, Replacement, and Refinement

Placing the modifier virtual in the parent class indicates that the given method can potentially be replaced by a function defined in a child class. This is only a potential, it need not be replaced, and if not the function in the parent will be used.

If a child class does override the parent class method, it is a complete replacement of the method from parent class. Sometimes, as in the initialization method shown, we instead want to combine the new code with that of the parent, making sure that both are executed. In C++ this is accomplished by invoking the function in the parent class from inside the code for the child class. In order to avoid confusion, the fully qualified name, in this case

```
backtrackFramework<Position*>::initialize();
```

is used to completely and fully specify exactly what function should be executed.

---

framework running. If success is reported, then the stack is popped in order to print the result.

```cpp
void knightsTour::solve ()
{
        // start framework
        if (run ()) {    // print solution
            cout << "solution is:\n";
            while (! theStack.empty ()) {
                cout << * theStack.top () << '\n';
                theStack.pop ();
                }
            }
        else
            cout << "no solution ";
}
```

11.4   AN IMPLEMENTATION

Of all the containers in the standard template library, the deque has the least obvious implementation approach. Techniques for implementing vectors, lists, queues, trees, and so on are all well known. But there are many possible techniques that can be used to implement a deque, and the language definition does not constrain the software developer of the abstraction in any significant regard. In this section we will describe one possible technique. The approach presented here has the advantage of being relatively simple, but is not the only possibility.

The basic idea in this implementation is to internally represent a deque as a pair of vectors. That is, although we visualize a deque as a linear structure, such as:

it actually can be stored internally as two vectors. This allows values to be added at either end. Note, however, that the first vector is "backwards," as the first element is at the top, while the last element is at the bottom, in position 0.

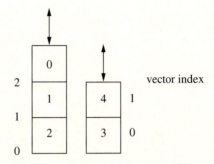

Figure 11.3 gives a class description for our simplified deque implementation, with many of the shorter methods being defined as in-line procedures.

The structure of most of the remaining operations is very similar. All are implemented by performing operations on one or the other of the underlying vectors. The complicating factor is that either vector could potentially be empty, in which case the operation must be performed on the other. The method front, which returns the first element in the collection, is typical:

```
template <class T> T & deque<T>::front ()
    // return first element in deque
{
    if (vecOne.empty ())
        return vecTwo.front ();
    else
        return vecOne.back ();
}
```

If vector one is empty, then the first value in the deque is the first value in vector two. If, on the other hand, vector one is not empty, then the first value in the deque is the *last* value in the first vector. The method back is similar. The methods to remove an element from either the front or the back of the collection are only slightly more complex:

```
template <class T> void deque<T>::pop_front ()
    // remove first element in deque
```

```
//
//    class deque
//        double ended queue

template <class T> class deque {
public:
    typedef dequeIterator<T> iterator;
    typedef T value_type;

        // constructors
    deque () : vecOne(), vecTwo() { }
    deque (unsigned int size, T & initial) : vecOne (size/2, initial),
        vecTwo (size - (size / 2), initial)  { }
    deque (deque<T> & d) : vecOne(d.vecOne), vecTwo(d.vecTwo) { }

        // operations
    T &  operator [ ] (unsigned int);
    T &  front ();
    T &  back ();
    bool empty () { return vecOne.empty () && vecTwo.empty (); }
    iterator begin () { return iterator(this, 0); }
    iterator end () { return iterator(this, size ()); }
    void erase (iterator);
    void erase (iterator, iterator);
    void insert (iterator, T &);
    int  size () { return vecOne.size () + vecTwo.size (); }
    void push_front (T & value) { vecOne.push_back(value); }
    void push_back (T & value) { vecTwo.push_back(value); }
    void pop_front ();
    void pop_back ();

protected:
    vector<T> vecOne;
    vector<T> vecTwo;
};
```

Figure 11.3 A simplified implementation of the class deque

```
{
    if (vecOne.empty ())
        vecTwo.erase(vecTwo.begin ());
    else
        vecOne.pop_back ();
}
```

If the first vector is empty, we must erase the first element in the second vector, otherwise we can simply reduce the size of the first vector by one. Note that this approach may not be the best solution, because the erase operation on vector two is almost undoubtedly very costly. Often, sequences of pushes and pops occur one after another. This would occur, for example, if the deque were used as a stack or as a queue. Rather than each pop_front causing an erase, a better alternative in this case would be to move some number of elements (for example, half) from the second vector back to the first. Subsequent pop_front operations would then encounter the more efficient pop_back alternative, rather than the erase. The development of this possibility will be explored in some of the exercises at the end of the chapter.

The subscript operator changes the index values into a subscript that is appropriate for one of the underlying vectors. Notice that the subscripts must be reversed for the first vector:

```
template <class T> T & deque<T>::operator [ ] (unsigned int index)
    // return given element from deque
{

    int n = vecOne.size ();
    if (index <= n)
        return vecOne [ (n-1) - index ];
    else
        return vecTwo [ index - n ];
}
```

11.4.1 Deque Iterators

An iterator for our deque abstraction is most easily constructed by using the subscript operator to access the underlying element. Such an approach is shown in the class description in Figure 11.4.

As with many of the iterator implementations we present, a major difficulty arises from the need to support both a prefix and a postfix form of the iterator operation. The prefix form is implemented in-line, as it simply changes the state of the current iterator and returns. The postfix form must change the current state, but return an iterator that describes the location prior to the change. This is most easily accomplished by cloning the current iterator, which will preserve the initial state, then updating the value, and finally returning the clone.

```
template <class T> deque<T>::iterator dequeIterator<T>::operator ++ (int)
    // postfix form of increment
{

        // clone, update, return clone
    deque<T>::iterator clone(theDeque, index);
    index++;
    return clone;
}
```

```
//
//        class dequeIterator
//             iterator protocol for deque

template <class T> class dequeIterator {
    friend class deque<T>;
    typedef dequeIterator<T> iterator;
public:
        // constructors
    dequeIterator (deque<T> * d, int i) : theDeque(d), index(i) { }
    dequeIterator (deque<T>::iterator & d)
        : theDeque(d.theDeque), index(d.index) { }

        // iterator operations
    T & operator * () { return (*theDeque)[index]; }
    iterator & operator ++ (int) { ++index; return this; }
    iterator operator ++ (); // prefix change
    iterator & operator -- (int) { --index; return this; }
    iterator operator -- (); // postfix change
    bool operator == (iterator & r)
        { return theDeque == r.theDeque && index == r.index; }
    bool operator < (iterator & r)
        { return theDeque == r.theDeque && index < r.index; }
    T & operator [ ] (unsigned int i)
        { return (*theDeque) [index + i]; }
    void operator = (iterator & r)
        { theDeque = r.theDeque; index = r.index; }
    iterator operator + (int i)
        { return iterator(theDeque, index + i); }
    iterator operator - (int i)
        { return iterator(theDeque, index - i); }

protected:
    deque<T> * theDeque;
    int index;
};
```

Figure 11.4 Implementation of a deque iterator

Having described the structure of deque iterators, we can now return to the description of those deque methods that make use of iterators. The method **erase** recovers the index position from the iterator, and erases an element from the appropriate vector. It uses the fact that vectors construct random access iterators, so we can easily create the iterator that corresponds to a given index position within a vector.

```
template <class T> void deque<T>::erase (deque<T>::iterator & itr)
    // erase value from deque
{
    int index = itr.index;
    int n = vecOne.size ();
    if (index < n)
        vecOne.erase (vecOne.begin () + ((n-1) - index));
    else
        vecTwo.erase (vecTwo.begin () + (n - index));
}
```

The `insert` method is similar, and will not be shown. The erase method that removes a range of values is more complicated, because the range may cross the boundary between the two vectors. The implementation of this method, therefore, divides into three cases, depending upon whether all the elements to be removed are in the first vector, are all in the second vector, or whether some are in the first vector and some are in the second. The development of this code will be left as an exercise.

11.5   CHAPTER SUMMARY

Key Concepts

- Deque
- Depth-first search
- Breadth-first search
- Backtracking
- Framework
- Inheritance
- Virtual member functions

The deque, or double-ended queue, is a data structure that provides a combination of features from both the `vector` and `list` data types. Like a `vector`, a deque is a randomly accessible and indexed data structure. Like a `list`, elements can be efficiently inserted at either the front or the end of the structure. Thus, a deque can be used in either a stacklike or a queuelike fashion.

We have illustrated the use of the deque by developing a program that can find a path through a simple maze. By storing the intermediate steps in a stack, the search technique will explore one path entirely to completion before examining alternatives. This is known as depth-first search. By changing the use of the deque to a queuelike form, all paths are explored in parallel. This is known as breadth-first search.

We have introduced backtracking as a general problem-solving technique, applicable whenever the "state" of the task at hand can be captured and stored at the point where one of many alternative possibilities must be selected.

Finally, we introduced the idea of a software framework. A framework describes the general structure of a solution to a problem, without defining any specific details. These details can then be filled in, typically using inheritance, to specialize the framework for the solution of a given problem. A framework thus provides reuse not only for code but also for the reuse of an idea or approach to solving a class of similar problems.

Study Questions & Exercises

Study Questions

1. Give a short characterization of the deque data type.

2. What vector operations are not supported by the class deque? What list operations?

3. Give the integer encoding of this simple six-cell maze:

4. Show the state of the deque in the maze example in Section 11.2 after five moves have been performed.

5. How does breadth-first search differ from depth-first search?

6. What requirements must be satisfied in order to use backtracking in the solution of a problem?

7. What is a framework?

8. What is the underlying representation used to hold the values in the implementation of the deque described in this chapter?

Exercises

1. Consider the following graph. Starting from node A, list the vertices as they might be visited in a breadth-first search and as they might be visited using a depth-first search. Note that there are many different sequences for both forms of search.

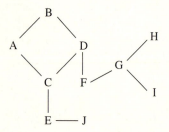

2. The maze-solving program exploits a redundancy in the maze encoding. This redundancy comes from the assumption that if one can move east from one cell to the next, one can also move west from the second cell back to the first. The constructor maze::maze makes use of this redundancy by only processing openings to the north and west.

However, this redundancy is not intrinsic to the numeric encoding of the maze. A "one-way" opening could easily be described as a cell with value 3, for example, being next to a call with value 7. From the 7 cell one could move to the 3 cell, but from the 3 cell one could not move back to the 7 cell.

To change our maze-solving program it is only necessary to change the constructor that translates the external encoding into the internal encoding. Show the modifications that must be provided to permit this form of maze.

3. A difficulty occurs when the first element is removed from a deque but the first vector in the internal representation is empty. The pop then causes the first element to be removed from the second vector. This is potentially costly if a number of pops are performed in sequence. A better alternative is to first move half the elements from the second vector into the first vector, so that subsequent pops are implemented as operations on the first vector. Write implementations for pop_front and pop_back that use this idea.

4. The implementation of the erase method that takes a range of values as argument must recognize three different cases:
   a. Both beginning and end of range are found in the first vector.
   b. Both beginning and end of range are found in the second vector.
   c. Beginning of range is found in first vector, end of range in second vector.

   Implement the code for the erase method that handles each of these cases.

12

Sets and Multisets

Chapter Overview

In this chapter we introduce the *set* first as a mathematical abstraction, and then as a realization in two different forms. The first form is a `bit-set`, used for maintaining a set of integer values from a limited range. The second is the standard library `set` data abstraction, which can hold values of more general types. After summarizing the operations that can be performed using the `set` abstraction, we describe the start of a simplified implementation. Providing good guaranteed performance for the `set` data type requires techniques that are sufficiently complex, so we will continue the development of this code over the next two chapters. Topics discussed in this chapter include:

▲ The set abstraction
▲ Bit vector sets
▲ The set data type
▲ An example implementation

12.1   THE SET DATA ABSTRACTION

The concept of a *set* underlies much of mathematics, and is an integral part of many algorithms. In its simplest form, a set is simply a collection of elements. The fundamental operations involved in the set abstraction include adding and removing elements, and testing for the inclusion of an element. The `set` data type is designed to perform all of these operations very quickly, in $O(\log n)$ steps (where n represents the number of elements in the collection). Recall that to determine whether a value that occurs in a `vector` or `list` requires, in the worst case, an examination of every value, a process that could take $O(n)$ steps.

More complex set operations include forming unions, intersections, and differences with another set. These latter operations are particularly characteristic of the idea of a set. Within this framework, there are, however, many possible variations. These are:

▲ Some types of sets maintain actual data values, while other formulations of the set data type merely maintain an indication of the presence or absence of an element. A set containing elements that are characters or small integers, for example, need only maintain enough information to tell whether an element is present in the set, because it can be easily regenerated if necessary. On the other hand, a set containing employee records, or floating-point numbers, must carry around the actual data values themselves, because they are not easily reconstructed.

▲ In most formulations of the abstract concept of a set, an element is not permitted to appear more than once. A `multi_set` (sometimes called a *bag*) is a setlike data structure that permits elements to be repeated. In practice, whether the implementation of a set data structure has a similar multiset counterpart is related to the first point; namely, those implementations that maintain only presence information generally can be used only for sets, while those that maintain entire values can be used (with slight modification) for either sets or multisets. It is conventionally assumed that no harm comes from adding an element to a set in which it already appears; the addition operation is simply ignored.

▲ The mathematical definition of a set is normally interpreted to imply that the elements are unordered, and the only comparison required of all values is a test for equality. Nevertheless, for the sake of a gain in efficiency, some set implementations, including the `set` and `multi_set` data types in the standard library, will use the ability to compare ordering between elements. Thus, when selecting a set implementation for a particular problem, an important question to be addressed is whether elements can or cannot be placed in order.

12.2   SET OPERATIONS

The characteristic new feature of a set is the inclusion of operations that act on entire collections of values. These operations are:

▲ **Union**. A union of two sets is formed by adding to one set all values from a second set that do not already appear in the first set.

generic algs:

resultSetItr = set_union(set1, set2, resultSet);

InputIterator   OutputIterator

▲ **Intersection**. The intersection of two sets is the collection of values that appear in both sets. An intersection of one set from another can be formed by removing from the first set all values that do not appear in the second set.

▲ **Difference**. The difference of two sets is the opposite of the intersection; it is the set of values from one set that do not appear in a second set.

▲ The *symmetric difference* is the union of two sets minus the intersection.

▲ **Subset**. A set is said to be a subset of another set if all values from the first set appear also in the second set.

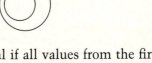

▲ **Equality**. Two sets are equal if all values from the first set appear in the second, and all values from the second also appear in the first. Stated another way, two sets are equal if they are both subsets of each other.

12.3   BIT VECTOR SETS *

In this chapter we will examine two different implementations of the set concept. The first of these is used to represent sets of small integer values. The second implementation technique is more general, and will be described in Section 12.6.

A bit vector is simply a sequence of 0/1 bit values. These values can be packed very efficiently into a larger structure, such as an integer value. A 32-bit integer, for example, can hold 32 binary values in the amount of storage required to store only a single integer value. Thus, a single integer value can be used to store a bit set with 32 or fewer locations, two integer values can store 64 or fewer values, and so on. The logical bitwise operations can then be used to determine the value of any given position.

Figure 12.1 gives a description for the standard library class `bitset`. The class is a template class; however, the template argument is not a type, but an integer. The integer represents the number of items to be stored in the bit set. Like index values, bit values are ordered starting with zero and extending to one less than the size of the collection. We assume here that integers have 32 bits; the code, however, could easily be modified to fit other integer sizes.

Two internal operations are used to determine the vector element that holds a particular bit position, and the bit number within the element. The member function `indexValue` returns the first of these values. Because each vector element holds 32 bits, it is sufficient to simply divide the index value by 32. For example, bit value 37 will be found in the data position with index value 1, because the integer division 37/32 yields the value 1.

The second internal function computes a mask into the selected value, with a one bit representing the bit at the position being manipulated, and zero values in all other bit positions. The mask is like a cover in which a slit has been opened that permits us to view only a single bit value. To create this mask, the function takes the remainder of the index value when divided by 32, and uses this result as an amount to shift left a numeric one value. If the original value was 37, for example, the remainder after dividing by 32 is 5. Thus, the value one is shifted left by five places, yielding the bit pattern 00100000. This will be the mask for each of the bit operations performed.

To turn a bit on (member function `set`), we simply mask the corresponding integer. This is illustrated by the following (we use 8 bit values for illustration, although a typical integer can hold 32 bit values):

---

* Section headings followed by an asterisk indicate optional material.

```
//
// bitset
// set of integer values
// assumes 32 bit integers
template <int N>
class bitset {
public:
        // constructors
    bitset() : data ((N+31)/32, 0) { }
    bitset (bitset<N> & b) : data (b.data) { }

        // bit level operations
    void flip  ();
    void flip  (int index);
    void reset ();
    void reset (int index);
    void set   ();
    void set   (int index)
    bool test  (int index);

        // bit testing operations
    bool any   ();
    bool none  ();
    int  count ();

        // set operations
    void operator |= (bitset<N> & rhs);
    void operator &= (bitset<N> & rhs);
    void operator ^= (bitset<N> & rhs);
    bool operator == (bitset<N> & rhs);

        // other operations
    void operator << (int);
    void operator >> (int);
    string to_string ();

protected:
    vector<int> data;
    int indexValue (int index) { return index / 32; }
    int mask (int index) { return 1 << (index % 32); }
};
```

Figure 12.1 A description of the standard library class `bitset`

Data	10011001
Mask	00100000
Result	10111001

```
template <int N> void bitset<N>::set(int index)
    // set (to 1) the given bit value
{
    data[indexValue(index)] |= mask(index);
}
```

The function `set()` with no arguments sets all bit values to the on position. An integer value that is all 1 can be created using the bitwise inverse operator (the tilde operator) with the value zero.

```
template <int N> void bitset<N>::set()
    \meta set all values to 1
{
    int n = data.size();
    for (int i = 0; i < n; i++)
        data[i] = ~ 0;
}
```

To test a bit position the vector data value is *and*-ed with the mask. If the result is nonzero, then the data byte must have had a 1 value in the selected position. If the result is zero, then the data type must have contained a zero bit.

Data	10011001
Mask	00100000
Result	00000000

```
template <int N> bool bitset<N>::test (int index)
    // test the indicated bit position
{
    return 0 != (data[indexValue(index)] & mask(index));
}
```

To clear the bit (member function `reset`), a bitwise *and* is performed with the corresponding word and the bitwise inverse of the mask. The member function with no arguments resets all bit values.

Data	10111001
Mask	00100000
Inverted mask	11011111
Result	10011001

```
template <int N> void bitset<N>::reset (int index)
    // reset (to zero) the corresponding bit value
{
    data[indexValue(index)] &= ~ mask(index);
}
```

```
template <int N> void bitset<N>::reset ()
    // reset all values to zero
{
    int n = data.size();
    for (int i = 0; i < n; i++)
        data[i] = 0;
}
```

Finally, to invert the value at the mask position, regardless of its current value, the *exclusive-or* bit level operation is used. The exclusive-or of a one and zero value is always one, while the exclusive-or of two one values is zero, as is the exclusive-or of two zero values. Thus, if the value in the position selected by the mask is one, it will become zero, and if it is zero, it will become one.

Data   10011001

Mask   00100000

Result 10111001

```
template <int N> void bitset<N>::flip (int index)
    // flip the corresponding bit value
{
    data[indexValue(index)]] ^= mask(index);
}
```

All values can be simultaneously inverted using the `flip` function with no arguments. Again, the bitwise invert operator is used to change the actual bit values.

```
template <int N> void bitset<N>::flip ()
    // flip all values
{
    int n = data.size();
    for (int i = 0; i < n; i++)
        data[i] = ~ data[i];
}
```

To generate the union of one bit vector set with another, the bitwise *or* operation is used. This is implemented as an assignment operator, because the semantics are to modify the left argument by including those elements from the right argument that are not already set. The binary or operator is also defined for bit sets, and operates by cloning the left argument into a temporary, performing the or assignment, then returning the temporary.

Data   10011001
Argument   00111000
Result   10111001

```
template <int N> void bitset<N>::operator |= (bitset<N> & rhs)
    // form the union of set with argument set
{
    int n = data.size();
    for (int i = 0; i < n; i++)
        data[i] |= rhs.data[i];
}
```

The intersection of one set with a second consists of those values from the first set that are also found in the second set. This can be discovered using the bitwise *and* operation:

Data   10011001
Argument   00111000
Result   00011000

```
template <int N> void bitset<N>::operator &= (bitset<N> & rhs)
    // form the intersection of set with argument set
{
    int n = data.size();
    for (int i = 0; i < n; i++)
        data[i] &= rhs.data[i];
}
```

The equality testing operator will determine if two sets are identically equal. To implement this, we simply compare the corresponding values in the two arrays.

```
template <class N> bool bitset<N>::operator == (bitset<N> & rhs)
    // test to see if two sets are the same
{
    // test to see if every position is equal to the argument
    int n = data.size();
    for (int i = 0; i < n; i++)
        if (data[i] != rhs.data[i])
            return false;

    // all equal, two sets the same
    return true;
}
```

Note that running time of each of these operations is proportional to the size of the set, but independent of the number of items (one bits) held in the set. This is not true of values maintained by, for example, a linked list.

The member functions none, any, and count are used to test the collection as a whole. The first is true if all bit values are off, the second is true if any bit value is true, and the third returns the number of bits that are on. The member function to_string converts a bit set into an object of type string. The string will have as many characters as elements in the bit set. Each zero bit will correspond to the character 0, while each one bit will be represented by the character 1.

The left and right shift operators (operator << and >>) can be used to shift a bit set left or right, in a manner analogous to the use of these operators on integer arguments. Zeros are shifted into the new positions. The bitset data structure in the standard library does not provide support for iterators.

The following illustrates the use of bit set operators by rewriting the sieve of Erastosthenes program (Section 8.3.1) using a bit vector, instead of a vector of integers.

```
//
//      sieve of Erastosthenes
//      algorithm for finding prime numbers
//      following execution,
//      one values in bit vector represent primes
//
const unsigned int max = 1000;

void sieve(bitset<max> & values)
{
        // first initialize all cells
        values.set();

        // now search for non-zero cells
        for (int i = 2; i*i <= max; i++) {
            if (values.test(i)) {
                // inv: i has no factors
                for (int j = i + i; j < max; j += i)
                    values.reset(j);
                // inv: all multiples of i have been cleared
                }
            // all nonzero values smaller than i are prime
    }
        // inv: all nonzero values are prime
}
```

12.4   THE SET DATA TYPE

While the `bitset` class simply stored a binary value that indicates whether or not the element was contained in the set, the more general `set` data type—like vectors, lists, and other container classes—stores actual values. As with many of the other container classes in the standard library, the `set` data structure is implemented as a combination of a relatively simple container class and a number of generic operations.

As we have done for the other container types we have examined, we will investigate the `set` data type in three steps. First, we will describe the solution of a typical problem that can be addressed using the data structure. Next, we will summarize the operations provided by the `set` data type, and a few of the more useful generic functions. Finally, we will provide the first of two simplified implementations of the data type. The implementation we will describe here will be correct, although not guaranteed to be efficient. A slightly more efficient implementation will subsequently be presented in Chapter 14.

12.4.1   A Spelling Checker

The basic idea of a spelling checker is to generate from a document a set of words that may be misspelled. We say "may be" because even the best spelling checkers cannot handle names or technical terms, so all one can do is indicate to the user a potential problem.

The spelling checker we describe will use three different sets of words. The first will be a set containing all the words found in the input document. The second is a set of words known to be correctly spelled. By producing a third set that represents the difference between these two sets, we can then generate the set of words that are found in the document but not known to be correctly spelled.

The input is read line by line, translated into lowercase and split into words using the functions `toLower` and `split` we have encountered previously (see Chapter 7). The split function will not only separate each line into words, but also remove punctuation characters. An iterator loop places each word into the set. Adding a new element to an instance of the `set` data type is accomplished using the `insert` member function.

```
void readWords (istream & input, set<string> & words)
    // read words from given input stream, placing into set
{
    string line;
        // while there is input, read a line
    while (getline(infile, line)) {
            // translate into lower case
        toLower(line);
```

```
            // split into individual words
        list<string> words_on_line;
        split(line, " .;?!:\t", words_on_line);
            // add each word to set
        list<string>::iterator start = words_on_line.begin();
        list<string>::iterator stop = words_on_line.end();
        for ( ; start != stop; ++start)
            words.insert (*start);
        }
}
```

We assume the list of correctly spelled words is stored in a file on disk. By simply changing the arguments passed to the procedure, we can read the dictionary from this file using the *same* algorithm that reads the input source. This is shown in the main program for our spelling checker, as follows:

```
void main () {
        // declare the two input files
    ifstream sourceFile ("text.txt"); // name of source file
    ifstream dictFile ("words.txt"); // dictionary file

        // create the three sets
    set<string> wordset, dictset, misspellings;

        // read the two files
    readWords (sourceFile, wordset);
    readWords (dictFile, dictset);

        // create the set difference
    set_difference (wordset.begin(), wordset.end(),
        dictset.begin(), dictset.end(),
        inserter (misspellings, misspellings.begin()));

        // write out the set of misspellings
    cout << "Misspelled words\n";
    set<int>::iterator start = misspellings.begin();
    set<int>::iterator stop = misspellings.end();
    for ( ; start != stop; ++start) {
        cout << *start << endl;
        suggestCorrection (*start, dictset);
        }
}
```

The generic algorithm `set_difference` generates the difference between the word list and the dictionary list, in effect removing the correctly spelled words from the word list and leaving only the misspelled words. The five arguments to this algorithm represent iterator ranges for the two source sets, and an iterator for the destination set. An `inserter` (Section 9.2.1) is used to change the iterator operations of this algorithm into insertions for the given set.

Once the set of misspelled words has been generated, an iterator loop is used to print each word on the standard output. Following each word, a set of suggested corrections is produced. The next section will describe the procedure that performs this task.

12.4.2   Spelling Correction

We can improve the spelling checker program by generating a list of suggested corrections. Although there are no guaranteed algorithms for correcting English spelling, various heuristics can be used to discover alternatives. We will describe here only one technique, but will suggest several others in the exercises at the end of the chapter.

The subroutine that controls the generation of alternatives simply prints a message, then executes the functions corresponding to each heuristic to create the set of suggested alternatives, and finally loops through the set of alternatives, printing each.

```
void suggestCorrection (string & word, set<string> & dictionary)
    // suggest alternatives to the misspelled word
{
    set <string> suggestions;
    cout << "Suggested alternatives for " << word << endl;
        // try each heuristic in turn
    transpositions(word, dictionary, suggestions);
        // ... other heuristics would go here
        // ...
        /// now print each suggestion
    set<string>::iterator start = suggestions.begin();
    set<string>::iterator stop = suggestions.end();
    for ( ; start != stop; ++start)
        cout << "Suggestion: " << *start << endl;
}
```

The heuristic we will describe is to simply transpose adjacent letters. After each transposition, the resulting word is tested against the dictionary. This is accomplished using the member function count, which returns the number of times a given entry is found in a set. If this value is larger than zero, it means the word is found in the dictionary, and should be considered to be an alternative.

```
void transposition
    (string & word, set<string> & dictionary, set<string> & suggestions)
    // try transpositions of characters in the word
{
    for (int i = 1; i < word.length(); i++) {
        swap (word[i-1], word[i]);
        if (dictionary.count(word) > 0)
            suggestions.insert (word);
                // put word back as before
            swap(word[i-1], word[i]);
        }
    }
}
```

Other heuristics include adding or removing letters from the word, or looking for words with similar characteristics.

12.4.3   Anagrams

An *anagram* is a rearrangement of the letters in a word to form a new word. In Exercise 6 of Chapter 7, it was suggested that to tell if two words were anagrams, the individual letters in the words could be sorted and the two resulting strings compared for equality. In this section we will describe a systematic technique for discovering all the anagrams of a word.

Like an anagram, a *permutation* of a set of values is simply a rearrangement. If the values can be compared against each other (such as if the values are integer, characters, or words), then it is possible to systematically construct all permutations of a sequence. The basic idea is to order the permutations, with the smallest permutation being the one in which values are listed smallest to largest, and the largest being the sequence that lists values largest to smallest.

Consider, for example, the permutations of the integers 1 2 3. The six permutations of these values are, in order:

$$
\begin{array}{ccc}
1 & 2 & 3 \\
1 & 3 & 2 \\
2 & 1 & 3 \\
2 & 3 & 1 \\
3 & 1 & 2 \\
3 & 2 & 1
\end{array}
$$

Notice that in the first permutation the values are all ascending, while in the last permutation they are all descending.

The generic algorithm `next_permutation` takes a set of values and rearranges them to form the next permutation in sequence. The algorithm returns a Boolean value, which is false when there are no further permutations. We can use this property to generate anagrams. Given a starting word, we first sort the word, placing the letters in ascending order. Then a loop is used to generate each new anagram. We can combine this with the dictionary used in the spelling correction program, and only output those words that are found in the dictionary.

```
void printAnagrams (string & word, set<string> & dictionary)
    // print all the anagrams of a word
{
    cout << "anagrams of " << word << endl;
        // first sort the word ascending
    sort (word.begin(), word.end());
        // then generate anagrams
    while (next_permutation (word.begin(), word.end()))
        if (dictionary.count(word) > 0)
            cout << word << endl;
}
```

12.5   SUMMARY OF OPERATIONS FOR CLASS SET

Table 12.1 summarizes the operations provided by the set and multiset data types. Both are template data structures, where the template argument represents the type of the elements the collection contains. An optional second template argument represents the operator used to compare keys.[1] The elements maintained in a set or multiset must recognize the less than comparison operator (operator <). An interesting feature of the set data abstraction is that the equality testing operator (operator ==) is *not* used to test values for equality. Instead, two values A and B are considered to be equal if both A < B and B < A are false!

The default constructor is used to create a collection with no elements. The copy constructor can be used to create a set that is a copy, or clone, of another set. Each element in the cloned set is a copy of the corresponding value in the original set. The assignment operator can be used to completely replace the values in a set with the contents of another set. The assignment operator copies the values from the right-hand argument set. This should be contrasted with the member function swap. The swap operation exchanges the values of the receiver with the argument set, so that the receiver contains the argument elements, and the argument set contains the receiver's values. The swap is performed in constant time. In the next section we will see an example use for this method.

Elements are inserted into a set using the insert member function. The function returns a pair, where the first element is the iterator that represents the location of the newly inserted value, and the second element is a Boolean that indicates whether the insertion was performed. (We will

---

1. See Section A.3 in Appendix A.

Table 12.1   Summary of set and multiset operations

Constructors

set<T> s;	Default constructor	$O(1)$
multiset<T> m;	Default constructor	$O(1)$
set<T> s (aSet);	Copy constructor	$O(n)$
multiset<T> m (aMultiset)	Copy constructor	$O(n)$
s = aSet	Assignment	$O(n)$
s.swap (aSet)	Swap elements with argument set	$O(1)$

Insertion and Removal

s.insert (value_type)	Insert new element	$O(\log n)$
s.erase (value_type)	Remove all matching element	$O(\log n)$
s.erase (iterator)	Remove element specified by iterator	$O(\log n)$
s.erase (iterator, iterator)	Remove range of values [a]	$O(\log n)$

Testing for Inclusion

s.empty ()	True if collection is empty	$O(1)$
s.size ()	Number of elements in collection	$O(n)$
s.count (value_type)	Count number of occurrences [b]	$O(\log n)$
s.find (value_type)	Locate value	$O(\log n)$
s.lower_bound (value_type)	First occurrence of value	$O(\log n)$
s.upper_bound (value_type)	Next element after value	$O(\log n)$
s.equal_range (value_type)	Lower and upper bound pair	$O(\log n)$

Iterators

set<T>::iterator itr	Declare a new iterator	$O(1)$
s.begin ()	Starting iterator	$O(1)$
s.end ()	Stopping iterator	$O(1)$
s.rbegin ()	Starting iterator for reverse access	$O(1)$
s.rend ()	Stopping iterator for reverse access	$O(1)$

a. Returning memory for removed elements requires time proportional to the number of elements removed.

b. The count operation is also bounded by the number of matching elements. This quantity can potentially be larger than $\log n$.

introduce the pair data type in Section 16.1.1.) Recall that an element will not be inserted into a set if it was already present in the collection, whereas an insertion will always be successful for a multiset. As in our sample program, this return value is often ignored in algorithms that use the set data type.

The erase member function can be used to remove values from a set.

There are several forms. The first form takes as argument a value, and removes all occurrences of the value. For a set, this quantity will be either zero or one, while in a multiset the value may occur multiple times. The number of elements removed is returned as an argument. A second form of `erase` takes as argument an iterator, and simply removes the associated value from the collection. A third form takes an iterator pair that represents a range of values, and removes all the values in the indicated range.

The member function `empty` indicates whether a collection is empty, while the member function `size` yields the number of elements in the set. The function `count` can be used to determine how many times a given value occurs in the collection. Unlike the generic algorithm, which uses a linear search, the `count` method for a multiset requires only $O(\log n)$ steps to find the first element, and time proportional to the number of matching elements to count how many fit the desired characteristic.

Similarly, the method `find`, which returns an iterator to a value (the end-of-range iterator if not found), requires only $O(\log n)$ steps, an improvement over the $O(n)$ generic algorithm. Because the same element can occur multiple times in a `multiset`, three other member functions used for locating elements are also provided. The function `lower_bound` returns the *first* occurrence of the argument value. The function `upper_bound` returns the first element *past* the given value. Both return the end-of-range iterator if the element is not present in the collection. The function `equal_range` returns a `pair`, containing both the values yielded by the lower- and upper-bound member functions. All three require only $O(\log n)$ operations.

As with all containers, the member functions `begin` and `end` return starting and ending iterator values. The member functions `rbegin` and `rend` return iterators that yield the values in reverse sequence, from largest to smallest, rather than the ascending order yielded by the normal iterator pair.

12.5.1   Generic Functions for Set Operations

An interesting feature of the `set` data type is that what we normally think of as set operations—set union, set intersection, set difference, and so forth—are not implemented directly as methods, but instead are provided by generic algorithms. By doing this, these algorithms can be used with any ordered collection, not just sets. The following summary describes how these functions can be used with the `set` and `multiset` container classes.

SUBSET TEST
The generic algorithm `includes` can be used to determine whether one set is a subset of another, that is, whether all elements from the first are contained in the second. In the case of multisets, the number of matching elements in the second set must exceed the number of elements in the first. The four arguments are a pair of iterators representing the (presum-

ably) smaller set, and a pair of iterators representing the (potentially) larger set.

```
if (includes(set_one.begin(), set_one.end(),
    set_two.begin(), set_two.end()))
        cout << "set is a subset" << endl;
```

The less than operator (operator <) will be used for the comparison of elements. Where this is inappropriate, an alternative version of the includes function is provided. This form takes a fifth argument, which is the comparison function used to order the elements in the two sets.

SET UNION OR INTERSECTION

The function set_union can be used to construct a union of two sets. The two sets are specified by iterator pairs, and the union is copied into an output iterator that is supplied as a fifth argument.

Note that the resulting values are copied into the output container, which must have sufficient room for the result. For example, the following combines two sets, and copies the result into a vector.

```
    // union two sets, copying result into a vector
    // declare the vector for the result values
vector<int> v_one (set_one.size() + set_two.size());

    // form union
set_union(set_one.begin(), set_one.end(),
    set_two.begin(), set_two.end(), v_one.begin());
```

Most of the time the size of the result set is not known in advance, and in any case it is more useful to store the values in another set. In this situation, an *insert iterator* is used to convert the iterator operations performed by the generic algorithms into insertions. (See the discussion of insert iterators in Section 9.2.1.)

Replacing one or the other set variables with the union of the two sets is one situation where the swap member function is applicable. First, a temporary set is constructed to hold the resulting union set. Then the values in this temporary are swapped with one or the other argument values. If the temporary is declared inside a compound statement, the temporary will be deleted at the end of the statement.

```
{       // form union in place
set<int> temp_set;      // create temporary
set_union (set_one.begin(), set_one.end(),
    set_two.begin(), set_two.end(),
    inserter(temp_set, temp_set.begin()));
    // exchange values with first set
set_one.swap (temp_set);   // temporary will now be deleted
}
```

The function set_intersection is similar, and forms the intersection

The function `lower_bound` finds the first occurrence of a given value, while the function `upper_bound` finds the first element larger than the argument value. Because the tree is maintained in order, to perform either of these it is only necessary to traverse a single path from root to leaf. Consider first the function `lower_bound`. If we compare a value to the root of a subtree and the root is smaller than the value, we know the first occurrence of the value, if it occurs at all, must be in the right subtree, because all values in the left subtree must be smaller than or equal to the root. Similarly, if the value we are seeking is less than the value held by the node, the first occurrence must be in the left subtree. Interestingly, however, if the value we are seeking is equal to the value held by the root node, it may nevertheless not be the *first* occurrence of this element, so we must still search the left subtree.

These ideas are captured in the following code. In the method in class node, we will pass around the ending iterator as a second argument, because instances of class node need not know how to construct this value. The creation of the ending iterator will be described in a later chapter.

```
template <class T> iterator set<T>::lower_bound (T & element)
     // find first occurrence of element in collection
{
     if (root == 0)
         return end();
     else
         return root->lower_bound(element, end());
}


template <class T> iterator node<T>::lower_bound
(T & element, iterator & end)
{
     if (value < element)
         if (rightChild != 0)
             return rightChild->lower_bound (element, end);
         else
             return end; // not found at all
     // check left child
     if (leftChild != 0) {
             // see if it is found along left child
         iterator result = leftChild->lower_bound (element, end);
         if (result != end) // found it, must be first
             return result;
     }
     // not found in left child, either we are it or not found at all
     if (element < value)
```

```
            return end; // not found at all
        else
            return setIterator(this); // make iterator that points to us
}
```

The code for `upper_bound` is almost the same. If the root value is less than the element being sought, then the upper bound, if it is found at all, must be in the right subtree. Otherwise, if there is a left subtree, we explore that. If not found there, then either the current node is the first larger node (if it satisfies the property) or there is no larger node.

```
template <class T> iterator node<T>::upper_bound
(T & element, iterator & end)
{
    if (value < element)
        if (rightChild != 0)
            return rightChild->upper_bound (element, end);
        else
            return end; // not found at all
    if (leftChild != 0) {
        iterator result = leftChild->upper_bound (element, end);
        if (result != end) return result;
        }
    if (element < value)
        return setIterator (this);
    return end;
}
```

Having defined the lower- and upper-bound procedures, the `count` method simply counts the number of values between these two. Note that although both `lower_bound` and `upper_bound` are $O(\log n)$, the count procedure could in principle be worse, because the number of matching elements could be as large as n.

```
template <class T> int set<T>::count (T & element)
    // count number of occurrences of element
{
    iterator first = lower_bound(element);
    iterator last = upper_bound(element);
    int counter = 0;
        // count number of elements between lower and upper
    while (first != last) {
        counter++;
        first++;
        }
    return counter;
}
```

To insert an element into a set, we first check to see if the value is already contained in the set. If so, then no insertion is performed. This step is omitted in the multiset implementation. Otherwise, to insert an element into a set we must first check to determine whether the set is empty. If so, then a new node is created. Only if the current collection is nonempty should the `insert` method in the root node be invoked. The `insert` method in class node takes as argument a new node, and not simply an element.

```
template <class T> void set<T>::insert (T & newElement)
    // insert a new element into a set
{
        // do not insert if already in set
    if (count(newElement) > 0)
        return;
        // create a new node
    node<T> * newNode = new node<T> (newElement, 0, 0, 0);
        // see if collection is empty
    if (root == 0)
        root = newNode;
    else
        root->insert (newNode);
}
```

The insertion routine for class node simply walks down the tree until the leaf position is found, then places the new node into location. Note that the procedure is the same whether or not the value is already present in the collection.

```
template <class T> void node<T>::insert (node<T> * newNode)
    // insert a new element into a binary search tree
{
    if (newElement < value)
        if (leftChild != 0)
            leftChild->insert (newNode);
        else {
            newNode->parent = this;
            leftChild = newNode;
            }
    else
        if (rightChild != 0)
            rightChild->insert (newNode);
        else {
```

```
                newNode->parent = this;
                rightChild = newNode;
            }
    }
```

Generalizing the insertion method slightly will simplify the implementation of the member function **erase**. A *merge* of two subtrees combines the trees into one structure. It is assumed that the two trees are originally children of a single node, so that every value in the left argument is smaller than or equal to every value in the right argument. Special cases occur if either the left or right subtree is empty, otherwise a recursive call merges the left subtree with the left child of the right-child node.

```
template <class T>
node<T> * node<T>::merge (node<T> * left, node<T> * right)
        // merge two subtrees into one
{
    if (left == 0)
        return right;
    if (right == 0)
        return left;
    node<T> * child = merge(left, right->leftChild);
    child->parent = right;
    right->leftChild = child;
    return right;
}
```

As with many data structures, removal of an item is more complicated than insertion. The task can be divided into two steps. The first step is to discover the node that needs to be deleted. Here the algorithm is very similar to addition and count, basically walking a path from root to leaf. The execution time for this step is again proportional to the length of the path from root to node. Once a node to be deleted is found, it must be removed. We cannot simply leave a hole in the data structure, so instead another node must be found to take the place of the eliminated value. The most important factor is to ensure the maintenance of the search tree property.

For example, suppose we wish to remove the value 5 from the following tree. Having found the node containing the value 5, the two choices for promotion to the new locations are the two children of node 5, which are nodes 4 and 7. The solution is to merge these two trees together, using the procedure we described earlier. In this manner, the left subtree will be pushed down the tree until it finds an appropriate insertion point. A recursive call on **remove** deletes any further values from the right subtree, prior to performing the merge.

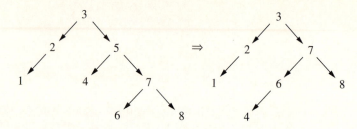

```
template <class T>
node<T> * set<T>::remove (node<T> * current, T & testElement)
    // remove all instances of testElement from collection
{
    if (current != 0) {
        node<T> * pa = current->parent;
        if (testElement < current->value)
            current->leftChild =
                remove (current->leftChild, testElement);
        else if (current->value < testElement)
            current->rightChild =
                remove (current->rightChild, testElement);
        else {    // found an item to remove
            node<T> * result = current->merge(current->leftChild,
                remove (current->rightChild, testElement));
            delete current;
            result->parent = pa;
                return result;
                }
        }
    return current;
}
```

12.6.1   Implementation of Generic Algorithms

The implementation of generic algorithms that provide the set operations
is similar to the algorithm merge that we have encountered already. As
with merge, a complicating factor is handling the situation when one of
the input sets becomes exhausted, and the remainder of the other set must
be processed.

```
template <IT1, IT2, IT3>
IT3 set_union (IT1 ele1, IT1 stop1, IT2 ele2, IT2 stop2, IT3 dest)
    // form the intersection of the two input sets, copy to destination
{
    while ((ele1 != stop1) || (ele2 != stop2)) {
```

```
                      // copy values from set 1 not in set 2
        if ((ele2 == stop2) || (*ele1 < *ele2))
            *dest++ = *ele1++;
                      // copy values from set 2 not in set 1
        else if ((ele1 == stop1) || (*ele2 < *ele1))
            *dest++ = *ele2++;
        else { // found two equal values, copy just one
            *dest++ = *ele1++;
            ele2++;
            }
        }
    return dest;
}
```

The code for set intersection is similar, but only copies values if they are found in both collections.

```
template <IT1, IT2, IT3>
IT3 set_intersection (IT1 ele1, IT1 stop1, IT2 ele2, IT2 stop2, IT3 dest)
        // form the union of the two input sets, copy to destination
{
    while ((ele1 != stop1) || (ele2 != stop2)) {
                // ignore values from set 1 not in set 2
        if ((ele2 == stop2) || (*ele1 < *ele2))
            *ele1++;
                // ignore values from set 2 not in set 1
```

Short Circuit Evaluation

The code for the set union, set intersection, and the other generic set operations depends in a critical fashion on the *short circuit* evaluation semantics for the logical *or* operator. This means that if the output of a logical expression can be determined solely by examining the left argument, then the right argument is completely ignored.

In this case, the left argument compares an iterator against the terminating value. Recall that it is illegal to dereference an end-of-range iterator. Thus, if the left argument expression is true, the right argument is illegal. But if the left argument *is* true, the short circuit semantics tell us that the right argument will simply be ignored.

If the left argument to the logical expression in the if statement *is* true, then to verify the legality of the conditional statement requires combining the test condition for the if statement with the test condition for the preceding while statement. If we assume that ele2 is equal to stop2, for example, then it must necessarily be true that ele1 is *not* equal to stop1, because otherwise the loop would have halted. It is therefore legal to dereference ele1, as is done by the conditional statement.

The reader should verify that for each of the statements using short circuit evaluation, if either the left argument *or* the right argument is true the associated statement is legal, and that the correct outcome is produced.

```
        else if ((ele1 == stop1) || (*ele2 < *ele1))
            *ele2++;
        else { // found two equal values, add to destination
            *dest++ = *ele1++;
            ele2++;
            }
        }
    return dest;
}
```

The code for the various forms of set difference are left as exercises.

12.7   CHAPTER SUMMARY

Key Concepts

- Set element operations: insertion, removal, test for inclusion
- Set collection operations: union, intersection, difference, subset
- Bit vector sets
- Multisets
- Binary search trees

There are two primary purposes for the set data type. The first is to provide a standard data structure for which all three of the operations of insertion, removal, and test for inclusion can be performed rapidly. This was not true for any of the data structures we have encountered previously.

The second use of the set data structure is the ability to perform operations that affect entire collections at one time. The basic set operations are union, intersection, difference, subset, and equality testing.

Values in sets are unique—inserting a value into a set more than once will have no effect. Sets are therefore a natural candidate data structure in any problem for which this uniqueness property is useful. For example, in any English language document the same words will occur many different times. By placing all the words in a document into a set, as we did with the spelling checker algorithm, we obtain a much shorter collection of words.

Because the elements of sets are maintained in sequence, the data structure is also useful in any problem for which order plays an important role. An obvious example is sorting, and in the next chapter we will see how sets can be used to create a sorting algorithm.

The class bitset is used to maintain a set of binary integer values.

The more general class set stores values, and can be used with any data type that can be ordered.

A multiset is a form of set in which values can occur more than one time.

Efficient execution time for set operations is assured through the use of a binary search tree as an underlying representation.

Further Reading

A good introduction to the use of sets in mathematics is provided by Ross and Wright [Ross 85]. Because sets form such an integral part of mathematics, it is somewhat surprising that sets are used relatively little in programming, at least in comparison to more basic types such as vectors, lists, and trees. The likely reason is that sets are almost by definition dynamic data structures, and the implementation of sets can be easily constructed out of lists, which are relatively common. One interesting computer language in which sets are a fundamental data type is the language SETL [Schwartz 86, Baxter 89].

Study Questions & Exercises

Study Questions

1. What are the basic operations performed by the set data abstraction?

2. What is a multiset (or bag), and how does it differ from a set?

3. What is the distinction between the set difference and the symmetric difference?

4. What data values are represented by a bit set?

5. What are the mask and location values produced by the bit set for index position 3? For 33? For 133?

6. There are four different sets of strings used in the spelling checking and correcting program. Describe the values held by each.

7. Why is it preferable to use the count member function with a set, rather than the generic algorithm we used with lists and vectors?

8. What is a binary search tree?

9. What do we mean when we say that the logical operators in C++ use short circuit evaluation?

Exercises

1. Describe the union, intersection, and differences for the following two sets:

    Set A : 1, 2, 5, 7, 12
    Set B : 1, 5, 12, 36, 52

2. The set data type can perform insertion, removal, and test for inclusion of an element in $O(\log n)$ steps, where n represents the number of elements in the set. Describe how these operations can be performed using a list and using a vector, and the asymptotic execution time for each.

3. Explain why it is not possible (or, at least, not easy) to generate a multiset version of a set that is implemented using bit vectors.

4. Prove that a set A is a subset of a set B if and only if the intersection of A and B is equal to A. Would this be a very good way to implement the subset test? Why or why not?

5. Prove that a set A is a subset of a set B if and only if the union of A and B is equal to B. Would this be a very good way to implement the subset test? Why or why not?

6. Provide an implementation of the member function bitset::to_string, which produces a string representation of a bit set.

7. Another heuristic for creating potential replacements for misspelled words is to either remove a single letter or insert a single letter. Implement functions similar to the transposition algorithm for each of these. For inserting a letter, simply try all twenty-six letters in turn in each potential location.

8. What values would need to be maintained by an iterator for the class bitset? Design and implement such a facility.

9. Write an implementation for the generic algorithm set_difference and for the generic algorithm set_symmetric_difference.

10. Starting with the binary search tree shown in Figure 12.2, show the tree that will result after each of the following insertions:
    a. Insert the value Abel.
    b. Then, insert the value Andrew.
    c. Then, insert the value Antonia.

11. Starting with the binary search tree shown in Figure 12.2, show the tree that will result after each of the following deletions:
    a. Delete the value Adela.
    b. Then, delete the value Angela.
    c. Then, delete the value Alex.

12. Sketch a proof of correctness for the member function node::insert. Verify that the binary

search tree property is preserved following the insertion.

13. Show that the routine `merge` would still preserve the binary search tree property if the recursive call were instead written as:

```
left->rightChild =
merge(left->rightChild, right);
```

14. Show the tree that would result from the deletion described in the book using the change proposed in the preceding question.

15. Sketch a proof of correctness for the member function `set::remove`. Verify that the binary search tree property is preserved following the deletion.

16. Using the Skew Heap data structure we will describe in Chapter 15, one can implement union very quickly (see the boxed text in Section 15.3). Explain why this would nevertheless not be a good data structure on which to base an implementation of sets. (Hint: Consider the asymptotic complexity of other operations.)

Chapter

13

Trees: A Nonlinear Data Structure

Chapter Overview

Previous chapters have been matched primarily with data structures found in the STL. This chapter diverts slightly from that pattern. Although binary trees underly the implementation of the `set` data structure in the standard library, the user of the library normally might not be aware of their presence. However, binary trees are a ubiquitous data structure in the solution of many problems in computer science. For this reason, an understanding of some of the basic properties of binary trees is an essential part of learning about basic data structures.

In this chapter we introduce many of these properties and illustrate the use of binary trees with several classic applications. Major topics include:

▲ Properties of trees
▲ Binary trees
▲ Operator precedence parsing
▲ Tree traversals

13.1   PROPERTIES OF TREES

In Chapter 12 we noted that the efficient execution time for operations on the set data type is made possible through the use of a binary tree as an underlying data structure. Trees, especially binary trees, are ubiquitous in computer algorithms. For this reason, it is important to understand a few basic properties of trees. Here we will present some of their more important characteristics.

Just as the intuitive concepts of a stack or a queue can be based on everyday experience with similar structures, the idea of a tree can be found frequently in everyday life also, and not just the arboreal variety. For example, sports events are often organized using trees, with each node representing a pairing of contestants, the winner of each pairing advancing to the next level. The winner of the last pairing is declared the winner of the tournament.

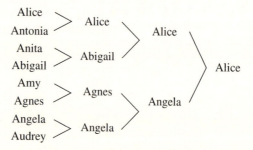

Similarly, information about ancestors and descendants is often organized into a tree structure. A typical family tree is shown in Figure 13.1. An arrow emanating from a node indicates that the individuals represented by the targets of the arrows are children of the individual described by the source node. For example, Persephone is a daughter of Demeter, and Zeus and Poseidon are both children of Cronus. As you will see, much of the terminology used in computer science to discuss trees is derived from such usage. For example, "child nodes" correspond to children in the family tree.

In a sense, the inverse of a family tree is an ancestor tree. While a family tree traces the descendants from a single individual, an ancestor tree records the ancestors of an individual. An example ancestor tree is shown in Figure 13.2. We could infer from this tree, for example, that Iphigenia is the child of Clytemnestra and Agamemnon, and Clytemnestra is in turn the child of Leda and Tyndareus. Shortly, we will have more to say about the characteristics of trees typified by these two forms.

After vectors and lists, trees are perhaps the data structure most frequently encountered in computer algorithms. Algorithms on trees illustrate many of the most important concepts in data structures and the

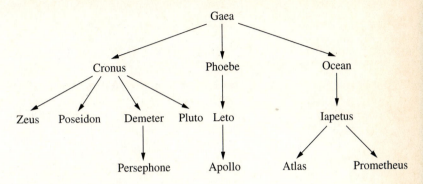

Figure 13.1   A typical family tree

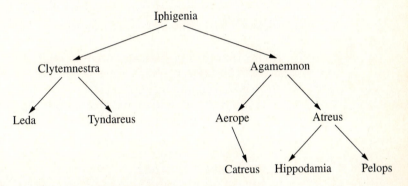

Figure 13.2   A typical ancestor tree

analysis of algorithms. For example, a tree is a natural representation for information that is organized in a hierarchical fashion. The table of contents of this book provides a good example of a hierarchical structure.

The general characteristics of trees can be illustrated using Figure 13.1. A tree consists of a collection of *nodes*, connected by directed arcs. A tree is headed by a single *root* which, in contradiction to nature, appears at the top of the structure.[1] A node that points to other nodes is said to be the *parent* of the nodes pointed to, which in turn are referred to as the *children* of the first node. Continuing the familial metaphor, the term *descendants* is used to describe the children of a node, and the children of those nodes, and their children, and so on. A characterization of the root node is, therefore, that the root is the single node in the structure that does not possess a parent, and from which all other nodes are descended. At the other end,

---

1. Donald Knuth claims that the convention of writing the root of the tree at the top stems from handwritten drawings, in which naturally it is easier to begin with the fixed root and proceed down the page.

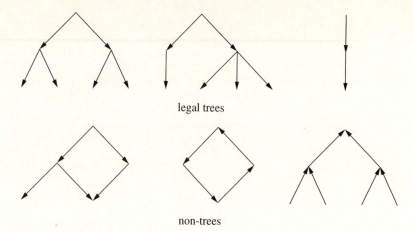

legal trees

non-trees

Figure 13.3 Various trees and non-trees

nodes that do not have children are called *leaf nodes*. A node that does possess children is often called an *interior node*. Information is associated with both leaf and interior nodes.

An important characteristic of trees is that there is a single unique path along arcs from the root to any particular node; that is, arcs do not join together. Figure 13.3 illustrates various trees, and various non-trees. The largest number of arcs traversed in moving from root to any leaf is known as the *height* of the tree.

Note that in a valid tree any node can be considered a root of the tree formed by considering only the descendants of the node (see Figure 13.4). We call this second tree the *subtree* rooted at the node. This recursive nature of trees leads naturally to an alternative, recursive, characterization of trees.

▲ A node with no children is a tree. Such a node is called a leaf. A leaf node has height zero.

▲ A node with a nonempty collection of trees is a tree. The trees in the collection are known as the children of the node. The tree so constructed is in turn called the parent to the children trees. A tree with a non-empty set of children is called an interior node. The height of an interior node is one greater than the maximum height of any child.

▲ There is a single node with no parent, called the root of the tree.

Trees appear in computer science in a surprising large number of different varieties and forms. A common example is the *parse tree*. Computer languages, including C++, are defined, in part, using a *grammar*. Grammars provide rules that explain how the tokens in the language can be put together. A portion of the grammar for C++ could be given as:

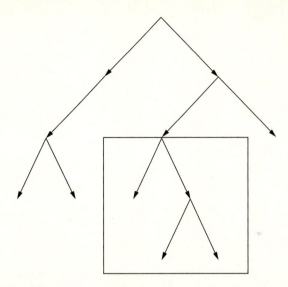

Figure 13.4   A subtree is also a tree

$$< statement > \ ::= \ < select\text{-}statement > \ | \ < expr >$$
$$< select\text{-}statement > \ ::= \ \texttt{if}(< expr >) < statement > \ \texttt{else} \ < statement >$$
$$< expr > \ ::= \ < relational\text{-}expr > \ | \ < assign\text{-}expr > \ |\texttt{identifier}$$
$$< relational\text{-}expr > \ ::= \ < expr > \ < \ < expr >$$
$$< assign\text{-}expr > \ ::= \ < expr > \ = \ < expr >$$

A C++ statement, such as:

```
if (a < b) max = b else max = a
```

is analyzed by constructing a tree (see Figure 13.5). Leaf nodes represent the tokens, or symbols, used in the statement. Interior nodes represent syntactic categories. A major task of a compiler is to construct a parse tree for an input program, then to associate information, such as types, with every node in the tree. As a last step in the compilation process, code is produced for the program by traversing the tree, that is, visiting each node in the tree in sequence. At each node encountered during this traversal, code is generated that will, when executed, perform the operation being described.

A slightly different form of a tree is an *expression tree*. As the name suggests, an expression tree (sometimes called an *abstract syntax tree*) is used to describe expressions. The two-dimensional nature of the tree eliminates the need for features such as parentheses or precedence. An expression tree for $A + (B + C) * D$ is shown in Figure 13.6.

Given our characterization of trees, there is an obvious implementation in which a tree is defined as a recursive structure, or tree node. Each tree node maintains some information and a list of pointers to children tree

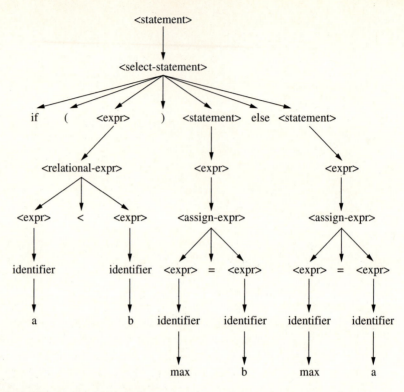

Figure 13.5 A typical parse tree

nodes (which follow). It turns out, however, that almost all trees used in computer algorithms are of a specialized form, called a binary tree, and for this form we can develop much more efficient algorithms.

```
template <class T> class treeNode {
public:
        .
        .
        .
protected:
        // data fields
        T value;
        list<treeNode *> children;
};
```

13.2   BINARY TREES

The defining characteristics of a binary tree can be illustrated by comparing the trees shown in Figures 13.1 and 13.2. An important characteristic of the tree shown in Figure 13.2 is that no node has more than two children.

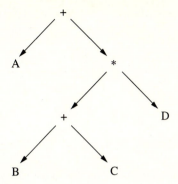

Figure 13.6 A typical expression tree

Furthermore, we have ordered the nodes; the mother is always represented by the left-child arc, and the father by the right-child arc. Because no individual can have more than two parents,[2] every node can be thought of as possessing exactly two child fields. In some situations the field may be empty, indicating, in this example, that the information is not known. A node can have only one subtree (indicating that only one of the parents is known), but it must be made clear whether the subtree represents a left or right child. For example, the information that Catreus is the father of Aerope is conveyed by the node Catreus as the right subtree of the node Aerope, and not the left subtree. A tree with these characteristics is known as a *binary tree*. The importance of binary trees stems from their frequency; they occur often in algorithms, and from the fact that they can be efficiently manipulated.

The most important properties of trees, and in particular binary trees, are related to the ratio of the number of nodes to the height of the tree. Thus, we first investigate this value.

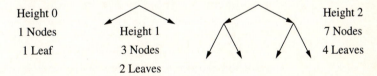

A binary tree with height zero can hold one node, which must be a leaf. The largest possible binary tree with height 1 holds 3 nodes, 2 of which are leaves. A complete binary tree of height 2 holds 7 nodes, including 4 leaves. It is not difficult to see that at each new level, the number of leaves will be twice the number of leaves of the preceding level.

---

2. At least prior to the advent of modern surrogate techniques.

Figure 13.7 A thin and unbalanced tree

Theorem 13.1   A complete binary tree of height n will have 2^n leaves.

The proof is by induction. The base cases for zero, one and two can be proven by inspection. Assume a tree of height n has 2^n leaves. To form a complete tree of height $n+1$, we create a new root with subtrees of height n. The number of leaf nodes is thus 2×2^n, or 2^{n+1}.

Theorem 13.2   The number of nodes in a complete binary tree of height n is $2^{n+1} - 1$.

This theorem is validated by noting that the number of nodes in a full binary tree is $1 + 2 + \ldots + 2^n$. That this sum is $2^{n+1} - 1$ can be easily verified by induction. An alternative illustration of this fact should also be obvious to computer scientists. The binary representation of 2^n is a 1 followed by n zeros. Thus, 2^5 is represented in binary as 100000. The sum $1 + 2 + \ldots 2^n$ is therefore represented in binary as a sequence of n one bits. Adding one additional value will force a carry in each position, yielding as a result a one followed by $n + 1$ zeros, or 2^{n+1}.

We have been careful in the preceding discussion to describe the trees as "full" binary trees. Without this property the results do not hold. Consider a tree with four nodes, all linked down the right-child arc (see Figure 13.7). The tree has height three, yet only four nodes, instead of the 15 nodes predicted by the theorem. The reason is obvious: The tree is "thin" because most of the nodes have only one child. Most of the algorithms associated with trees possess a running time proportional to the height of the tree. Thus, attaining good performance will require ensuring that long thin trees do not occur. One approach is to require trees to maintain a certain form. A common requirement is that every node have exactly two children, except on the bottommost two levels. A binary tree that is completely filled, with the possible exception of the bottom level that is filled from left to right, is known as a *complete binary tree*. Figure 13.8 gives an example of such a tree.

It can be seen that a complete binary tree of height h has between 2^h and $2^{h+1} - 1$ nodes. Inverting this shows that a complete binary tree containing n nodes must have a height greater than or equal to $\lfloor \log n \rfloor$, and less than $\lceil \log n \rceil$. From this we see that the longest path from root to leaf in a complete binary tree is $O(\log n)$.

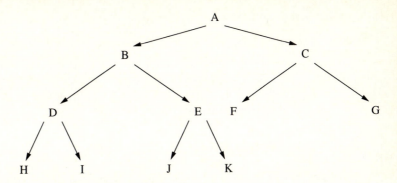

Figure 13.8   A complete binary tree

Figure 13.9   A height-balanced binary tree

Complete binary trees provide the maximal number of leaves with the minimal path length. This observation is behind a pair of theorems we will use to obtain lower-bound values in later chapters.

Theorem 13.3   A binary tree containing n nodes must have at least one path from root to leaf of length $\lfloor \log n \rfloor$.

Theorem 13.4   In a complete binary tree containing n nodes, the longest path from root to leaf traverses no more than $\lceil \log n \rceil$ nodes.

Another type of tree that we will study in Chapter 14 uses a slightly different structural property in order to guarantee that trees do not get too far out of balance. A *height-balanced* binary tree has the property that for each node the *difference* in heights of the right and left child is no larger than one. This property assures that locally, at each node, the balance is roughly maintained, although globally over the entire tree differences in path lengths can be somewhat larger. Figure 13.9 shows an example of a height-balanced binary tree.

Clearly, a complete binary tree is also height-balanced. Thus, the *largest* number of nodes in a balanced binary tree of height n is $2^{n+1} - 1$. An interesting question is to discover the *smallest* number of nodes in a height-balanced binary tree. For height zero there is clearly only one tree. For height 1 there are three trees:

The smallest of these has 2 nodes. In general, for a tree of height n, the smallest number of nodes is found by connecting the smallest tree of height $n - 1$ and $n - 2$.

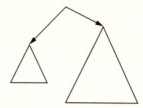

If we let M_n represent the function yielding the minimum number of nodes for a height balanced tree of height n, we obtain the following equations:

$$M_0 = 1$$
$$M_1 = 2$$
$$M_{n+1} = M_{n-1} + M_n + 1$$

These equations are very similar to the famous *Fibonacci numbers* defined by the formula $f_0 = 0, f_1 = 1, f_{n+1} = f_{n-1} + f_n$. Each value M_n is one larger than the corresponding Fibonacci number. It is easy to show using induction that we can bound the Fibonacci numbers by 2^n. In fact, it is possible to establish an even tighter bounding value. Although the details need not concern us here, the Fibonacci numbers have a closed form solution, that is, a solution defined without using recursion (see Exercise 7). Using this information, we can show that the function M also has an approximate closed form solution:

$$M_n \approx \frac{1}{\sqrt{5}} \left[\frac{1 + \sqrt{5}}{2} \right]^n + 1$$

By taking the logarithm of both sides and discarding all but the most significant terms, we obtain the result that $n \approx 1.44 \log M_n$. This tells us that the longest path in a height-balanced binary tree with n nodes is at worst only 44 percent larger than the $\log n$ minimum length. Hence algorithms on height-balanced binary trees that run in time proportional to the length of the path are still $O(\log n)$.

We have only touched the surface in describing the known properties of binary trees. Many other interesting characteristics are described in the literature. However, these few properties will be sufficient for our purposes for the remainder of the book.

13.2.1   Vector Implementation

Because a complete binary tree possesses such a regular structure, the data values can easily be maintained in a vector. Just as the vector implementations of stack and queues were more efficient than the linked list versions, because they avoided the necessity of dynamic memory allocation, so too is the vector implementation of a tree very efficient.

To represent a tree in a vector, we will store the root of the tree in position 0. The children of the node stored at position i will be stored in position $2 \times i + 1$ and $2 \times i + 2$. In this manner, the complete binary tree shown in Figure 13.8 would be stored as follows:

0	1	2	3	4	5	6	7	8	9	10
A	B	C	D	E	F	G	H	I	J	K

Accessing the parents is easy. The parents of the node stored at position i will be found at position $(i - 1)/2$. Thus, as the storage for pointers is not required in this representation, the operations used to move up and down the tree are simple arithmetic operations that can be performed very rapidly. We will use the vector representation of complete binary trees when we discuss the *heap* data structure in Chapter 15.

The difficulty with this representation, of course, is the requirement that the trees be complete. Representing the thin unbalanced tree in Figure 13.7 would require a vector of 15 elements, the same as for the complete binary tree of height 3. Yet most of these would be "unused." Some indication would need to be maintained in order to know which elements in the vector are valid, and which represent "holes." Such a scheme is occasionally encountered. But in most cases where the complete binary tree structural property cannot be easily maintained, the more general dynamic memory implementation described in the next section will be used to implement operations on trees.

0	1	2	3	4	5	6	7	8	9	10	11	12	13	14
A	ε	B	ε	ε	ε	C	ε	ε	ε	ε	ε	ε	ε	D

13.2.2   Dynamic Memory Implementation

The obvious representation for a node in a binary tree is a structure containing a value field, pointers to right and left children, and a pointer to the parent node. Such a class description was presented in Chapter 12 (see Figure 12.4). Here we will describe the implementation of some of the features of this class that were not described in the previous chapter.

The copy method is used to duplicate an entire tree rooted at a given node. The argument is the parent node for the newly created copy. The procedure first recursively duplicates the child subtrees, then creates a new root node. Note that this operation does not change the original tree, and that the parent for the new node is passed as an argument.

```
template <class T> node<T> * node<T>::copy(node<T> * newparent)
    // return copy of tree rooted at node
{
        // duplicate node, copy children
    node<T> * newnode = new node<T> (value, newparent, 0, 0);
    if (leftChild)
        newnode->leftChild = leftChild->copy(newnode);
    if (rightChild)
        newnode->rightChild = rightChild->copy(newnode);
    return newnode;
}
```

The `release` method frees the memory associated with the children of a node. The `copy` and `release` methods will be used in subsequent chapters to build new data structures that make use of binary trees.

```
template <class T> void node<T>::release()
{   // release memory associated with children
    if (leftChild) {
        // release left child
        leftChild->release();
        delete leftChild;
        leftChild = 0;
        }
    if (rightChild) {
        // release right child
        rightChild->release();
        delete rightChild;
        rightChild = 0;
        }
}
```

13.2.3   Application: "Guess the Animal" Game

We will illustrate the use of binary trees with a program that plays a simple interactive game, called "Guess the Animal." The player thinks of an animal. The computer then poses a number of questions, attempting to discover the animal the player has in mind. An example session might look like this:

```
Does it live in water?
no
Does it bark?
```

```
no
I know.  Is it a cat?
yes
I won!
Try again?
```

The database of animal facts is stored in a binary tree of strings. Interior nodes represent questions, and leaf nodes represent answers (animals). Initially, the game database has very little information. In our game, we start with simply one answer, namely the animal "cat." When the computer fails to match the animal the player has in mind, it "learns" by asking for the name of the user's animal, and for a distinguishing question to differentiate the animal from some known animal. An example session might look like this:

```
Does it live in water?
yes
I know.  Is it a fish?
no
What is the animal you had in mind?
a duck
What is a yes/no question that I can use to tell a fish from a duck?
Does it have webbed feet?
For a duck is the answer yes or no?
yes
Try again?
```

The main program stores the database of animal facts in the tree held by the variable root, although this is used only during reinitialization of the game. The current node is referred to by the variable current, which travels down the tree asking questions.

```
void animalGame() {
    // initialize the database with one animal
    node<string> * root  = new node<string> ("cat", 0, 0, 0);
    node<string> * current = root;
    // now start the game
    cout << "let's play guess the animal.\n";
    while (current != 0) {
        // if current node has children it is a question
        if (current->leftChild != 0) {
            cout << current->value << '\n';
            if (answer())
                current = current->leftChild;
            else
                current = current->rightChild;
        }
```

```
        // if no children it is an answer
        else {
            cout << "I know.  Is it a " << current->value << " ?\n";
            if (answer())
                cout << "I won.\n";
            else {
                // we didn't get it.
                // time to learn something
                learnNewAnimal(current);
            }
            cout << "Try again?\n";
            if (answer())
                current = root;
            else
                return;
        }
    }
}
```

The majority of questions are designed to have simple yes/no answers. The decoding of the user responses is performed by the routine named answer, as follows:

```
bool answer() {
    // get yes/no answer
    while (1) {
        string ans;
        getline(cin, ans);
        if ((ans[0] == 'y') || (ans[0] == 'Y'))
            return true;
        else if ((ans[0] == 'n') || (ans[0] == 'N'))
            return false;
        cout << "please answer yes or no.\n";
    }
}
```

The only other procedure is the code used to learn about a new animal when the computer makes a wrong guess. This is performed by the procedure learnNewAnimal. The procedure asks for the name of the new animal and the distinguishing question. The current node, which must be a leaf node, is then changed into a question node, and the two animals are installed as child nodes.

```
void learnNewAnimal(node<string> * current)
{   // learn about a new animal type

    string currentAnimal = current->value;
```

```
cout << "what is your animal?\n";
string newAnimal;
getline(cin, newAnimal);
cout << "What is a yes/no question that I can use to tell a "
    << current->value << " from a " << newAnimal << " ?\n";
string newQuestion;
node<string> * node1 = new node<string>(newAnimal, current, 0, 0);
node<string> * node2 = new node<string>(currentAnimal, current, 0, 0);
// make sure allocation worked
assert ((node1 != 0) && (node2 != 0));

getline(cin, newQuestion);
cout << "For a " << newAnimal << " is the answer yes or no?\n";
if (answer() != 0) {
    current->leftChild = node1;
    current->rightChild = node2;
    }
else {
    current->leftChild = node2;
    current->rightChild = node1;
    }
current->value = newQuestion;
}
```

13.3 OPERATOR PRECEDENCE PARSING*

In Section 10.3.2, we described an algorithm to convert an infix string into a postfix polish representation. The basic technique employed by that algorithm, called *operator precedence parsing*, can be used, as well, to convert a string representation of an expression into an expression tree. In this section we will describe the details of this transformation.

The first step is to describe the representation for the expression tree. As before, we will simplify the task somewhat by dealing only with binary operators. In addition, we will also assume the only operands are one-character identifier names. (The exercises explore the removal of some of these simplifying assumptions.) We will represent nodes in the expression tree with a class named expressionInformation, represented as:

```
enum operators {identifier, leftparen, plus, minus, times, divide};

class expressionInformation {
public:
    // data areas, type, other information
    operators type;
    string name;
```

```
    // constructors
    expressionInformation(char n) : type(identifier), name(n) { }
    expressionInformation(operators op) : type(op) { }
};
```

The global type `operators` describes the set of tokens in our language. Instances of `expressionInformation` hold an operator type. If the node represents an identifier, the name of the identifier will be stored in a string. The name field is otherwise unused.

The infix to postfix conversion routine required a single stack, which held pending operators that had not yet been processed. The expression parsing algorithm will use a *pair* of stacks. The first is the operand stack, similar to the earlier algorithm. The second stack contains expressions trees, representing expressions that have *already* been processed.

We will illustrate the operation of this algorithm by working through the recognition of the expression a * b + c * d. The various steps involved in the creation of the expression tree are shown in Figure 13.10.

Operators are always immediately made into nodes and pushed on to the operator stack. This is shown in the first step in Figure 13.10. As in the earlier infix to postfix algorithm, the multiplication operand is immediately pushed on the operator stack. By the time the addition operator is read, two values have been pushed on to the operand stack. Because the addition operator has lower precedence than the multiplication operator already on the operator stack, the multiplication operator is popped from the stack. In this algorithm, unlike in the infix to postfix conversion algorithm, when a binary operator is popped from the operator stack, the two arguments for the operator are also popped from the operand stack. A new tree is formed by creating a new node for the binary operator and using the two popped operands as the left and right child.

Execution proceeds following this pattern. When the end of input is encountered, the operator stack contains two values, and the operand stack contains three. As in the earlier algorithm, the final step is to simply empty the operator stack by repeatedly popping and processing operators. When the stack is empty there will be one remaining value in the operand stack, which is the desired expression tree.

The following procedure implements the popping of a binary operator from the operator stack. The two operands are popped from the operand stack, a new node is created, and the new expression is pushed back on to the operand stack.

```
void doBinary(operators theOp,
        stack < node<expressionInformation> *> & operandStack)
{       // build a binary operator node by combining child nodes
        // pop the argument expressions
    node<expressionInformation> * right = operandStack.top();
    operandStack.pop();
    node<expressionInformation> * left = operandStack.top();
```

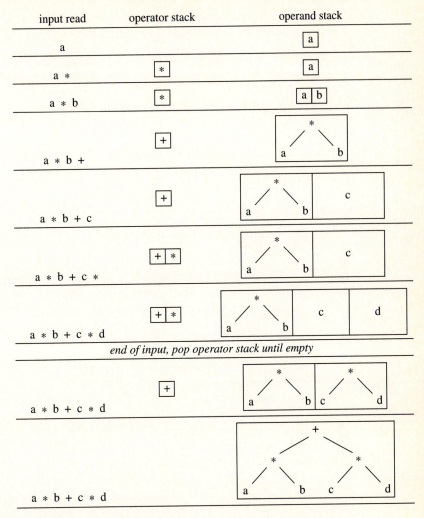

Figure 13.10 Execution of operator precedence parsing algorithm

```
operandStack.pop();
// build the new binary operator node
node<expressionInformation> * newNode =
    new node<expressionInformation>(theOp, 0, left, right);
assert(newNode != 0);
// push new expression back on stack
operandStack.push(newNode);
}
```

As in the earlier algorithm, a function named `processOp` is used to compare a newly encountered operator to the existing binary operators on the operator stack. Operators on the stack are popped and processed as long as they have higher priority than the argument operator.

```
void processOp(operators theOp, stack <operators> & operatorStack,
            stack <node<expressionInformation> *> & operandStack)
{
    // pop stack while operators have higher precedence
    while ((! operatorStack.isEmpty()) && (theOp < operatorStack.top()))
        {
        doBinary(operatorStack.top(), operandStack);
        operatorStack.pop();
        }

    // then push operator
    operatorStack.push(theOp);
}
```

The following procedure is the main program for the parsing process. The structure of the program is similar to the structure of the infix to postfix conversion routine (see Figure 10.2).

```
node<expressionInformation> * parse(string & inputString)
{
    // stacks for both operators and operands
    stack <operators> operatorStack;
    stack <node<expressionInformation> *> operandStack;

    int i = 0;
    while (inputString[i] != '\0')
        if (isAlphabetic(inputString[i])) {
            // create an operand node for an identifier
            node<expressionInformation> * newNode =
            new node<expressionInformation>
                (expressionInformation(inputString[i++]));
        assert(newNode != 0);
        operandStack.push(newNode);
        }
    else
        switch(inputString[i++]) {
            case '(':
                operatorStack.push(leftparen);
                break;
            case ')':
                while (operatorStack.top() != leftparen) {
                    doBinary(operatorStack.top(), operandStack);
                    operatorStack.pop();
```

```
                    }
                    // pop the right parenthesis
                    operandStack.pop();
                    break;
                case '+':
                    processOp(plus, operatorStack, operandStack);
                    break;
                case '-':
                    processOp(minus, operatorStack, operandStack);
                    break;
                case '*':
                    processOp(times, operatorStack, operandStack);
                    break;
                case '/':
                    processOp(divide, operatorStack, operandStack);
                    break;
            }

        // pop all operators remaining on the stack
        while (! operatorStack.isEmpty())  {
            doBinary(operatorStack.top(), operandStack);
            operatorStack.pop();
        }
        // return the final expression
        return operandStack.pop();
    }
```

13.4   TREE TRAVERSALS

Just as it is often necessary to examine each node of a linked list in sequence, it is frequently necessary to examine every node in a binary tree. But while a list has an obvious linear ordering, no single ordering is the obvious "correct" way to iterate over the elements of a tree. If we consider each of the n nodes of a binary tree as independent, then there are $n!$ different orderings, or sequences in which one could visit every node. ($n!$ is n factorial, or $n \times (n-1) \times \ldots \times 1$). Of course, most of these sequences have little regularity, and are thus of dubious use in practice. Generally, traversal algorithms are defined recursively out of three steps:

1. Process a node.
2. Recursively visit and process the left-child subtree.
3. Recursively visit and process the right-child subtree.

But even within this framework, there are six possible ways to arrange these tasks:

1. Process value, then left-child subtree, then right-child subtree.
2. Process left-child subtree, then value, then right-child subtree.
3. Process left-child subtree, then right-child subtree, then value.
4. Process value, then right-child subtree, then left-child subtree.
5. Process right-child subtree, then value, then left-child subtree.
6. Process right-child subtree, then left-child subtree, then value.

In almost all cases of interest, the subtrees are analyzed left to right. Thus, the six possibilities are reduced to the first three. These three are given names. Visiting the node first, followed by the left child and then the right child is called *preorder traversal*. Visiting the left child first, followed by processing the node, followed by visiting the right child is called *inorder traversal*. Finally, visiting the left child first, then the right child, and lastly processing the node is known as *postorder traversal*.

Just as the "post" in postfix polish notation implied that we viewed the arguments before encountering the operator in an arithmetic expression, here the "post" means that we will process the child nodes prior to processing the parent. In fact, a simple relationship exists between these tree traversals and pre- and postfix polish notation. Consider a tree traversal of the expression tree shown in Figure 13.6, printing out the value of each node when it is processed. A prefix traversal will result in the following output:

$$+ \ a^* + b \ \ c \ \ d$$

This is simply the prefix polish form of the tree, where operators are written first, followed by their operands. An inorder traversal results in the following:

$$a + b + c^* d$$

This is the infix form of the expression, minus parenthesis (see Exercise 11). A postfix traversal, as you might expect, produces the postfix polish expression:

$$a \ \ b \ \ c + d^* +$$

The translation of these into recursive functions that operate on instances of class node is relatively simple, as illustrated by the following:

```
// preorder processing of tree rooted at current
void preorder(node<T> * current)
{      // visit node, left child, right child
    if (current) {
        process(current->value); // process current
        // then visit children
        preorder(current->left());
        preorder(current->right());
```

```
            }
    }


    // inorder processing of tree rooted at current
    void inorder(node<T> * current)
    {       // visit left child, node, right child
        if (current) {
            inorder(current->left());
            process(current->value); // process current
            inorder(current->right());
            }
    }


    // postorder processing of tree rooted at current
    void postorder(node<T> * current)
    {       // visit left child, right child, node
        if (current) {
            postorder(current->left());
            postorder(current->right());
            process(current->value); // process current
            }
    }
```

Outside of the recursive calls, each function is performing only a constant amount of work at every node. Thus, iterating over all n elements in a tree can be performed in $O(n)$ steps, regardless of the order used.

Unfortunately, these functions suffer from the same problems that motivated the development of iterators in Chapter 6. The functions must be rewritten for each task to be performed. Furthermore, the writing of these methods exposes the internal representation details of the structure. To avoid this, we define a family of iterator classes for traversing trees. By means of these, a normal iterator loop can be used to access each element of the tree.

The iterators we will define will all have a similar structure, as shown in Figure 13.11. Each iterator value will maintain a pointer to the current node. Dereferencing an iterator will yield the value of the current node. Assigning an iterator the value of another iterator will copy the data field. Testing an iterator against another iterator is performed by testing the values of their current pointers. If the two pointers are referencing the same node, then the iterators are equal.

As we have seen in previous iterator implementations, a complicating factor is the need to support both prefix and postfix increment operators. The prefix form is the more basic, and simply changes and returns the current iterator value. The postfix form also changes the current iterator, but must return the previous iterator value prior to the increment. This is

```
template <class T>
class inorderTreeTraversal {
public:
    typedef inorderTreeTraversal<T> iterator;

        // constructor
    inorderTreeTraversal (node<T> * s);
    inorderTreeTraversal (iterator & itr)
        : current (itr.current) { }

        // iterator protocol
    iterator & operator ++();
    iterator operator ++(int);
    T & operator * ()
        { return current->value; }
    void operator = (iterator & itr)
        { current = itr.current; }
    bool operator == (iterator & rhs)
        { return current == rhs.current; }

protected:
    node<T> * current;
};


template <class T>
inorderTreeTraveral<T> inorderTreeTraversal<T>::operator ++ (int)
{
        // clone ourselves using the copy constructor
    inorderTreeTraversal<T> clone (*this);
    operator ++ ();  // increment ourselves
    return clone;    // return copy
}
```

Figure 13.11 Structure of iterator class

generally accomplished by cloning the current iterator, then incrementing the current iterator, then returning the clone. Iterators will differ in the additional data fields they maintain, and in the implementation of the increment operator.

13.4.1 Postorder Tree Traversal Iterator

The first traversal algorithm we examine is the postorder traversal. The postorder traversal examines the left child first, then the right child, and finally processes a node. The following illustration numbers the nodes in the order they would be processed by a postorder traversal.

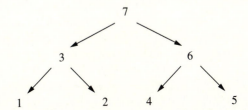

The first node to return in this traversal is the leftmost descendant of the root. The constructor assigns the value to the data field `current`, locating the leftmost descendant using a while loop that we will see again in several iterators. We call the action performed by this loop a *left slide*.

```
template <class T>
postorderTreeTraversal<T>::postorderTreeTraversal (node<T> * root)
        // initialize postorder tree traversal iterator
{
        // start at root
    current = root;
        // slide left to find leftmost descendant
    while (current && current->leftChild)
        current = current->leftChild;
}
```

The next node to process is always either the parent node for the current node or a right child of the parent. However, when we access the parent, we need to assure that we are not already the right child of the parent. So the `if` statement in the increment operator is really checking three conditions:

1. Is there a parent node? If there is no parent node, we are finished.

2. If there is a parent node, was the current node the right child? If so, then the next node to be processed should be the parent node.

3. Finally, if there is a parent node, and the current node was the left child of the parent node, *and* there is a right child for the parent node, then the next node will be found down the right-child subtree. We first move to the right child, then find the leftmost descendant of this child.

```
template <class T>
postorderTreeTraversal<T> & postorderTreeTraversal<T>::operator ++ ()
      // iterator increment for postorder traversal
{
      node<T> * child = current;
      current = current->parent;
      if (current && current->rightChild && current->rightChild != child) {
          current = current->rightChild; // move to right child
          while (current->leftChild) // perform left slide
              current = current->leftChild;
      }
      return *this;  // return ourself
}
```

We would like to claim that a complete iterator traversal of a binary tree with n nodes could be performed in $O(n)$ steps. One way to assure this would be if the increment operation required only a constant number of steps. However, clearly this is not so. The while loop performing the left slide in the increment (as well as in the constructor) can, in the worst case, traverse a complete path from root to leaf, potentially requiring $O(\log n)$ steps. It would seem, therefore, that the best bound we could make for n invocations of the increment operator would be $O(n \log n)$.

However, this worst case behavior for the increment operator does not occur in every case; in fact, it does not occur in most cases. A more careful accounting of how time is spent in traversing a tree will suffice to show that, while we cannot bound the time for each iteration operation, the total time for a tree traversal is still satisfactory.

To see how this could be so, first note that every node is eventually selected as the current node, and no node is selected more than once. If every node is "assigned" a constant amount of time, then the total time to perform a complete iteration must be no larger than n times this constant, or $O(n)$. This is true even if some nodes "borrow" time from other nodes, as long as the records are kept even.

We next argue that no node is ever passed over more than once in a left slide. The left slide is used simply to find the leftmost descendant of a node, and, once found, the next sequence of iterations will slowly move back up a tree.

The secret then is for the increment operation that is performing a left slide to "borrow" the time from those nodes over which it is sliding. The nodes passed over will never themselves perform a left slide, and so must always produce their result in constant time.

An argument of this sort, that bounds a sequence of events without bounding the time for any single event, is called an *amortized analysis*.

13.4.2 Preorder Tree Traversal Iterator

A preorder traversal visits the current node first, then visits nodes associated with the left child, and finally visits nodes associated with the right child. The following figure indicates the sequence in which nodes would be visited using a preorder traversal.

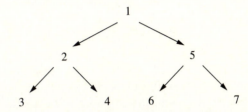

The preorder tree traversal starts at the root of the tree, so the constructor simply sets the current node to the argument value.

```
template <class T>
preorderTreeTraversal<T>::preorderTreeTraversal (node<T> * root)
    // initialize iterator
{
    current = root;
}
```

The increment operation divides into several cases. If there is a left child for the current node, the left child becomes the current node. Otherwise, if there is a right child, the right child becomes the current node. If there is neither a left nor right child, we must move back up the tree. We move backwards until we find a node with a right child that we have not yet processed. This involves checking whether the current node is a left or right child of its parent, as well as checking whether the parent has a right-child field. As long as the current node was a right child, *or the right-child field is empty*, we move upwards.

```
template <class T>
preorderTreeTraversal<T> & preorderTreeTraversal<T>::operator ++ ()
{
    if (current->leftChild)
        current = current->leftChild;
    else if (current->rightChild)
        current = current->rightChild;
    else {
        node<T> * child = current;
        current = current->parent;
```

```
    while (current &&
      ((current->rightChild == child)||(current->rightChild == 0)))
      {
      child = current;
      current = current->parent;
      }
    if (current && current->rightChild)
      current = current->rightChild;
    }
  return *this; // return ourself
}
```

An amortized analysis similar to that presented for postorder traversal shows that the total execution time of an iteration is $O(n)$, despite the fact that we cannot bound the time for any individual increment step.

13.4.3   Inorder Tree Traversal Iterator

An inorder traversal visits the left child first, then visits the current node, and finally visits the right child. The following diagram illustrates the order in which nodes would be processed using an inorder traversal.

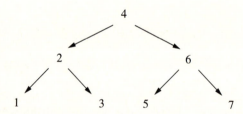

To initialize the traversal, the current node is placed at the leftmost child of the root. The time required to perform this step is proportional to the length of the associated path, but we will argue that over time this cost can be ignored.

```
inorderTreeTraversal<T>::inorderTreeTraversal (node<T> * root)
    // initialize inorder traversal
{
    current = root;
        // perform a left slide
    while (current && current->leftChild)
        current = current->leftChild;
}
```

The algorithm to move to the next location divides into one of two cases. If there is a right child to the current node, then the right tree has not been processed. We move down the right branch, and slide along until we encounter the leftmost child of the right branch. If there is no right child, then we must move back up the tree. The parent pointer makes locating the parent field trivial, but we must determine whether the parent should be processed. If the current node is the left child of the parent, then the answer is yes. If, on the other hand, the current node is the right child of the parent, then the parent has already been processed, and we need to continue moving up the tree.

```
inorderTreeTraversal<T> & inorderTreeTraversal<T>::operator ++ ()
    // increment inorder traversal operator
{
    if (current->rightChild) {
            // do left slide from right child
        current = current->rightChild;
        while (current->leftChild)
            current = current->leftChild;
    }
    else {
        node<T> * child = current;
        current = current->parent;
        while (current && current->rightChild == child) {
            child = current;
            current = current->parent;
        }
    }


    return *this; // return ourself
}
```

The analysis of the running time for the increment operator is slightly more subtle than for pre- and postorder traversals, but similar in structure and result. We "charge" the cost of the traversal not to the loop in which it occurs, but to the step in which it is eventually returned as a value. Therefore, a constant amount of processing time is assigned to each node. This is sufficient to show that, in total, the amount of time performed by an inorder tree traversal iteration loop is $O(n)$, even though we cannot bound the execution of any single instance of the increment operator.

Inorder traversals are the appropriate form to use in creating an iterator for the set data type described in the previous section. We could implement the iterator creating operations for sets as follows:

```
class set<T> {
public:
    typedef inorderTreeTraversal<T> iterator;
        .
        .
        .
    iterator begin() { return inorderTreeTraversal<T> (root); }
```

```
    iterator end() { return inorderTreeTraversal<T> (0); }
         .
         .
         .
};
```

The traversal required to implement the backward iterators, rbegin and rend, is similar to the inorderTreeTraversal, but reverses the role of left and right children.

13.4.4   Level-Order Tree Traversal Iterator

Now we will examine a fourth type of tree iterator. This form is encountered occasionally, although less frequently than the previous three. It does, however, provide yet another example of the use of the queue data type. A *level-order* traversal of a tree examines all nodes at level 1 (namely, the root) before examining nodes at level 2. Next, all nodes of level 2 are examined. In general, all nodes of level i are examined before any node of level $i + 1$. A level-order traversal would visit nodes of a complete binary tree of height three in the following order:

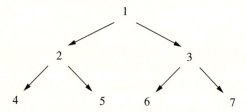

Unlike the other tree traversals, which required only a pointer to the current node, the level-order traversal must also maintain a queue of pending nodes. To initialize the level-order traversal the root node is inserted into an empty queue. To increment each step, a node is removed from the front of the queue, and the children of the removed node are inserted into the end of the queue. The nature of the queue will ensure the level-order property.

```
levelorderTreeTraversal<T>::levelorderTreeTraversal (node<T> * root)
    : dataQueue ()
{
    current = root;
    if (current != 0) {
        if (current->leftChild != 0)
            dataQueue.push (current->leftChild);
        if (current->rightChild != 0)
            dataQueue.push (current->rightChild);
```

```
        }
    }

    levelorderTreeTraversal<T> & levelorderTreeTraversal<T>::operator ++ ()
    {
        if (dataQueue.empty())
            current = 0;
        else {
            current = dataQueue.front();
            dataQueue.pop();
            if (current->leftChild != 0)
                dataQueue.push (current->leftChild);
            if (current->rightChild != 0)
                dataQueue.push (current->rightChild);
        }
        return *this; // return ourself
    }
```

The execution time of the increment operator can be bounded by a constant, and thus the total execution time is $O(n)$. The maximum number of elements in the queue is bounded by the maximum number of elements at any one level. Unfortunately, as an examination of a complete binary tree will show, this value can be as large as $n/2$.

13.5   BINARY TREE REPRESENTATION OF GENERAL TREES

Note that the binary tree abstract data type is actually sufficient to represent any tree structure. To illustrate this, consider an example tree such as:

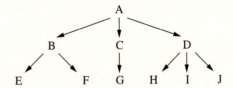

In the general case, the concept of an inorder traversal is not well defined. However, preorder, postorder, and level-order traversals can be described. For this example, preorder and postorder traversal algorithms would visit the nodes in this sequence:

Preorder   A B E F C G D H I J
Postorder   E F B G C H I J D A

To represent this tree using binary nodes, use the left pointer on each node to indicate the first child of the current node. Then use the right pointer to indicate a "sibling," a child with the same parents as the current node. The tree would thus be represented as follows:

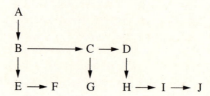

Turning the tree 45 degrees makes the representation look more like the binary trees we have been examining in earlier parts of this chapter:

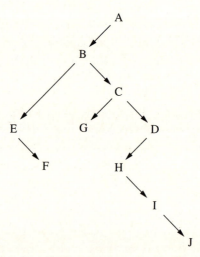

Now note that the order nodes would be examined in the various traversal strategies:

Preorder	A B E F C G D H I J
Inorder	E F B G C H I J D A
Postorder	F E G J I H D C B A

An interesting observation is that a preorder traversal of the binary tree representation corresponds to the preorder traversal of the original tree. Even more surprising, a postorder traversal of the original tree corresponds to an inorder traversal of the binary tree representation.

13.6   CHAPTER SUMMARY

Key Concepts

- Tree
  - Node
  - Root
  - Arc
  - Parent
  - Child
  - Leaf
  - Interior node
  - Subtree
  - Height
- Binary tree
- Vector implemen-
  tation of complete
  binary tree
- Operator precedence
  parsing
- Tree traversals
  - Preorder
  - Inorder
  - Postorder
  - Level-order

In this chapter we have introduced the concept of a binary tree. Along with vectors and lists, trees are a fundamental building block for many important data structures. The importance of trees stems from their ability to hold a great deal of information and yet access the information very quickly; in a balanced tree, the longest path from root to any node is approximately proportional to the logarithm of the number of elements held by the tree.

In a binary tree, each node has at most two children. The children of a tree are themselves trees. We have examined two implementation techniques for binary trees: an encoding that packs elements of a binary tree into a vector, and a more general technique that uses pointers and dynamically allocated nodes.

One use of trees is in the representation of expressions. We have presented an algorithm, called operator precedence parsing, that can be used to convert an expression from a textual representation into a tree form.

There is no obvious linear order for the elements in a tree. We have examined four different traversal strategies for a binary tree. The differences are characterized by the order in which each node is processed relative to the processing of the nodes in the subtrees associated with the left and right children.

▲ A preorder traversal visits each node, followed by a preorder traversal of the left child, and finally a preorder traversal of the right child.

▲ An inorder traversal performs an inorder traversal of the left child, followed by visiting the node, and finally an inorder traversal of the right child.

▲ A postorder traversal performs a postorder traversal of the left and right children, then visits the node.

▲ A level-order traversal visits all nodes of a specific depth or path length from the root before considering any nodes of a further distance.

Finally, we noted how arbitrary trees with any number of children per node can be encoded using binary trees. Because algorithms making use of binary trees are common and easy to use, this encoding makes it easy to extend these processes to general tree structures.

Study Questions & Exercises

Study Questions

1. What is the root of a tree? What is a leaf node? What is an ancestor node?

2. When referring to trees, what is the definition of the term height? How is the height related to the number of arcs traversed when moving from root to leaf?

3. How is the structure of a family tree different from the structure of an ancestor tree?

4. What is a complete binary tree?

5. What is a height-balanced binary tree?

6. Why are vectors generally used only to maintain complete binary trees?

7. Give an example that illustrates each of the four different types of tree traversals.

Exercises

1. What are some of the ways that trees are used as descriptive devices in non-computer science applications?

2. Write the expression tree for $(a + b) * (c + d * e)$.

3. Write the prefix and postfix representations of the expression given in the previous question.

4. Write the parse tree for the statement

   ```
   if (x < y) then a = x else if (y < z) then a
   = z else z = y
   ```

5. The Fibonacci numbers are described by the formula $F(0) = 0$, $F(1) = 1$, and the recursive formula $F(n) = F(n - 2) + F(n - 1)$. Write two routines for computing the nth Fibonacci number. The first routine should compute the value iteratively; given an argument value n, it first computes $F(0)$, then $F(1)$, and from these each value $F(i)$ until i reaches n. The second algorithm should work recursively. Given an argument n, if n is larger than 1 it will recursively call itself to compute the two earlier Fibonacci numbers, then return their sum. Calculate and compare execution timings for these two algorithms.

6. Many students mistakenly believe that examples such as the one analyzed in the previous question show that recursion is an inherently inefficient technique. This is not true. The problem with the recursive solution in the previous question was not the recursion, but that the same values were being repeatedly regenerated. This can be observed by writing a third Fibonacci calculator, one that does not recalculate values if they have already been computed. (This technique is sometimes known as *dynamic programming*.)

   The third Fibonacci routine allocates a vector of $n + 1$ values, initialized to the value -1. If then calls a recursive routine to fill in the elements of this vector, finally returning the last computed value. It could be written as:

   ```
   int Fibonacci (unsigned int n)
   {    // vector is initialized to -1
        vector<int> values(n+1, -1);
        fibCalculator (values, n);
        return values[n];
   }
   ```

   The routine `fibCalculator` first checks the vector to see if the entry indexed by the second argument is something other than -1. If so, it merely returns the value. If not, it computes the value by making recursive calls, then assigns the computed value to the appropriate index position. Write the routine `fibCalculator`, then compare its execution time with the two algorithms you wrote in the previous question.

7. Prove that the following formula describes the Fibonacci numbers. (The first three parts of this question are repeated from Chapter 4.)

   $$Fib_n = \frac{1}{\sqrt{5}} \left[\left(\frac{1+\sqrt{5}}{2} \right)^n - \left(\frac{1-\sqrt{5}}{2} \right)^n \right]$$

   a. Verify that the formula works for values 0, 1, and 2.

   b. Show that $(\frac{1+\sqrt{5}}{2})^2$ is the same as $1 + \frac{1+\sqrt{5}}{2}$, and similarly $(\frac{1-\sqrt{5}}{2})^2$ is the same as $1 + \frac{1-\sqrt{5}}{2}$.

   c. By substituting the formula verify that $Fib_{n+1} = Fib_{n-1} + Fib_n$. (Hint: Rewrite $(\frac{1+\sqrt{5}}{2})^{n+1}$ as $(\frac{1+\sqrt{5}}{2})^{n-1} \times (\frac{1+\sqrt{5}}{2})^2$, then use the property you verified in the previous step.)

   d. Argue why as n gets larger, the second term in the subtraction contributes less and less to the result. (Hint: consider the values of the second term as n increases.)

   e. From (d) we know that, for large values of n, the value of Fib_n is approximately $\frac{1}{\sqrt{5}} \left(\frac{1+\sqrt{5}}{2} \right)^n$.

   Let c represent the constant value $\frac{1+\sqrt{5}}{2}$. Compute the decimal approximation to c, giving at least two digits to the right of the decimal point.

   f. Taking the logarithm of both sides, we have that $\log Fib_n \approx \log \frac{1}{\sqrt{5}} + n \log c$. We can ignore the left argument to the addition as insignificant. Compute the value of $\log c$.

   g. Dividing both sides by $\log c$, we obtain the final result, which is that $n \approx \frac{1}{\log c} \log Fib_n$. Compute the value of $\frac{1}{\log c}$.

8. Modify the `expressionInformation` data structure to also accommodate integer values. Then modify the parsing algorithm so that it will recognize integer constants.

9. Modify the expression tree parsing algorithm so that it will recognize identifiers of more than one character in length.

10. The following is a complete binary tree of height 3.

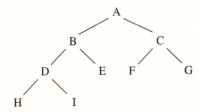

For each of the traversal algorithms we have described (preorder, inorder, postorder, and level order), list the sequence in which nodes would be processed.

11. Recall that the inorder traversal of an expression tree did not yield the original expression, because parentheses grouping was lost. One possible solution to this problem is to print out an opening parenthesis prior to visiting every child node, and a closing parenthesis after visiting each child. This, however, results in far too many parentheses. For the expression tree shown in Figure 13.6, the result would be $((a) + (((b) + (c)) * (d)))$. Describe a recursive algorithm that prints out the minimal number of parenthesis necessary. For this example expression tree, it should produce the original expression $a + (b + c) * d$.

12. Investigate empirically the relative execution speeds of the various iteration techniques. Do this by constructing a somewhat large tree, then iterating over the nodes several times. Make several timings of the program execution using the different iteration techniques.

13. The set data structure produces bi-directional iterators in response to the functions `begin()` and `end()`. This requires adding support for the decrement member function `--`, as well as the increment member function `++`. Describe the algorithm for the inorder traversal that will move an iterator backwards one step.

14. Notice that left nodes in binary trees do not use their child pointer fields, although space is allocated for these. The late Alan J. Perlis described an ingenious algorithm to make use of this otherwise wasted space [Perlis 60]. Suppose we have a means of distinguishing two types of pointers; one possibility is to maintain a one-bit field with each pointer, another possibility is to use positive and negative values for pointers. One type of pointer will be used for ordinary purposes. The second type, called a *thread*, will be used in child nodes, in which case the pointer will refer to the next node in the inorder traversal of the list.

   a. Describe an inorder iterator for these lists, and show that this data structure needs to maintain no more than a single pointer field.

   b. (Harder) Describe the new insertion algorithm for this data structure that maintains the threads.

   c. (Harder still) Describe the removal algorithm for this data structure.

15. Rewrite the family tree shown in Figure 13.1 using the binary tree representation of general trees described in Section 13.5. What is the height of the resulting tree?

16. In Section 13.5, we described how general trees could be represented as binary trees; however, we did not produce working code for the data abstraction. Create a class definition that implements this technique for representing general tree structures. What methods should your class provide?

14

Searching

Chapter Overview

In this chapter we will investigate data structures that are useful when a predominate task in a problem is discovering whether a particular element is contained in a collection, and if so, perform an operation on this element. Let us first review the data structures we have seen. We can search for elements in either a vector or a list using either the find or count generic algorithms. However, to determine whether a particular value is contained in the collection requires, in the worst case, examining every element, an $O(n)$ task. The set data type introduced in Chapter 12 is better, permitting operations in $O(\log n)$ steps, but only if the binary tree used internally to maintain the values is well balanced. In this chapter we will revisit all of these data structures. We will describe techniques that can be used to improve the access time for vectors, as well as methods that can be used to guarantee that trees remain well balanced.

Major topics discussed in this chapter include the following:

▲ Divide and conquer
▲ Ordered vectors
▲ Balanced binary search trees
▲ Tree sort
▲ Partition and quick sort

```
template <class Iterator, class ValueType>
Iterator lower_bound (Iterator start, Iterator stop, ValueType & value)
     // perform binary search on data, returning true if found
{
     unsigned int low = 0;
     unsigned int max = stop - start;
     unsigned int high = max;

     while (low < high) {

          // inv: start[0..low-1] are all less than value
          // start[high..max] are all greater than value
          unsigned int mid = (low + high) / 2;
          if (start[mid] < value)
               low = mid + 1;
          else
               high = mid;
     }

     // return element for which start[0..low-1] less than value
     // and value less than or equal to start[low]
     // or ending iterator if no such value
     if (low < max)
          return start + low;
     return stop;
}
```

Figure 14.1   An implementation of a binary search algorithm

of the loop we examine the midpoint. For the purposes of showing correctness, it is only necessary that the midpoint be larger than or equal to `low` and smaller than or equal to `high`. If the data item at `mid` is smaller than the test element, then all values smaller than the midpoint must be smaller than the element, and thus we can make `low`, which represents the lowest value that could possibly match the element, be `mid + 1`. On the other hand, if the data value is larger than or equal to the test element, then we can set the value of `high` to the midpoint with the certainty that all elements associated with index values high or greater are larger than the test element.

To prove termination we must ensure that either `low` or `high` is changed on each iteration of the loop. This depends upon a property of integer division—that for nonnegative values, division rounds *down* to the next lower value in cases where a fractional value would result. Thus, if *low* < *high* then (*low* + *high*)/2 must be strictly smaller than *high* (although it could be the same as *low*). With this assumption, we then know that either low is being set to mid + 1, in which case it is clearly increasing in value, or high is being set to mid, in which case it is decreasing.

14.1.2   Application: Root Finding

The idea behind the binary search technique can be used in many applications, not simply in searching vectors of values. We illustrate this by describing how binary search can be used to discover a root of a function. (A root is a point where the function has value zero.) Figure 14.2 shows a portion of the graph for the function $x^3 - 14x^2 + 59x - 65$. If we evaluate the function at 0, and again at 8, we can readily see that the *signs* of the two results are different. That is, one value is positive and the other is negative. Because it is continuous, the function must cross the zero axis somewhere in between. The invariant maintained by our root finding algorithm will be to preserve this property. That is, at each step we compute the midpoint value. Either the low or high value is changed to this midpoint value in order to maintain the property that the sign of the function at the low value is different from the sign of the function at the high value. When the low and high positions are sufficiently close (a condition determined by a factor provided by the user), we return the result, which is presumably close to the root value.

A procedure that implements this idea is shown in Figure 14.3. To determine if two quantities have different signs, the values are multiplied together. If the result is less than or equal to zero, then the quantities must have different signs, otherwise they have the same sign. When applied to the function shown in Figure 14.2, the algorithm first examines location 4. Because the value of the function at 4 is also positive, we know the root

---

Comparisons

It goes without saying that for binary search, search trees, or almost any other searching algorithm to work one needs the ability to compare two elements. Note that this was not true for the list data structure. The only operator we used in developing lists was the equality test operator, ==, used to tell if two values were equal. Here we require in addition the relational operator, <, to determine if one value is less than another. As always, when a new data type is created these can be overridden by programmers to have any desired meaning. Usually when comparisons are overridden, programmers want to define all the

four relational operators, <, <=, >= and >, as well as the two equality testing operators, == and !=. It is also important that whatever meaning is attached to these operators they satisfy the transitivity relation, which is if $x < y$ and $y < z$ then $x < z$, and the inverse relation, which is if $x < y$ is true then $y < x$ is false.

The algorithms in the standard template library use only the operators < and ==. Thus, a minimal data type need only define these two in order to be used with the data structures described in this book.

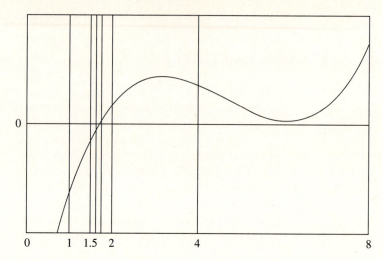

Figure 14.2 Steps in discovering a root of a function

must be between 0 and 4. So location 2 is examined next, with the same result. The value of the function at location 1 is negative, so the lower bound can be changed to that value. The sequence of values examined next continues in this fashion, examining 1.5, 1.75, 1.625, 1.71875, and so on. Within ten iterations the root can be determined to within 0.01.

14.2 ORDERED VECTORS

Although the `set` data type provides rapid insertion and removal, because it only provides bi-directional iterators, there are generic algorithms that cannot be used with sets. The random access iterators provided by the `vector` data type can be used with all generic algorithms. By keeping the elements in the vector ordered, we can also provide rapid access to elements. However, insertion of new elements and removal of values is still a relatively slow $O(n)$. Nevertheless, there are situations where this is acceptable. Imagine an internal representation for a telephone book, for example. Here, access is performed much more frequently than insertions or removals. In such situations, a vector representation might be preferable, because a vector of n elements requires less storage than the same number of values stored in a `set`.

We can use the ability to perform binary search, add it to the ability of our `vector` data structure to dynamically change size, and from these create a variety of vector that can be very efficiently searched to determine if it contains a specific element. (This is similar to the `orderedList` class we introduced in Section 9.5.1.) We will once again use inheritance, intro-

```
double rootSearch
      (double (&f)(double), double low, double high, double epsilon)
      // search the function argument for a root between low and high
      // assume f is a continous function
{
      // make sure there is a root in the range
      assert(f(low) * f(high) <= 0);

      // search while range is larger than epsilon
      while (epsilon < (high - low)) {
            // inv: f(low) and f(high) have different signs
            // examine mid point
            double mid = (high + low) / 2.0;
            // replace either high or low
            if (f(mid) * f(high) <= 0)
                  low = mid;
            else
                  high = mid;
            // inv: f(low) and f(high) have different signs
            }

      // return midpoint of last region
      return (high + low) / 2.0;
}
```

Figure 14.3   A binary search root-finding algorithm

duced in Chapter 9, in the development of our new data abstraction. By using inheritance, all the previous work that went into the development of the `vector` data type (described in Chapter 8) will be made available to the new abstraction with no additional effort.

The interface to this data type will be similar to that provided by the data type `set`. The declaration for our new data structure can be given as follows:

```
//
// class orderedVector
//  vector maintained in sorted order
//

template <class T> class orderedVector : public vector<T> {
public:
        // constructors
      orderedVector() : vector<T>() { }
      orderedVector(orderedVector & v) : vector<T>(v) { }
```

```
        // additional methods
    int       count   (T & value);
    iterator  find    (T & value);
    void      insert  (T & value);
    void      erase   (T & value);
};
```

The actual values are stored in the vector buffer provided by the parent class. As we will see when we describe the insertion algorithm, the values will be maintained in order. The default constructor initializes the size of the vector to zero, while the copy constructor copies values from the data area in the argument vector.

The remaining operations all use binary search. To see if a particular value is present in the collection, we perform a binary search on the data vector. If we find the appropriate element we return it, otherwise we return the end-of-range iterator.

```
template <class T>
iterator orderedVector<T>::find (T & value)
    // find the location of the given value
{
    iterator where = lower_bound (begin(), end(), value);
    iterator stop = end();
    if ((where != stop) && (*where == value))
        return where;
    else
        return stop;
}
```

The method to count the number of occurrences of a value is similar. The value returned by the binary search is the first location that could possibly hold the element. We move forward from there, counting the values that match. As soon as we have found an element that does not match, we can return the count.

```
template <class T>
int orderedVector<T>::count (T & value)
    // count the number of times the given value occurs
{
    vector<T>::iterator stop = end();
    vector<T>::iterator start = lower_bound (begin(), stop, value);
        // count number of matching values
    int counter = 0;
    while ((start != stop) && (*start++ == value))
        counter++;
    return counter;
}
```

Using these procedures, we can search a collection of n elements in $O(\log n)$ steps. Unfortunately, adding a value to the collection is more difficult. To illustrate the procedure, consider adding the value *Adam* to the following collection:

0	1	2	3	4	5
Abigail	Adela	Agnes	Alex	Alice	Audrey

To insert a new value, we first make the collection one element larger, creating a "hole" at the end.

0	1	2	3	4	5	6
Abigail	Adela	Agnes	Alex	Alice	Audrey	

Next, all the elements in index positions larger than the location for the new element are moved over one location, thereby moving the "hole" down to the desired location. This will be performed automatically by the `insert` member function in the class `vector`.

0	1	2	3	4	5	6
Abigail		Adela	Agnes	Alex	Alice	Audrey

Finally, the new value is placed into the hole. Again, this is performed for us by the `insert` member function.

0	1	2	3	4	5	6
Abigail	Adam	Adela	Agnes	Alex	Alice	Audrey

The code to perform this insertion operation is:

```
template <class T> void orderedVector<T>::insert (T & value)
    // add a new element to an ordered vector collection
{
        // find the location for the insertion
    iterator where = upper_bound(begin(), end(), value);
        // perform the insertion
    vector<T>::insert (where, value);
}
```

The binary search algorithm is used to find the location for the insertion. The enlargement of the vector, the movement of elements, and the insertion of the new value are all performed by the vector member function insert. A fully qualified name is required because we are overriding the original name, and need to access the method in the parent class. However, asymptotic analysis of this procedure is not encouraging. Although the binary search can be performed very quickly, the insert operation requires, in the worst case, $O(n)$ steps for a vector of n elements. Even if dynamic memory allocation is not performed, the loop to shift elements right by one position can still require $O(n)$ iterations. Thus, insertions are considerably slower than lookup for this data structure (which, as we noted earlier, could be acceptable if lookup is performed much more frequently than insertion or removal). The removal procedure is similar, and will not be presented.

14.3   BALANCED BINARY SEARCH TREES

Binary search over a vector of values is an appropriate technique for the problem of *static* searching, where the data values are known in advance and it is not possible to add or delete elements from the collection (or where addition and removal of elements is very infrequent). In the more general *dynamic* search problem, additions and deletions to the collection are permitted. In these cases a vector may not be an appropriate structure. As we noted in the previous section, both addition and deletion to an ordered vector require, in the worst case, the movement of all elements with index values larger than the affected position, and are thus $O(n)$ operations.

As we noted in the previous two chapters, a binary search tree can provide very good performance, but only if the tree is kept well balanced. We have been careful to note that the complexity of each of the operations performed on search trees is proportional to the length of the path from root to the node being manipulated. In a well-balanced tree, such as that shown in Figure 14.4, the length of the longest path is roughly $\log n$. A well-balanced tree could have a million entries, for example, and still maintain a maximum path length no larger than 20.

On the other hand, if we happen to insert elements into the tree in order, we can easily create the tree shown in Figure 14.5. This is still a search tree, but the expected time to perform an operation will be $O(n)$, or linear in the number of nodes. This is simply a very expensive way to implement a linked list. To avoid this difficulty, we require a method to ensure that our search trees remain balanced. In this section we will investigate one simple technique to preserve this property.

An *AVL tree* attempts to guarantee efficient performance by maintaining the height-balanced characteristic discussed in Chapter 13. That is, for each node we maintain the property that the difference in heights between

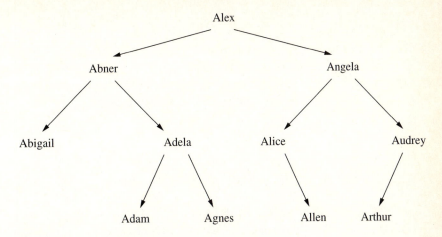

Figure 14.4 A binary search tree

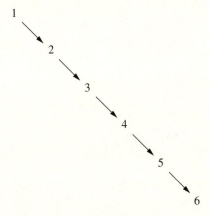

Figure 14.5 A very unbalanced search tree

the left and right subtrees is no larger than one. The method for doing this was first described in 1962 by two Russian mathematicians, G. M. Adel'son-Vel'skiĭ and E. M. Landis, and the resulting binary search trees are named in their honor.

As we noted in the last chapter, in a height-balanced binary tree containing n nodes, the longest path cannot exceed roughly $1.5 \log n$. To maintain the height-balanced property, it is actually not necessary to know the height of each subtree. We can get by with only maintaining at each node a *balance factor* that indicates the difference in heights of the left and right subtrees. A value of -1 indicates the left child is "heavier"; that is, there is a path from root to leaf in the left-child subtree of length h, for some value of h, whereas the longest path in the right child subtree is length $h - 1$. (It cannot be any smaller than $h - 1$ and still maintain the height-balanced

```
//
// class avlNode
// a single node in an avl tree
//

template <class T> class avlNode {
public:
        // constructor
    avlNode (T & value, avlNode<T> * p)
        value(v), parent(p),
        leftChild(0), rightChild(0), balanceFactor(0) { }

        // operations
    node<T> * copy ( node<T> *);
    void release ();
    int count (T & testElement);
    void insert (T &);
    int size ();

        // data fields
    T value;
    node<T> * parent;
    node<T> * leftChild;
    node<T> * rightChild;

protected:
    short   balanceFactor;  // balance factor, either -1, 0 or 1

    avlNode *       singleRotateLeft        ();
    avlNode *       singleRotateRight       ();
    avlNode *       balance                 ();
};
```

Figure 14.6   Class definition of an AVL tree node

property.) A balance factor of 0 will indicate that the longest paths in the two child subtrees are equal, while a value of 1 will indicate that the right child possesses the longest path.

The class definition for a node in our AVL tree is shown in Figure 14.6. The class definition is similar to the earlier class node (Section 12.6). With appropriate changes, iterators defined for the earlier class can be used with AVL nodes. The AVL node class defines a large number of private facilitator methods, which we will describe.

First, we will consider the problem posed by the addition of a new node to an AVL tree, and how transformations must be applied to maintain the height-balanced property. We will do so by working through a simple example, and then abstracting the general algorithm from the specific problems we encounter. Consider inserting the integer values 1 to 7 in order into an empty tree. Inserting 1 into an empty tree, of course, causes no difficulty. An insertion of 2 yields the following structure. The value preceding the colon is the element, while the value following the colon is the balance factor.

As with the earlier binary search trees, we first walk down the path until we discover a leaf node or interior node with only one child where the value can be inserted. The insertion is either along a left link or along a right link. In the case of the addition of 2, the insertion is along the right link.

Actually, two cases can occur at the leaf. The situation we have seen occurs when the leaf node originally had no children, and thus becomes unbalanced. On the other hand, the node could have been an interior node with a child along the other branch. For example, suppose we were to insert the value 0. The root would now become balanced.

Instead of inserting 0, imagine that we continue the addition of ascending numbers. When we try to insert the value 3 we run into our first problem. The child node 2 has balance factor 1, and as a consequence the balance factor on the root is increased to 2. To rectify this we perform a *rotation* to the left, making the node 2 into the new root.

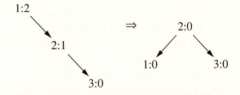

The question then becomes what the new balance factors should be for the node following the rotation. Rather than simply answering the

question for this specific case, let us investigate the solution to the more general problem. Assume we are performing a rotation on a node A with right child B. Let the maximum height of the right subtree for A be h. If we let A_{bf} represent the balance factor for A, then the height of the left subtree must be $h - A_{bf}$. The heights of the child subtrees of B depend upon the balance factor for node B. If B_{bf} is positive, then we know the right subtree of node B must be $h - 1$ (because the right subtree is larger than the left, and with the addition of one more node the length of the subtree rooted at B must be h). Thus, the height of the left subtree must be $(h - 1) - B_{bf}$. If B_{bf} is negative, the reverse argument can be given.

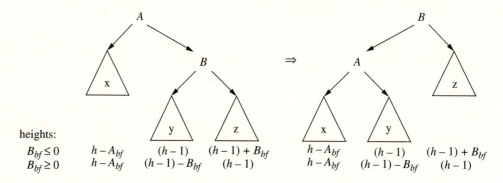

heights:

$B_{bf} \leq 0$ $h - A_{bf}$ $(h - 1)$ $(h - 1) + B_{bf}$ $h - A_{bf}$ $(h - 1)$ $(h - 1) + B_{bf}$
$B_{bf} \geq 0$ $h - A_{bf}$ $(h - 1) - B_{bf}$ $(h - 1)$ $h - A_{bf}$ $(h - 1) - B_{bf}$ $(h - 1)$

Now suppose we perform a left rotation, moving node A to a subordinate position and elevating node B to the root. The rotation preserves the search tree property, because all values in the left subtree of B (labeled y in our illustration) must be both greater than the value associated with A and less than the value associated with B. Because we know the heights of the two children, it is a simple matter to discover the balance factor for the new node A, expressed in terms of the balance factors A_{bf} and B_{bf}.

Condition	Balance factor for A	
$B_{bf} \leq 0$	$(h - 1) - (h - A_{bf})$	$= A_{bf} - 1$
$B_{bf} \geq 0$	$((h - 1) - B_{bf}) - (h - A_{bf})$	$= A_{bf} - B_{bf} - 1$

Discovering the balance factor for B involves knowing the height of the new subtree rooted at A. Unfortunately, we don't know which of the children for A is the larger. Thus, the previous two cases must each be further subdivided, yielding four cases. In the case where the balance factor of B is less than or equal to zero, the right subtree of A is larger if the balance factor of A is greater than or equal to 1, otherwise the left subtree is larger. Similarly, if the balance factor of B is greater than or equal to zero, the right subtree is larger if the balance factor of A is less than or equal to that of B, otherwise the left subtree is the larger of the two.

Condition	Height of A
$B_{bf} \leq 0 \wedge A_{bf} \geq 1$	n
$B_{bf} \leq 0 \wedge A_{bf} < 1$	$(h+1) - A_{bf}$
$B_{bf} \geq 0 \wedge A_{bf} \leq B_{bf}$	$(h+1) - A_{bf}$
$B_{bf} \geq 0 \wedge A_{bf} > B_{bf}$	$h - B_{bf}$

Knowing the size of the subtree rooted at node A provides all the information we need to compute the new balance factor for B.

Condition	Balance factor for B	
$B_{bf} \leq 0 \wedge A_{bf} \geq 1$	$(h-1) + B_{bf} - h$	$= B_{bf} - 1$
$B_{bf} \leq 0 \wedge A_{bf} < 1$	$(h-1) + B_{bf} - ((h+1) - A_{bf})$	$= A_{bf} + B_{bf} - 2$
$B_{bf} \geq 0 \wedge A_{bf} \leq B_{bf}$	$(h-1) - ((h+1) - A_{bf})$	$= A_{bf} - 2$
$B_{bf} \geq 0 \wedge A_{bf} > B_{bf}$	$(h-1) - (h - B_{bf})$	$= B_{bf} - 1$

In the situation that prompted our investigation of rotations, we had initially $A_{bf} = 2$ and $B_{bf} = 1$. Following the rotation all balance factors were zero. The reader should verify that the equations we developed will also yield the value zero.

The code used to perform a left rotation on a node is given next. The code to perform a right rotation is similar. Both procedures return the new balanced root and update the balance factors according to the equations we have developed.

```
template <class T>
avlNode<T> * avlNode<T>::singleRotateLeft ()
    // perform single rotation rooted at current node
{
    avlNode * nodeA = this;
    avlNode * nodeB = nodeA->rightChild;
    avlNode * nodeC = nodeB->leftChild;

    nodeA->rightChild = nodeC;
    nodeB->leftChild = nodeA;
    if (nodeC != 0)
        nodeC->parent = nodeA;
    nodeB->parent = nodeA->parent;
    nodeA->parent = nodeB;

    // now update the balance factors
    int Abf = nodeA->balanceFactor;
    int Bbf = nodeB->balanceFactor;
    if (Bbf <= 0) {
        if (Abf >= 1)
```

```
            nodeB->balanceFactor = Bbf - 1;
        else
            nodeB->balanceFactor = Abf + Bbf - 2;
        nodeA->balanceFactor = Abf - 1;
        }
    else {
        if (Abf <= Bbf)
            nodeB->balanceFactor = Abf - 2;
        else
            nodeB->balanceFactor = Bbf - 1;
        nodeA->balanceFactor = (Abf - Bbf) - 1;
        }
    return nodeB;
}
```

Returning to our example, the insertion of the value 4 causes no diffi-culty. The insertion of the value 5 forces another left rotation, this time rooted at the right-child node.

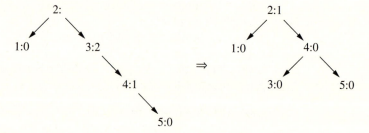

The insertion of 6 does not cause a balance problem for the child sub-trees, but does generate a problem for the root, because the left subtree has height 0 but the right subtree would have height 2. A single rotation re-stores the correct balance by making the previous root, 2, a child of the new root 4. The insertion of 7 causes one last rotation, leaving us with a balanced tree.

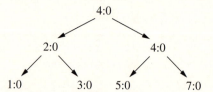

Occasionally single rotations are not sufficient. To see this, let us con-tinue inserting the values 15 and 16 in reverse order. The insertion of 16 is simple; however, the insertion of 15 causes a height imbalance. Unlike the earlier cases, a single rotation is not sufficient to restore the height-balanced property.

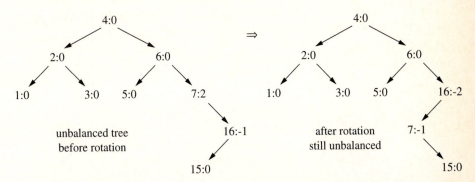

The problem arises when an insertion is made into the left child, causing the left child to become heavy, of a node that is itself a heavy right child. Using the equations derived earlier, the reader can verify that this case, and the symmetric case for right child insertions, are the only two instances in which a single rotation will produce a value that is not balanced. Fortunately, this situation is both easy to recognize and easy to handle. The solution is a combination of *two* single rotations, and is thus called a *double* rotation. First, we perform a right rotation on the right child. This is followed by a left rotation at the point of the earlier imbalance.

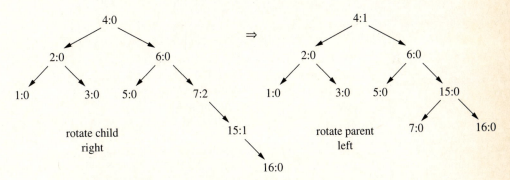

The following procedure is used to rebalance a subtree, selecting either a single or double rotation as necessary.

```
template <class T>
avlNode<T> * avlNode<T>::balance()
{       // balance tree rooted at node
        // using single or double rotations as appropriate
        if (balanceFactor < 0) {
            if (leftChild->balanceFactor <= 0)
                // perform single rotation
```

```
                return singleRotateRight();
            else {
                // perform double rotation
                leftChild = leftChild->singleRotateLeft();
                return singleRotateRight();
                }
            }
        else {
            if (rightChild->balanceFactor >= 0)
                return singleRotateLeft();
            else {
                // perform double rotation
                rightChild = rightChild->singleRotateRight();
                return singleRotateLeft();
                }
            }
    }
```

Using this, we are finally in a position to present the code for insertion into an AVL tree:

```
template <class T>
avlNode<T> * avlNode<T>::insert (T & val)
{       // add new element into balanced avl tree
    if (val < value) { // insert into left subtree
        if (leftChild != 0) {
            int oldbf = leftChild->balanceFactor;
            leftChild = leftChild->add(val);
            // check to see if tree grew
            if ((leftChild->balanceFactor != oldbf) &&
                leftChild->balanceFactor)
                    balanceFactor--;
            }
        else {
            leftChild = new avlNode(val, this);
            // 0 becomes -1, 1 becomes 0
            balanceFactor--;
            }
        }
    else { // insert into right subtree
        if (rightChild != 0) {
            int oldbf = rightChild->balanceFactor;
            rightChild = rightChild->add(val);
            // check to see if tree grew
            if ((rightChild->balanceFactor != oldbf)
                && rightChild->balanceFactor)
```

```
                        balanceFactor++;
            }
        else {
            rightChild = new avlNode(val, this);
            // 0 becomes 1, -1 becomes 0
            balanceFactor++;
            }
        }

        // check if we are now out of balance, if so balance
        if ((balanceFactor < -1) || (balanceFactor > 1))
            return balance();
        return this;
    }
```

The method in class `avlNode` inserts into either the left or right subtree, updates the balance factors, and then rebalances if necessary.

Both single and double rotations can be performed in constant time independent of the size of the subtrees they are manipulating. Because insertion basically walks a path from root to leaf and then performs insertions when returning, when coupled with the observation concerning the longest path in a height-balanced tree this shows that insertion can be performed in $O(\log n)$ time. In fact, rotations are relatively rare. It can be shown that one rotation, either single or double, is the most that is ever required to bring a height-balanced tree back into form following an insertion. This follows

---

$O(\log n)$ Not a Lower Bound on Searching

It is tempting to conjecture that the $O(\log n)$ performance of the AVL tree is asymptotically the best that is possible for the searching problem. An argument to this effect might be made somewhat along the following lines. The element being matched could be any one of the n values in the collection, or it might not appear in the collection. Thus, there are $n + 1$ possible outcomes. The execution of the program itself as a tree can be represented with leaves as the final result and interior nodes as statements in which a choice is made. Because we know there are $n + 1$ different outcomes, there must be at least $n + 1$ leaves in this tree. But then we know there must be at least one path of length $\lceil \log n \rceil$ in this tree. Hence traversing the tree, that is, executing the program, requires at least $O(\log n)$ steps.

This argument is reasonably valid if the only operations permitted are comparisons of elements in the collection to the item being examined. The fallacy is to assume that this is the only possibility. Just as we used binary search to rule out large numbers of elements in the beginning of this chapter, we can use an alternative technique, hashing, to avoid many comparisons. Recall from Chapter 8 that a hash function was a mapping from element values into the integers. In Chapters 18 and 20 we will see how hash functions can be used to implement very efficient data structures, called hash tables. By making use of an appropriate hash function, we can reduce the complexity of searching to almost constant time.

from the observation that a single or double rotation always results in a balanced subtree.

As was true with the binary search tree class presented in Chapter 12, removal of a value from an AVL tree is more complex than insertion. You will recall that removing a value from the middle of a tree left a "hole," and the problem was finding an appropriate value to fill the gap. One candidate that preserves the search tree property is the leftmost descendant of the right child. The general approach in the removal algorithm for AVL trees is finding and removing this value from the subtree, rebalancing as necessary, then placing this value in the location of the removed cell, and finally traversing back up the tree, rebalancing as necessary. Unlike the situation in insertion, during deletion several rotations may be necessary to bring the tree back into balance.

14.4   APPLICATION: TREE SORT

The search tree data structure naturally suggests a sorting algorithm. The basic idea behind the tree sort algorithm is simple: Elements of a collection are added, one by one, into a search tree. The addition process will naturally order the elements. Once all the elements have been ordered, an iterator is constructed to remove the elements and place them back into the argument container.

```
template <class T>
void treeSort(vector<T> & data)
{
    // declare a search tree of the correct type
    multiset<T> sorter;
    vector<T>::iterator itr, stop;
    stop = data.end();

    // copy the entire vector into the tree
    for (itr = data.begin(); itr != stop; ++itr)
        sorter.insert(*itr);

    // now copy the values back into the array
    multiset<T>::iterator tree;
    for (itr = data.begin(); itr != stop; ++itr)
        *itr = *tree++;
}
```

The addition of all n elements of the vector input into the search tree can be performed in $O(n \log n)$ steps. Because the traversal to copy the values back into the vector is linear, this means the total running time of the algorithm is $O(n \log n)$.

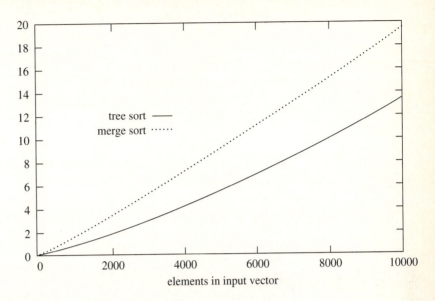

Figure 14.7   A comparison of merge sort to tree sort

Figure 14.7 compares the running time of tree sort to that of merge sort, the fastest algorithm we have seen up to now. Recall that merge sort was also an $O(n \log n)$ algorithm.

14.5   FINDING THE *NTH* LARGEST

In this section we will consider a slightly different searching problem, which is to find the Nth largest element in a vector of values. To simplify matters, we will match N to the range of valid vector index positions. Thus, the smallest element will be discovered by asking for element 0, the next smallest by element 1, the median (midpoint) by asking for element $n/2$ (where n is the length of the vector), and so on.

A simple and obvious algorithm is first to sort the vector. The Nth largest value would then be the value contained at index position N. Using the tree sort algorithm we just encountered, the sorting process can be performed in $O(n \log n)$ operations. Because indexing of a vector can be performed in constant time, we can discover the Nth largest value in a vector of n elements in no more than $O(n \log n)$ steps.

But sorting is doing much more work than is necessary. The sorted vector will tell us the position of each value in the ordered array, not simply the single value we are seeking. If we are interested in only *one* position (the median, for example), then we might think there is a better (that is, faster) algorithm that can be employed. In fact, there is a faster algorithm. Even more interesting, an investigation of this new algorithm will lead to the development of an elegant and fast sorting algorithm.

The key step in the improved searching algorithm will be to *partition* the vector into two components. Suppose, for example, that we have the following vector of eleven values and wish to discover the median value, which would be the element in index position 5 of the sorted vector.

2	97	17	37	12	46	10	55	80	42	39

To start, we will simply guess an answer. Let us guess that the value found in index position 3, that is, 37, is the answer. To see if we are correct, we will systematically compare every element in the collection to our guess. We rearrange the elements of the vector into two sections. The first section will be those elements that are smaller than or equal to the guess. Those elements in the second section will be those elements that are strictly larger than the guess. When we are finished, we will put the guess element back between the two groups, and return the new index position for the guess element (which may or may not be the position we are seeking).

				pivot ↓		> pivot				
< = pivot										
12	10	17	2	37	97	46	55	80	42	39

An algorithm to perform this task is shown in Figure 14.8. Traditionally, the value of the "guess" is known as the *pivot*, because all other elements will pivot around the value. The first step in the pivot algorithm, and one that distinguishes the algorithm from a simple partition, is to move the pivot to the beginning of the array, by swapping the pivot position with the first element. Having moved this value out of the way, the partition can then be safely conducted by comparing against this value. As before, the partition algorithm will then divide the input into two groups, those that are known to be less than or equal to the pivot, and those that are known to be greater than the pivot. When the pivoting is finished, the result can be visualized as:

pivot ↓   low ↓

	< = pivot	> pivot

Note that the value returned by the partition step is the beginning of the larger group, while what we need is the previous value, the end of the

```
template <class T>
unsigned int pivot (vector<T> & v, unsigned int start,
     unsigned int stop, unsigned int position)
     // partition vector into two groups
     // values smaller than or equal to pivot
     // values larger than pivot
     // return location of pivot element
{
        // swap pivot into starting position
     swap (v[start], v[position]);

        // partition values
     unsigned int low = start + 1;
     unsigned int high = stop;
     while (low < high)
         if (v[low] < v[start])
             low++;
         else if (v[--high] < v[start])
             swap (v[low], v[high]);

        // then swap pivot back into place
     swap (v[start], v[--low]);
     return low;
}
```

Figure 14.8 The vector pivot algorithm

smaller group. The partition value is decremented to obtain this position, and the value is swapped with the pivot.

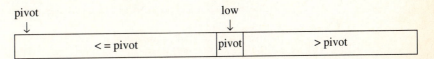

We return now to the problem of finding the Nth largest value in a vector. The resulting position yielded by the pivot algorithm is either the index value we were seeking, or it is not. If it is, then we are finished. If it is not, then it might at first appear that little information has been gained. But this is not necessarily the case. We have, in fact, divided the vector into two portions. Just as with binary search, we can in one step immediately rule out a large number of possible answers. By comparing the resulting index position for the pivot to the position we are seeking, we can recursively search either the lower or the upper portion of the transformed vector. The algorithm that results from this insight is as follows:

```
template <class T>
T findElement(vector<T> & v, unsigned int N,
        unsigned int low, unsigned int high)
{
        // partition the vector
    unsigned int pivotPosition =
        pivot (v, low, high, (high + low) / 2);

        // see if we are done
    if (pivotIndex == N)
        return v[N];

        // else try again
    if (N < pivotIndex)
        return findElement(v, N, low, pivotPosition);
    else
        return findElement(v, N, pivotPosition + 1, high);
}
```

How fast is this algorithm? It is relatively easy to see that the partition step will run in time proportional to the section of the vector it is processing. (To see this, note that each element in this section is examined only once.) The worst-case running time of the findElement algorithm, however, depends upon how lucky one is in finding good pivot positions. The best case occurs if we only happen to stumble upon the answer before we have recursed very many times. The next best case occurs when the algorithm recursively calls itself until a partition consisting of only a single element is found, but the algorithm is fortunate in the selection of pivot elements. This happens when every pivot divides the vector roughly in half.

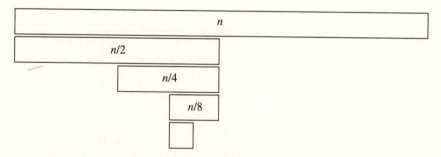

Execution time in this case is proportional to the sum $n + \frac{n}{2} + \frac{n}{4} + \ldots + 1$. If we factor out the common n term, the remaining sum can be expressed as $1 + \frac{1}{2} + \frac{1}{4} + \ldots$. The infinite series given by this pattern is bounded by the value 2, and thus any finite initial portion of the series must be similarly bounded. This is sufficient to show that in the best case the `findElement` algorithm will run in $O(n)$ steps.

But what if we make a series of bad choices for the pivot value? The worst choice for a pivot would be one that represents either the largest or the smallest element in the collection. In this situation, one or the other of the vectors will be empty, and with $O(n)$ work we will have succeeded in eliminating only *one* element.

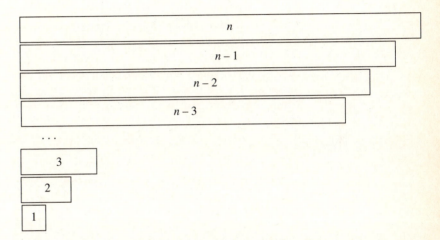

The series that results from this string of poor choices is $n + (n - 1) + (n - 2) + \ldots + 1$. As we have seen in earlier chapters, this series characterizes an algorithm with $O(n^2)$ operations. This is even worse than our naive approach that first sorted the vector.

So `findElement` is an algorithm that has terrific best case performance and terrible worst case performance. How does it perform in the "average" case? Are there techniques that can be used to ensure that the worst-case performance is relatively rare? The answer to the first question is that, on average, the `findElement` algorithm performs very quickly. Unfortunately, the mathematics necessary to formally prove this is beyond our presentation here.

The key to positively ensuring fast performance is to try to intelligently select the pivot value. Various authors have proposed different strategies to do this, including:

▲ Simply use the first element as the pivot value. This avoids the need for the initial swap, but is a relatively poor choice if the vector is somewhat, but not completely, ordered.

▲ Select the pivot at random from the range of values.

▲ Select the pivot as the value in the midpoint of the range of elements (this is the option used in our version of the algorithm).

▲ Select three values from the range, and compute the median (middle) value from these three.

Readers interested in more complete analysis of these, and many other, possibilities can investigate the references cited at the end of this chapter.

14.5.1   Application: Quick Sort

The pivoting algorithm shown in Figure 14.8 is at the heart of one of the smallest, fastest, most elegant, and interesting sorting algorithms known. The algorithm was named *quick sort* by its originator, Tony Hoare, now of Oxford University. The idea behind quick sort is simple: After one partition step, we have not entirely sorted a vector, but we have made some progress. For example, following the partitioning of the eleven-element vector we described in the last section, the vector held the following values:

				pivot ↓						
<= pivot							> pivot			
2	17	12	10	37	97	46	55	80	42	39

Although not sorted, elements are at least closer to their final destination. More importantly, no elements need be exchanged across the pivot, thus yielding two separate areas that can now be sorted independently of each other. To obtain a full sorting, we simply recursively call the quick sort procedure, in order to sort each of the two subvectors resulting from the partition. This divide-and-conquer algorithm can be given as follows:

```
template <class T>
void quickSort(vector<T> & v, unsigned int low, unsigned int high)
{
    // no need to sort a vector of zero or one elements
    if (low >= high)
        return;

    // select the pivot value
    unsigned int pivotIndex = (low + high) / 2;

    // partition the vector
    pivotIndex = pivot (v, low, high, pivotIndex);

    // sort the two sub vectors
    if (low < pivotIndex)
        quickSort(v, low, pivotIndex);
```

```
    if (pivotIndex < high)
        quickSort(v, pivotIndex + 1, high);
}
```

To make an algorithm that takes only a single vector argument, matching the format for the other sorting algorithms we have seen, we can overload the function name and create an alternative procedure that merely invokes the recursive routine.

```
template <class T> void quickSort(vector<T> & v)
{
    unsigned int numberElements = v.size ();
    if (numberElements > 1)
        quickSort(v, 0, numberElements - 1);
}
```

As with the `findElement` algorithm, the asymptotic execution time of the `quickSort` algorithm depends in part on how lucky one is in selecting a pivot position. The best case occurs when the pivot breaks the vector exactly in half. The recursive calls then sort two arrays of approximately $n/2$ elements. Similarly, each of these is divided roughly in half, resulting in four arrays of approximately $n/4$ elements. The number of times one can divide a vector of size n in half is approximately $\log n$. Because each partition step executes in time proportional to the length of the array, the total time is $O(n \log n)$.

The other extreme occurs when the pivot is always either the smallest or the largest element. One partition is then empty, and the other contains $n - 1$ elements. In this case, n recursive calls will be performed, and the total execution time is proportional to $n + (n - 1) + (n - 2) + \ldots + 1$. As we have seen, this is $O(n^2)$.

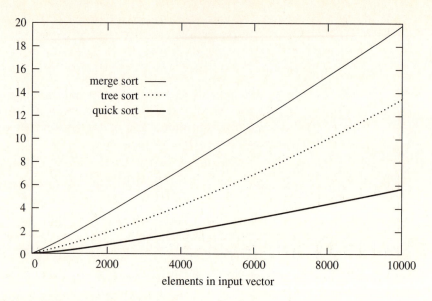

Figure 14.9   Execution time of quick sort versus tree sort

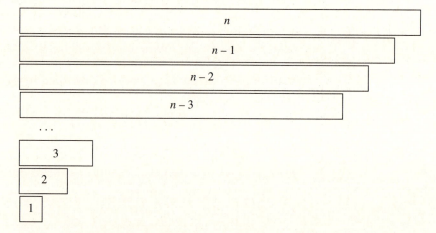

Once again we have vastly different best and worst case execution behavior. To determine the average execution time, either we can resort to sophisticated mathematics (see the references at the end of this section) or perform empirical timings.

EXECUTION TIMINGS FOR QUICK SORT

In actual timings on random input values, the quick sort algorithm lives up to its name. Figure 14.9 graphs execution time in comparison to merge sort over the same range used in Figure 14.7. At the far right edge of the graph, the quick sort algorithm is almost three times faster than merge sort.

Empirical timings are, in a certain sense, almost as coarse a measuring device as asymptotic analysis. As we noted in Chapter 4, factors that can alter the actual timing of an algorithm include the quality of the code generation for the compiler in use, the hardware and operating system for the computer on which the program is run, and the load balance (that is, other processes also in execution) of the computer at the time the measurements are taken. In addition, the quick sort algorithm is influenced very profoundly by the algorithm used to select the pivot value, and by the degree to which the input values are ordered or random. Thus, execution timings of the algorithm on random values may or may not be a good predictor for the execution time of the algorithm in any particular circumstance.

14.6   CHAPTER SUMMARY

Key Concepts

- Divide and conquer
- Binary search
- Ordered vectors
- Search trees
- AVL trees
- Tree sort
- Partition, findElement
- Quick sort

The solution of many problems involves searching a collection of values to find a specific element. In this chapter we have explored techniques that can be used to permit this operation to be performed quickly. In all cases, the speed is obtained by maintaining values in some sort of order.

If a vector of values is maintained in order, then binary search can be used to quickly locate a specific value. At each step in a binary search, the middle element is compared to the test value, and half the values in the collection are thereby eliminated from consideration.

Binary search of a vector is efficient if the data values are fixed, and insertions and removal of items is infrequent or does not occur at all. To insert or remove an item into or from an ordered vector requires, in the worst case, the movement of every value in the collection. In the more general dynamic search situation, these operations can be performed more rapidly using a search tree.

A search tree is a binary tree that maintains the property that for every node, all the values associated with the descendants of the left child are less than or equal to the value of the node, and the values associated with descendants of the right child are greater than the value of the node. By maintaining this property, it is possible to very quickly search for an item, and insertions and deletions can be performed rapidly as well, as long as the tree does not become too unbalanced.

To ensure that a search tree remains balanced, an additional requirement is necessary. We have explored one form of tree, the AVL tree, that maintains the height-balanced property. This guarantees that the difference in heights between the left and right child of any node is never larger than one. This property is then sufficient to guarantee efficient tree operations.

A slightly different variation on the searching problem is finding a single value in an ordered collection without ordering the entire collection, for example, finding the median (middle) value. Using the technique of partitioning, an algorithm can be created that will very rapidly discover this single value from a vector of elements. This same partitioning process is the key idea behind an elegant and fast recursive sorting algorithm, quick sort.

Further Reading

Searching large quantities of data was one of the first applications for modern digital computers. Thus, trees and search trees have been extensively studied, and have a large associated literature. Most of the classic algorithms are examined in Volumes 1 and 3 of Knuth [Knuth 73, Knuth 75]. The book by Weiss [Weiss 92] also provides an extensive bibliography.

AVL trees were first proposed by Adel'son-Vel'skiĭ and Landis in 1962 [Velskii 62]. A slightly more accessible discussion is found in Weiss [Weiss 92].

The tree sort algorithm was first described by Robert Floyd in 1964 [Floyd 64].

The partition, findElement, and quick sort algorithms were first described by Tony Hoare [Hoare 61, Hoare 62]. In his ACM Turing Award lecture published in [Ashenhurst 87], Hoare recounts how the algorithm was first developed in a nonrecursive form. The nonrecursive version was extremely difficult to code or understand. It was only with the introduction of recursion in the language Algol-60 that the elegance of the algorithm became clear. Sedgewick [Sedgewick 78] provides an extremely thorough analysis of the quick sort algorithm. A slightly more accessible discussion of the relative merits of various techniques for selecting the pivot element is provided by Weiss [Weiss 92]. Several variations are described by Gonnet and Baeza-Yates [Gonnet 91].

Study Questions & Exercises

Study Questions

1. What does the principle of "divide and conquer" mean? Under what circumstances will it lead to an efficient problem solution?

2. What operations does the class `orderedVector` inherit from class `vector`?

3. What are the asymptotic execution times for the four new methods defined in class `orderedVector`?

4. What do the initials AVL stand for in the name AVL tree?

5. What additional information is stored by a node in an AVL tree that is not used by the binary search tree nodes introduced in Chapter 12?

6. Under what circumstances is it necessary to use a double rotation in rebalancing an AVL tree?

7. Why does the tree sort algorithm use a `multiset` and not a `set`?

8. What are various techniques that have been proposed for selecting a pivot value to partition a vector of random values?

9. What is the name of the person who discovered the quick sort algorithm?

10. What is the best-case asymptotic execution time of the quick sort algorithm? What is the worst-case execution time? Under what circumstances will the best time be achieved? Under what circumstances will the worst-case time be achieved?

11. Why are actual timings on random vectors not necessarily a good predictor of the performance of the quick sort algorithm?

Exercises

1. Trace the values of low and high in Figure 14.1 during the course of a binary search for element 7 in the following vector:

   2 4 5 7 8 12 24 37 40 41 42 43 50 68 67

2. How many elements will be examined in performing a binary search on a vector of 10,000 values?

3. The binary search algorithm shown in Figure 14.1 will continue searching until the values low and high meet, even if by chance the element being targeted is discovered sooner. For example, if we were searching the vector of names for the value "Alex," we would discover the element on the first comparison. Modify the algorithm so that it will halt if the element is discovered.

4. Assuming the function f is continuous, give a proof of correctness for the root finding algorithm described in Figure 14.3.

5. Write the method erase for the ordered vector data structure. First, perform a binary search to find the location of the argument. Test this location to make sure the value is actually contained in the collection. If so, then use the erase member function from the class vector to eliminate the value.

6. Modify the way the new element insertion routine for binary search trees handles duplicate elements:
   a. The detection of duplicate elements produces an error message.
   b. A duplicate value inserted into a tree replaces the existing value.

7. Verify the formulas used in the single right rotation algorithm.

8. Assume a node has a balance factor of 2. Assuming this is the first such unbalanced node encountered in a walk back up a path from leaf to root, there are nine possible values for the child subtrees (-1, 0, or 1 in each). Verify that for each of these nine values, the method balance will restore the height-balanced property of the search tree.

9. Is the tree sort algorithm stable? (See Chapter 8, Exercise 9.)

10. Using the techniques described in Exercise 19, Chapter 4, test the hypothesis that tree sort is an $O(n \log n)$ algorithm. Using the coefficient c you compute, estimate for the tree sort algorithm how long it would take to sort a vector of 100,000 elements.

11. A nonrecursive form of quick sort can be written by stacking pairs of indices (lower- and upper-bound) that represent sections of the vector waiting to be sorted. Thus, after partitioning, both the lower and upper ranges would be placed on the stack. At each step of the algorithm, a range of values is removed from the stack and partitioned. Use the stack data structure from Chapter 10 to implement this algorithm.

12. Trace the series of recursive calls performed by quick sort during the process of sorting the following vector: 3, 1, 4, 1, 5, 9, 2, 6, 5, 3, 5.

13. Is the quick sort algorithm stable? (See Exercise 9.)

14. What is the execution time of the quick sort algorithm when all elements in a collection are equal? Compare this to the execution time for tree sort in the same situation.

15. What is the execution time of the quick sort algorithm when the input is already sorted? How would this be different if instead of the midpoint we selected the first element as the pivot value?

16. Construct a vector of 10 elements that makes quick sort exhibit the worst-case $O(n^2)$ behavior when we use the pivot selection strategy presented in this chapter.

Chapter

15

Priority Queues

Chapter Overview

A *priority queue* is a data structure useful in problems in which it is important to be able to rapidly and repeatedly find and remove the largest element from a collection of values. In this chapter we will present two different implementations of priority queues. The first technique uses an abstraction called a *heap*, and is constructed as an *adaptor* built on top of another form of container, typically a vector or deque. The heap data structure is then used to demonstrate yet another approach to sorting a collection of values. The second implementation strategy is the *skew heap*. The skew heap is notable because it does not provide guaranteed performance bounds for any single operation, but if a number of operations are performed over time, the average execution time of operations will be small.

To demonstrate a common use of a heap, the chapter concludes with a discussion of discrete event-driven simulation. This topic is approached by first developing a general *framework* for simulations, then specializing the framework using *inheritance*.

Major topics discussed in this chapter include the following:

▲ The priority queue data abstraction
▲ Heaps and heap sort
▲ Skew heaps
▲ A framework for simulation
▲ Discrete event-driven simulation

The second data structure, a skew heap, avoids the maximum size difficulty by maintaining the heap values in a binary tree. But solving one problem comes only at the cost of introducing another, namely the difficulty of keeping the tree relatively well balanced. Skew heaps are interesting because the worst-case cost for insertions and deletions is a relatively slow $O(n)$, but this worst case behavior does not occur frequently and cannot be sustained. In particular, the occurrence of a worst-case situation must necessarily be followed by several insertions and deletions that are much faster. Thus, amortized over a number of insertions and deletions, the average cost of operation is still relatively good. Another advantage of the skew heap is that it provides a fast implementation for the operation of merging two priority-queue heaps to form a new queue.

15.2   HEAPS

A heap is a binary tree in which every node possesses the property that its value is larger than or equal to the value associated with either child node. This is referred to as the *heap order property*. A simple induction argument establishes that the value associated with each node in a heap must be the largest value held in the subtree rooted at the node. It follows from this property that the largest element in a heap will always be held by the root node. This is unlike a search tree, where the largest element was always held by the rightmost node. Discovering the maximum value in a heap is therefore a trivial operation.

Recall from Chapter 13 that a *complete binary tree* is a binary tree that is entirely filled (in which every node has two children), with the exception of the bottom level, which is filled from left to right. Figure 15.1 shows a complete binary tree that is also a heap. The key insight behind the heap data structure is the observation, which we noted in Chapter 13, that because a complete binary tree is so regular, it can be represented efficiently in an array. The root of the tree will be maintained in position 0 of the array. The two children of node n will be held in positions $2n + 1$ and $2n + 2$. The array corresponding to the tree in Figure 15.1 is the following:

0	1	2	3	4	5	6	7	8	9	10
16	14	9	10	12	7	8	5	2	11	3

Note that a vector that is sorted largest to smallest is also a heap, but the reverse is not true. That is, a vector can maintain a heap and still not be ordered.

Given the index to a node, discovering either the parent or the children of that node is a simple matter of division or multiplication. No explicit pointers need be maintained in the array structure, and traversals of the

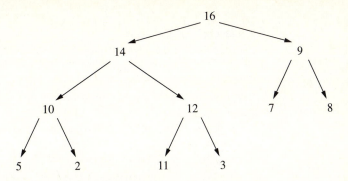

Figure 15.1   A complete binary tree in heap form

heap can be performed very efficiently. Notice that the property of completeness is important to ensure there are no "gaps" in the array representation.

The standard library class `priority_queue` constructs a heap on top of a randomly accessible data structure, usually either a `vector` or a `deque`. Like the `stack` and queue data types (Chapter 10), the underlying container is provided as a template argument. An optional second template argument (not shown) represents the function to be used in comparing two elements.[1] We will see an example that uses this argument in Section 15.4. To declare a priority queue, the user must state both the priority queue type and the type of the underlying container, as in this example:

```
// create a priority queue of integers
priority_queue < vector<int> > aQueue;
```

Figure 15.2 gives the class declaration and member functions for this data type. Notice that operations are either defined by the underlying structure, or by one of the generic heap functions we will define.

The operations of insertion (performed by `push(newElement)`) and deletion (performed by `pop()`) are more complex than the others, and involve calling an auxiliary function. We will discuss insertion first. When a new element is added to the priority queue, it is obvious that *some* value must be moved to the end of the array, to maintain the complete binary tree property. However, it is likely that the new element cannot be placed there without violating the heap order property. This violation will occur if the new element is larger than the parent element for the location. A solution is to place the new element in the last location, then move it into place by repeatedly exchanging the node with its parent node until the heap order property is restored (that is, until the new node either rises to the top or until we find a parent node that is larger than the new node). Because the

---

1. See Section A.3 in Appendix A.

```
//
// class priority_queue
//    a priority queue managed as a vector heap
//

template <class Container> class priority_queue {
public:
    typedef Container::value_type value_type;

    // priority queue protocol
    bool        empty () { return c.empty(); }
    int         size  () { return c.size(); }
    value_type & top  () { return c.front(); }
    void        push  (value_type & newElement)
                { c.push_back(newElement);
                    push_heap(c.begin(), c.end()); }
    void        pop   ()
                { pop_heap (c.begin(), c.end());
                    c.pop_back(); }
protected:
    Container     c; // container of values
};
```

Figure 15.2   Declaration for the class `priority_queue`

new element rises until it finds a correct location, this process is sometimes known as a *percolate up*.

The insertion method for percolating a value into place is shown in
Figure 15.3. We have added the invariants required to prove the correctness
of the procedure (see following box). Because the `while` loop moves up one
level of the tree each cycle, obviously it can iterate no more than log n
times. The running time of the insertion procedure is $O(\log n)$. (Note that
before calling `push_heap`, the new element is pushed on to the end of
the container. For the vector data structure, this operation could, in the
worst case, require $O(n)$ steps, if a new buffer is allocated and elements

---

Heaps and Heaps

The term *heap* is used for two very different
concepts in computer science. The heap *data
structure* is an abstract data type used to implement priority queues, as well as being used in a
sorting algorithm that we will discuss in a later
chapter. The terms *heap*, *heap allocation*, and so
on, are also frequently used to describe memory
that is allocated and released directly by the user,
using the `new` and `delete` operators. You should
not confuse the two uses of the same term.

```
template <class Iterator>
void push_heap(Iterator start, Iterator stop)
        // initial condition:
        // iterator range describes a heap, except that
        // final element may be out of place
{

            // position is index of out of place element
            // parent is index of parent node
        unsigned int position = (stop - start) - 1;
        unsigned int parent = (position - 1) / 2;


        // now percolate up
        while (position > 0 && start[position] < start[parent]) {
            // inv: tree rooted at position is a heap
            swap (start[position], start[parent]);
            // inv: tree rooted at parent is a heap
            position = parent;
            parent = (position - 1) / 2;
            }
        // inv: entire structure is a heap

}
```

Figure 15.3 Method for insertion into a heap

are copied. This could potentially increase the execution time of the entire operation.)

The deletion procedure is handled in a manner similar to insertion. We swap the last position into the first location. Because this may destroy the heap order property, the element must *percolate down* to its proper position by exchanging places with the larger of its children. For reasons that will soon become clear, we invoke another routine named adjust_heap to do this task.[2] Figure 15.4 shows an intermediate step in this process. The value 3 has been promoted to the root position, where it subsequently has been swapped with the larger of its two children. The value 3 will now be compared to the values 10 and 12, and will be swapped with the larger value. This will continue until either the value is larger than both children, or until we reach the leaf level of the tree. The code to perform the deletion is shown in Figure 15.5.

Because at most three comparisons of data values are performed at each level, and the while loop traces out a path from the root of the tree to the leaf, the complexity of the deletion procedure is also $O(\log n)$.

---

2. The procedure adjust_heap is not defined by the standard library, and is therefore not guaranteed to exist in all implementations.

15.2.1   Application: Heap Sort

The heap data structure provides an elegant technique for sorting an array. The basic idea is to first form the array into a heap. To sort the array, the top of the heap (the largest element) is swapped with the last element of the array, and the size of the heap is reduced by one. The effect of the swap, however, may be to destroy the heap property. But this is exactly the same condition we encountered in deleting an element from the heap. And, not surprisingly, we can use the same solution. Heap order is restored by invoking the adjust_heap procedure.

Slightly more surprising is that we can use the adjust_heap procedure to construct an initial heap from an unorganized collection of values held in a vector. To see this, note that a subtree consisting of a leaf node by itself satisfies the heap order property. To build the initial heap, we start with the smallest subtree containing interior nodes, which corresponds to the

---

Proof of Correctness: push_heap

The proof of correctness for the algorithm named push_heap begins with the assumption that the collection represented by the iterator range represents a valid heap, with the possible exception of the very last element, which may be out of order. The sole task of the algorithm is to move this one element into place.

Throughout the algorithm, the variable position will maintain the index position of this value, while the variable parent will maintain the index position of the parent node.

The while loop at the heart of the algorithm has two test conditions. Both must be true for the loop to execute. Together, the two conditions assert that the position has a parent (that is, the position is not yet the root node) and that the parent value is smaller than the position, in contradiction to the heap order property. The following illustrates this situation:

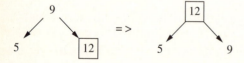

The invariant at the top of the loop body asserts that the subtree rooted at position repre-

sents a heap. This will trivially be true the first time the while loop is executed, because the subtree represents only a leaf. Because the parent node is already larger than the other child (if the parent has two children), simply swapping the position with the parent is sufficient to locally reestablish the heap order property. (To see why, note that any children of node position must have originally been children of node parent, and must therefore be smaller than the parent.) Following the swap, the tree rooted at the index value parent will therefore be a heap. This value becomes the new position, and we determine the new parent index.

The while loop terminates either when the value percolates all the way to the top of the heap, or when a node is encountered that is larger than the new value. In the first case the final loop invariant is asserting that the entire structure represents a heap. If, on the other hand, the loop terminates because of the second case, we know that the subtree rooted at parent has the heap order property. But because this subtree holds the only value that could have been out of order, we therefore can conclude that the entire structure must have the heap order property.

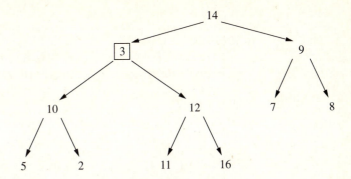

Figure 15.4 A value percolating down into position.

middle of the data array. Invoking the `adjust_heap` method for this value will ensure that the subtree satisfies the heap order property. Walking back toward the root of the tree, we repeatedly invoke the `adjust_heap`, thereby ensuring all subtrees are themselves heaps. When we finally reach the root, the entire tree will have been made into a heap. This algorithm is implemented by the following procedure:

```
template <class Iterator>
void make_heap (Iterator start, Iterator stop)
{
    unsigned int heapSize = stop - start;
    for (int i = heapSize / 2; i >= 0; i--)
            // assume children of node i are heaps
        adjust_heap(start, heapSize, i);
            // inv: tree rooted at node i is a heap
    // assert: structure is now a heap
}
```

To convert a heap into a sorted collection, we simply repeatedly swap the first and last positions, then readjust the heap property, reducing the heap size by one element. This is performed by the following procedure:

```
template <class Iterator>
void sort_heap (Iterator start, Iterator stop)
{
    unsigned int lastPosition = stop - start - 1;
    while (lastPosition > 0) {
        swap(start[0], start[lastPosition]);
        adjust_heap(start, lastPosition, 0);
        lastPosition--;
        }
}
```

```
template <class Iterator>
void pop_heap (Iterator start, Iterator stop)
{
    unsigned int lastPosition = (stop - start) - 1;
    // move the largest element into the last location
    swap (start[0], start[lastPosition]);
    // then readjust
    adjust_heap(start, lastPosition, 0);
}


template <class Iterator>
void adjust_heap
    (Iterator start, unsigned heapSize, unsigned position)
    // initial conditions:
    // collection represents a heap, except that element
    // at index value position may be out of order
{
    while (position < heapsize) {
        // To fix, replace position with the larger
        // of the two children
        unsigned int childpos = position * 2 + 1;
        if (childpos < heapsize) {
            if ((childpos + 1 < heapsize) &&
                start[childpos + 1] > start[childpos])
                    childpos++;
            // childpos is larger of two children
            if (start[position] > start[childpos])
                    // structure is now heap
                return;
            else
                swap (start[position], start[childpos]);
        }
    position = childpos;
    }
}
```

Figure 15.5 Method for deletion from a `heap`

Combining these two, the heap sort algorithm can be written as:[3]

```
template <class Iterator>
void heap_sort(Iterator start, Iterator stop)
{       // sort the vector argument using a heap algorithm
```

---

3. Note that `make_heap` and `sort_heap` are generic algorithms in the standard library, but `heap_sort` is not.

```
// first build the initial heap
make_heap (start, stop);

// then convert heap into sorted collection
sort_heap (start, stop);
}
```

To derive the asymptotic running time for this algorithm, recall that the `adjust_heap` procedure requires $O(\log n)$ steps. There are n executions of `adjust_heap` to generate the initial heap, and n further executions to reheap values during the sorting operation. Combining these tells us that the total running time is $O(n \log n)$. This matches that of the merge sort algorithm (Section 8.3.3) and the quick sort algorithm (Section 14.5.1), and is better than the $O(n^2)$ bubble and insertion sort algorithms (Section 5.1.4).

Of a more practical benefit, note that the heap sort algorithm does not require any additional space, because it constructs the heap directly in the vector input value. This was not true of some of the previous sorting algorithms. Those algorithms must pay the cost not only of the sorting itself, but of the allocation and deallocation of the data structures formed during the process of ordering the elements.

An empirical analysis of the running time of the heap sort algorithm illustrates that for almost all vector sizes, heap sort is comparable in speed

---

Proof of Correctness: `adjust_heap`

The `adjust_heap` algorithm is in some ways the opposite of the `push_heap` procedure. Here, the assumption is that the structure of the given size beginning at the starting iterator is a heap, except that the value with the index value position may be out of order.

To reestablish the heap order property, the two children of node position are examined. The value indexed by `childpos` is set to the larger of the two children. If this value is smaller than the value in question, then the heap order property holds, and therefore the entire structure must be a heap. If, on the other hand, the larger child is also larger than the value in question, then they must be swapped. This is illustrated as:

Note that because the element was swapped with the larger of the two children, the new root must therefore be not only larger than the element in question, but also larger than the smaller child. Thus we need not consider the subtree rooted at the smaller child. But it is now necessary to continue to examine the subtree rooted at the position into which the value in question was swapped. The larger child position becomes the new value held by the variable `position`, and the while loop continues.

The algorithm terminates either when the value in question finds its location (being larger than both children) or when it reaches a point where it has no children.

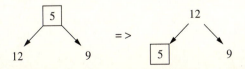

to quick sort (see Figure 15.6). An advantage of heap sort over quick sort is that the heap sort algorithm is less influenced by the initial distribution of the input values. Recall that a poor distribution of values can make quick sort exhibit $O(n^2)$ behavior, while heap sort is $O(n \log n)$ in all circumstances.

15.3   SKEW HEAPS*

The obvious method to avoid the bounded-size problem of heaps is to use a tree representation. This is not, however, quite as simple as it might seem. The key to obtaining logarithmic performance in the heap data structure is that at each step we were able to guarantee that the tree was completely balanced. Finding the next location to be filled in an array representation of a completely balanced binary tree is trivial—it is simply the next location following the current top of the array. In a tree form this is not quite as easy. Consider the tree shown in Figure 15.1. Knowing the location of the last element (the value 3) is of no help in discovering where the next element should be inserted to maintain the balanced binary tree property. In fact, the next element is part of an entirely different subtree than that containing the current last element.

A *skew heap* avoids this problem by making no attempt to maintain the heap as a completely balanced binary tree. As seen when we examined search trees, this means that a tree can potentially become almost linear,

---

Proof of Correctness: `make_heap`

To prove that the `make_heap` algorithm creates a heap it is necessary to understand the task being performed by the loop that is at the heart of the algorithm. At each step of this algorithm, the assumption is that the subtrees representing the children of node i are proper heaps, and the task to be performed is to make the subtree rooted at node i into a heap.

Note that the value i is initialized to the value `heapSize / 2`, and moves downwards. Observe that all subtrees with index values larger than `heapSize / 2` represent leaf nodes, and that leaf nodes possess the heap property (trivially, because they have no children). Thus, the first time execution moves from the start of the procedure to the assertion in the body of the loop, the assertions must be true. We have already proven the `adjust_heap` procedure, and therefore the

invariant following the procedure call must be true.

Now consider the case in which we encounter the assertion at the beginning of the loop body, after having executed some number of previous iterations of the loop. In this case, the children of node i must either be leaves, or they must have been previously processed. In either case, the subtrees rooted at the child nodes must be heaps and, therefore, following execution of the body of the loop, the subtree rooted at node i must be a heap.

The establish the final condition, we simply note that either the loop was executed, in which case the final condition matches one of the loop invariants we previously established, or the loop was never executed, which can only happen if the heap contains only a single leaf. In the latter case, we have already noted that a leaf node is a heap.

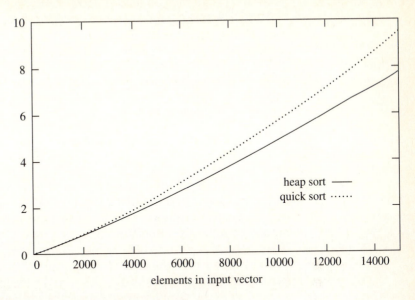

Figure 15.6 Empirical timing of heap sort

and we can place no guarantee on logarithmic performance for any individual operation. But another critical observation can be made concerning heaps, which is that the order of the left and right children for any node is essentially arbitrary. We can exchange the left and right children of any node in a heap without destroying the heap order property. We can make use of this observation by systematically swapping the left and right children of a node as we perform insertions and deletions. A badly unbalanced tree can affect the performance of one operation, but it can be shown that subsequent insertions and deletions must as a consequence be very rapid. In fact, if m insertions or deletions are performed, it can be shown (although the details are beyond the discussion here) that the total time to perform all m operations is bounded by $O(m \log n)$. Thus, amortized over time, each operation is no worse than $O(\log n)$.

The second observation critical to the implementation of skew heaps is that both insertions and deletions can be considered special cases of merging two trees into a single heap. This is obvious in the case of the deletion process. Removing the root of the tree results in two subtrees. The new heap can be constructed by simply merging these two child trees.

```
template <class value_type> void  skewHeap<value_type>::pop ()
{    // remove the minimum element from a skew heap
    assert (! empty());
    node<value_type> * top = root;
    root = merge(root->right(), root->left());
    delete top;
}
```

Similarly, insertion can be considered a merge of the existing heap and a new heap containing a single element.

```
template <class value_type>
void skewHeap<value_type>::push (value_type & val)
        // to add a new value, simply merge with
        // a tree containing one node
{
        root = merge(root, new node<value_type>(val));
}
```

The skewHeap data structure, shown in Figure 15.7, implements both insertions and deletions using an internal method merge. The recursive merge operation follows. If either argument is empty, then the result of a merge is simply the other tree. Otherwise we will assume the largest value is the root of the first tree, by returning the merge of the arguments reversed if this is not the case. To perform the merge, we move the current left child of the left argument to the right child of the result, and recursively merge the right argument with the old right child.

```
template <class value_type>
node<value_type> * skewHeap<value_type>::merge
        (node<value_type> * h1, node<value_type> * h2)
        // merge two skew heaps to form a new heap
{
            // if either tree is empty, return the other
        if (! h1) return h2;
        if (! h2) return h1;

            // assume largest is root of h1
        if (h2->value > h1->value)
            return merge(h2, h1);

            // reverse children and recurse
        node<value_type> * lchild = h1->left();
        if (lchild) {
            h1->left(merge(h1->right(), h2));
            h1->right(lchild);
            }
        else      // no left child
            h1->left(h2);
        return h1;
}
```

For example, suppose we are merging a heap containing the elements 2, 5, and 7 with a heap containing the two elements 4 and 6. Because the

```
//
//    class skewHeap
//       heap priority queue implemented using skew heap merge
//       operations
//

template <class value_type> class skewHeap {
public:
        // constructors
        skewHeap         () : root(0) { }
        ~ skewHeap       ();

            // priority queue protocol
        bool        empty () { return root == 0; }
        int         size  () { return root->size(); }
        value_type & top  () { return root->value; }
        void        pop   ();
        void        push  (value_type & value);

            // additional method: splice two heaps together
        void        splice        (skewHeap & secondHeap);


protected:
            // root of heap
        node<value_type> *       root;

            // internal method to merge two heaps
        node<value_type> * merge (node<value_type> *, node<value_type> *);
};
```

Figure 15.7 The skewHeap class declaration

element at the top of the left heap, 7, is larger, it becomes the new root. At the same time, the old left child of the root becomes the new right child. To form the new right child, we recursively merge the old right child and the original right argument.

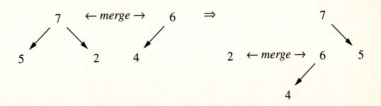

The first step in the recursive call is to flip the arguments so that the largest element is held in the first argument. The top element of this heap then becomes the new root. As before, the old left child of this value becomes the new right child. A recursive call is made to insert the right argument, 7, into the now empty former right child of the node 4. This results in the node 7 being returned, and the final result produced.

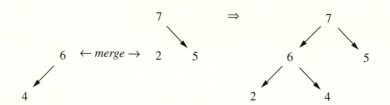

To illustrate why the amortized analysis of skew heaps can be so good, note that the worst-case situation occurs when the left subtree contains a long path along the right child links. For example, consider the merging of the singleton 2 into such a tree.

Merging Heaps

Skew heaps basically operate by merging two heaps to form a new heap. This means that it is relatively easy to combine two instances of the data structure. We have taken advantage of this by providing a splice method that takes another instance of skew heap as argument.

```
template <class value_type>
void skewHeap<value_type>::splice
   (skewHeap<value_type> & secondHeap)
{
   // merge elements from a second heap
   // into current heap
   root = merge(root, secondHeap.root);
   // empty values from second heap
   secondHeap.root = 0;
}
```

The merge procedure used is the same as the merge used in implementing the addition and removal methods. It can thus be expected to run very rapidly, in time proportional to the longest path in the largest heap, not the number of elements in the argument heap, as would be the case if the values were simply added one by one.

An important feature to note, however, is that this operation effectively empties the argument heap, by setting its root value to zero. This is necessary because of the way in which our data structures are performing memory management. In our scheme, each node in a tree must be "owned" by only one data structure. This data structure is responsible for performing a deletion to free the memory used by the node when it is no longer being used as part of the structure. If a single node were to be used in two different structures, it is possible, indeed inevitable, that it would be deleted at two different times by two different structures.

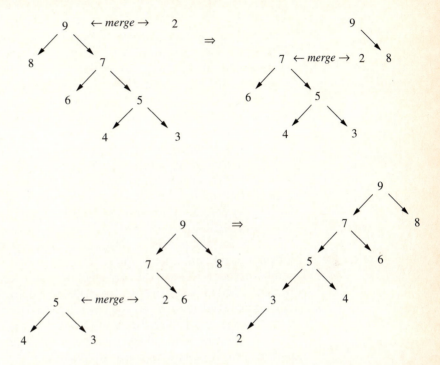

The merge requires 4 steps. However, note that now the long right path has been converted into a long left path. Thus, the next insertion will be relatively quick. Assume, for example, we now insert the value 1.

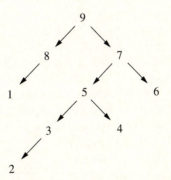

It is tempting to conjecture that after two insertions we would be back to the original poor configuration, but note that this has not occurred. The longest path is still a left path, although it is now on the right side. Quite a few steps must take place before the situation can arise where a long right path can slow insertions.

15.4 APPLICATION: DISCRETE EVENT-DRIVEN SIMULATION

Imagine you are considering opening an ice-cream store on a popular beach. You need to decide how large the store should be, how many seats you should have, and so on. If you plan too small, customers will be turned away when there is insufficient space and you will lose profits. On the other hand, if you plan too large, most of the seats will be unused and you will be pay useless rent on the space, and hence lose profits. So you need to choose approximately the right number, but how do you decide?

One approach would be to perform a simulation. You first examine similar operations in comparable locations and form a model that includes, among other factors, an estimation of the number of customers you can expect to arrive in any period of time, the length of time they will take to decide upon an order, and the length of time they will stay after having been served. Based on this you can design a simulation.

A *discrete event-driven simulation* is a popular simulation technique. Objects in the simulation model mirror objects in the real world, and are programmed to react as the real objects would react, as much as possible. A priority queue is used to store a representation of "events" that are waiting to happen. This queue is stored in order based on the time the event should occur, so the smallest element will always be the next event to be modeled. As an event occurs, it can spawn other events. These subsequent events are placed into the queue as well. Execution continues until all events have occurred, or until a preset time for the simulation is exceeded.

To see how we might design a simulation of our ice-cream store, consider a typical scenario. A group of customers arrive at the ice-cream store. From our measurements of similar stores we derive a probability that indicates how frequently this occurs. For example, suppose we assume that groups will consist of from one to five people, selected uniformly over that range. (In actual simulations the distribution would seldom be uniform. For instance, groups of size two and three might predominate, with groups of size one and groups larger than three being relatively less frequent. The mathematics involved in forming nonuniform distributions is subtle, and not particularly relevant to our discussion. We will therefore use uniform distributions throughout.) These groups will arrive at times spaced from one to ten minutes apart, again selected uniformly. Once they arrive, a group will either be seated, or see that there are no seats and leave. If seated, they will take from two to ten minutes to order, and once they order they will remain from fifteen to thirty-five minutes in the store. We know that every customer will order from one to three scoops of ice cream, and that the store makes a profit of $0.35 on each scoop.

To create a random integer between two values, we can write a simple function that uses the `randomInteger` class we introduced in Chapter 2.

```
class IceCreamStore {
public:
    IceCreamStore()
        : freeChairs(35), profit(0.0) { }

    bool canSeat (unsigned int numberOfPeople);
    void order(unsigned int numberOfScoops);
    void leave(unsigned int numberOfPeople);

    unsigned int freeChairs;
    double profit;
};
```

Figure 15.8   The class `IceCreamStore`

This new function takes the integer endpoints, and returns a new value from a uniform distribution between the two points:

```
integer randBetween (integer low, integer high)
    // return random integer between low and high
{
    randomInteger randomizer;
    return low + randomizer(high - low);
}
```

The primary object in the simulation is the store itself. It might seem odd to provide "behavior" for an inanimate object such as a store; however, we can think of the store as a useful abstraction for the servers and managers who work in the store. The store manages two data items: the number of available seats and the amount of profit generated. The behavior of the store can be described by this list:

▲ When a customer group arrives, the size of the group is compared to the number of seats. If insufficient seats are available, the group leaves. Otherwise the group is seated and the number of seats decreased.

▲ When a customer orders and is served, the amount of profit is computed.

▲ When a customer group leaves, the seats are released for another customer group.

A class description for `IceCreamStore` is shown in Figure 15.8. The implementation of the methods are shown in Figure 15.9.

```
bool IceCreamStore::canSeat (unsigned int numberOfPeople)
    // if sufficient room, then seat customers
{
    cout << "Time: " << time;
    cout << " group of " << numberOfPeople << " customers arrives";
    if (numberOfPeople < freeChairs) {
        cout << " is seated" << endl;
        freeChairs -= numberOfPeople;
        return true;
        }
    else {
        cout << " no room, they leave" << endl;
        return false;
        }
}


void IceCreamStore::order (unsigned int numberOfScoops)
    // serve ice-cream, compute profits
{
    cout << "Time: " << time;
    cout << " serviced order for " << numberOfScoops << endl;
    profit += 0.35 * numberOfScoops;
}


void IceCreamStore::leave (unsigned int numberOfPeople)
    // people leave, free up chairs
{
    cout << "Time: " << time;
    cout << " group of size " << numberOfPeople << " leaves" << endl;
    freeChairs += numberOfPeople;
}
```

Figure 15.9   The methods implementing the class `IceCreamStore`

15.4.1   A Framework for Simulations

Rather than simply code a simulation of this one problem, we will generalize the problem and first produce a generic *framework* for simulations. This is similar to the framework for backtracking problems we presented in Chapter 10.

At the heart of a simulation is the concept of an *event*. An event will be represented by an instance of class event. The only value held by the class will be the time the event is to occur. The method processEvent will be invoked to "execute" the event when the appropriate time is reached.

```
//
//      class event
//          execution event in a discrete event-driven simulation
//

class event {
public:
          // constructor requires time of event
     event (unsigned int t) : time(t) { }

          // time is a public data field
     unsigned int time;

          // execute event by invoking this method
     virtual void processEvent() { }
};
```

The simulation queue will need to maintain a collection of different types of events. Each different form of event will be represented by different derived classes of class event. Not all events will have the same type, although they will all be derived from class event. (This is sometimes called a *heterogeneous* collection, and the value that points to an event is sometimes called a *polymorphic* variable.) For this reason, the collection must store *pointers* to events, instead of the events themselves.

Because comparison of pointers cannot be specialized on the basis of the pointer types, we must instead define an explicit comparison function for pointers to events. When using the standard library, this is accomplished by defining a new structure, the sole purpose of which is to define the function invocation operator (the ( ) operator) in the appropriate fashion.

Polymorphic Variables

A variable that can hold many different types of values is called *polymorphic* ("poly" = many, "morph" = form). In object-oriented languages, such as C++, polymorphic variables are linked to the class-derived class hierarchy. A variable declared as a pointer to a parent class, such as the class event, can in fact hold a value that is a derived class type, such as arriveEvent.

In C++, polymorphic variables can only occur through the use of pointers or references. This is due to the way memory is allocated by the C++ system. Note that the storage required by the child class is *larger* than the storage required by the parent class. (The parent class has only one integer data field, while the child class has two). Memory for all elements of a *vector* must be the same—this is necessary for the efficient indexing ability characteristic of vectors. These two requirements conflict with one another. However, the space required to hold a pointer is fixed, regardless of the type of value to which it points. For this reason C++ only allows pointer values to be polymorphic.

Because in this particular example we wish to use the priority queue to return the *smallest* element each time, rather than the largest, the order of the comparison is reversed, as follows:

```
class eventComparison {
public:
    bool operator () (event * left, event * right)
        { return left->time > right->time; }
};
```

We are now ready to define the class `simulation`, which provides the basic structure for the simulation activities. The class `simulation` provides two basic functions. The first is used to insert a new event into the queue, while the second runs the simulation. A data field is also provided to hold the current simulation "time."

```
class simulation {
public:
    simulation () : eventQueue(), currentTime(0) { }

    void scheduleEvent (event * newEvent)
        { eventQueue.push (newEvent); }

    void run();

    unsigned int currentTime;

protected:
    priority_queue<vector<event *>, eventComparison> eventQueue;
};
```

Notice the declaration of the priority queue used to hold the pending events. In this case, we are using a vector as the underlying container. We could easily have used a deque. Note also the way in which the comparison function class is provided as the second template argument.

The heart of the simulation is the member function `run()`, which defines the event loop. This procedure makes use of three of the five priority queue operations, namely `top()`, `pop()`, and `empty()`. It is implemented as:

```
void simulation::run()
    // execute events until event queue becomes empty
{
    while (! eventQueue.empty()) {
        event * nextEvent = eventQueue.top();
        eventQueue.pop();
        time = nextEvent->time;
```

```
        nextEvent->processEvent();
        delete nextEvent;
        }
}
```

ICE-CREAM STORE SIMULATION

Having created a framework for simulations in general, we now return to the specific simulation in hand, the ice-cream store. An instance of class `simulation` is defined as a global variable, called `theSimulation`. An instance of `iceCreamStore` is accessible via the name `theStore`.

As we noted already, each activity is matched by a derived class of event. Each derived class of event includes an integer data field, which represents the size of a group of customers. The arrival event occurs when a group enters. When executed, the arrival event creates and installs a new order event:

```
class arriveEvent : public event {
public:
    arriveEvent (unsigned int time, unsigned int gs)
        : event(time), groupSize(gs) { }
    virtual void processEvent ();
protected:
    unsigned int groupSize;
};


void arriveEvent::processEvent()
{
    if (theStore.canSeat(groupSize))
        theSimulation.scheduleEvent
            (new orderEvent(time + randBetween(2,10), groupSize));
}
```

An order event similarly spawns a leave event:

```
class orderEvent : public event {
public:
    orderEvent (unsigned int time, unsigned int gs)
        : event(time), size(gs) { }
    virtual void processEvent ();
protected:
    unsigned int groupSize;
};


void orderEvent::processEvent()
{
        // each person orders some number of scoops
```

```
        for (int i = 0; i < groupSize; i++)
            theStore.order(1 + rand(3));
        theSimulation.scheduleEvent
            (new leaveEvent(time + randBetween(15,35), groupSize));
};
```

Finally, leave events free up chairs, but do not spawn any new events:

```
class leaveEvent : public event {
public:
    leaveEvent (unsigned int time, unsigned int gs)
        : event(time), groupSize(gs) { }
    virtual void processEvent ();
protected:
    unsigned int groupSize;
};


void leaveEvent::processEvent ()
{
    theStore.leave(groupSize);
}
```

The main program simply creates a certain number of initial events, then sets the simulation in motion. In our case, we will simulate two hours (120 minutes) of operation, with groups arriving with random distribution between two and five minutes apart.

```
void main() {
    // load queue with some number of initial events
    unsigned int t = 0;
    while (t < 120) {
        t += randBetween(2,5);
      theSimulation.scheduleEvent(new arriveEvent(t, randBetween(1,5)));
        }

    // then run simulation and print profits
    theSimulation.run();
    cout << "Total profits " << theStore.profit << endl;
}
```

An example execution might produce a log such as this:

```
customer group of size 4 arrives at time 11
customer group of size 4 orders 5 scoops of ice cream at time 13
customer group size 4 leaves at time 15
customer group of size 2 arrives at time 16
customer group of size 1 arrives at time 17
```

```
customer group of size 2 orders 2 scoops of ice cream at time 19
customer group of size 1 orders 1 scoops of ice cream at time 19
customer group size 1 leaves at time 22
          .
          .
          .

customer group of size 2 orders 3 scoops of ice cream at time 136
customer group size 2 leaves at time 143
total profits are 26.95
```

15.5   CHAPTER SUMMARY

Key Concepts

- Priority queue
- Heap
- Heap order property
- Heap sort
- Skew heap
- Discrete event-driven simulation

A priority queue is not a queue at all, but is a data structure designed to permit rapid access and removal of the largest element in a collection. Priority queues can be structured by building them on top of lists, sets, vectors, or deques. The vector or deque version of a priority queue is called a heap. The heap structure forms the basis of a very efficient sorting algorithm.

A skew heap is a form of heap that does not have the fixed-size characteristic of the vector heap. The skew heap data structure is interesting because it can potentially have a very poor worst-case performance. However, it can be shown that the worst case performance cannot be maintained, and following any occurrence the next several operations of insertion or removal must be very rapid. Thus, when measured over several operations, the performance of a skew heap is very impressive.

A common problem addressed using priority queues is the idea of discrete event-driven simulation. We have illustrated the use of heaps in an example simulation of an ice-cream store. In Chapter 19, we will once more use a priority queue in the development of an algorithm for computing the shortest path between pairs of points in a graph.

Further Reading

The binary heap was first proposed by John Williams in conjunction with the heap sort algorithm [Williams 64]. Although heap sort is now considered to be one of the standard classic algorithms, a thorough theoretical analysis of the algorithm has proven to be surprisingly difficult. Only in 1991 was the best case and average case execution time analysis of heap sort reported [Schaffer 91].

Skew heaps were first described by Donald Sleator and Robert Tarjan in [Sleator 86]. An explanation of the amortized analysis of skew heaps is presented in [Weiss 92]. The ice-cream store simulation is derived from a similar simulation in my earlier book on Smalltalk [Budd 87].

Study Questions & Exercises

Study Questions

1. What is the primary characterization of a priority queue?

2. Why is a priority queue not a true queue?

3. How could a priority queue be constructed using a list?

4. What is the heap data structure?

5. What are the two most common uses of the term heap in computer science?

6. What is the heap order property?

7. What is a complete binary tree?

8. Give a vector of ten elements ordered largest to smallest, then show the corresponding complete binary tree. Why will the tree always be a heap?

9. What is the difference between the procedures sort_heap and heap_sort?

10. In the skew heap data structure, what is similar about the push and pop routines?

11. What is a discrete event-driven simulation?

12. What is a heterogeneous collection?

13. What is a polymorphic variable?

Exercises

1. Complete the design of a priority queue constructed using lists. That is, develop a data structure with the same interface as the priority_queue data type, but that uses lists as the underlying container and implements the interface using list operations.

2. Although it is possible to implement iterators for the heap data structure, argue why it makes little sense to do so.

3. Give an example of a priority queue that occurs in a non-computer science situation.

4. Explain how the skewHeap data structure could be changed so that the smallest item was the value most easily accessible, instead of the largest value.

5. Show what a heap data structure looks like subsequent to insertions of each of the following values:

$$4\ 2\ 5\ 8\ 3\ 6\ 1\ 10\ 14$$

6. Show what a skewHeap data structure looks like subsequent to insertions of each of the following values:

$$4\ 2\ 5\ 8\ 3\ 6\ 1\ 10\ 14$$

7. Consider the following alternative implementation of push_heap:

```
template <class Iterator>
void push_heap (Iterator start,
        Iterator stop)
{

    unsigned int heapsize = stop - start;
    unsigned int position = heapsize - 1;

    // now restore the possibly lost heap property
    while (position > 0) {
        // reheap the subtree
        adjust_heap(data, heapsize,
            position);
        // move up the tree
        position = (position-1)/2;
    }
}
```

a. Prove that this algorithm will successfully add a new element to the heap.

b. Explain why as a practical matter this algorithm is less desirable than the algorithm presented earlier in the book.

8. Using the techniques described in Exercise 19, Chapter 4, test the hypothesis that heap sort is an $O(n \log n)$ algorithm. Using the coefficient c that you compute, estimate for the heap sort algorithm how long it would take to sort a vector of 100,000 elements. Is your value in agreement with the actual time presented in the second table in Appendix B? Why do you think the values computed for small vectors represent a better predictor of performance for heap sort than did the equivalent analysis performed for tree sort?

9. Another heap-based sorting algorithm can be constructed using skew heaps. The idea is to simply copy the values from a vector into a skew heap, then copy the values one-by-one back out of the heap. Write the C++ procedure to do this.

10. Perform empirical timings on the algorithm you wrote for the previous question. Use input vectors of various sizes containing random numbers. Compare the running time of this algorithm to that of tree sort and heap sort.

11. Design a simulation of an airport. The airport has two runways. Planes arrive from the air and request permission to land, and independently planes on the ground request permission to take off.

12. One alternative to the use of uniform distributions is a weighted discrete probability. Suppose we observe a real store and note that 65 percent of the time customers will order one scoop, 25 percent of the time they will order two scoops, and only 10 percent of the time will they order three scoops. This is certainly a far different distribution from the uniform distribution we used in the simulation. In order to simulate this behavior, we can add a new method to our class random.
    a. Add a method named `weightedDiscrete` to the class `random`. This method will take, as an argument, a vector of unsigned integer values. For example, to generate the distribution above, the programmer would pass the method a vector of three elements, containing 65, 25, and 10.
    b. The method first sums the values in the array, resulting in a maximum value. In this case the value would be 100. A random number between 1 and this maximum value is then generated.
    c. The method then decides in which category the number belongs. This can be discovered by looping through the values. In our example, if the number is less than 65, then the method should return 0 (remember, index values start at 0), if less than or equal to 90, return 1, and otherwise return 2.

13. Modify the ice-cream store simulation so that it uses the weighted discrete random number generated function implemented in the previous question. Select reasonable numbers for the weights. Compare a run of the resulting program to a run of the program using the uniform distribution.

Chapter **16**

Maps and Multimaps

Chapter Overview

Like a vector, a *map* is an indexed data structure in which values are obtained by association with an index, or key value. However, unlike a vector, with a map the index elements are not restricted to an integer range, but instead can be any ordered data type. Thus, a map could be indexed, for example, by words represented as strings. In this chapter we introduce the map data type and illustrate its use in the solution of several problems. We then construct a simplified example implementation, using inheritance to build the map data type on top of the set data abstraction. This once again illustrates the power of inheritance as a technique for creating new data abstractions out of existing classes. Major topics discussed in this chapter include the following:

- ▲ The map data abstraction
- ▲ Example programs: a telephone directory, sentence generation, a concordance
- ▲ An example implementation

16.1   THE MAP DATA ABSTRACTION

Indexed collections occur frequently in the development of computer programs; however, the index values are not always integers or easily mapped onto integers. For example, a dictionary is most easily described as a collection that is indexed by words (strings) and contains definitions.

Abstractly, a map (sometimes called a *table*, *dictionary*, or *associative array*) is an indexed structure, similar to a vector. Unlike a vector, in a map the index values, as well as the elements, can be any type. Elements are accessed by means of the subscript operator, just as with a vector. Like a list or a set, but unlike a vector, a map does not limit the number of elements that can be held in the structure.

A multimap is similar to a map, but does not require that key values be unique. That is, each key must be associated with only one value in a map, but may be associated with many values in a multimap.

16.1.1   Pairs

The development of the map data structure is, perhaps surprisingly, made almost trivial by building on top of the existing set data type. Internally, a map will maintain items as pairs of values. Both the key and the element value are stored as part of the data structure. This differs from the vector data type, where only the element values, and not the indices, were explicitly stored. The data type we will use for this purpose is the class pair, shown in Figure 16.1.

The two data fields for a pair are called first and second, and are publicly accessible. The index value for a pair is often called the *key*. When used with a map, the key field is fixed; once set, it cannot be altered. The value field, on the other hand, is public and can be changed. A pair can be compared to another pair, and the ordering is determined entirely by the key field.

16.2   EXAMPLE PROGRAMS

We will present three example programs that illustrate the use of the map data type.

16.2.1   A Telephone Directory

We will illustrate the use of the map data type by describing a program for maintaining a telephone directory. The directory is simply an indexed structure, in which the name of the person or business (a string) is the key

```
//
//      class pair
//          A single key/value pair,
//

template <class Key_type, class Value_type>
class pair {
public:
            // both key and value are public accessible
    Key_type first;
    Value_type second;


        // constructors
    pair  (Key_type initialKey, Value_type initialValue)
        : first (initialKey), second (initialValue) { }
    pair  () { }

        // comparisons
    bool operator < (pair<Key_type, Value_type> & p)
        { return first < p.first; }
};
```

Figure 16.1   Definition of the class pair

value, and the telephone number (a long integer) is the associated entry. We might write such a class as shown in Figure 16.2.

Simple operations on our database are directly implemented by map commands. Adding an element to the database is simply an `insert`, removing an element is an `erase`, and updating is a combination of the two. To print all the entries in the database we can use the `for_each()` generic algorithm, which takes as argument an iterator range and a function, and applies the function to each value in the range. To achieve the desired effect we apply this simple utility routine:

```
void printEntry (telephoneDirectory::entry_type & entry)
    // print a single entry in the telephone database
{
    cout << entry.first << ":" << entry.second << endl;
}
```

The implementation of the next pair of operations will illustrate how a few of the generic algorithms can be used with maps. Suppose one wanted

```
//
//    telephoneDirectory
//       a class that maintains a dictionary of
//       name-number pairs

class telephoneDirectory {
public:
        // shorthand names for different types
    typedef map<string, long integer> database_type;
    typedef database_type::value_type entry_type;
    typedef database_type::iterator iterator;

        // add a new entry to database
    void addEntry (string name, long number)
        { database[name] = number; }

        // remove an entry from the database
    void remove (string name)
        { database.erase(name); }

        // update value in database
    void update (string name, long number)
        { remove(name); addEntry(name, number); }

        // display all names in database
    void displayDatabase()
        { for_each(database.begin(), database.end(), printEntry); }

        // display names with given prefix
    void displayPrefix(int);

        // display names in prefix order
    void displayByPrefix();

protected:
    database_type database;
};
```

Figure 16.2 The telephoneDirectory class

to display all the phone numbers with a certain three-digit initial prefix.[1] We will use the `find_if()` generic algorithm (which is different from the `find()` member function in class `map`) to locate the first entry. Starting from this location, subsequent calls on `find_if()` will uncover each successive entry.

```
void telephoneDirectory::displayPrefix (int prefix)
    // display all entries with given prefix
{
    cout << "Listing for prefix " << prefix << endl;
    telephoneDatabase::iterator where;
    where = find_if
        (database.begin(), database.end(), checkPrefix(prefix));
    while (where != database.end()) {
        printEntry(*where);
        where = find_if
            (++where, database.end(), checkPrefix(prefix));
        }
    cout << "end of prefix listing" << endl;
}
```

For the predicate to this operation, we require a Boolean function that takes only a single argument (the pair representing a database entry) and tells us whether it is in the given prefix. There is no obvious candidate function, and in any case the test prefix is not being passed as an argument to the comparison function. The solution to this problem is to employ a technique that is commonly used with the standard library—defining the predicate function as an instance of a class, and storing the test predicate as an instance variable in the class, initialized when the class is constructed. The desired behavior is then defined as the function call operator for the class:

Directory

```
int prefix(telephoneDatabase::entry & entry)
    // return prefix from database entry type
    // by removing the last four digits
{
    return entry.second / 10000;
}


class checkPrefix {
public:
```

---

1. I apologize to international readers for this obviously North-American-centric example.

```
        checkPrefix (int p) : testPrefix(p) { }
        int testPrefix;
        bool operator () (telephoneDatabse::entry & entry)
            { return prefix(entry) == testPrefix; }
};
```

Our final example will be to display the directory sorted by prefix. It is not possible to alter the way in which maps are themselves ordered. So, instead, we first copy the entire map into a vector, and then sort the vector. The generic sorting algorithm allows us to specify an alternative comparison function to be used to order elements. Once sorted, we use the for_each() function on the vector to print each entry.

```
void telephoneDirectory::displayByPrefix()
    // display all entries ordered by prefix
{
    cout << "Display by prefix" << endl;
    vector<telephoneDatabase::entry> sortedData (database.size());
    copy(database.begin(), database.end(), sortedData.begin());
    sort (sortedData.begin(), sortedData.end(), prefixCompare);
    for_each(sortedData.begin(), sortedData.end(), printEntry);
    cout << "end display by prefix" << endl;
}
```

The function used by the sorting operation to compare prefix values is the following:

```
bool prefixCompare
    (telephoneDatabase::entry & a, telephoneDatabase::entry & b)
    // compare the prefix values of two database entries
{
    return prefix(a) < prefix(b);
}
```

16.2.2   Silly Sentence Generation Revisited

In Chapter 8 we described a program that would generate a sequence of nonsense English sentences. By using a map to represent a more complex grammar, we can greatly improve the power of this program. This grammar can be described as shown in Figure 16.3. The left column represents an index into the table, and the right column represents a list of potential replacements. Each line is, in turn, a list of words.

Let us see how this grammar can generate the sentence, "My sister loves eating with the man next door." Our start symbol for the grammar is the nonterminal "SENTENCE." Of the four possible sentence types, one is selected randomly. In this case, it is the sentence of the form "PERSON

SENTENCE	PERSON DOES SOMETHING
	PERSON thinks that I am PROPERTY
	I DO SOMETHING
	you think that I am PROPERTY
ACTIVITY	dancing
	eating
	sleeping
OBJECT	PERSON
	life
	my computer
	my friends
DO	hate
	am jealous of
	love
DOES	hates
	loves
PERSON	my sister
	my father
	my girl friend
	the man next door
PROPERTY	creative
	intelligent
SOMETHING	ACTIVITY
	ACTIVITY with PERSON
	OBJECT

Figure 16.3 Grammar for silly sentences

DOES SOMETHING." Each of the terms in this line will be recursively tested in turn. For PERSON our grammar selects (again, choosing randomly) the text "my sister." For DOES the text "loves" is chosen, and for SOMETHING the text "ACTIVITY WITH PERSON" is chosen. One of the possibilities for ACTIVITY is the text "eating," while for PERSON the string "the man next door" can be used.

We will read the grammar from an input file. Each line of the file will begin with one word representing the category, and the rest of the line will be the remainder of the grammar rule. Internally, the grammar

```
typedef map<string, vector< list<string> > > grammarType;

void readGrammar (istream & ifile, grammarType & grammar)
    // read a silly sentence grammar into the given structure
{
    string line;
    while (getline(ifile, line)) {
        list<string> words;
        split (line, " ", words);
        string category = words.front();
        words.pop_front();
            // add a new grammar rule
        grammar[category].push_back(words);
        }
}
```

Figure 16.4 Reading the silly sentence grammar

will be stored in a map. The key to the map will be the category, while
the value will be a `vector` of `list`s. Each entry in the vector will be
a different rule, and each rule is represented as a list of words. A procedure that reads this input grammar and translates it into the internal
form is shown in Figure 16.4. In the final line of the loop, note how
one statement checks for an existing grammar rule with the given category name, creating it if necessary; creates a new vector for holding
the grammar rule; and fills the value of this vector with the list that
represents the grammar rule. So much activity represented with so few
symbols graphically illustrates the power of the standard library abstractions.

The heart of the procedure (Figure 16.5) is a simple recursive algorithm that takes as input a word, and returns a silly sentence generated
from the word. The procedure checks to see if the given word is a category name. If not, it is simply returned. If it is a category name, a
randomly selected element of the vector is selected (the procedure `rand-
Between` was described in Section 15.3). Each part of the selected grammar

---

Reference Variables

The `generateSentence` program is the first
example we have seen in this text of the use
of *reference variables* being used other than as
pass-by-reference parameters. The local variable
rules is defined as a reference to the value grammar[start]. The use of the ampersand implies

that the reference is simply an *alias* for the larger
expression. In this case, the use of the reference
allows us to refer to the grammar rule without
having to repeatedly execute the subscript expression.

```
string generateSentence (string & start, grammarType & grammar)
    // generate silly sentence from given start string
{
    if (grammar.count(start) != 0) {
        vector< list<string> > & rules = grammar[start]; // see box
        int n = rules.size();
        list<string> & rule = rules[randBetween(0, n-1)];
        list<string>::iterator start, stop;
        stop = rule.end();
        string result;
        for (start = rule.begin(); start != stop; ++start)
            result += generateSentence (*start);
        return result;
        }
    else  // not a category, simply return string
        return start;
}
```

Figure 16.5 Silly sentence generation algorithm

rule is then independently processed, because it could potentially expand further.

The following table illustrates the sequence of recursive calls invoked in producing the sentence, "My sister loves eating with the man next door." The first column represents the argument to the procedure gen-erateString. The second column is the level of recursive call. The final column is the item randomly selected as matching the value, if the first argument is an index into the table; if the item in the first column is not an index into the table, then it is simply printed.

word	level	selection
SENTENCE	1	PERSON DOES SOMETHING
PERSON	2	my sister
my sister	3	*not index in table, return:* my sister
DOES	2	loves
loves	3	*not index in table, return:* loves
SOMETHING	2	ACTIVITY with PERSON
ACTIVITY	3	eating
eating	4	*not index in table, return:* eating
with	4	*not index in table, return:* with
PERSON	4	the man next door
the man . . .	5	*not in table, return:* the man next door

The following lines illustrate some of the sentences that can be generated in this fashion:

my father hates dancing with my father
my sister loves eating with the man next door
I love my computer
I hate life
my sister thinks that I am intelligent
the man next door thinks that I am creative
my father thinks that I am intelligent
the man next door loves dancing
I love sleeping with my girl friend
you think that I am creative

16.2.3   A Concordance

Our final example program to illustrate the use of the map data type is a concordance. A concordance is an alphabetical listing of words in a text that indicates the line numbers on which each word occurs. The data values will be maintained in the concordance by a multimap, indexed by strings (the words), and will hold integers (the line numbers). A multimap is employed because the same word will often appear on multiple different lines; indeed, discovering such connections is one of the primary purposes of a concordance. An alternative possibility would have been to use a map, and use a set of integer elements as the associated values.

```
class concordance {
    typedef multimap<string, int> wordDictType;
public:
    void addWord (string, int);
    void readText (istream &);
    void printConcordance (ostream &);

protected:
    wordDictType wordMap;
};
```

Note that the class definition does not include a constructor function. Recall that in such situations a default constructor will be created automatically, and this will in turn invoke the default constructor for the wordMap data field. The default constructor for a map creates a collection with no entries.

The creation of the concordance is divided into two steps: first the program generates the concordance (by reading lines from an input stream), and then the program prints the result on the output stream. This is reflected in the two member functions readText() and printConcordance(). The first of these, readText(), is written as:

```
void concordance::readText (istream & in)
    //read all words from input stream, entering into concordance
{
    string line;
    for (int i = 1; getline(in, line); i++) {
        // translate into lower case, split into words
        allLower(line);
        list<string> words;
        split(line, " ,.;:", words);
            // enter each word on line into concordance
        list<string>::iterator wptr;
        for (wptr = words.begin(); wptr != words.end(); ++wptr)
            addWord(*wptr, i);
    }
}
```

Lines are read from the input stream one by one. The text of the line is first converted into lowercase, then the line is split into words using the function `split()` (described earlier in Section 7.2.2). Each word is then entered into the concordance. The method used to enter a value into the concordance is as follows:

```
void concordance::addWord (string word, int line)
    // add a new word to the concordance
{

        // see if word occurs in list
        // first get range of entries with same key
    wordDictType::iterator low = wordMap.lower_bound(word);
    wordDictType::iterator high = wordMap.upper_bound(word);
        // loop over entries, see if any match current line
    for ( ; low != high; ++low)
        if ((*low).second == line)
            return; // word already appeared on this line
        // didn't occur, add now
    wordMap.insert(wordDictType::value_type(word, line));
}
```

The major portion of `addWord()` is concerned with ensuring that values are not duplicated in the word map should the same word occur twice on the same line. To assure this, the range of values matching the key is examined; each value is tested, and if any match the line number, then no insertion is performed. Only if the loop terminates without discovering the line number will the new word/line number pair be inserted.

The final step is to print the concordance, as performed in this fashion:

```
void concordance::printConcordance (ostream & out)
    // print concordance on the given output stream
{
```

```
            string lastword = "";
            wordDictType::iterator pairPtr;
            wordDictType::iterator stop = wordMap.end();
            for (pairPtr = wordMap.begin(); pairPtr != stop; ++pairPtr)
                    // if word is same as previous, just print line number
                if (lastword == (*pairPtr).first)
                    out << " " << (*pairPtr).second;
                else {
                        // first occurrence of word
                    lastword = (*pairPtr).first;
                    cout << endl << lastword << ": " << (*pairPtr).second;
                    }
            cout << endl; // terminate last line
    }
```

An iterator loop is used to cycle over the elements being maintained by the word list. Each new word generates a new line of output; thereafter line numbers appear separated by spaces. If, for example, the input was the text:

It was the best of times,
it was the worst of times.

The output, from best to worst, would be:

best: 1
it: 1 2
of: 1 2
the: 1 2
times: 1 2
was: 1 2
worst: 2

16.3   OPERATIONS ON MAPS

Table 16.1 summarizes the member functions provided by the map and multimap data types. Each will shortly be described in more detail.

16.3.1   Include Files

Whenever you use a map or a multimap, you must include the map header file.[2]

```
# include <map>
```

---

2. On some systems the include file is named map.h.

Constructors		
`map<T> m;`	Default constructor	$O(1)$
`multimap<T> m;`	Default constructor	$O(1)$
`map<T> m (aMap)`	Copy constructor	$O(n)$
`multimap<T> m (aMultiMap)`	Copy constructor	$O(n)$
`m = aMap`	Assignment	$O(n)$
Insertion and Removal		
`m [ key ]`	Return reference to value with key	$O(\log n)$
`m.insert (key_value_pair)`	Insert given key value pair	$O(\log n)$
`m.erase (key)`	Erase value with given key	$O(\log n)$
`m.erase (iterator)`	Erase value at given iterator	$O(\log n)$
Testing for Inclusion		
`m.empty ()`	True if collection is empty	$O(1)$
`m.size ()`	Return size of collection	$O(n)$
`m.count (key)`	Count number of elements with given key	$O(\log n)$
`m.find (key)`	Locate element with given key	$O(\log n)$
`m.lower_bound (key)`	First occurrence of key	$O(\log n)$
`m.upper_bound (key)`	Next element after key	$O(\log n)$
`m.equal_range (key)`	Lower and upper bound pair	$O(\log n)$
Iterators		
`map<T>::iterator itr;`	Declare new iterator	$O(1)$
`m.begin()`	Starting iterator	$O(1)$
`m.end()`	Ending iterator	$O(1)$
`m.rbegin()`	Backwards moving iterator start	$O(1)$
`m.rend()`	Backwards moving iterator end	$O(1)$

Table 16.1   Summary of operations for map **data type**

16.3.2   Creation and Initialization

The declaration of a map follows the pattern we have seen repeatedly in the standard library. A map is a template data structure, specialized by the type of the key elements and the type of the associated values. There is an optional third template argument that specifies the function to be used in comparing key values.[3] A map created with the default constructor ini-

---

3. See Appendix A, Section A.3.

tially contains no elements, while a map created from the copy constructor will contain copies of the values in the argument container.

```
    // map indexed by doubles containing strings
map<double, string> map_one;

    // map indexed by integers, containing integers
map<int, int> map_two;

    // create a new map, initializing it from map two
map<int, int> map_three (map_two);
```

A map can be assigned the value of another map.

```
map_three = map_two;
```

16.3.3   Type Definitions

The classes `map` and `multimap` define a number of type definitions. These are most commonly used in declaration statements. For example, an iterator for a map of strings to integers can be declared in this fashion:

```
map<string, int>::iterator location;
```

In addition to `iterator`, the following other types are defined:

`key_type`   The type associated with the keys used to index the map.

`value_type`   The type of the `pair` used to store entries in the map. The constructor for this type is used in create new entries.

16.3.4   Insertion and Access

Values can be inserted into a map or a multimap using the `insert()` operation. Note that the argument must be a key-value pair. This pair is easily generated using the constructor for the `value_type` specification.

```
map_three.insert (map_three::value_type(5, 7));
```

With a map (but not a multimap), values are usually accessed and inserted using the subscript operator. Simply using a key as a subscript creates an entry—the default element is used as the associated value. Assigning to the result of the subscript changes the associated binding.

```
cout << "Index value 7 is " << map_three[7] << endl;
    // now change the associated value
map_three[7] = 5;
cout << "Index value 7 is " << map_three[7] << endl;
```

16.3.5   Removal of Values

Values can be removed from a map or a multimap by providing the key value. In a multimap, the erasure removes all elements with the associated key. An element to be removed can also be denoted by an iterator, as, for example, the iterator yielded by a find() operation. A pair of iterators can be used to erase an entire range of elements.

```
// erase element 4
map_three.erase(4);
```

```
// erase element five
mtesttype::iterator five = map_three.find(5);
map_three.erase(five);
```

```
// erase all values between seven and eleven
mtesttype::iterator seven = map_three.find(7);
mtesttype::iterator eleven = map_three.find(11);
map_three.erase (seven, eleven);
```

16.3.6   Iterators

The member functions begin() and end() produce bi-directional iterators for both maps and multimaps. Dereferencing an iterator for either a map or a multimap will yield a pair of key/value elements. The fields names first and second can be applied to these values to access the individual fields. The first field is constant, and cannot be modified. The second field, however, can be used to change the value being held in association with a given key, and will modify the value being maintained in the collection. Elements will be generated in sequence, based on the ordering of the key fields.

The member functions rbegin() and rend() produce iterators that yield the elements in reverse order.

16.3.7   Searching and Counting

The member function size() will yield the number of elements held by a container. The member function empty() will return a Boolean true value if the container is empty, and is generally faster than testing the size against zero.

The member function find() takes a key argument, and returns an iterator denoting the associated key/value pair. In the case of multimaps, the first such value is returned. In both cases, the past-the-end iterator is returned if no such value is found.

```
if (map_one.find(4) != map_end.end())
    cout << "contains a four" << endl;
```

The member functions `lower_bound()`, `upper_bound()`, and so on are analogous to their form in sets. The function `lower_bound`, for example, yields the first entry that matches the argument key, while the member function `upper_bound()` returns the first value past the last entry matching the argument. Finally, the member function `equal_range()` returns a `pair` of iterators, holding the lower and upper bounds. The concordance program, presented earlier, demonstrated the use of these functions.

The member function `count()` returns the number of elements that match the key value supplied as the argument. For a map, this value is always either zero or one, whereas for a multimap it can be any nonnegative value. To simply determine whether or not a collection contains an element, using `count()` is often easier than using the `find()` function and testing the result against the end-of-sequence iterator.

```
if (map_one.count(4) > 0)
    cout << "contains a four" << endl;
```

16.4   AN EXAMPLE IMPLEMENTATION

As we indicated in the early part of this chapter, a `map` can be viewed as nothing more than a `set` of `pairs`. By using inheritance to derive `map` from `set`, many of the `map` operations are provided by the parent class with no additional effort required. (As always, note that this implementation technique is not required by the language definition, and implementations of the standard library are free to use other techniques. Our example implementation of class `set` was described in Chapter 12.) The major new operation is the subscript operator, while a few other member functions must be redefined because their parameter types differ from the function that would otherwise be inherited from the class `set`.

```
template <class Key, class Value>
class map : public set <pair<Key, Value> > {
public:
    typedef set<pair<Key, Value> > parent;

        // constructors
    map () : parent () { }
    map (map<Key, Value> & m) : parent (m) { }

        // definition for subscript operator
    Value & operator [ ] (Key &);
```

```
            // methods that change parameter types
            // from methods inherited from class set
        void erase (Key &);
        void erase (iterator & itr) { parent::erase(itr); }
        int  count (Key &);
        iterator find (Key &);
        iterator lower_bound (Key &);
        iterator upper_bound (Key &);
        pair<iterator, iterator> equal_range (Key &);
};
```

The implementation of all the member functions is similar, and we will present only a few characteristic examples here. The `find()` member function is typical. The function first creates a new set entry, using the `value_type` data type inherited from the class `set`. The `first` field of this is then set to the given key, while the `second` field is left with its default value. Because `pairs` are compared only by their keys, a search of the set (accessed using the fully qualified name) will return the associated entry, if it exists.

```
template <class Key, class Value>
map<Key, Value>::iterator find (Key & key)
        // find the entry with the associated key
{
        value_type test;
        test.first = key;
        return parent::find (test);
}
```

The `find` function is used by the member function `erase`. There are two forms of `erase`. The first takes as argument an iterator, and is simply the function inherited from the class `set`. The second takes as argument a key, and first searches the collection using the key. Only if the key is found is the entry removed. (In the class `multimap`, the conditional would be replaced by a loop, as all elements should be removed).

```
template <class Key, class Value>
void map<Key, Value>::erase (Key & key)
        // remove entry with the given key
{
        iterator where = find(key);
        if (where != end())
            erase(where);
}
```

The subscript operator first creates a new key/value pair using the given key and the default element for value. This new structure is then inserted into the set. Because pairs are compared only by their keys, and because sets only allow a single instance of any value, the insertion will fail if an entry with the same key already exists. Whether or not the insertion succeeds, the `insert` member function inherited from the class `set` will return a pair, the first field of which is an iterator that denotes the location of the element in the collection (either the location of the existing element or the location of the newly entered value). The second field of the structure denoted by this iterator is the reference to the value indexed by the given key.

```
template <class Key, class Value>
Value & map<Key, Value>::operator [ ] (Key & key)
    // return reference associated with given key
{
        // create a pair with the given key field
    value_type test;
    test.first = key;
        // insert will return an iterator and a bool
    pair<iterator, bool> where = insert(test);
    return (*(where.first)).second;
}
```

The user should be careful when using the subscript operator. Subscripting causes the associated element to be added to the container, even if the subscript result is not used as a target for an assignment but is only on the righthand side of an expression. A programmer should never use the subscript operator to test whether the collection contains a value using a given key, but should instead use the `find` operation for this purpose.

The implementation of all other operations is provided by inheritance. Iterators for class `map` are even easier, because the `set` data abstraction provides iterators that can be used without modification, as long as the programmer remembers that iterator elements are instances of class `pair`. Finally, note that an implementation for `multimap` can be created in a similar fashion, inheriting from class `multiset` rather than set.

16.5   CHAPTER SUMMARY

Key Concepts

- Map and multimap
- Pairs
- Concordance
- Implementation using inheritance

A map is an indexed collection, similar to a vector. Unlike a vector, the index keys can be any ordered type, and element types can be any value whatsoever. In this chapter we have explored one implementation technique that can be used in the realization of the `map` abstraction, although there are many others.

A high level data structure, such as a `map`, can simplify the solution of many problems. An illustration of this is the concordance constructed in Section 16.2.3. Generating concordance requires little in the way of lines of code. Nevertheless, in these few lines the program makes use of no less than a dozen different data structures:

▲ The input consists of an input stream, `istream`.

▲ The output is written to an output stream, type `ostream`.

▲ The data for the concordance is built on top of a `multimap`, the index elements of which are `strings`, while the stored values are `integer`.

▲ Elements in the `multimap` are instances of the class `pair`.

▲ The multimap itself is built on top of the `set` data type.

▲ The `split` procedure requires as arguments a `string`, and returns a `list` of strings.

▲ Iterators are constructed for both `lists` and `maps`.

We have not even counted facilitator classes, such as `link`.

Further Reading

Although dictionaries and tables are not basic to C and C++, they are found in a number of other programming languages. They are one of the fundamental data structures in the string processing language SNOBOL [Griswold 71], and in the more recent language by the same author, Icon [Griswold 90]. The dictionary type is also a basic part of the Smalltalk standard library [Goldberg 83].

The silly sentence generators are adapted from an example *ABC* program originally written by Steven Pemberton [Geurts 85].

Study Questions & Exercises

Study Questions

1. What are the characteristics of a map?

2. How is a map similar to a `vector`? How is it different?

3. How does a `multimap` differ from a `map`?

4. What is a `pair`?

5. What does the generic algorithm `for_each` do?

6. Give three more example sentences that could be generated by the grammar in Figure 16.3.

7. Extend the grammar in Figure 16.3 so that it can generate questions.

8. What is the purpose of a concordance?

9. How is the example implementation of the map data type tied to the implementation of the set data type?

Exercises

1. Concordances often filter out common words, such as "the" or "and." Suppose you have a file of common words, which is then read into a set. Modify the concordance program so that it checks words from this set and, if found, does not enter them into the database.

2. Rewrite the sample map implementation to use composition, rather than inheritance. That is, a map should hold as part of its state a `set`. How does your implementation differ from the one presented in the text? Which is easier to understand? What features do you need to provide that are not explicitly provided in the implementation discussed in the text?

3. Write a procedure that scans an input stream and produces an alphabetized list of the words in the input along with their frequency of occurrence.

4. Extend the grammar for the silly sentence

generation program so that it generates questions as well as statements.

5. Individuals unfamiliar with a foreign language will often translate a sentence from one language to another using a dictionary and word-for-word substitution. Although this does not produce the most elegant translation, it is usually adequate for short sentences, such as, "Where is the train station?" Write a program that will read from two files. The first file contains a series of word-for-word pairs for a pair of languages. The second file contains text written in the first language. Examine each word in the text, and output the corresponding value of the dictionary entry.

## Part III

OTHER CONTAINERS

17

Hash Tables

Chapter Overview

A *hash table* is a natural embodiment of the concept of divide and conquer. Although not provided as a basic data structure in the standard library, hash tables can nevertheless be easily constructed using other containers. In this chapter we introduce the idea of a hash table, and illustrate the use of hash tables in sorting, as well as other applications. The hash table implementation we develop is constructed as an adaptor for another container, similar to the stack and priority queue adaptors described in earlier chapters. Inheritance can then be used to simplify the interface to this structure. Major topics discussed in this chapter include the following:

▲ The hash table abstraction

▲ Hash functions

▲ Buckets

▲ Hash table sorts: counting sort, radix sort, bucket sort

▲ An example implementation

17.1 THE HASH TABLE ABSTRACTION

The power of the binary tree as a data structure comes through the application of the principle of *divide and conquer*. For most operations on a binary tree, at each step the tree is divided into two roughly equal parts, thereby reducing the complexity of the task by half. But what if the problem could be reduced by a factor larger than two? Suppose in a single constant-time operation a problem could be reduced by a factor of 10, or by 1000. Intuitively, it would seem that this would offer even greater benefits than those provided by binary trees.

In a certain sense, this benefit is exactly what is being made possible when we use a vector. When a subscript is applied to a vector, a single constant time operation allows access to any element. We move from thinking about the vector as an entire collection, to thinking about just a single element. But two primary problems are implicit in the use of vectors. The first is that a vector must be indexed using an integer value, and the second is that each element of a vector can hold only a single value. The *hash table* is a data structure that overcomes both of these difficulties. The first problem is addressed through the use of a *hash function*, a function that maps values into integer locations. This allows the programmer to think of a problem in terms of values, instead of indices. The second difficulty is addressed through the use of *buckets*, table locations that can hold more than one element.

The next two sections will describe in more detail these two features of hash tables. We will then illustrate the use of hash tables by considering several sorting algorithms, each very different from the other but similar in their use of hash tables. Finally, we will conclude the chapter by developing hash tables as a general-purpose container class.

17.2   HASH FUNCTIONS

Suppose six friends, Alfred, Alex, Alice, Amy, Andy and Anne, have started a club and wish to maintain a database containing the amount of club dues they each have paid. Dues are paid each time a member attends a meeting, but not all members attend all meetings, nor do they pay the same amount each time they meet. The club programmer, Amy, is in charge of writing programs to do the bookkeeping.

Initially, Amy uses the integer values 0 to 5 to represent each of the individual members. However, one day Amy discovers an interesting fact. If she takes the third letter of each of the their names, treats the letter as representing an integer by letting "a" represent the value 0, "b" represent the value 1, and so on up to "z" which represents 25, then computes the remainder yielded after dividing each value by 6, each returns a different integer value between 0 and 5.

Chapter 17

name			value	remainder
Al	f	red	5	5
Al	e	x	4	4
Al	i	ce	8	2
Am	y		24	0
An	d	y	3	3
An	n	e	13	1

What Amy has just discovered is called a *perfect hash function*. A hash function is a function that takes as input an element from some set of values and returns an unsigned integer result. The term "to hash" evokes an image of random mixing and shuffling. This is appropriate, because hash functions are permitted wide latitude in the manner of transformations they may employ. (We will have much more to say about hash functions in our subsequent discussion.) A perfect hash function is a hash function that in addition yields a one-to-one mapping from the index elements to the integers starting at zero and extending to the number of elements in the set, so that each element maps onto a *different* integer value.

Using her hash function, Amy writes the simple program shown in Figure 17.1 to manage her club finances. Input consists of a series of names and amounts, such as:

```
Alfred 2.32
Alex 1.76
Alice 4.87
Alfred 3.71
Amy 0.51
Andy 7.59
Alex 2.63
Anne 3.62
```

The output of the program is a summary of the amount each member has paid in dues.

Of course, Amy's carefully worked out system falls apart when the set of index values changes. Suppose, for example, that Alan wishes to join the club. The nameHash calculation for Alan will yield 0, the same value as for Amy. Two values that have the same hash value are said to have

```
//
//      Amy's program to compute club finances
//

unsigned int nameHash( string & name)
{   // perfect hash function for
    // Alfred, Alex, Alice, Amy, Andy and Anne
    return name[2] - 'a';
}

void main() {
    string name;
        // funds are stored in a vector, initialized to zero
    vector<double> funds(6, 0.0);
    double totalDues = 0; // total dues paid
    double amount;

    // loop while there are records
    while (cin >> name >> amount) {
        // add the new amount to the data record
        funds[nameHash(name)] += amount;
        // add to the total dues paid
        totalDues += amount;
        }

    // report the result
    cout << "Dues paid:\n";
    cout << "  Alfred: $" << funds[nameHash("Alfred")] << '\n';
    cout << "  Alex: $" << funds[nameHash("Alex")] << '\n';
    cout << "  Alice: $" << funds[nameHash("Alice")] << '\n';
    cout << "  Amy: $" << funds[nameHash("Amy")] << '\n';
    cout << "  Andy: $" << funds[nameHash("Andy")] << '\n';
    cout << "  Anne: $" << funds[nameHash("Anne")] << '\n';
    cout << "total dues paid: $" << totalDues << '\n';
}
```

Figure 17.1 Amy's program to compute club finances

collided.[1] Although it would seem that collisions would preempt the use of the hashing technique, we will see in the next section how this difficulty can be overcome.

---

1. Therefore another definition of a perfect hash function is a hash function that operates on a set of n elements, generating result values between 0 and $n - 1$, and for which no two values cause a collision.

It might appear at this point that the discovery of a hash function, and in particular a perfect hash function, is simply a matter of blind luck. This is in part true, and in part not true. It is true that there is no known systematic procedure that can be used to generate a perfect hash function from an arbitrary set of values. However, there are techniques that can be used in the majority of cases of practical interest. The reference section at the end of this chapter will point the interested reader to some of the related literature. Further discussion on techniques used to create hash functions will be postponed until after we have covered a more general use of hash tables.

17.3 COLLISION RESOLUTION USING BUCKETS

The true power of the hashing technique comes when each element in the hash table is itself a collection. Basically, the idea is to separate the elements to be maintained into one of several *buckets*. Each bucket can hold an arbitrary number of elements. Thus, for example, the addition of a new element is a two-step process: First, choose the bucket into which the element is to be inserted, and then place the element into the bucket. The inclusion test and removal of an element from the collection are handled similarly. Because buckets can hold multiple elements, the problem of collisions effectively goes away.

Generally, the bucket is formed using one of the data structures we have previously examined. For example, the bucket sort algorithm we will subsequently describe uses a `multiset` to hold the bucket values, while the radix sort algorithm uses a `list`.

17.3.1 Asymptotic Analysis of Hash Table Operations

A major motivation for using hash tables is the speed with which operations can be performed. To illustrate this, let us consider the asymptotic complexity of determining whether or not a value is contained in a hash table.

An analysis of the asymptotic running time of hash table operations is complicated by the uncertainty involved in the hash function. The worst-case hash function would be one that always returned a single value, for example, zero. Although this behavior is certainly permissible under our definition of a hash function, the effect would be to place all elements into a single bucket. This does imply, however, that our worst-case complexity is certainly no slower than the execution behavior of the underlying data structure used to represent the buckets. If we were to use a `set` for the buckets, for example, the worst case-asymptotic complexity of lookup would be $O(\log n)$.

The best possible hash function would be one that uniformly distributes elements over the range of hash values; that is, a function that has the effect of maintaining approximately the same number of elements in each bucket. Discovering such a function is not always easy, but is the key to obtaining the best performance from a hash table. We will present the asymptotic run-time analysis of our hash table assuming this case.

If we let m represent the size of our hash table, then there are approximately n/m elements in each bucket. If we assume the time to compute the hash function itself is constant, and the time to discover which bucket an element corresponds to is constant, then the time to access an element is the search time for an underlying container of size n/m. Because searching for an element in a `set` of size k can be performed in $O(\log k)$ steps, this means that seeing whether or not an element occurs in a well-balanced hash table can be performed in $O(\log(n/m))$ steps.

We next assume that the number of hash table entries is roughly *proportional* to the total number of elements; that is, the number of elements in the table will never exceed, say, $m * 10$. Thus, n/m is no larger than $\frac{10m}{m}$ or 10. Hence, $O(\log(n/m))$ is $O(\log 10)$. The logarithm of any constant is itself a constant, so we can simply say that the asymptotic complexity of search is $O(1)$.

Hence, the worst-case performance for a hash table is essentially the worst-case performance of the underlying bucket data structure. The best-case performance permits operations to be performed in constant time. Analysis of the "average" case is complicated, in part because of the uncertainty involved in defining the meaning of the term "average" for various hash functions and distributions of key values. Nevertheless, in practice when used with a reasonable hash function the performance of hash tables is quite good.

17.4   HASH TABLE SORTING ALGORITHMS

We will illustrate the use of hash tables by describing three very different sorting algorithms that use the same idea, hashing into buckets, in very different fashions.

17.4.1   Counting Sort

The first algorithm is applicable only to the task of sorting positive integer values from a limited range. For example, suppose you need to sort 1,000 elements, but you know the values are each between zero and 19. One approach would be to simply count the number of zeros, the number of ones, and so on. In the end, you might come up with a table such as:

0 : 47	5 : 114	10 : 36	15 : 93
1 : 92	6 : 16	11 : 92	16 : 12
2 : 12	7 : 37	12 : 43	17 : 15
3 : 14	8 : 41	13 : 17	18 : 63
4 : 32	9 : 3	14 : 132	19 : 89

This would tell you that the sorted vector would contain 47 zeros, followed by 92 ones, then 12 twos, and so on. Simply stated, there is no need to manipulate the actual values themselves, only their count.

The algorithm that embodies these ideas is shown in Figure 17.2. The input is a vector of values, and the integer that represents the largest value in the array. The hash table in this case is simply a vector of integer values, initially zero. The algorithm loops through the input vector, incrementing the counts. When the counts have all been determined, the program loops through the counts vector, and overwrites the original data vector. (A set of such counts is sometimes called a *histogram*. If the input sequence is letters, for example, the histogram will indicate the frequency of occurrence of different letters. The intent of gathering such information might not be sorting, but the techniques are similar.)

To determine the asymptotic execution time efficiency of this algorithm we need to consider both the values n, the number of data elements, and m, the largest data value. The first loop, the loop that copies values into the data vector, is clearly $O(n)$. The analysis of the nested loops

---

Fast Searching Using Buckets

Back in Chapter 14 we noted that hash tables would, in theory, provide us with a means to perform searches for elements in faster than $O(\log n)$ time, but only under certain conditions. Having described the hash table technique, the idea is obvious. To determine whether a certain element is contained in a collection, it is only necessary to select the appropriate bucket to which the element would be assigned if it were present, and search just the one bucket. The hash operation is typically fast, and if the element is present it must be in only one bucket. Thus, the time to search for a single element is the time to search just a single bucket, which is potentially much faster than the time to search the entire collection.

For this to be a nontrivial gain in execution time, the number of buckets is required to be a significant percentage of the number of elements being maintained (so that each bucket contains only a few elements), and the hash function must distribute elements from the collection relatively uniformly to each of the buckets. Because it is frequently difficult to discover a hash function having these characteristics, using an asymptotically less efficient data structure, such as a `set`, will often be more practical.

```
void countSort (vector<unsigned int> data, unsigned int m)
    // sort the vector of values, each element no larger than m
{

        // allocate the hash table of counts
    vector<unsigned int> counts (m, 0);
    vector<unsigned int>::iterator start, stop;
    start = data.begin();
    stop = data.end();

        // count the occurrences of each value
    for (; start != stop; ++start)
        counts[*start]++;

        // now put values back into vector
    start = data.begin();
    for (int i = 0; i < m; i++)
        for (int j = counts[i]; j > 0; j--)
            *start++ = i;
}
```

Figure 17.2 The counting sort algorithm

that end the algorithm is more subtle. Clearly, the outer loop will execute m times. In the worst case, the inner loop could execute n times. This might lead us to suspect the execution time is $O(m \times n)$; however, this is not the case. Indeed, you can easily convince yourself that the assignment statement will be executed exactly n times. Thus, the total execution time is the *maximum* of n and m. This is often written as $O(n + m)$.

This is extremely fast compared to the other sorting algorithms we have seen. Figure 17.3 compares the execution time of counting sort to quick sort. Whereas quick sort exhibits a quadratic behavior, counting sort is, as predicted, almost linear. However, the execution timings are also influenced by the range of values being sorted. Figure 17.3 shows timings for sorting values smaller than 100, smaller than 1,000, and smaller than 10,000. As the range of values becomes larger, the execution time increases.

This simple algorithm has been rediscovered many times, and has often been cited as a counterexample to the assertion that sorting requires $O(n \log n)$ operations. However, it is important to point out that this algorithm can only be used in a narrow set of circumstances. In particular, the elements must be integers, and must be drawn from a small range. The bucket sort algorithm described next is similar in structure to the integer counting sort algorithm, but removes some of these limitations.

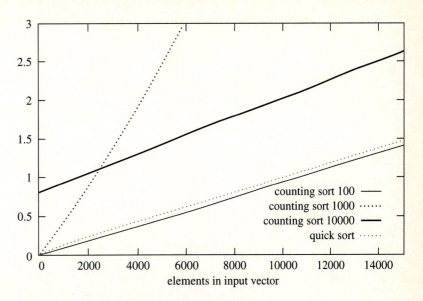

Figure 17.3 Execution Timings for Counting Sort

17.4.2 Bucket Sorting

We have seen in earlier chapters how various data structures each naturally suggested an associated sorting algorithm. In the same way, the hash table data structure suggests a novel approach to sorting, at least under certain conditions.

As with all hash table based algorithms, the general idea will be to separate elements into the different buckets, process each of the buckets, then append the sorted elements together to form the final answer. For this to be effective, it must be possible to merge very efficiently into the final list the results of sorting each of the buckets individually. One way to ensure this is to insist that the hash function supplied by the user has the property that all values assigned to the first bucket be smaller than any values assigned to the other buckets, and that all values assigned to the second bucket be smaller than the values in subsequent buckets, and so on. Thus, to form the final list it is sufficient to merely append end-to-end the sorted lists from each of the separate buckets.

The *bucket sort* algorithm shown in Figure 17.4 utilizes this idea. The user is required to supply an appropriate size and function for the hash table that satisfies the properties we have outlined. For our buckets we use

```
template <class T, class HashFun>
void bucketSort
    (vector<T> & values, unsigned tablesize, HashFun hash)
    // sort the values of the given vector into ascending order
{
    vector< multiset<T> > bucket(tablesize);
    int max = values.size();

    // put each element into the appropriate bucket
    for (int i = 0; i < max; i++) {
        unsigned int hashIndex = hash(values[i]);
        bucket[hashIndex].insert(values[i]);
        }

    // now put elements back into vector
    int k = 0;
    for (int j = 0; j < tablesize; j++) {
        multiset<T>::iterator start = bucket[j].begin();
        multiset<T>::iterator stop = bucket[j].end();
        while (start != stop)
            values[k++] = *start++;
        }
}
```

Figure 17.4   The bucket sort algorithm

the multiset data structure, because inserting values into a multiset will automatically place them in order.

Unfortunately, actual timings of the bucket sort algorithm are usually disappointing. When the number of values being sorted is small in relation to the number of buckets, execution time is dominated by the need to initialize all the buckets. When the number of values is large in relation to the buckets, the advantage of using buckets at all becomes marginal. In almost no case will the execution speed of bucket sort be better than that of quick sort.

17.4.3   Radix Sorting

An entirely different way of using hash tables and buckets is illustrated by the radix sort algorithm. Like counting sort, *radix sorting* is a technique for ordering a list of positive integer values. The values are successively ordered on digit positions, from right to left. This is accomplished by copying the values into buckets, where the index for the bucket is given by the position of the digit being sorted. Once all digit positions have been examined, the collection must be sorted.

The sequences of values found in each bucket during the four steps involved in sorting the list are:

624 762 852 426 197 987 269 146 415 301 730 78 593

During pass 1, the one's place digits are ordered. Each value that ends in a 2 is placed into the same bucket, as are all elements that end in a 3, and so on. During pass 2, the ten's place digits are ordered, retaining the relative positions of values set by the earlier pass. Again, all values that have a 2 in the ten's position are placed into the same container, as are all values that have a 3 in the ten's position, and so on. On pass 3, the hundred's place digits are ordered, again retaining the previous relative ordering. After three passes the result is an ordered collection.

Bucket	Pass 1	Pass 2	Pass 3
0	730	301	78
1	301	415	146, 197
2	762, 852	624, 426	269
3	593	730	301
4	624	146	415, 426
5	415	852	593
6	426, 146	762, 269	624
7	197, 987	78	730, 762
8	78	987	852
9	269	593, 197	987

In this case, we are using a `list` as the data type for the underlying bucket. This is because the relative order of the elements is vitally important. Each pass must preserve the relative order of the elements established by the previous pass. If we were to use a `set`, as in the bucket sort algorithm, we would lose this ordering.

The radix sorting algorithm, shown in Figure 17.5, has a slightly more complex structure than the previous two algorithms. A `while` loop is used to cycle through the various passes. The value of the variable `divisor` indicates which digit is currently being examined. A Boolean flag is used to determine when execution should halt. Each time the while loop is executed, a vector of lists is declared. By placing the declaration of this structure inside the while loop, it is reinitialized to empty each step. Each time the loop is executed, the values in the input are copied into the appropriate bucket. Once distributed into the buckets, the values are gathered back into the input. As long as more than one bucket is used

```
void radixSort(vector<unsigned int> & values)
{
    bool flag = true;
    int divisor = 1;
    vector<unsigned int>::iterator start, stop;
    list<unsigned int>::iterator lstart, lend;

    while (flag) {
        vector< list<unsigned int> > buckets(10);
        flag = false;
            // first copy values into buckets
        start = values.begin();
        stop = values.end();
        while (start != stop) {
            int hashIndex = (*start / divisor) % 10;
            if ((*start / divisor) > 0)
                flag = true;
            buckets[hashIndex].push_back(*start++);
        }

            // then copy buckets back into array
        start = values.begin();
        for (int i = 0; i < 10; i++) {
            lstart = buckets[i].begin();
            lend = buckets[i].end();
            while (lstart != lend)
                *start++ = *lstart++;
        }

            // update divisor for next loop
        divisor *= 10;
    }
}
```

Figure 17.5   The radix sort algorithm

the program must continue. The flag is finally set to false, and execution halted, when all values map into the first bucket.

An examination of the radix sort algorithm shows that the nested loops are proportional to the number of elements in the data array, while the number of executions of the surrounding loop is controlled by the maximum number of digits in the largest data value. Thus, the execution time performance of radix sort is, like value sort, tied to the range of values being sorted. This is shown in Figure 17.6, which illustrates the execu-

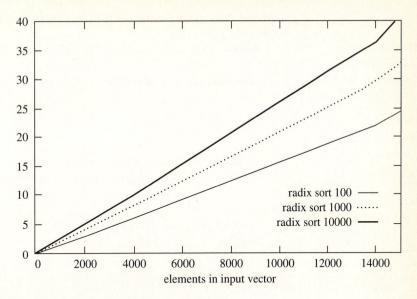

Figure 17.6 Execution timings for radix sort

tion time on values between 0 and 100, between 0 and 1,000, and between 0 and 10,000. As the value of the numbers become larger, the execution times increase. However, performance remains roughly linear.

17.5   THE HASH_TABLE DATA TYPE

Although the idea of hash tables can be embedded in an algorithm, such as in the bucket sort or radix sort algorithms, it is also possible to create a general-purpose hash table class. Figure 17.7 shows one example. In this class description, as in the `stack` and `priority queue` data structures seen in earlier chapters, the underlying container used to represent the buckets is provided by a template parameter. The advantage of doing so is that it permits the development of a very general abstraction, one that can be used with lists, vectors, sets, or maps. The disadvantage is that the operations provided by the hash table can only be those common to all data structures. The hash function is also passed as a template parameter, which implies that the hash functions must be written in the form of a function object (a class that implements the function call operator).

The member function `bucket`, shown in Figure 17.7, returns the bucket into which an element is hashed. It is this function that the programmer invokes when using a hash table. For example, if we have a hash table constructed out of an underlying collection of sets, the programmer could

```
template <class Container, int Size, class HashFun>
class hash_table {
    typedef Container::value_type value_type;
public:
    hash_table() : buckets(Size) { }

        // operations
    bool        empty();
    int         size ();
    Container & bucket( value_type & element)
        { return buckets[hash(element) % Size]; }


protected:
    vector<Container> buckets;
    HashFun           hash;
};
```

Figure 17.7 The class `hash_table`

determine the number of times a value appeared in the collection using
something like this:

```
class hashFun {
public:
    unsigned int operator() (int n) { ... }
 };


hash_table< set<int>, 12, hashFun> aHashTable;


if (aHashTable.bucket(247).count(247)) ....
```

The few member functions that are implemented by the `hash_table`
data structure operate by iterating through each of the buckets. Here, for
example, is the implementation of the member function `size`:

```
template <class Container, int Size, class HashFun>
int hash_table<Container, Size, HashFun>::size()
    // return number of elements in hash table
{
    int result = 0;
        // sum number of elements in each bucket
    for (int i = 0; i < Size; i++)
        result += buckets[i].size();
    return result;
}
```

The implementation of iterators for hash tables is somewhat complex,
so we will omit them from our presentation (see Exercise 12).

We could improve the interface seen by the programmer by using inheritance to specialize a hash table for a particular type of bucket. For example, the following shows a specialization created using the set data type. As illustrated, new member functions can be defined to hide from the user the invocation of the bucket member function.

```
template <class value_type, int Size, class HashFun>
class hash_set : public hash_table<set<value_type>, Size, HashFun> {
public:
    int    count    (value_type & element)
            { return bucket(element).count(element); }
    void   insert   (value_type & element)
            { bucket(element).insert(element); }
};
```

17.6   HASH FUNCTIONS

The application of a hash function is almost always a two-step process:

1. Transform the key into an integer value.
2. Map the resulting integer into a valid index for the hash table.

There are a number of well-known methods to accomplish the first task. Often these are used in combination.

Mapping   Integer values that occur in the key can be transformed or mapped into other integer values. This is the technique Amy used in her hash function. The character 'a' was mapped on to 0, the character 'b' on to 1, and so on. Often more complex maps are defined using an array. The elements of the array are specified ahead of time, when the program is compiled. Hashing a value is simply a matter of indexing into the array. This idea is the basis for the most commonly used algorithm for generating a perfect hash function from a known set of identifiers.

Folding   Using folding, the key is partitioned into several parts, and the (perhaps hashed) integer values for the individual parts are combined. The combination is usually accomplished using an efficient operation, such as addition, multiplication, shifting, or the logical exclusive or operation. For example, the following loop converts a string into an integer value by summing the integers corresponding to each character.

```
unsigned int hashval = 0;
int i = str.length();
while (i > 0)
        hashval += str[--i];
```

Shifting   Often the application of these methods results in values for which the low-order bits are not random. For example, printable character values are only a small range of the total integer values. In these situations, a shift operation can be used to eliminate these bits.

Shifting can also be used to avoid a problem that occurs when folding is performed using a commutative operator, such as addition. The problem is that a commutative operator will produce the same hash value for permutations of the arguments. Thus, the loop just given will produce the same hash value for the strings 'apt', 'tap' and 'pat.' By shifting the results of the previous calculation before performing the addition we can eliminate this difficulty.

```
unsigned int hashval = 0;
int i = str.length();
while (i > 0)
        hashval = (hashval << 1) + str[--i];
```

Casts   A cast can be used to convert almost any type into an integer. Most frequently this is used when the location of an object in memory—that is, its pointer address—is used as a hash value. A cast is applied to convert this pointer value into an integer.

Almost always, the second step of transforming the hashed key value into a legal index is accomplished simply by taking the remainder (or mod) after dividing by the table size. While this is easy, it is not the only

---

The Birthday Paradox

The frequency of collisions when performing hashing is related to a well-known mathematical puzzle. How many randomly chosen people need to be in a room before it becomes likely that two people will have the same birth date? Most people would guess the answer would be in the hundreds, because there are 365 possible birthdays (excluding leap years). In fact, the answer is only 24 people.

To see why, consider the opposite question. With n randomly chosen people in a room, what is the probability that no two have the same birth date? Imagine we take a calendar, and mark off each individual's birth date in turn. The probability that the second person has a different birthday from the first is 364/365, because there are 364 different possibilities not already marked. Similarly, the probability that the third person has a different birthday from the first two is 363/365.

Since these two probabilities are independent of each other, the probability that they are *both* true is their product. If we continue in this fashion, if we have $n - 1$ people all with different birthdays, the probability that individual n has a different birthday is:

$$\frac{364}{365} \times \frac{363}{365} \times \frac{362}{365} \times \ldots \times \frac{365 - n + 1}{365}$$

When $n \geq 24$ this expression becomes less than 0.5. This means that if 24 or more people are gathered in a room, the odds are better than even that two individuals have the same birthday.

The implication of the birthday paradox for hashing is to tell us that for any problem of reasonable size, we are almost certain to have some collisions. Functions that avoid duplicate values are surprisingly rare, even with a relatively large table.

possibility. In the bucket sort algorithm in Figure 17.4, we used a shift instruction. Shift instructions have a speed advantage over divisions, but they can only be used in situations where the number of buckets is a power of two. Another alternative is to use bitwise operations to select just a few binary digits from an integer key.

Special care must be taken to guarantee that the value returned by the modular division operation is a legal index. In particular, a negative value for the left argument could result in a negative (and hence, out-of-range) index. The safest approach is to use unsigned arithmetic in computing hash values.

If division is used, the only source of variation is the size of the table. Let us consider the effect of a computation to take the remainder by dividing by n, the hash table size:

$$index = key \bmod n$$

Some values of n are much better than others in shuffling the key values. If n is even, for example, then the index will be even for even key values and odd for odd key values. In many cases this is unacceptable. For example, on most machines pointer addresses are always even, and often always multiples of 4. If the key is simply an address, this would result in the odd-numbered buckets being totally unused.

If n is a power of two, then the mod is simply the low-order bits of the key value. Not only is the mod instruction an inefficient way to obtain this value, but usually these bits are not as random as we would like.

Empirical evidence suggests that better scattering is achieved in cases where n is a prime number. Thus, if one wants a hash table of "about" 1,000 elements, then a size of 997 or 1,009 is preferable.

17.7   CHAPTER SUMMARY

Key Concepts

- Hashing
- Hash functions
- Collisions
- Hash tables
- Buckets
- Asymptotic analysis of hash tables
- Counting sort
- Bucket sorting
- Radix sorting

Hashing a value means simply applying a function that transforms a non-integer key into an integer value. This simple idea is the basis for a very powerful data structuring technique. If it is possible to discover a function that transforms a set of keys via a one-to-one mapping on to a set of integer index values, then it is possible to construct a vector using non-integer keys. More commonly, several key values will map into the same integer index. Two keys that map into the same value are said to have collided. The problem of multiple key values for each index can be accommodated by maintaining a bucket for each possible hash (key) value. The bucket will hold all values with the same hash value. Such a structure is known as a hash table.

The process of hashing permits access and testing operations that potentially are the fastest of any data structure we have considered. Unfortunately, this potential depends upon the wise choice of a hash function, and luck with the key set. A good hash function must uniformly distribute key values over each of the different buckets. Discovering a good hash function is often the most difficult part of using the hash table technique.

We illustrated the use of hash tables by describing three different sorting algorithms. Each of these algorithms uses the idea of distributing values into different buckets, but each uses the buckets for a different purpose.

Further Reading

The hash table technique described here is technically known as *collision resolution by chaining*, and is but one of a great number of hash table techniques. Probably the most important technique we do not discuss involves *open table hashing*, or *open addressing*, where the actual element values are stored in the hash table, instead of the table being an array of buckets. A practical disadvantage of the open table technique (and the reason why we do not present it here) is the requirement that it be possible to determine whether a position has been filled or not. Despite this, for hashing values for which this is not difficult (for example, pointers or integers), then open addressing is an acceptable approach that has the merit of using less space. We will discuss a simple version of open addressing in Chapter 20.

Another topic we do not address is *extendible hashing*, which occurs when the hash table is maintained in memory but the data items themselves are maintained on disk. Here the main consideration is to reduce the number of disk accesses. Again, we will discuss a simple external hashed data structure in Chapter 20.

As with most data structures, the exposition by Knuth [Knuth 75] provides a wealth of information on hashing. Good analysis of the average time complexity of hashing is found in Cormen et al. [Cormen 90], and in Gonnet et al. [Gonnet 91]. Other explanations can be found in Aho et al. [Aho 83], and Weiss [Weiss 92]. The merits of various hash functions in a practical setting (namely, compiler symbol tables) are discussed in Aho et al. [Aho 86]. Drozdek [Drozdek 96] describes a number of hashing algorithms written in C++.

Study Questions & Exercises

Study Questions

1. What is a hash function?

2. What is a hash function collision?

3. What is a perfect hash function?

4. What are hash table buckets?

5. What properties must be satisfied for a hash table to permit constant time insertion, access, and removal of values?

6. Give a short English language description of the bucket sort algorithm.

7. For what type of input values would it be appropriate to use the bucket sorting algorithm?

8. Give a short English language description of the radix sort algorithm.

9. For what type of input values would it be appropriate to use the radix sorting algorithm?

10. Give an example, different from those described in the book, for the hash function techniques of mapping and folding.

Exercises

1. Give an explanation of each of the following terms: hashing, collision, bucket.

2. When Alan wishes to join the circle of six friends, why can't Amy simply increase the size of the vector to seven?

3. Give a class definition for a hash table that uses the list data type for the individual bucket elements. What new member functions could you then add to this new data type?

4. Amy's club has grown, and now includes the following members:

Abel	Abigail	Abraham	Ada
Adam	Adrian	Adrienne	Agnes
Albert	Alex	Alfred	Alice
Amanda	Amy	Andrew	Andy
Angela	Anita	Anne	Antonia
Arnold	Arthur	Audrey	

   a. Find what value would be computed by Amy's hash function for each member of the group.
   b. Assume we use Amy's hash function and assign each member to a bucket by simply dividing the hash value by the number of buckets. Determine how many elements would be assigned to each bucket for a hash table of size 5. Do the same for a hash table of size 11.

5. Can you come up with a perfect hash function for the names of the week? The names of the months? The names of the planets?

6. Examine a set of twelve or more telephone numbers, for example the numbers belonging to your friends. Suppose we want to hash into seven different buckets. What would be a good hash function for your set of telephone numbers? Will your function continue to work for new telephone numbers?

7. Using the techniques described in Exercise 19, in Chapter 4, test the hypothesis that bucket sort is an $O(n)$ algorithm for small values of n. Use the data presented in the first table in Appendix B. Then use the same techniques, but use the data from the second table.

8. Is the bucket sort algorithm shown in Figure 17.4 stable?

9. Is the radix sort algorithm shown in Figure 17.5 stable?

10. Another variation on the bucket sort algorithm shown in Figure 17.4 uses an array of skew heaps. Elements are first inserted into the different heaps. Then elements are taken out of the heaps, using the pop function. Write the C++ procedure that implements this algorithm.

11. Using empirical timings, compare the execution time of the algorithm you constructed for Question 10 against the execution time of the bucket sort algorithm shown in Figure 17.4.

12. In this exercise we will develop an iterator for the hash_table data type.
   a. The hash_table_iterator class must maintain three data fields: a reference to the underlying vector of buckets from a hash table, an index that records the number of buckets, and an iterator for the underlying container. Write the class description that includes these three fields.
   b. There are two constructors for the hash table iterator class. The first takes as argument only the buckets and size, and must search for the first valid element. (This search will use the increment operator, defined in the following part.) The alternative constructor will take in addition an iterator, and set all three data fields from the arguments. The latter is used in implementing the end() hash table operation, which sets the iterator to point to the end() iterator generated by the final bucket. Write these two operators.
   c. When the current element is requested, the value referenced by the iterator to the underlying container is yielded. Write this operator.
   d. The increment operator for a hash table iterator first tries to move the current bucket iterator to a new element. If there are no further elements in the current bucket, the index value is advanced to the next bucket. If there are no further buckets, the past the end iterator for the final bucket is returned. Otherwise, the beginning iterator for the new bucket is created. If this yields a valid

element, it is then returned. Otherwise, if the bucket is empty, then the next bucket is examined. This process continues until either all buckets have been examined or an element is located. Write this operator.

e. Write the decrement operator that performs a similar task, but moving backwards.

18

Matrices: Two-Dimensional Data Structures

Chapter Overview

The term *matrix* is used to describe a two-dimensional array of values. Although not provided directly as a data abstraction in the standard library, matrices can easily be constructed in a variety of ways using other containers. In this chapter we illustrate some of these techniques, and discuss the type of problems that make one implementation approach preferable over another. Major topics discussed in this chapter include the following:

▲ The matrix data abstraction

▲ Vectors of vectors

▲ Sparse matrices

▲ Matrices with non-integer indices

18.1 THE MATRIX DATA ABSTRACTION

A *matrix* is a two-dimensional array of values. Matrices occur frequently in a variety of mathematical and financial problems. Matrices are related to arrays and vectors, and just as it is useful to create the `vector` data type on top of the underlying C++ array, it is also useful to create a variety of matrix data abstractions.

In this chapter we will first describe how matrices can be created as arrays of arrays in C++. We then describe some of the problems implicit in this representation, and describe a number of alternative representation techniques for two-dimensional structures.

18.1.1   C++ Matrices

A simple matrix in C++ is created by declaring the extent of each dimension. Consider this statement:

```
double d[3][4];
```

The value `d` is a three-by-four matrix of double precision value. It consists of three rows and four columns. The space set aside by the compiler for this data type will constitute twelve double precision values. These will be placed end-to-end in memory, and might be visualized as follows:

element	element	element	element
d[0][0]	d[0][1]	d[0][2]	d[0][3]
element	element	element	element
d[1][0]	d[1][1]	d[1][2]	d[1][3]
element	element	element	element
d[2][0]	d[2][1]	d[2][2]	d[2][3]

Because elements are placed in memory in order, with the second subscript changing more quickly than the first, it is possible to view this as a vector of vectors. That is, a singly subscripted value, such as `d[1]`, will evaluate to the address of `d[1][0]`, in the middle row of this structure. The placement of elements in memory for each row is exactly the same as the placement of elements in a four-element vector. We will later use this observation when we create an alternative matrix data abstraction.

Like C++ arrays, matrices can be initialized by the declaration statement in which they are created, by placing the initial values in a list of quantities surrounded by curly braces. Each row of values is given a separate set of braces. The following initializes a three-by-four element matrix:

```
double prices[3][4] =
    { { 1.25, 1.09, 0.58, 0.25 },
    { 1.35, 0.98, 0.62, 0.35 },
    { 1.40, 1.12, 0.43, 0.19 } };
```

```
template <class MatrixType1, class MatrixType2, class MatrixType3>
void matrixMultiply
        (MatrixType1 a, MatrixType2 b, MatrixType3 c,
            unsigned n, unsigned m, unsigned p)

    // multiply a times b, placing result into c
    // a is n by m, b is m by p, c is n by p
{
    for (int i = 0; i < n; i++)
        for (int j = 0; j < p; j++) {
            c[i][j] = 0;
            for (int k = 0; k < m; j++)
                c[i][j] += a[i][k] * b[k][j];
            }
}
```

Figure 18.1 A matrix multiplication algorithm

As with the `vector` data type in comparison to C++ arrays, one of the few redeeming features of the construct compared to the data abstractions we will present shortly is that two-dimensional matrices can be easily initialized in this fashion.

Individual elements of a matrix are accessed using two applications of the subscript operator. This is illustrated by Figure 18.1, which describes the conventional matrix multiplication operation. You will recall that when multiplying two matrices, each row of the first matrix is combined with each column of the second, multiplying paired values and summing the results. A trio of template parameters are provided for the matrix arguments so that the resulting algorithm can be used both with standard C++ matrices and with the new matrix types we will subsequently define.

To illustrate the use of the matrix data type, consider the following problem. The matrix named `prices` described previously is an encoding of the following table of prices for various items from three different grocery stores:

Price per unit	Hamburger	Chicken	Tomato	Lettuce
Store A	$ 1.25	$ 1.09	$ 0.58	$ 0.25
Store B	$ 1.35	$ 0.98	$ 0.62	$ 0.35
Store C	$ 1.40	$ 1.12	$ 0.43	$ 0.19

Three families in a typical week consume different quantities of these items, represented by the following chart:

Family	Smith	Brown	Jones
Hamburger	5	2	0
Chicken	4	5	0
Tomatoes	2	1	6
Lettuce	1	2	4

We can discover which store would be least expensive for each family by solving a matrix multiplication problem. The matrix of stores by items is multiplied by the matrix of items by family, resulting in a new matrix of stores by family. This process could be performed by this short program:

```
void main() {
    double prices[3][4] = { ... as above };
    double quantity[4][3] = { ... };
    double cost[3][3];

        // perform the matrix multiplication
    matrixMultiply (prices, quantity, cost, 3, 4, 3);

        // output the result
    cout << "cost per family, Smith, Brown Jones\n";
    matrixOutput (cost, 3, 3);
}
```

The results would indicate that family Smith would be better off shopping at store A, while family Brown should go to store B, and family Jones to store C. The routine `matrixOutput` is a simple procedure we can use to print two-dimensional matrix values. By declaring the matrix type with a template parameter, we can use the same routine for both conventional C++ arrays and the matrix datatypes we will shortly define.

```
template <class MatrixType>
void matrixOutput (MatrixType mat, unsigned int n, unsigned int m)
    // output an n by m matrix
{
    for (int i = 0; i < n; i++)  {
        for (j = 0; j < n; j++)
            cout << m[i][j] << " ";
        cout << endl;
        }
}
```

Problems with the C++ matrix as a data type mirror those with the vector data type. The size of a C++ matrix must be known at compile time, and cannot be modified dynamically as a program executes. However, most importantly, simple matrices are not "self-describing." By this we mean

```
template <class value_type>
class matrix {
public:
    matrix  (unsigned int nor, unsigned int noc);

    vector<value_type> &     operator [ ]     (unsigned int index)
        { return rows[index]; }

    unsigned int    numberOfRows       () { return rows.size(); }
    unsigned int    numberOfColumns    () { return rows[0].size(); }

protected:
    vector< vector<value_type> > rows;
};
```

Figure 18.2 Definition of the class `matrix`

that they do not contain within them information about their structure. This is why, for example, we must pass the dimensions of the matrices as arguments to the procedure shown in Figure 18.1. We can solve this problem by creating a new matrix data abstraction.

18.2   MATRICES AS VECTORS OF VECTORS

One way to create a new matrix data type would be to build on the `vector` data type described in Chapter 8. A matrix is conceptually simply a two-dimensional array of values, each of which is a vector of data values:

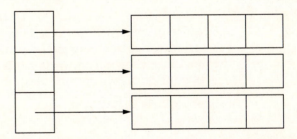

The class description for this abstraction is shown in Figure 18.2. A protected data area holds a vector of vectors. The constructor must allocate space for each row. The constructor function takes two arguments, which represent the number of rows and the number of columns, respectively. The implementation of the constructor, which follows, resizes each row vector to the appropriate size:

```
template <class value_type>
matrix<value_type>::matrix
     (unsigned int nor, unsigned int noc) : numberOfRows(nor)
{
        // resize each row vector to the appropriate size
     for (unsigned int i = 0; i < numberOfRows; i++)
          rows[i].resize(numberOfColumns);
}
```

To determine the number of rows it is sufficient to compute the length of the `rows` vector. To determine the number of columns one simply computes the number of elements held in the first row. Both of these member functions are sufficiently short that they can be defined in the class declaration (Figure 18.2).

The C++ language only permits a single argument to be used with the subscript operator. When using multidimensional structures, separate subscript operations are applied for each dimension. The subscript operator for the matrix class simply returns a reference to a vector. The vector can then be subscripted to access an individual element.

The assignment of one matrix to another is implemented by performing an element by element copy. By defining this as an ordinary function, not a member function, and using a template parameter for the right argument, we can use the assignment operator with either another `matrix` or with a C++ array.[1]

```
template <class value_type, class matrixType>
void operator = (matrix<value_type> & left, matrixType & right)
{
     for (int i = 0; i < left.numberOfRows(); i++)
          for (int j = 0; j < left.numberOfColumns(); j++)
               left[i][j] = right[i][j];
}
```

Because the `matrix` data type is more self-describing, we can overload the arithmetic operators when they are used with matrices. For example, the procedure shown next overloads the multiplication operator to mean matrix multiplication, making use of the procedure defined earlier:

```
template <class value_type>
matrix<value_type> operator *
     (matrix<value_type> & left, matrix<value_type> & right)
     // overload * operator to perform matrix multiplication
{
```

---

1. The definition of the C++ language permits member functions to have template parameters separate from the class templates; however, few compilers at present support this. If such facilities were available, it would be possible to define the assignment operator as a member function in the `matrix` class. See Section A.5 in Appendix A.

```
            // allocate space for the result
        matrix<value_type> result(left.numberOfRows(),
                right.numberOfColumns());

            // perform the multiplication
        matrixMultiply (left, right, result,
            left.numberOfRows(), left.numberOfColumns(),
                    right.numberOfColumns());

        // return the result
        return result;
}
```

The grocery store cost minimization problem solved previously could be rewritten to use these matrix operators, resulting in the following:

```
void main() {
        matrix<double> pmatrix(3, 4);
        matrix<double> qmatrix(4, 3);
        matrix<double> costs(3, 3);

            // assign initial values from C++ array of data
        pmatrix = prices;
        qmatrix = quantities;
            // now perform multiplication
        costs = prices * quantities;

            // output the result
        cout << "cost per family, Smith, Brown Jones\n";
        matrixOutput (cost, 3, 3);
}
```

18.2.1   Combining Matrices and Vectors

The class matrix combines naturally and easily with the class vector. For example, the following overloads the multiplication operator again, so that when the left argument is a matrix and the right argument a vector, the result is a vector value.

```
template <class value_type>
vector<value_type> operator *
  (matrix<value_type> & a, vector<value_type> & v)
{
        // check compatibility
    assert(a.numberOfColumns() == v.size());
        // allocate result
    vector<value_type> result (a.numberOfRows());
```

```
        // compute result
    for (int i = 0; i < a.numberOfRows(); i++) {
        result[i] = 0.0;
        for (int j = 0; j < a.numberOfColumns(); j++)
            result[i] += a[i][j] * v[j];
    }

        // return result
    return result;
}
```

To be useful for numeric problems we would need to define many more functions and arithmetic operators, such as arithmetic assignment, matrix inversion, and the calculation of a determinant. In addition, we would have to consider the effects of round-off errors; in many cases, algorithms that differ from the "classic" definitions of operations will yield more reliable results. Such topics are beyond our discussion here; a good text on numerical analysis will provide an explanation of these and many other issues.

Another issue of concern in a more complete implementation would be memory management. Operations such as multiplication and assignment produce temporary values, which exist only while the operation is being performed and are then released. This can cause unnecessary dynamic memory allocation. A more careful (and complex) design could minimize these by saving the dynamically allocated storage areas across assignments. However, the details necessary to accomplish this are subtle, and not relevant to our discussion here.

18.3   SPARSE MATRICES

In many numeric problems, matrices arise that have nonzero values in only a few positions. An example is shown in Figure 18.3. Such matrices are termed *sparse*. Storing all values in a sparse matrix may be unnecessarily costly. Instead, one could simply store information that indicates which values are indeed nonzero, and return zero for all other values.

The problem with this approach is that elements are accessed using the subscript operator, and at the point where the subscript operator is applied we do not know whether a particular value is being requested or whether a location is being modified. This means that the subscript operator by itself cannot tell which of the two following uses is occurring:

```
c[i][j] = ....
.... = c[i][j]
```

We cannot simply return a reference to an element, as we do with the `vector` and `matrix` classes. In the first situation we only want to create a new element if the assigned value is nonzero, while in the second there is

0	0	0	0	0	0	0	0	0	0	0	0	0	0	0
0	2	0	0	0	0	0	0	0	0	0	0	0	0	0
0	0	0	0	0	0	0	0	0	0	0	0	0	0	0
0	0	0	0	0	0	7	0	0	0	0	0	0	0	0
0	0	0	0	0	0	0	0	0	0	0	0	0	0	0
0	0	0	0	9	0	0	0	0	0	0	4	0	0	0
0	0	0	0	0	0	0	0	0	0	0	0	0	0	0
0	0	0	0	0	0	0	0	0	0	0	0	0	0	0
0	0	0	0	0	0	0	0	3	0	0	0	0	0	0
0	0	1	0	0	0	0	0	0	0	0	0	0	0	0

Figure 18.3   An example sparse matrix

also no need to create a reference if the associated position contains only the default value.

The solution to this problem is to create an intermediary class that exists only for the brief span of time between when the subscript is applied and when it can be determined which of these two uses is appropriate. Instances of this class can perform only two types of operations—they can complete an assignment or they can convert themselves into a value. These correspond to the two situations described previously.

A class that embodies these ideas is shown in Figure 18.4. Instances of the class `sparse_matrix_element` maintain a reference to a row and the index value that describes the column being referenced within the row. The only operations that can be performed with these values are assignment and conversion to an expression. (To simplify the presentation, our sparse matrix will store only double precision values.) By placing the

Yet Another Time-Space Tradeoff

A characteristic of the vector data type is that access to any element can be performed in constant time. Recall, however, that access to elements in a map requires in the worst case $O(\log n)$ steps, where n represents the number of elements in the collection. Sparse arrays therefore represent yet another example of a time–space tradeoff.

A sparse array is used when too many ele-ments in the conventional representation would have the value zero. Thus, the conventional representation uses too much space in relation to the amount of information being stored. The sparse array uses less memory, but requires greater time to access each element. Deciding which representation to select for any particular problem requires balancing the competing requirements for these two resources.

```
class sparse_matrix_element {
public:

        // elements can be assigned
     void operator = (double newValue);
     void operator += (double newValue);

        // or they can be used as expressions
     operator double ();


protected:
     friend class sparse_matrix_row;
     sparse_matrix_element (map<int, double> & r, int i)
        : row(r), index(i) { }
     map<int, double> & row;
     int index;
};
```

Figure 18.4   Definition of the class `sparse_matrix_element`

constructor for the class in the protected portion, and declaring the class `sparse_matrix_row` as a *friend*, we can guarantee that matrix elements can only be created as a result of indexing a sparse matrix row.

The actual data for the row will be stored in a map. Recall from Chapter 16 that a map can be considered a generalization of a vector, but one in which the index values can be any expression. Through the use of a map, we need to store only the values that are actually being used.

The class `sparse_matrix_row` is shown next. Note that this class is even simpler than sparse matrix element. The sparse matrix row class maintains the row data values in a map, the same map that will be referenced by the sparse matrix elements constructed in response to subscripts.

Conversion Operators

The class `sparse_matrix_element` is the first time we have seen a *type* used as an *operator*. An operator used in this fashion defines how a value can be converted, and is hence named a *conversion operator*. In this case, the operator indicates that a sparse matrix element can be converted into a double precision value.

Conversion operators are applied automatically and implicitly by the compiler when necessary. For example, when a sparse matrix element occurs in the middle of an expression, the compiler will discover that it lacks any operators that know how to handle this particular data type. So the compiler then searches to determine if it can convert the value into a type that it can use. Finding the conversion operator for double precision values, the compiler will automatically apply this function to convert the subscript element into a double, then proceed in generating code to make use of the double precision value.

The only operation permitted by the class `sparse matrix row` is to recognize a subscript, and return a sparse matrix element.

```
class sparse_matrix_row {
public:
      sparse_matrix_element operator [ ] (int index)
          { return sparse_matrix_element (row, index); }
protected:
      map<int, double> row;
};
```

The implementations of the member functions for `sparse_matrix_element` are shown in Figure 18.5. Operations on the underlying map are used to determine whether the indexed element exists in the matrix. Similarly, if a value is assigned a quantity that matches the default value (zero), the corresponding index is simply removed from the map. In this fashion, the map stores only those elements which contain nonzero entries.

In the same way that the `matrix` class maintained a vector of vectors, the `sparse_matrix` class (Figure 18.6) maintains a vector of sparse matrix rows. When a subscript operator is invoked, a sparse matrix row is returned. When another subscript operator is invoked, a sparse matrix element is returned. Finally, when either the sparse matrix element is assigned to or used, one of the sparse matrix element member functions is processed.

Because the interface for the sparse matrix matches the interface for the `matrix` class, a sparse matrix can be used in any situation in which a `matrix` is used, by changing only the declarations.

18.4   NON-INTEGER INDEX VALUES

In the previous section we used the map data type to implement sparse arrays, making use of the property that a map will only store those index positions that are actually being used. Another property of the map that we did not use in the sparse matrix example is that the index values need not be integer. In this section we will make use of this property, creating two-dimensional matrices indexed by non-integer values.

Just as a two-dimensional matrix can be envisioned as a vector in which each element is a vector, we can create a more general matrix class by defining a map in which each element is another map. For example, suppose we want to represent the following table of average temperature for various cities:

```
void sparse_matrix_element::operator = (double newValue)
    // only create entry if value is nonzero
{
    if (newValue == 0.0)
            // remove value with given index
        row.erase(index);
    else
        row[index] = newValue;
}


void sparse_matrix_element::operator += (double newValue)
    // increment entry, create if result is nonzero
{
    if (row.count(index) == 0) {
        if (newValue != 0.0) {
            row[index] = newValue;
        }
        else {
            row[index] += newValue;
            if (row[index] == 0.0)
                row.erase(index);
        }
    }
}


sparse_matrix_element::operator double ()
    // convert entry into value, using default if necessary
{
    if (row.count(index) == 0)
        return 0.0; // use default
    else
        return row[index]; // use value in table
}
```

Figure 18.5   Implementation of member functions for `sparse_matrix_element`

City	January	April	July	October
Bismark	9.9	43.5	71.7	46.7
Denver	28.5	46.4	72.9	51.4
Wichita	32.0	56.7	80.9	59.9
San Francisco	50.7	55.7	58.8	61.4

One approach would be to declare a map, indexed by strings, containing elements that are themselves maps, again indexed by strings and this time

```
class sparse_matrix {
public:
    sparse_matrix (int nor, int noc)
        : numberOfRows(nor), numColumns(noc) { }

    sparse_matrix_row &  operator [ ]  (int index)
            { return rows[index]; }

    unsigned int  numberOfRows    () { return rows.size(); }
    unsigned int  numberOfColumns () { return numColumns; }

protected:
    vector < sparse_matrix_row > rows;
    int numColumns;
};
```

Figure 18.6 Definition of the class `sparse_matrix`

containing numbers. Let us call such a data type a `chartType`, and the underlying row type a `chartRowType`. These could be defined as:

```
typedef map<string, map<string, double> > chartType;
typedef map<string, double> chartRowType;
```

To create a chart, we simply declare a new variable, then initialize the variable with a sequence of assignment statements:

```
    // declare the new chart
chartType temps;
    // then initialize it
temps["Bismark"]["January"] = 9.9;
temps["Bismark"]["April"] = 43.5;
    .
    .
    .
temps["San Francisco"]["January"] = 50.7;
temps["San Francisco"]["April"] = 55.7;
temps["San Francisco"]["July"] = 58.8;
```

The operations provided by the underlying map data type can then be used to construct programs. The following program fragment, for example, prints the average yearly temperature for each city represented in the database:

```
    // loop over each city
chartType::iterator city_itr;
for (city_itr = temps.begin(); city_itr != temps.end(); ++city_itr) {
    string city = (*city_itr).first;
    chartRowType & cityTemps = (*city_itr).second;
```

```
        double aveTemp = 0.0;
            // sum the temperatures recorded for each month
        chartRowType::iterator m_itr; // month iterator
        for (m_itr = cityTemps.begin(); m_itr != cityTemps.end(); m_itr++)
            aveTemp += (*m_itr).second;
            // output the average of all temperatures
        cout << "Average temperature for " << city << " is "
            << (aveTemp / cityTemps.size()) << endl;
    }
```

Matrices can be generated in a similar fashion using any type of index value.

18.5   CHAPTER SUMMARY

Key Concepts

- Matrix
- Matrix multiplication
- Sparse matrix
- Matrix with non-integer keys

A matrix is a two-dimensional array of values. Matrices occur in a number of mathematical and financial problems. The C++ language provides a primitive matrix facility; however, this data type suffers from problems similar to the vector data type. Most notably, there is no way to determine the extent (number of rows and columns) of a primitive C++ array merely by examining the data values themselves.

We can construct more general matrix abstractions in a variety of ways. A simple form of matrix is a vector of vectors. By using a map in place of a vector, we can implement the idea of a sparse matrix, a matrix that stores only the values that are being used. Finally, a map of maps provides a means of implementing a two-dimensional matrix structure where the index values are not integers.

Study Questions & Exercises

Study Questions

1. What is a matrix?

2. How many elements will be contained in a matrix with four rows and six columns?

3. What is the asymptotic execution time of the matrix multiplication algorithm shown in Figure 18.1?

4. What is a sparse matrix?

5. What are the two ways in which a matrix element is used?

6. What property of a map makes it useful in implementing the sparse matrix class? What property makes it useful in implementing the data type chartType in Section 18.4?

7. What is a conversion operator?

Exercises

1. Assume that two-dimensional matrices are laid out in memory as shown at the beginning of Section 18.1.1. Write a formula that will determine the memory offset for location i, j relative to the start of the matrix, assuming the matrix has n rows of m elements. (For example, for the given 3 by 4 matrix, element d[1][2] is found at offset 6, while element d[2][1] has offset 9.)

2. The vector data type allows the programmer to specify an initial value for each vector position when declaring a new data structure. Add

a constructor to the `matrix` data type that provides similar functionality.

3. We can define the addition of two matrices as element-by-element combination. That is, each element in the result is the sum of the corresponding elements with the same index values in the two arguments. Overload the addition operator for two matrix arguments so it will produce a result with this meaning.

4. In the `vector` data type, the member function `resize()` changes the number of elements that can be stored in the container. We used this member function, for example, in the constructor for the class `matrix`. Implement a variation on `resize()` for two-dimensional matrices. Your function should take two integer arguments, and alter both the number of rows and the number of columns.

5. Using the chart representation described in Section 18.4, write short programs to perform the following:

   a. Compute the mean temperature for all cities and all months.
   b. For each month, compute the mean temperature across all cities.
   c. Find the cities with the highest and the lowest average temperatures.
   d. Find the city with the greatest temperature variation.

6. A two-dimensional matrix is said to be *symmetric* if the value held at index position i, j is the same as that held at position j, i. Given such a structure, it is not necessary to store both values. Instead, we might only store those values that correspond to positions i, j where $i <= j$. A request for j, i, where $j < i$, would then be turned around and the element i, j returned. Show how to modify the `sparse_matrix` data type in order to represent symmetric matrices in this fashion. (Hint: The sparse matrix element type will need to store a reference to the entire array, not simply one row.)

Chapter

19

Graphs

Chapter Overview

Graphs occur in a variety of different problems in computer science. In this chapter we provide a brief introduction to the concept, illustrating how graphs can be represented in a variety of different forms using the containers in the standard library. Example problems are then solved to illustrate the benefits as well as the limitations of each of the different representations. That complex algorithms can be solved in a concise fashion illustrates well the power of the standard template library. The chapter concludes with two classic examples of the use of graphs, *finite automata* and *Turing machines*. Major topics discussed in this chapter include the following:

▲ The graph data abstraction

▲ Adjacency matrix representation

▲ Edge list representation

▲ Sparse matrix representation

▲ Finite automata

▲ Turing machines

19.1 THE GRAPH DATA ABSTRACTION

In this chapter we will explore the idea of a *graph* as it is represented using a number of different data structures. Our purpose is not to summarize

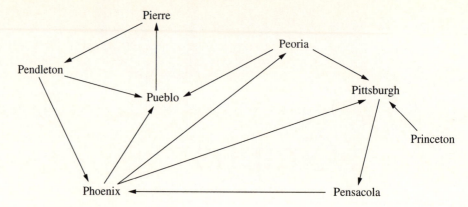

Figure 19.1   A typical graph

the field of graph theory, which is a rich and complex cross between mathematics and computer science; rather, the objective of this chapter is to illustrate the use of many of the data structures developed in earlier chapters to solve realistic nontrivial problems.

A graph, such as the one shown in Figure 19.1, can be considered to be composed of *vertices* and *edges*. Either may carry additional information. If the graph is being used to model real-world objects, for example, a roadmap, then the value of a vertex might represent the name of a city, whereas an edge could represent a road from one city to another.

There are a variety of different types of graphs. A graph is said to be *directed* if the edges have a designated beginning and ending point; otherwise, a graph is said to be undirected. We will restrict our discussion in this chapter to directed graphs. But this is actually no restriction at all since an undirected graph can always be simulated by a directed graph where each edge is represented by two arcs traveling in opposite directions:

A second source of variation in the idea of a graph is the distinction between a *weighted* or *labeled* graph and an *unweighted* graph. In a weighted graph, each edge is given a numerical value. For example, the value might represent the distance of the highway connecting two cities, or the cost of the airfare between two airports. An unweighted graph carries no such information. We will begin by considering algorithms for unweighted graphs. This discussion will then be followed by a pair of algorithms that operate on the weighted forms.

19.2   ADJACENCY MATRIX REPRESENTATION

One of the most common ways of representing a graph is to use a matrix, such as those studied in Chapter 18. The vertices in the graph are used as index values for the matrix. This means the vertices must either be numbered in the original graph or some mechanism must be provided to associate each vertex with an integer value. To represent the graph shown in Figure 19.1, we could simply list the cities in alphabetical order and number the list. Entries in the matrix are Boolean values, represented by 0 and 1. A one value in the position indexed by i and j in the matrix indicates that there is an edge from vertices i to j, while a zero values indicates there is no such connection. By convention a node is always considered to be connected to itself, and thus all positions in the major diagonal (that is, positions with the same row and column index value) are 1. The adjacency matrix representation for the graph in Figure 19.1 is:

City	0.	1.	2.	3.	4.	5.	6.	7.
0. Pendleton	1	0	0	1	0	0	0	1
1. Pensacola	0	1	0	1	0	0	0	0
2. Peoria	0	0	1	0	0	1	0	1
3. Phoenix	0	0	1	1	0	1	0	1
4. Pierre	1	0	0	0	1	0	0	0
5. Pittsburgh	0	1	0	0	0	1	0	0
6. Princeton	0	0	0	0	0	1	1	0
7. Pueblo	0	0	0	0	1	0	0	1

One could define the adjacency matrix as a C++ array in the following fashion:

```
int adjacency [8][8] = { { 1, 0, 0, 1, 0, 0, 0, 1},
        { 0, 1, 0, 1, 0, 0, 0, 0},
        { 0, 0, 1, 0, 0, 1, 0, 1},
        { 0, 0, 1, 1, 0, 1, 0, 1},
        { 1, 0, 0, 0, 1, 0, 0, 0},
        { 0, 1, 0, 0, 0, 1, 0, 0},
        { 0, 0, 0, 0, 0, 1, 1, 0},
        { 0, 0, 0, 0, 1, 0, 0, 1} };
```

A number of questions could be asked concerning any particular graph. One of the fundamental problems is the question of *reachability*. What set of vertices can be reached by starting from a particular vertex and moving only along the given edges in the graph? Conversely, are there any vertices that cannot be reached by traveling in such a fashion?

There are two basic variations on this question. The *single-source* question poses a specific initial starting vertex, and requests the set of vertices reachable from this vertex. The *all-pairs* question seeks to generate this information simultaneously for all possible vertices. Of course, a solution to the all-pairs question will answer the single-source question as well. For this reason, we would expect that an algorithm that solves the all-pairs problem will require at least as much effort as any algorithm for the single-source problem. In the next section we will present a solution to the all-pairs reachability problem. A solution to the single-source reachability problem will subsequently be presented in Section 19.3.

19.2.1 Warshall's Algorithm

The algorithm we will describe to illustrate the use of the adjacency matrix representation of graphs is known as Warshall's algorithm, after the computer scientist credited with its discovery. Warshall's algorithm is designed to generate a *reachability* matrix. A reachability matrix is similar to an adjacency matrix, only a 1 value in location i,j indicates that vertex j can be reached by some path starting from vertex i, even if the two vertices are not directly connected. The heart of Warshall's algorithm (see Figure 19.2) is a trio of loops, which operate very much like the loops in the classic algorithm for matrix multiplication presented in Chapter 18. The key idea is that at each iteration through the outermost loop (index k), we add to the graph any path of length 2 that has node k as its center.

The following illustrates executing Warshall's algorithm on the adjacency matrix defined earlier:

```
void main () {
        // execute the algorithm
    warshall (adjacency, 8);
        // print the result
    matrixOutput (adjacency, 8, 8);
}
```

The process of adding information to the graph is performed through a combination of bitwise logical operations. The expression a[i][k] & a[k][j] is true if there is a path from node i to node k, and if there is a path from node k to node j. This tells us that there is therefore a path from node i to node j. By using the bitwise-or assignment operator, we add this information to position a[i][j]. The use of bitwise-or ensures that if there was a 1 bit already in the position, indicating we had already discovered a previous path, then the earlier information will not be erased. Figure 19.3 gives the intermediate values of the matrix a as we execute Warshall's algorithm on the adjacency matrix from the graph of Figure 19.1.

The easiest way to understand Warshall's algorithm is to simulate a few iterations through the outer loop. In the first iteration we are looking

```
//
// warshall
//    solve the all pairs reachability problem
//     using the adjacency matrix representation of a graph
//     converts adjacency matrix into a reachability matrix
//


template <class matrixType>
void warshall (matrixType & a, unsigned int n)
     // a must be an n by n matrix
{
        // each step through the outer loop
        // see if it is possible to make a connection
        // from vertex i to vertex j through vertex k

     for (int k = 0; k < n; k++) {
        for (int i = 0; i < n; i++)
           for (int j = 0; j < n; j++)
               a[i][j] |= a[i][k] & a[k][j];
           // inv: if there is a path from vertex i to vertex j
           // that does not go through any vertex higher than k
           // then a[i][j] is 1.
           }
}
```

Figure 19.2   Warshall's algorithm

for paths that flow through node 0, which represents Pendleton. Because Pierre has the only edge flowing into Pendleton, it is the source of the only possible new paths. In this case there are two new paths discovered, one that links Pierre with Phoenix and another that links Pierre with Pueblo.

In the second iteration we investigate paths that travel through node 1, Pensacola. We discover one new edge, which links Pittsburgh with Phoenix. It turns out in the next step that there are no new paths that flow through Peoria, and thus we have omitted this table from Figure 19.3.

The next step is to discover paths through Phoenix, and it is here that we can see how Warshall's algorithm really operates. From the original graph we can derive the edges from Pendleton to Peoria, and Pendleton to Pittsburgh, just as we did in the earlier steps. But now we can do more. From the previous steps we now know that one can travel from Pierre to Phoenix and from Pueblo to Phoenix. Thus, by extending paths we have earlier encountered, we can now say that it is possible to travel from Pierre to Peoria and Pittsburgh, and from Pueblo to the same two destinations.

```
1 0 0 1 0 0 0 1              1 0 0 1 0 0 0 1
0 1 0 1 0 0 0 0              0 1 0 1 0 0 0 0
0 0 1 0 0 1 0 1              0 0 1 0 0 1 0 1
0 0 1 1 0 1 0 1              0 0 1 1 0 1 0 1
1 0 0 0 1 0 0 0              1 0 0 1 1 0 0 1
0 1 0 0 0 1 0 0              0 1 0 0 0 1 0 0
0 0 0 0 0 1 1 0              0 0 0 0 0 1 1 0
0 0 0 0 1 0 0 1              0 0 0 0 1 0 0 1
```
Initial matrix   Matrix after iteration 0

```
1 0 0 1 0 0 0 1              1 0 1 1 0 1 0 1
0 1 0 1 0 0 0 0              0 1 1 1 0 1 0 1
0 0 1 0 0 1 0 1              0 0 1 0 0 1 0 1
0 0 1 1 0 1 0 1              0 0 1 1 0 1 0 1
1 0 0 1 1 0 0 1              1 0 1 1 1 1 0 1
0 1 0 1 0 1 0 0              0 1 1 1 0 1 0 1
0 0 0 0 0 1 1 0              0 0 0 0 0 1 1 0
0 0 0 0 1 0 0 1              0 0 0 0 1 0 0 1
```
Matrix after iteration 1   Matrix after iteration 3

```
1 0 1 1 0 1 0 1              1 1 1 1 0 1 0 1
0 1 1 1 0 1 0 1              0 1 1 1 0 1 0 1
0 0 1 0 0 1 0 1              0 1 1 1 0 1 0 1
0 0 1 1 0 1 0 1              0 1 1 1 0 1 0 1
1 0 1 1 1 1 0 1              1 1 1 1 1 1 0 1
0 1 1 1 0 1 0 1              0 1 1 1 0 1 0 1
0 0 0 0 0 1 1 0              0 1 1 1 0 1 1 1
1 0 1 1 1 1 0 1              1 1 1 1 1 1 0 1
```
Matrix after iteration 4   Matrix after iteration 5

```
1 1 1 1 0 1 0 1              1 1 1 1 1 1 0 1
0 1 1 1 0 1 0 1              1 1 1 1 1 1 0 1
0 1 1 1 0 1 0 1              1 1 1 1 1 1 0 1
0 1 1 1 0 1 0 1              1 1 1 1 1 1 0 1
1 1 1 1 1 1 0 1              1 1 1 1 1 1 0 1
0 1 1 1 0 1 0 1              1 1 1 1 1 1 0 1
0 1 1 1 0 1 1 1              1 1 1 1 1 1 1 1
1 1 1 1 1 1 0 1              1 1 1 1 1 1 0 1
```
Matrix after iteration 6   Matrix after iteration 7

Figure 19.3   Some intermediate graphs while executing Warshall's algorithm

---

Proof of Correctness: Warshall's Algorithm

To prove the correctness of Warshall's algorithm, note that if there is a path from vertex i to vertex j, then there is a path that never travels through any vertex more than once. (Simply remove such loops, resulting in a shorter path.)

The heart of the algorithm then involves establishing the invariant shown at the end of the outermost loop in Figure 19.2. We will use a technique similar to mathematical induction.

To establish the base case, note that any path that goes through vertex zero and uses no vertices with labels larger than zero will be marked at the end of the first iteration through the loop. Such a path must consist of only two legs—vertex i to vertex zero, then vertex zero to vertex j. Each of the steps must be present as edges in the initial graph. But therefore they will be recognized when the index values match the given vertex numbers, and we have that a[i][j] must be set to 1.

Next, we consider the induction step. Assume we are on the k*th* iteration, and all paths that traverse only vertices labeled k or less have been marked. Assume there is a path from vertex i to vertex j that goes through vertex k, and that uses no vertices numbered larger than k. But this means there is a path from vertex i to vertex k that does not go through any vertices larger than k. Therefore, by our induction hypothesis a[i][k] must be 1. Similarly, there must be a path from vertex k to vertex j, which also cannot use vertex k. Therefore a[k][j] must be 1. But at the point the index values match the vertex numbers, the value a[i][j] will therefore be set to 1. So the invariant remains true at the end of the loop.

Therefore, once the variable k finishes cycling through all vertices, we know that for all i, j pairs, if there is a path from vertex i to vertex j that goes through vertices labeled n or less (that is, all vertices) then a[i][j] will be 1. But this implies that all possible paths will have been discovered.

Even though at each step we consider only paths of length 2, by repeatedly extending existing edges the algorithm discovers paths of any length.

It is easy to see that Warshall's algorithms is $O(n^3)$, where n is the number of nodes in the graph. In the sidebar we provide a proof of correctness for the algorithm.

19.3   EDGE LIST REPRESENTATION

The adjacency matrix representation has the disadvantage that it always requires $O(n^2)$ space to store a matrix with n vertices, regardless of the number of edges.[1] An alternative representation stores only the edges, and is thus advantageous if the graph is relatively sparse.

The basic idea is for each vertex to maintain both a name (held in a string), and a set of pointers to vertices to which it is connected. This is accomplished by the following class declaration:

---

1. Unless, of course, a sparse matrix representation such as the one presented in Chapter 18 is used to hold the adjacency values.

```
//
//      class vertex
//              an unweighted graph vertex
//

class vertex {
public:
    // constructors
    vertex () { }
    vertex (string & init) : name(init) { }

    // add a new edge
    void addEdge (vertex & v) { edges.insert (&v); }

    // data fields are public
    string name;
    set <vertex *> edges;
};
```

The one method, named addEdge, is used to create a new edge that originates at the vertex. Note that this method takes a reference as argument, but must store a pointer in the edges data structure. The address operator (operator &) is used to obtain the address (pointer) of the referenced item. For example, the graph in Figure 19.1 could be created by the following sequence of statements.

```
// make the initial vertices
vertex pendleton("pendleton");
vertex pensacola("pensacola");
vertex peoria("peoria");
vertex phoenix("phoenix");
vertex pierre("pierre");
vertex pittsburgh("pittsburgh");
vertex princeton("princeton");
vertex pueblo("pueblo");

// create the initial links
pendleton.addEdge(phoenix); pendleton.addEdge(pueblo);
pensacola.addEdge(phoenix);
peoria.addEdge(pittsburgh); peoria.addEdge(pueblo);
phoenix.addEdge(peoria); phoenix.addEdge(pittsburgh); phoenix.addEdge(pueblo);
pierre.addEdge(pendleton);
pittsburgh.addEdge(pensacola);
princeton.addEdge(pittsburgh);
pueblo.addEdge(pierre);
```

```
//
//    findReachable
//        single source reachability
//        find all the vertices that are reachable
//        from the given starting position
//        uses a depth first search algorithm
//

void findReachable (vertex & source, set<vertex *> & reachable)
     // assume the set of reachable vertices is initially empty
{
        // create a stack of pending vertices
        // initialized with the starting vertex
     stack < list<vertex *> > pendingVertices;
     pendingVertices.push (&source);

        // pull vertices from stack one by one
     while (! pendingVertices.empty()) {
        vertex * vertx = pendingVertices.top();
        pendingVertices.pop();
            // if we haven't visited it yet, then do so now
        if (reachable.count(vertx) == 0) {
           reachable.insert(vertx);
               // add the cities now reachable
           set<vertex *>::iterator start = vertx->edges.begin();
           set<vertex *>::iterator stop = vertx->edges.end();
           for (; start != stop; ++start)
              pendingVertices.push (*start);
        }
     }
}
```

Figure 19.4   Single-source reachability algorithm

19.3.1   Reachability Using Depth-First Search

We will illustrate the use of the vertex data type by presenting an algorithm for the single-source reachability problem—that is, a procedure to discover which vertices may be reached by a sequence of edges starting from a single-source vertex.

The procedure used to compute this is shown in Figure 19.4. The algorithm uses depth-first search, a technique we have encountered previously in Chapter 11. You will recall that the depth-first search algorithm utilizes a stack of vertices that are known to be reachable, and through which other vertices may be reachable. In this case, the stack is constructed using a `list` for the underlying container, and initially contains only the source vertex.

One node is removed from the stack at each step of processing. If it is a node that has not previously been reported as reachable, then it is added to the set of reachable vertices, and the neighbors of the node are pushed on the stack. When the stack is finally empty, then all nodes that can be reached will have been investigated.

Depth-and Breadth-First Search

In the `findReachable` algorithm, simply changing the declaration of the `stack` to a `queue` changes the search technique from a depth-first search to a breadth-first search. The reader should try simulating the program with this change, and note the difference in the order that vertices are visited.

Proof of Correctness: Reachability Algorithm

The proof of correctness of the reachability algorithm is an inductive argument, in which the induction quantity is the length of the smallest path from the source vertex to the vertex in question.

A trivial base case is provided by the starting vertex itself. There is a path of length zero from the source vertex to itself, and thus the source is reachable. If we examine the code, we will see that the starting vertex is placed into the queue immediately after the queue is created. The queue is therefore not empty, and the `while` loop must execute at least once.

As the starting node is the only value in the queue, it must be the value first pulled from the queue. Because the set of values in `reachable` is empty (an assumption, not part of the code), the count will be zero and the source vertex placed into the set. Thus, we have traced the execution to the point where we can assert that the source vertex must always be placed into the set of reachable vertices.

The induction step assumes that all vertices reachable along a path of length n or less will eventually be placed into the queue, and subsequently pulled from the queue. (Note that we have just established this for $n = 0$.) The first time such a vertex is removed from the queue, it will not be found in the set of reachable vertices, and hence the `if` statement will be executed. But the body of the if statement places back into the queue all vertices reachable in one step from the vertex just pulled from the queue. Thus, vertices that are reachable along a path of length $n + 1$ must eventually be placed into the queue (because a path of length $n + 1$ is simply one step more than a path of length n).

It is simple to observe that all vertices placed into the queue must eventually be removed from the queue (because the `while` loop executes until the queue becomes empty). These two together prove that all vertices reachable along a path of length $n + 1$ must eventually be pulled from the queue.

By induction, we have therefore proved that all vertices reachable along a path of any length will eventually be pulled from the queue. Because the first time this happens the vertex will be added to the set of reachable vertices, all reachable vertices will eventually be added to the set.

For example, executing the following instructions will reveal that in our example graph it is possible to get from Pierre to any city except Princeton.

```
// find which cities are reachable from pierre
set<vertex *> reachable;
findReachable(pierre, reachable);

// print them out
cout << "reachable cities:\n";
set<vertex *>::iterator itr;
for (itr = reachable.begin(); itr != reachable.end(); ++itr)
    cout << (*itr)->name << endl;
```

To obtain a running time for this algorithm, observe that each entry placed into the stack corresponds to an edge, and that no edge will be placed into the stack more than once. Therefore, the while loop will execute no more than E times, where E represents the number of edges. Because the set operations are $O(\log E)$ in the worst case, the total worst case execution time is $O(E \log E)$. An upper bound on E is n^2, where n is the number of vertices, although frequently graphs have far fewer edges. However, this shows that even in the worst case, the single-source reachability problem can be solved more quickly than can the all-pairs variation.

19.4   WEIGHTED ADJACENCY MATRIX

Just as important as the question of what cities can be reached by starting at a given location is the question of how much the trip will cost. But to determine this, we must somehow encode the "cost" of traversing an edge. To accommodate this, we have the notion of a weighted graph, in which every edge has an associated value. For example, we might weight the edges in Figure 19.1, producing a graph such as that shown in Figure 19.5.

Just as there were two major representations of unweighted graphs, there are also two primary techniques of encoding weighted graphs. These are the weighted adjacency matrix and the labeled edge list representation. We will explore each of these in turn.

The weighted adjacency matrix is a two-dimensional matrix, just like the unweighted form. Instead of simply using 0/1 values, now the value in each position is the cost of moving from the vertex associated with the row to the vertex associated with the column. There are two special cases. The cost to move from any vertex to itself is zero, and the cost to move from any vertex to a vertex to which it is not connected is infinity (by convention, written ∞). In practice, any value larger than any quantity expected to arise during computation can be used to represent infinity. The weighted adjacency matrix representation of the graph shown in Figure 19.5 is:

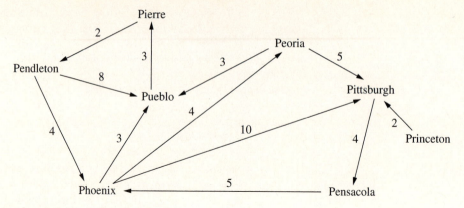

Figure 19.5   A weighted graph

```
//
//      floyd
//              Floyd's algorithm for finding the shortest
//              path between all pairs of vertices
//

template <class MatrixType>
void floyd (MatrixType & a, unsigned int n)
     // assume a is an n by n matrix
{
     for (unsigned int k = 0; k < n; k++)
          for (unsigned int i = 0; i < n; i++)
               for (unsigned int j = 0; j < n; j++)
                    a[i][j] = min(a[i][j], a[i][k] + a[k][j]);
}
```

Figure 19.6   Floyd's algorithm

City	0.	1.	2.	3.	4.	5.	6.	7.
0. Pendleton	0	∞	∞	4	∞	∞	∞	8
1. Pensacola	∞	0	∞	5	∞	∞	∞	∞
2. Peoria	∞	∞	0	∞	∞	5	∞	3
3. Phoenix	∞	∞	4	0	∞	10	∞	3
4. Pierre	2	∞	∞	∞	0	∞	∞	∞
5. Pittsburgh	∞	4	∞	∞	∞	0	∞	∞
6. Princeton	∞	∞	∞	∞	∞	2	0	∞
7. Pueblo	∞	∞	∞	∞	3	∞	∞	0

19.4.1 Floyd's Algorithm

The weighted adjacency matrix version of Warshall's algorithm is called Floyd's algorithm, again, named for the computer scientist credited with the discovery of the algorithm (the same Robert Floyd who first described the tree sort algorithm presented in Section 14.4). The procedure is shown in Figure 19.6. In place of the bitwise-and operation in Warshall's algorithm, an addition is used in Floyd's; in place of the bitwise-or used to update the path matrix, Floyd's algorithm uses a minimum value calculation.

If we apply this algorithm to the data in our sample graph, we obtain the intermediate values shown in Figure 19.7. These can be contrasted with the similar output from Warshall's algorithm. Note that each time a value was changed in Warshall's matrix, the same value is being modified here. Now, however, the value held in the matrix is not simply an indication that there is a path, but is the lowest known cost of the path.

19.5   SPARSE MATRIX REPRESENTATION

The adjacency matrix representation of a graph is often sparse, and thus it is not surprising that some of the sparse matrix manipulation techniques described in Chapter 18 are also applicable to graphs. For example, the representation of a chart as a map of maps described in Section 18.4 is a simple technique, well suited to representing graphs. To create the graph shown in Figure 19.5, we could use the following sequence of statements:

```
typedef map<string, map<string, unsigned int> > graph;

graph cityMap;

cityMap["Pendleton"]["Phoenix"] = 4;
cityMap["Pendleton"]["Pueblo"] = 8;
cityMap["Pensacola"]["Phoenix"] = 5;
cityMap["Peoria"]["Pittsburgh"] = 5;
cityMap["Peoria"]["Pueblo"] = 3;
cityMap["Phoenix"]["Peoria"] = 4;
cityMap["Phoenix"]["Pittsburgh"] = 10;
cityMap["Phoenix"]["Pueblo"] = 3;
cityMap["Pierre"]["Pendleton"] = 2;
cityMap["Pittsburgh"]["Pensacola"] = 4;
cityMap["Princeton"]["Pittsburgh"] = 2;
cityMap["Pueblo"]["Pierre"] = 3;
```

The type **graph** is, in effect, a two-dimensional sparse array, indexed by

```
0  ∞  ∞  4  ∞  ∞  ∞  8          0  ∞  ∞  4  ∞  ∞  ∞  8
∞  0  ∞  5  ∞  ∞  ∞  ∞          ∞  0  ∞  5  ∞  ∞  ∞  ∞
∞  ∞  0  ∞  ∞  5  ∞  3          ∞  ∞  0  ∞  ∞  5  ∞  3
∞  ∞  4  0  ∞  10 ∞  3          ∞  ∞  4  0  ∞  10 ∞  3
2  ∞  ∞  ∞  0  ∞  ∞  ∞          2  ∞  ∞  6  0  ∞  ∞  10
∞  4  ∞  ∞  ∞  0  ∞  ∞          ∞  4  ∞  ∞  ∞  0  ∞  ∞
∞  ∞  ∞  ∞  ∞  2  0  ∞          ∞  ∞  ∞  ∞  ∞  2  0  ∞
∞  ∞  ∞  ∞  3  ∞  ∞  0          ∞  ∞  ∞  ∞  3  ∞  ∞  0
```

Initial matrix   Matrix after iteration 0

```
0  ∞  ∞  4  ∞  ∞  ∞  8          0  ∞  8  4  ∞  13 ∞  7
∞  0  ∞  5  ∞  ∞  ∞  ∞          ∞  0  9  5  ∞  14 ∞  8
∞  ∞  0  ∞  ∞  5  ∞  3          ∞  ∞  0  ∞  ∞  5  ∞  3
∞  ∞  4  0  ∞  10 ∞  3          ∞  ∞  4  0  ∞  9  ∞  3
2  ∞  ∞  6  0  ∞  ∞  10         2  ∞  10 6  0  15 ∞  9
∞  4  ∞  9  ∞  0  ∞  ∞          ∞  4  13 9  ∞  0  ∞  12
∞  ∞  ∞  ∞  ∞  2  0  ∞          ∞  ∞  ∞  ∞  ∞  2  0  ∞
∞  ∞  ∞  ∞  3  ∞  ∞  0          ∞  ∞  ∞  ∞  3  ∞  ∞  0
```

Matrix after iteration 1   Matrix after iteration 3

```
0  ∞  8  4  ∞  13 ∞  7          0  17 8  4  ∞  13 ∞  7
∞  0  9  5  ∞  14 ∞  8          ∞  0  9  5  ∞  14 ∞  8
∞  ∞  0  ∞  ∞  5  ∞  3          ∞  9  0  14 ∞  5  ∞  3
∞  ∞  4  0  ∞  9  ∞  3          ∞  13 4  0  ∞  9  ∞  3
2  ∞  10 6  0  15 ∞  9          2  19 10 6  0  15 ∞  9
∞  4  13 9  ∞  0  ∞  12         ∞  4  13 9  ∞  0  ∞  12
∞  ∞  ∞  ∞  ∞  2  0  ∞          ∞  6  15 11 ∞  2  0  14
5  ∞  13 9  3  18 ∞  0          5  22 13 9  3  18 ∞  0
```

Matrix after iteration 4   Matrix after iteration 5

```
0  17 8  4  ∞  13 ∞  7          0  17 8  4  10 13 ∞  7
∞  0  9  5  ∞  14 ∞  8          13 0  9  5  11 14 ∞  8
∞  9  0  14 ∞  5  ∞  3          8  9  0  12 6  5  ∞  3
∞  13 4  0  ∞  9  ∞  3          8  13 4  0  6  9  ∞  3
2  19 10 6  0  15 ∞  9          2  19 10 6  0  15 ∞  9
∞  4  13 9  ∞  0  ∞  12         17 4  13 9  15 0  ∞  12
∞  6  15 11 ∞  2  0  14         19 6  15 11 17 2  0  14
5  22 13 9  3  18 ∞  0          5  22 13 9  3  18 ∞  0
```

Matrix after iteration 6   Matrix after iteration 7

Figure 19.7   Intermediate steps in Floyd's algorithm

strings and holding integer values. The sequence of assignment statements initializes the graph.

19.5.1 Dijkstra's Algorithm

We illustrate the use of the sparse array representation of a graph by describing a solution to the *single-source shortest path* problem. As the name suggests, the problem consists of discovering the shortest distance from a specific starting vertex to all other reachable nodes in a graph. The program, named `dijkstra` in honor of Edsger Dijkstra, the computer scientist credited with discovering the algorithm, is shown in Figure 19.8. Just as Floyd's algorithm has obvious similarities with Warshall's algorithm, there are similarities between Dijkstra's algorithm and the single-source reachability algorithm as presented earlier in Figure 19.4. The most obvious difference is that the reachability algorithm stores the collection of vertices waiting to be analyzed in a stack, while Dijkstra's algorithm stores the vertices in a priority queue.

Dijkstra's algorithm begins from a specific city given as an initial location. A `priority_queue` of distance/city pairs is then constructed and initialized with the distance to the starting city (namely, zero). To more easily manage the pair of values representing a city and a distance, this simple class is used:

```
//
//      DistancePair
//           a distance/city pair of values
//              two DistancePairs can be compared,
//              and are ordered based on the distance field
//

class DistancePair {
public:
        // constructors
     DistancePair () : distance(0) { }
     DistancePair (unsigned int ds, string & dt)
        : distance(ds), destination(dt) { }

        // comparisons
     bool operator < (DistancePair & right)
        { return distance < right.distance; }

        // data fields
     unsigned int distance;
     string destination;
};
```

```
//
//      dijkstra
//          Dijkstra's algorithm for finding the length of
//          the shortest path to each reachable destination
//          starting from a given source
//

void dijkstra (graph & cityMap,
        string & start, map<string, unsigned int> & distances)
{
        // process a priority queue of distances to cities
        priority_queue < vector<DistancePair>, greater<DistancePair> > que;
        que.push (DistancePair (0, start));

        while (! que.empty()) {
                // pull nearest city from queue
            int distance = que.top().distance;
            string city = que.top().destination;
            que.pop();
                // if we haven't seen it already, process it
            if (distances.count(city) == 0) {
                    // then add it to shortest distance map
                distances[city] = distance;
                    // and put values into queue
                map<string, unsigned int>::iterator start, stop;
                start = cityMap[city].begin();
                stop = cityMap[city].end();
                for (; start != stop; ++start) {
                    unsigned int destDistance = (*start).second;
                    string destCity = (*start).first;
                    que.push(DistancePair(distance + destDistance,
                            destCity));
                }
            }
        }
}
```

Figure 19.8 Dijkstra's single-source shortest path algorithm

A DistancePair records a distance and a destination. Two instances of
the class can be compared and are ordered on their distance values.

Dijkstra's algorithm manipulates a priority queue of distance pairs. Note
that we have included the optional second template argument in the declaration of this queue. This argument reverses the comparison test used in
ordering the queue, because at each step we wish to remove the smallest

distances	priority queue
	Pierre: 0
Pierre: 0	Pendleton: 2
Pendleton: 2	Phoenix: 6, Pueblo: 10
Phoenix: 6	Pueblo: 9, Peoria: 10, Pueblo: 10, Pittsburgh: 16
Pueblo: 9	Peoria: 10, Pueblo: 10, Pierre: 12, Pittsburgh: 16
Peoria: 10	Pueblo: 10, Pierre: 12, Pueblo: 13, Pittsburgh: 15, Pittsburgh: 16
	Pierre: 12, Pueblo: 13, Pittsburgh: 15, Pittsburgh: 16
	Pueblo: 13, Pittsburgh: 15, Pittsburgh: 16
	Pittsburgh: 15, Pittsburgh: 16
Pittsburgh: 15	Pittsburgh: 16, Pensacola: 19
	Pensacola: 19
Pensacola: 19	Phoenix: 24
	empty

Figure 19.9 Trace of execution of Dijkstra's algorithm

value from the collection, not the largest. On each traversal around the loop we pull a city from the queue. If we have not yet found a shorter path to the city (determined by noting whether the city occurs in the map of shortest distances), the current distance is recorded, and by examining the graph we can compute the distance from this city to each of the adjacent cities. This process continues until the priority queue becomes exhausted.

In addition to the graph, input to the procedure is the starting node, the "single source" named in the problem description. The output is returned in the last argument, which is a map keyed by city names and holding distance values. The algorithm is a form of breadth-first search centered around a priority queue, and thus is similar to the simulations we examined in Chapter 15.

Figure 19.9 illustrates the changes, to both the priority queue and the result dictionary of distances, as the program is executed on our example graph. Initially, the distance collection is empty and the queue contains the starting vertex, Pierre. At each step, the smallest element in the priority queue is removed. If the vertex removed from the queue is not yet present in the distances collection, then we have found the length of the shortest path to a new node. The newly discovered node is added to the distances collection. Knowing the shortest distance to this node, and knowing the distance to each neighbor of the node, we can compute the distances to each of the neighbor nodes.

In the first step we discover that the distance to the starting node is zero. The distance to its only neighbor, namely the city Pendleton, is 2. This value is computed and placed into the queue, where it is immediately removed.

Next, the destination Pendleton is removed. Adding the distance to Pendleton to the distance from Pendleton to its neighbors, Phoenix and Pueblo, we discover two new paths and place them into the priority queue. Note that the queue maintains values in order based on their distance, so the entry representing Phoenix will be in front of the entry representing Pueblo.

The processing of the entry for Phoenix illustrates the importance for this algorithm of the use of a priority queue, rather than a stack, as in depth-first search, or a simple queue, as in breadth-first search. From Phoenix we discover paths to Peoria, Pittsburgh, and Pueblo. The latter is, in fact, a shorter path than the entry placed earlier into the queue that

---

Proof of Correctness: Dijkstra's Algorithm

The proof that Dijkstra's algorithm discovers the shortest paths from the source to each reachable vertex uses a technique we encountered earlier in Chapter 8, *proof by contradiction*.

First, we make the following simple observation. The values pulled from the priority queue are each larger than or equal to their immediately preceding value. Note that this property is not inherent simply because we are using a priority queue. In the middle of execution it might be possible, for example, to insert a value into the queue that was smaller than the values previously removed from the queue. But this cannot happen in Dijkstra's algorithm because the values represent positive distances between vertices. Values inserted into the queue must be strictly larger than the value removed in the step in which they are created.

To prove that the distances discovered by Dijkstra's algorithm are indeed the shortest, we assume the opposite, and prove a contradiction. That is, we assume that the distance to at least one vertex is not the shortest. Let x be the *first* vertex that is so mislabeled. This means that Dijkstra's algorithm discovers a path of length c from the source to vertex x, but there is an alternative path with shorter distance. Let v be the next-to-last node in this alternative path. That is,

there is a path of length w_1 from the source to v, and an edge of length w_2 from v to x, and the sum $w_1 + w_2$ is less than c.

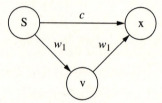

Because v is reachable, it will be discovered by Dijkstra's algorithm. Because w_1 is less than c, the analysis of v will occur prior to the analysis of x (otherwise x would not be the *first* vertex mislabeled). But at the point v was considered, the path to x with cost $w_1 + w_2$ would have been inserted into the queue, and therefore the path to x with cost $w_1 + w_2$ would of necessity have been discovered before the path with cost c was even considered.

But this contradicts the assertion that the first time we removed vertex x from the queue it has a path of length c. Therefore, there cannot exist a *first* vertex that is mislabeled, and therefore all vertices must be correctly labeled with their shortest distance.

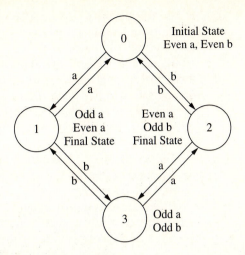

Figure 19.10   A typical finite automaton

represented the edge from Pendleton. Because the priority queue maintains values in order of their least cost, it will be the shortest path to Pueblo, the path through Phoenix, that will be removed first from the queue. Subsequent deletion from the queue of cities that have already been processed will simply be ignored. In this manner, the shortest distance to each city will be discovered.

The proof that with Dijkstra's algorithm all reachable vertices will eventually be pulled from the priority queue is similar to the induction proof presented for the reachability algorithm. The proof that the paths so uncovered are indeed the shortest paths is slightly more difficult, and is presented in the nearby box. An analysis similar to the reachable algorithm shows that the running time of this algorithm is $O(E \log E)$ as well.

19.6   FINITE AUTOMATA

Another common use of graphs is in the representation of *finite automata*. A finite automaton is a very simple model of a computing device. Like a labeled graph, an automaton consists of a sequence of vertices, called *states*, and a series of labeled edges connecting the states. One state is special, and is designated the *initial state*. Other states may be designated as *final states*.

Finite automata are devices used to recognize sequences of symbols with certain properties. For example, the finite automaton shown in Figure 19.10 processes strings of a and b symbols, and recognizes those strings with either an odd number of a symbols, or an odd number of b symbols, but not an odd number of both.

The automaton consists of four states, labeled 0, 1, 2, and 3. State 0 is the initial state. To understand how the automaton operates, we can give alternative descriptions for each of the states. State 0, the initial state, corresponds to having already processed an even number of a symbols and an even number of b symbols. If the automaton is in this state and the next symbol is an a, then we will move from having seen an even number of a symbols to the state the corresponds to having seen an odd number of a symbols. This is state 1. Similarly, state 2 corresponds to the situation where there is an even number of a symbols, but an odd number of b symbols.

Once in state 1, if the next symbol is another a, then we can move back into state 0 since the two a symbols balance out, and thus we have once more seen an even number of a symbols. If, however, the next symbol is a b, then the automaton must move into a state that records that we have seen both an odd number of a symbols and an odd number of b symbols. This is state 3. Any symbol read in this state will return the automaton to either state 1 or state 2.

We can encode the transition information for a finite automaton in a tabular form. The row indices correspond to the current state of the automaton, whereas the column indices correspond to an input symbol. The values in the table indicate the new state the automaton will move into when the input symbol is accepted.

Current State	Next state	
	Input a	Input b
0	1	2
1	0	3
2	3	0
3	2	1

This tabular representation suggests the use of a map of maps, similar to the chart datatype presented in Section 18.4 of Chapter 18 and the sparse matrix representation of Section 19.5. Adding data structures for a start state and a set of final states, we arrive at this representation of a finite automata:

```
//
//      finiteAutomata
//           a class used to represent a finite automaton
//

template <class TransitionType>
class finiteAutomata {
public:
        // constructor - takes start state
    finiteAutomata   (int st) : startState (st) { }
```

```
                  // methods to build the automata table
       void addFinal      (int fs) { finalStates.insert(fs); }
       void addTransition (int st, TransitionType t, int ns)
            { transitions[st][t] = ns; }


                  // methods to simulate the finite automaton
       void placeInStart () { currentState = startState; }
       int  advance       (TransitionType arcvalue);
       int  inFinal       ()
            { return finalStates.count(currentState) > 0; }


protected:
       int        startState;
       int        currentState;
       set <int>  finalStates;
       map < int, map<TransitionType, int> > transitions;
};
```

The data areas for the class hold the representation of the automaton. The constructor provides the start symbol, while set of final states and the transitions are provided by calls on member functions.

The simulation of the automaton is provided by a second series of member functions. These functions manipulate a value that represents the current state of the automaton. The method `placeInStart` sets this pointer to the start state. Thereafter, the method `advance` can be used to move the automaton from one state to the next. The method `inFinal` tests to see if the current state is a final state. The advance method can be written to determine whether there is an appropriate transition:

```
template <class TransitionType>
bool finiteAutomata<TransitionType>::advance (TransitionType value)
       // try to advance automaton along an arc
       // labeled with the given symbol
       // produce an error message is no appropriate transition
{
       if (transitions.count(currentState) != 0)
           if (transitions[currentState].count(value) != 0) {
               currentState = transitions[currentState][value];
               return true;
               }
       return false;
}
```

The advance method searches the map for arcs labeled with the argument token. If one is found, the current state is changed to the vertex at the end of the associated arc, and the function returns a true value. If no appropriately labeled arc is found, the false value is yielded as the function result.

To simplify moving the finite automaton through a sequence of steps, we can write a function `simulateAutomata` that takes a pair of iterators describing an input sequence and moves the automaton through the various steps, returning true if the final state is an acceptable state, and false if not.[2]

```
//
//    simulateAutomata
//         simulate the finite automata on given input values
//

template <class TranstionValue, class IteratorType>
bool simulateAutomata (finiteAutomata<TranstionValue> & automaton,
        IteratorType start, IteratorType stop)

{
        // place automaton in start state
    automaton.placeInStart();

        // run through all the transitions
    for (; start != stop; ++start)
        if (! automaton.advance(*start))
        return false;

        // return true if we are in a final state
    return automaton.inFinal();
}
```

The following sequence of statements can be used to generate a data structure that will simulate the finite automaton shown earlier in Figure 19.10:

```
    // create the finite automaton
finiteAutomata<char> fa (0);
    // add the final states
fa.addFinal(1); fa.addFinal(2);
    // add the transitions
fa.addTransition(0, 'a', 1); fa.addTransition(0, 'b', 2);
fa.addTransition(1, 'a', 0); fa.addTransition(1, 'b', 3);
fa.addTransition(2, 'a', 3); fa.addTransition(2, 'b', 0);
fa.addTransition(3, 'a', 2); fa.addTransition(3, 'b', 1);
```

---

2. This function can not be written as a member function in the class `finiteAutomata`, because it requires additional template arguments. Currently, few compilers support this feature.

To determine whether the finite automaton will accept various strings, we can create a string iterator as argument for the `simulateAutomata` function:

```
string testInput("ababa");
if (simulateAutomata (fa, testInput.begin(), testInput.end()))
    cout << "accepted\n";
else
    cout << "not accepted\n";
```

The result would indicate that the string `"ababa"` is recognized as matching the specifications defined by this automaton.

19.7   TURING MACHINES*

A *Turing machine* (named for its inventor, the British computer scientist Alan Turing) is another simple theoretical model of a computing device. However, despite this simplicity, the expressive power of a Turing machine is equivalent to that of any computing device. (The comparison between a Turing machine and a computer is analogous to a comparison between a hand shovel and a bulldozer. In theory, the former can do anything the latter can do, if we ignore issues such as ease of use and performance time.)

In many ways, a Turing machine is simply a combination of a finite automata and a (theoretically) infinite tape of symbols. The tape is used to represent both the input and the output of the computation, and takes the place of memory in conventional machines. We can represent the tape using a `list`, simulating the infinite nature of the tape by simply adding symbols to either end of the list as necessary.

We can illustrate the working of a Turing machine by examining the execution of a simple program written in Turing machine format. The program assumes that when it begins, the tape head is positioned so that it is at the left end of a binary number. We will simplify matters by assuming the tape can hold only three different values, either 0, 1, or a blank. The purpose of the program is to increment this number by one.

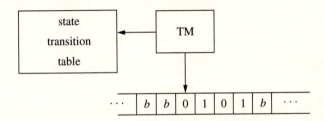

A Turing machine is programmed by describing how it should act in every combination of state and input symbol. For each state, input symbol pair, three pieces of information are recorded. These three pieces of information are the new values to be written to the tape, the new state to move into, and the direction the tape head should move. We will use four possibilities for the latter, representing Left, Right, Stay, and Halt the program.

The first task to perform is to move over the digits to locate the least significant bits of the number. This can be performed using only a single state (we will assume the program begins in state 0) with the following table:

Input	0	1	b
State 0	0/0/R	1/0/R	b/1/L

       new symbol/new state/action

The entries in the table indicate that if the input symbol is a 0, the 0 is written back to the tape and the tape head moves right. If the input is a 1, then 1 is written back and the tape head moves right. When the blank symbol that indicates that the end of the number is encountered, the blank is written back, the state is changed to state 1, and the tape head moves left, back over the least significant digit.

The second part of the program performs the increment operation. This can be described by three different states. State 1 represents "starting to increment." State 2 represents "carrying a digit," while state 3 represents "no carry." As soon as the blank at the left end of the tape is encountered, the program halts.

Input	0	1	b
State 0	0/0/R	1/0/R	b/1/L
State 1	1/3/L	0/2/L	b/1/H
State 2	1/3/L	0/2/L	1/2/H
State 3	0/3/L	1/3/L	b/3/H

We now describe how to represent a Turing machine using the containers in the standard library. In order to simplify the representation, we will use the integer value 2 to represent a blank symbol. Each entry of the state transition table will be represented by an instance of class `Transition`, which we can describe as:

```
//
//      class Transition
//              one transition in a Turing Machine representation

enum moves {Left, Right, Stay, Halt};

class Transition {
public:
        // constructors
```

```
        Transition () { } // needed for vector class
        Transition (int sy, int st, moves a)
            : newSymbol(sy), newState(st), action(a) { }

    int newSymbol;
    int newState;
    moves action;
};
```

The state table itself will be represented using the `matrix` class introduced in Section 18.2. The initialization of the state table can then be performed as follows:

```
matrix<Transition> states(4,2);

states[0][0] = Transition (0, 0, Right);
states[0][1] = Transition (1, 0, Right);
states[0][blank] = Transition(blank, 1, Left);
    .
    .
    .
```

The procedure to execute a Turing machine, shown in Figure 19.11, takes as input the state table and a list representing the input tape. The only significant complication in the program is simulating the infinite tape, by testing to see if the end of the list has been encountered when a move is made either left or right.

To execute the program, a list is filled with the input symbols, the simulation routine is executed, and the final list values are printed.

```
void main () {
    matrix <Transition> states(4,3);
    states[0][0] = Transition(0, 0, Right);
    .
    .
    .

    list <int> input;
    input.push_back(1); // input symbol values
    input.push_back(0);
    input.push_back(1);
        // perform simulation
    executeTuringMachine (states, input);
        // write output
    cout << "Final tape values ";
    list<int>::iterator start, stop;
    stop = input.end();
    for (start = input.begin(); start != stop; ++start)
        cout << *start << " ";
    cout << endl;
}
```

```
void executeTuringMachine (matrix<Transition> & states, list<int> & input)
    // simulate the execution of a Turing machine on the given inputs
{
    bool done = false;
    int currentState = 0;
    list<int>::iterator currentInput = input.begin();

    while (! done) {
            // get the new state information
        Transition & moveTo = states[currentState][*currentInput];
            // change the current state values
        currentState = moveTo.newState;
        *currentInput = moveTo.newSymbol;
        switch (moveTo.action) {
            case Left:
                    // add blank if at left end of tape
                if (currentInput == input.begin())
                    input.push_front(blank);
                --currentInput;
                break;

            case Right:
                    // add blank if at right end of tape
                ++currentInput;
                if (currentInput == input.end()) {
                    input.push_back(blank);
                    currentInput = input.end();
                    currentInput--;
                    }
                break;

            case Stay:
                break

            case Halt:
                done = true;
                break;
            }
        }
}
```

Figure 19.11   Procedure to simulate a Turing machine

19.8   CHAPTER SUMMARY

Key Concepts

- Graphs, vertices, and edges
- Adjacency matrix representation, weighted and unweighted
- Edge list representation, unweighted and weighted (or labeled)
- Warshall's algorithm—all pairs reachability
- Depth-first search used to compute single-source reachability
- Floyd's algorithm—all pairs shortest distance
- Dijkstra's algorithms—single-source shortest distance
- Finite automata
- Turing machine (optional)

The major theme of this chapter has been to demonstrate the use of many of the data structures described in this book in the solution of realistic problems. Graphs are ubiquitous, and the processing of graphs is a common occurrence. By making use of some of the data structures that we have developed here, algorithms on graphs can be succinctly and elegantly described.

Consider the data structures used in Dijkstra's algorithm (Figure 19.8):

▲ The starting location for the search is encoded as a `string`.

▲ The set of reachable vertices is returned as a `map`, indexed by `strings` and holding `integer` values.

▲ The graph is represented as a `map`, indexed by strings and holding elements that are themselves `map` of string/integer pairs.

▲ The algorithm makes use of a `priority_queue`, which is built on top of a `vector` of `DistancePairs`.

▲ The comparison operator for the priority queue is constructed using the `greater` function object, which generates a greater than comparison test for comparing two distance pairs.

In total, more than half a dozen different data types are used in the execution of this one algorithm.

Finally, in this chapter we introduced two theoretical models of computation. Finite automata, among the simplest and most basic models of computation, are used extensively in both theoretical computer science and in practical applications. The Turing machine is only slightly more complex, but can be shown in theory to be able to execute the same algorithms as any computer.

Further Reading

Algorithms on graphs are described in a number of books dealing with algorithms. Examples include [Aho 83], [Cormen 90], [Sedgewick 92], and [Weiss 92]. Further information on graph theory as a discipline in itself can be found in the book by Hartsfield and Ringel [Hartsfield 90].

Dijkstra's algorithm was first described in 1959 [Dijkstra 59]. Floyd's and Warshall's algorithms both appeared in 1962 [Floyd 62, Warshall 62]. The concept of a finite automata was first described in the 1940s [McCulloch 43].

More complete information on finite automata can be found in a book by Hopcroft and Ullman [Hopcroft 69]. The use of finite automata in compiler construction is described by Aho, Sethi, and Ullman [Aho 86]. The

use of automata in other areas of computer science has been described by
Wulf et al. [Wulf 81].

Study Questions & Exercises

Study Questions

1. What are the two components of a graph?

2. What is the difference between a directed and an undirected graph?

3. How can directed graphs simulate undirected graphs?

4. What is the difference between a weighted (or labeled) and an unweighted graph?

5. What is an adjacency matrix?

6. What are the two varieties of reachability questions for graphs?

7. How does the edge list representation of a graph differ from the adjacency matrix representation?

8. What is the difference between Floyds' algorithm and Warshall's algorithm?

9. What problem is solved using Dijkstra's algorithm?

10. Why is it important that Dijkstra's algorithm stores the intermediate results in a priority queue, rather than an ordinary stack or queue?

11. What is a finite automata?

12. Which of the following strings will be recognized as legal by the finite automata presented in Section 19.6?
    a. a
    b. aab
    c. aabba
    d. ababaabba

Exercises

1. Construct the adjacency matrix representation for the following graph:

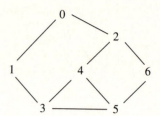

2. Suppose Warshall's algorithm is implemented using a sparse matrix representation described in Chapter 18. What is the time complexity of the algorithm? How much space does it use? Are there any changes to the algorithm that can be made to improve efficiency?

3. Suppose there is a path from some vertex v_i to some other vertex v_j in a graph. Argue why there must then be a path that never travels through any vertex more than once. (Hint: Assume a path does travel through some vertex two or more times. Show how the path can be shortened to eliminate one of the visits.)

4. Trace the depth-first search path followed by the algorithm given in Figure 19.4 through the graph given in Figure 19.1, numbering the vertices in the order they are visited by the algorithm.

5. An induction proof of correctness for Floyd's algorithm is very similar to the induction proof of correctness for Warshall's algorithm. Following the steps outlined in the sidebar proving Warshall's algorithm, provide a proof of correctness for Floyd's algorithm.

6. Redraw the graph shown in Figure 19.5, and number the vertices in the order they are visited by Dijkstra's algorithm.

7. Using the following graph as an illustration, argue why Dijkstra's algorithm requires the input graph to have non-negative edge weights.

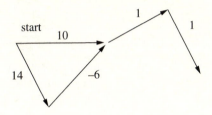

8. Give a sequence of tokens that will cause the finite automata in Figure 19.10 to move in the following patterns:
   a. First left, then right, then left, then right.
   b. In a clockwise direction, moving twice through each state.
   c. In a counter-clockwise direction, moving twice through each state.
   d. Clockwise once through all four states, then counter-clockwise once through all four states.

9. Construct a finite automata that will accept a sequence of a symbols if and only if the length of the input is a multiple of 3. Valid strings include aaa, and aaaaaaaaa. Invalid strings include a, aaaa and aaaaaaa.

10. Construct a finite automata that will accept a string consisting of two a symbols and one b symbol, in any order.

11. Using either depth-first search or breadth-first search, generate an iterator for a graph represented in an unweighted edge list representation. Your data structure should return vertex values, must not return the same vertex twice, and must be guaranteed to terminate for any finite graph.

12. Write a Turing machine program that decrements the number found in the current input tape.

13. (Harder) By combining the increment and decrement programs, write a Turing machine program that reads two integers from the input tape, and writes their sum.

## Chapter 20

Files: External Collections

Chapter Overview

When either the amount of data to be processed is too large to be maintained in memory at one time, or when the data must be maintained for longer than the execution time of one program, then values must be stored on an external medium, such as a file. In this chapter we discuss files as an abstract data type, and illustrate how files can be used in the solution of common problems. Major topics discussed in this chapter include:

▲ The file data abstraction

▲ Character streams and files

▲ Lexical analysis

▲ File merge sort

▲ Binary files

▲ Open table hashing

20.1 THE FILE DATA ABSTRACTION

The data structures discussed in this book have all been designed to reside in local or global memory. Such abstractions are known as *internal* data structures. Although these are by far the most common form of data structures, there are, nevertheless, two major drawbacks with this arrangement:

▲ Memory is always a fixed and finite resource. Given enough items to hold, a data structure may grow so large that it cannot be maintained in memory.

▲ The data held by the structure exists only as long as a program is running. As soon as a program exits, any internal data structures are lost.

To circumvent these problems, a programmer can use an *external* storage media, such as a file. At the most fundamental level, a file is simply a sequence of character values. The advantage of a file is that it is not held in memory, and is thus not limited in size by the amount of available memory, and a file can exist even after a program has finished execution.

In Chapter 1 we introduced streams, and have since been using stream operations throughout this book. Streams are the principle means of access to files in C++. In the next section we will discuss some additional operations on streams.

20.2   CHARACTER STREAM OPERATIONS

As noted in Chapter 1, stream input is accomplished using instances of the class `istream`, and stream output using instances of the class `ostream`. Two derived classes of these data structures can be used to attach a stream to a file. These classes are `ifstream`, for input file streams, and `ofstream`, for output file streams. The constructor for both classes takes a string representing the name of the file, and during initialization tries to open the file. The success of the initialization operation can be tested using the unary logical not operator. For example, the following program simply copies words from one file (named "infile") to another (named "outfile"). Because the string input operator uses white space to separate words, the << operator ignores white space, and in writing the output each word is followed by a newline, the effect will be to produce an output file in which each word is written on a separate line. If a failure is encountered while opening either file, then an error message is printed on the standard output.

```
ifstream ifile ("infile");
ofstream ofile ("outfile");
string word;

if (! ifile)
    cout << "cannot open input file\n";
else if (! ofile)
    cout << "cannot open output file\n";
else while (ifile >> word)
    ofile << word << '\n';
```

In addition to the stream operator >>, the following operations can be used with input streams:

`get()` The get operation returns the next character. Unlike the `>>` operator, white space is not ignored. The operation returns the symbolic value EOF on end of input. On most systems the value of EOF is −1, which does not correspond to any character value. For this reason, the return type for the get operation is declared as integer, and not character.

`peek()` The peek operation "peeks" at the next character, returning the character value but not processing the operation as a read. A subsequent read operation will then yield the value of the peeked character. We will examine a use for this operation in a later section.

`putback(c)` The putback operation pushes a character back into the input stream. The next input operation will then yield the value of the pushed back character. A simple implementation of peek can be constructed using a combination of `get` and `putback`. When streaming over a file, the putback function has no actual effect on the external file; it merely changes the sequence of characters read from the file.

`getline(buffer, size, terminator)` This operation reads a line of input into the buffer. A line is a sequence of characters terminated with the third argument, which by default is the newline character. The buffer must be able to hold at least as many characters as indicated by the second argument. No more than this number of characters will be read.

`read(buffer, size)` This operation reads the indicated number of characters into the buffer, if sufficient characters remain in the input stream. The actual number of characters input (which may be less than the requested size, if the end of the input stream was encountered) can be determined by invoking the function `gcount()`.

Similarly, in addition to the stream operator `<<`, the following operations can be used with output streams:

`put(c)` The put operation places a single character into the output stream.

`write(buffer, size)` This operation writes the indicated number of characters from the buffer into the output stream.

20.2.1 Streams and Iterators

Streams and iterators perform similar tasks (cycling over the elements in a collection) but utilize different function names. However, the standard library provides a technique that is used to interface between the two mechanisms. Adapter classes are defined that make use of the iterator protocol, but implement the member functions using stream operations.

The result is an object that acts like an iterator, but operates on a stream instead a collection.

INPUT STREAM ITERATORS

The class used to convert an input stream into an iterator is named `istream_iterator`. The class requires a template argument that defines the type being read from the file.[1] The following declaration creates an input stream iterator named `intStream` that reads integer values from a file named `inFile`:

```
istream_iterator<int> intStream (inFile);
```

Each time the iterator increment operator (operator ++) is invoked a new value from the stream is read (using the >> operator) and stored. This value is then available through the use of the dereference operator (operator *). The value constructed by the class `istream_iterator` using the default constructor (the constructor with no arguments) can be used as an ending iterator value. The following, for example, searches for the first value 7 in the file stream processed by the declaration provided previously:

```
istream_iterator<int> endOfStream;
istream_iterator<int>::iterator where = find (intStream, endOfStream, 7);
```

The element denoted by an iterator for an input stream is valid only until the next element in the stream is requested. An input stream iterator is an input iterator. This means that elements from the collection described by the iterator can only be accessed, they cannot be modified by assignment. Finally, elements can be accessed only once, and only in a forward direction. To read the contents of a stream more than once, you must create a separate iterator for each pass.

OUTPUT STREAM ITERATORS

The output stream iterator mechanism is analogous to the input stream iterator. Each time a value is assigned to the iterator, it will be written on the associated output stream, using the << operator. To create an output stream iterator you must specify, as an argument with the constructor, the associated output stream. Values written to the output stream must recognize the stream << operation. An optional second argument to the constructor is a string that will be used as a separator between each pair of values. The following, for example, copies all the values from a vector into the standard output, and separates each element by a space:

```
copy (aVector.begin(), aVector.end(), ostream_iterator<int> (cout, " "));
```

Simple file transformation algorithms can be created by combining input and output stream iterators and the various generic algorithms provided by the standard library. The short program that follows, for example,

---

1. A second, optional argument characterizes the type of the value that represents a difference between two pointer values. See Section A.3 in Appendix A.

reads a file of integers from the standard input, removes all occurrences of the value 7, and copies the remainder to the standard output, separating each value by a newline:

```
void main()
{
    istream_iterator<int> input (cin), eof;
    ostream_iterator<int> output (cout, "\n");
    remove_copy (input, eof, output, 7);
}
```

Table 20.1 summarizes a few of the generic algorithms that can be constructively used with file iterators.

20.3   APPLICATION: LEXICAL ANALYSIS

A compiler is typically structured in many layers, or phases. One of the first phases is devoted to the task of reading the sequence of characters from an input file and converting them into a sequence of tokens, such as identifiers and integers. This task is known as *lexical analysis*. A description of a function that can be used to perform lexical analysis of numeric values illustrates the use of some of the stream functions described in the previous section.

When a request is made for the next input token, the lexical analysis class will read characters from an input stream and form a single token. The structure of the token-forming function is rather simple: An `if` statement finds the next input character, automatically skipping whitespace. If the end of input is reached, then a false value is returned from the function.

We will illustrate only the portion of the function concerned with recognizing numeric values, which can either be integer or double-precision values. A complicating factor in the processing of these tokens is that integer and floating-point constants both begin in the same fashion. If a period follows an integer number, then the token is a floating-point constant. Even without a fractional part, a floating-point number can have an exponent field, which can optionally have a sign part.

```
if (isDigit(c)) {
    while (isDigit(input.peek()))     // read initial digits
        token += char(input.get());
    if (input.peek() == '.') { // read fractional part
        token += char(input.get());
        while (isDigit(input.peek()))
            token += char(input.get());
    }
    if ((input.peek() == 'e') || (input.peek() == 'E')) {
            // read exponent part
        token += char(input.get());
```

// continued on p. 481

`copy (iterator start, iterator stop, iterator destination)`
Copy a range of values to a given destination

`find (iterator start, iterator stop, value)`
Find first occurrence of given value

`find_if (iterator start, iterator stop, predicate)`
Find first occurrence of element that satisfies predicate

`adjacent_find (iterator start, iterator stop)`
Find first equal adjacent elements

`max_element (iterator start, iterator stop)`
Find largest element in file

`min_element (iterator start, iterator stop)`
Find smallest element in file

`replace_copy (start, stop, destination, value, replacement)`
Replace all occurrences of value with replacement

`count (iterator start, iterator stop, value, counter)`
Count number of instances of value

`count_if (iterator start, iterator stop, predicate, counter)`
Count number of instances that satisfy predicate

`equal (iterator start1, iterator stop1, iterator start2)`
Test two files for pairwise equality

`for_each (iterator start, iterator stop, function)`
Apply function on each element of file

`accumulate (iterator start, stop, initial_value)`
Reduce elements to a single value

`merge (iterator start1, stop1, start2, stop2, destination)`
Merge two ordered files together, copying to destination file

`set_union (iterator start1, stop1, start2, stop2, destination)`
Copy union of two ordered files to destination file

`set_intersection (iterator start1, stop1, start2, stop2, destination)`
Copy intersection of two ordered files to destination file

Table 20.1   Generic Algorithms Useful with Files

```
                    // optional sign
        if ((input.peek() == '+') || (input.peek() == '-'))
            token += char(input.get());
    // read exponent digits
    while (isDigit(input.peek()))
        token += char(input.get());
    }
}
```

The peek function is used to peek at the next character. If it is a period, then any following numeric fields must be part of a decimal constant. The peek is also used to determine whether the number is followed by an exponent part, and whether the exponent part includes a sign.

20.4   APPLICATION: FILE MERGE SORT

We noted earlier how the generic merge() routine could be used to merge two sorted files into one. In this section we will expand on this idea, building a complete sorting algorithm. Unlike previous sorting algorithms, this sorting algorithm is not limited by memory size, and can thus be used to sort very large files. A sorting algorithm that works with external storage devices is called an *external sorting algorithm*. The algorithms studied in previous chapters are technically known as *internal sorting algorithms*.

Both input and output for the file merge sort algorithm is specified using streams. The basic idea behind the algorithm is quite simple. The input stream is divided into small pieces, and each piece is small enough to be sorted using an internal sorting algorithm. The sorted portion of the input is then written to a temporary file. When this first phase is finished, there will be some number of temporary files, each holding a sorted portion of the input:

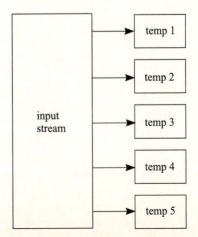

The next phase is the *merge* step. In this step we make use of the generic merge utility to merge two sorted streams to form a new sorted file. Recall that at each step of merging it is only necessary to compare the current element from each stream and output the smaller of the two. In this manner, the first two temporary files are merged to form a new temporary file, which is added to the end of the list.

This process is repeated again and again. At each step, two temporary files are deleted and one new temporary file is created. The process halts when only one temporary file exists. This temporary file is then copied to the output stream.

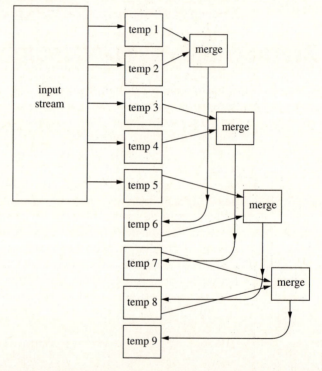

The first step in the realization of this program is a means to create a temporary file. We will number these files consecutively as temp1, temp2, and so on. Using this scheme, we can uniquely describe a file using an integer index. The following procedure converts an integer value into a file name. The low-order digits are stripped off the number and appended to the string. Because digits are discovered right to left, the concatenation operator is used to build the string representation of the number.

```
string tempFileName(int i)
     // create a temporary file name from integer i
{
     string name = "temp";
```

```
    string num = "";
        // convert i into a string name
    while (i > 0) {
        char val = (i % 10) + '0';
        num = string(val) + num;
        i = i / 10;
        }
        // return temp name and number
    return name + num;
}
```

A second small utility procedure takes a vector of strings, sorts them, then writes the sorted vector to a temporary file. A global variable named `topFile` keeps track of the number of temporary files that have been created. The routine `tempFileName` returns a string based on the integer value. Because the argument used to open an output stream must be an ordinary C string, the member function `c_str()` is used to extract the character buffer from the `string` data value. The conditional tests whether the file was successfully opened, printing an error message if not. Otherwise, and output stream iterator is constructed, and the copy utility is used to copy the entire vector into the file.

```
int topFile = 0;

void copyToTemporary(vector<string> & words)
    // copy the sorted list of words to a new temporary file
{
        // first sort the list of words
    sort (words.begin(), words.end());

        // then copy to temporary file
    ofstream tempfile (tempFileName(++topFile).c_str());
    if (! tempFile)
        cerr << "error: cannot open temporary file after sort\n";
    else
        copy (words.begin(), words.end(),
            ostream_iterator<string> (tempFile, "\n"));
}
```

This procedure is used in the first phase of the merge sort algorithm. You will recall that this first phase consisted of reading the input stream and dividing it into sorted components.

```
void phase1(istream & infile)
    // phase 1 of external heap sort
    // read all lines from input file,
    // and separate into temporary files

{
```

```
    string buffer;
    int wordVectorSize = 1000;
    vector<string> words(wordVectorSize);
    int wordcount;

        // read words and put them into temporary files
    wordcount = 0;
    while (getline(infile, buffer)) {
        words[wordcount++] = buffer;
        if (wordcount >= wordVectorSize) {
            copyToTemporary(words);
            wordcount = 0;
            }
        }
        // if word count is greater than zero, it means there were leftover words
    if (wordcount > 0) {
        words.resize(wordcount);
        copyToTemporary(words);
        }
}
```

The heart of the second phase is a procedure that takes two input streams and one output stream, and merges the input files into the output file. The merge idiom discussed previously does the majority of the work, but this is only possible after all the appropriate files have been created and opened, and converted from streams into iterators.

```
void phase2 ()
    // phase 2 of external merge sort
{
    int i = 1;
    while (i < topFile) {
            // open input and output files
        ifstream temp1 (tempFileName(i++).c_str());
        ifstream temp2 (tempFileName(i++).c_str());
        if ((! temp1) || (! temp2))
            cerr << "cannot open temporary input file\n";
        ofstream temp3 (tempFileName(++topFile).c_str());
        if (! temp3)
            cerr << "cannot open output file in merge\n";

            // now define the associated iterators
        istream_iterator<string> file1 (temp1);
        istream_iterator<string> file2 (temp2);
        istream_iterator<string> endOfFile;
        ostream_iterator<string> outFile (temp3, "\n");
```

```
            // then do the file merge
        merge (file1, endOfFile, file2, endOfFile, outFile);
        }
}
```

The main program ties these procedures together. The merge sort procedure takes two stream arguments, and invokes the phase1 procedure to divide the input into sorted pieces. It then merges the pieces together until only one file remains. The last step is to copy the final temporary file onto the output stream.

```
void mergeSort(istream & infile, ostream & outfile)
    // sort input stream, placing result on output stream
{
        // phase 1, break input into temporary files
    phase1 (infile);

        // phase 2, merge files back together
    phase2 ();

        // phase 3, copy from final temporary file to output file
    ifstream from(tempFileName(topFile).c_str());
    char ch;
    while (from.get(ch))
        outfile.put(ch);
}
```

20.5   BINARY FILES

A file is in many ways similar to a vector of characters. The analogy can be made even closer using two new features. The first feature is the fstream data type, which permits the creation of file streams that can be used simultaneously for both input and output. The second feature is the seekg method, which permits a stream to be positioned at an arbitrary location within a file. Using the latter we can perform random access operations on a file, just as a vector permits random access to any data element.

Using these features we can design a class that will permit a programmer to think of a file as a vector of arbitrary types of elements. The only restriction is that the elements held by the vector must have a fixed size, known at compile time. Although this rules out elements represented by dynamic data structures, such as strings and lists, in practice the limitation is not generally a problem.

We will call the data structure a random access stream, or rstream. Instances of rstream can be used as vectors, assigning values to specific locations using the method put, and retrieving the value of specific locations using the method get. The class description for this method is:

```
//
//     class rstream
//             randomly accessible streams of elements
//

template <class T> class rstream {
public:
     // constructor
     rstream      (string & name);

     // access to element
     int          get     (unsigned int index, T & value);

     // placement of element
     void         put     (unsigned int index, T & value);

     // number of elements
     unsigned int length ();


protected:
     fstream      theStream;
};
```

The actual data values will be accessed using an instance of fstream. The constructor for our class establishes the connection to the file stream. To do this, the method uses the function open. This function takes as argument a name and an access mode. There are three access modes, defined in a parent class named ios. These three modes are ios::in, for input; ios::out, for output; and ios::app, for appending new values to the end of an existing file. Modes can be combined using the bitwise-or operator. In this case, we wish to open the file for both input and output.

```
template <class T> rstream<T>::rstream(string & name)
{     // construct an instance of rstream
      // convert string into C-style pointer variable
      char * cName = name.c_str();
      // open the file for both input and output
      theStream.open(cName, ios::in | ios::out);
}
```

To write to the stream we use the method put. This method uses the function seekg to position the file pointer at a given location. Because index values are given in terms of the element values (instances of class T), and the seekg function requires a byte position, we multiply the index

value by the size of an element of type T. The latter quantity can be determined using the built-in function `sizeof`, which is the only function in C++ that takes a type name as argument. For historical reasons, the type of the argument used by the `write` procedure is a pointer to a character; therefore, we must cast the argument value into this form before writing.

```
template <class T>
void rstream<T>::put(unsigned int index, T & value)
{    // place a value into a random access stream
     // first position the stream
     theStream.seekg(sizeof( T ) * index);

     // then write the value
     char * valuePtr = (char *) & value;
     theStream.write(valuePtr, sizeof( T ));
}
```

The `get` method is similar. It must first position the stream, then read the value found at the given location. Whereas a `write` can be used to extend a file, a `read` operation will never work past the end of the file. The number of characters processed by a `read` can be determined by invoking the function gcount. We can use this to determine if the read operation was successful. The integer value returned as the result of this function will be nonzero if the read operation worked, and zero if the operation was unsuccessful.

```
template <class T> int rstream<T>::get(unsigned int index, T & value)
{    // read a value from a random access stream
     // first position the stream
     theStream.seekg(sizeof( T ) * index);
     // then read the value
     char * valuePtr = (char *) & value;
     theStream.read(valuePtr, sizeof( T ));
     // return the number of characters read
     return theStream.gcount();
}
```

The final operation provided is a method to determine the number of elements contained in a random access file. To compute the length of the file, we first move the file pointer to the end of the file. This can be accomplished using the `seekg` function with a second argument, indicating that we want to measure starting from the end of the file. Moving zero bytes from the end will position the file at the end of the file. The function `tellg` then returns the byte position in the file. By dividing this by the size of each entry, we can determine the number of elements held by the collection.

```
template <class T> unsigned int rstream<T>::length()
{    // return number of elements held in collection.
     // first, seek to end
     theStream.seekg(0, ios::end);
     // then divide current byte offset by size of elements
     return theStream.tellg() / sizeof( T );
}
```

To construct an iterator for the random access stream data structure, we merely maintain an index for the current element. The increment operator simply increments this value. If the read operation for this index is successful, then the element exists. If the read operation fails, then we have reached the end of the collection.

20.5.1   Open Table Hashing

We will illustrate the use of the random access stream data abstraction by developing a data structure that uses another form of hashing, called open table hashing. Like the hash table data structure we examined in Chapter 17, open table hashing uses a hash function to try to uniformly distribute elements over a range of values. Unlike the hash table structures we examined earlier, with open table hashing all values are stored in the table itself, which is actually an external file. Thus, the size of the hash table strictly limits the number of elements that can be maintained by the data structure.

As an example of the use of open table hashing, assume we are placing string values containing the names of Amy's club from Chapter 17, using again the hash function that took the third character of a name and converted the value into an integer between 0 and 25 (and, of course, using the remainder when the result is divided by the size of the collection). Let us insert in order the names *Alex, Amanda, Albert, Alice, Amy, Anne, Alfred, Andy, Arthur,* and *Abraham* into a ten-element collection.

Inserting the names *Alex, Amanda, Albert,* and *Alice* causes no difficulty. They each hash into a distinct location in the collection. Following the insertion of the last, we can visualize the collection as follows:

0	1	2	3	4	5	6	7	8	9
Amanda hash: 0	Albert hash: 1			Alex hash: 4				Alice hash: 8	

Now let us insert the name *Amy*. You will recall that the difficulty with the hash table mechanism occurred when two names hashed to the same location, which is called a collision. We see this here, because *Amy* hashes to the same location, 4, currently occupied by *Alex*. To avoid having two values at the same location, we will simply examine succeeding positions, in order, until we find an empty location. Doing this, we find that position 5 is currently empty, and place the record for *Amy* at that location.

0	1	2	3	4	5	6	7	8	9
Amanda hash: 0	Albert hash: 1			Alex hash: 4	Amy hash: 4			Alice hash: 8	

The value *Anne* hashes to location 3, which is unoccupied, and is thus easily inserted. The value *Alfred*, on the other hand, hashes to location 5, which is now occupied by *Amy*. The next empty position is location 6, which is where the record for *Alfred* is stored. The table now looks like this:

0	1	2	3	4	5	6	7	8	9
Amanda hash: 0	Albert hash: 1		Anne hash: 3	Alex hash: 4	Amy hash: 4	Alfred hash: 5		Alice hash: 8	

The entry for *Andy* hashes to location 3. Unfortunately, that position is already occupied, by the value *Anne*. Similarly, positions 4, 5, and 6 are also occupied. The value *Andy* can finally be inserted into location 7.

0	1	2	3	4	5	6	7	8	9
Amanda hash: 0	Albert hash: 1		Anne hash: 3	Alex hash: 4	Amy hash: 4	Alfred hash: 5	Andy hash: 3	Alice hash: 8	

The entry for *Arthur* can be inserted with no difficulty into location 9. The final entry, *Abraham*, hashes to index value 7. Values 7, 8, and 9 are all filled. To find the next position, we cycle the index values around to the beginning of the collection, to test position 0. Positions 0 and 1 are also filled. We finally find the last empty position at position 2. The final collection is as follows:

0	1	2	3	4	5	6	7	8	9
Amanda hash: 0	Albert hash: 1	Abraham hash: 7	Anne hash: 3	Alex hash: 4	Amy hash: 4	Alfred hash: 5	Andy hash: 3	Alice hash: 8	Arthur hash: 9

To better understand the advantage gained by using the hashing technique, consider the number of file accesses required to find a given record.

If the file was totally unorganized, a linear search would be required to determine if a specific record was contained in the file. If the record was not found in the file, then all ten records would need to be searched, and this is the same for the open hash table.

But consider the situation when searching for a record that *is* found in the data base. If the file was unorganized, then on average half the entries, or five values, would be examined until we found the correct element. But over half the elements in the open hash table (namely, the records for *Amanda*, *Albert*, *Anne*, *Alex*, *Alice*, and *Arthur*) hash immediately to the location where the values are stored, and thus can be located with a single access. Two more values, the records for *Amy* and *Alfred*, require only two file access operations.

As is often the case, the elements inserted into an almost-full hash table require more operations. To recover the record for *Andy* requires five operations, and to read the record for the last inserted value, *Abraham*, uses six file operations.

Nevertheless, on average, recovering a record for an element that is contained in the data base requires only slightly more than two file operations, which is less than half the work that would be required if hashing was not employed.

THE OPEN HASH TABLE DATA STRUCTURE

We will implement this idea in a data structure called an `openHashTable`. The class declaration for this structure can be given as:

```
//
//      class openHashTable
//          external hash table
//          template type must supply equality test
//          and function isEmpty

template <class T> class openHashTable {
public:
    // constructor
    openHashTable(string & name, unsigned int (&f)(T &));

    // operations
    void    create      (unsigned int size);
    int     add         (T & value);
    int     includes    (T & value);

protected:
    // data areas - hash function, random access stream, and size
    unsigned int  (&hashfun)(T &);
    rstream<T>    rfile;
    unsigned int  size;
};
```

The data areas maintained by the structure include a reference to the hash function, the size of the collection, and a random access stream that will contain the actual values. Because values are not stored in memory, but are instead maintained using an external file, the structure can hold a large number of elements.

The constructor takes as an argument the name of the file to be associated with the random access stream and the name of the hash function. The length of the file is used to determine the size of the collection. If the file does not exist, then the length function will return a zero value.

```
template <class T> openHashTable<T>::openHashTable
    (string & name, unsigned int (&f)(T &))
        : hashfun(f), rfile(name)
{    // set size to length of stream
    size = rfile.length();
}
```

The `create` method is used to initially create a collection with a fixed number of entries. The size is stored in the appropriate data area, and a number of elements are placed into the data file. It is assumed that the default constructor for the template type creates a value that will test as being null.

```
template <class T> void openHashTable<T>::create(unsigned int sz)
{    // create a new open hash table with sz records
    size = sz;

    // assume default constructor creates an empty value
    T initialValue;
    for (unsigned int i = 0; i < sz; i++)
        rfile.put(i, initialValue);
}
```

New elements are added to the collection using the method `add`. The function first computes the hash value for the new element. It must then examine, or *probe*, the collection until an empty location is found. If no empty location is found, the method does nothing and returns a false value (zero). Otherwise, the value is placed into the collection and a true (one) value returned. To determine whether a position has been assigned a value, the function `isEmpty` is invoked. Each template type used with the open hash table abstraction must provide a definition for this function.

```
template <class T> int openHashTable<T>::add(T & value)
{    // add record to an open hash table

    // find initial hash value
    unsigned int hashValue = hashfun(value) % size;
    unsigned int index = hashValue;
```

```
// see if occupied
T currentValue;
rfile.get(index, currentValue);
while (! isEmpty(currentValue)) {
    // it's filled, see if next record is empty
    index = index + 1;
    if (index >= size)
        index = 0;
    if (index == hashValue)
        return 0;
    rfile.get(index, currentValue);
    }
// found an empty position, place argument value
rfile.put(index, value);
return 1;
}
```

Elements can be extracted from an open hash table in one of two ways. In the exercises we will develop an iterator that will permit a loop to cycle over all the values of a collection. The alternative mechanism is a method, `includes`, that will determine whether an element matching the argument is contained in the collection.

```
template <class T> int openHashTable<T>::includes(T & value)
{   // see if the hash table includes a value matching argument
    unsigned int hashValue = hashfun(value) % size;
    unsigned int index = hashValue;
    T currentValue;
    rfile.get(index, currentValue);
    // loop as long as we don't see value
    while (! (currentValue == value)) {
        index = index + 1;
        if (index >= size)
            index = 0;
        if (index == hashValue)
            return 0;
        rfile.get(index, currentValue);
        }

    // found it, set value
    rfile.get(index, value);
    return 1;
}
```

If a matching element is found, the value is read twice, once to establish the value for the purposes of comparison, and the second time to copy the value into the argument variable. (Usually the equality testing operator will examine only a few fields, and the remaining fields will contain useful information.)

20.5.2 Application: A Simple Database

We will illustrate the use of the open hash table data structure by describing a simple database. This database will be used by Amy's club to keep track of each member's favorite flavor of ice cream. Because each record in an external file must be a fixed length, we cannot use our string abstraction directly. Instead, the actual information in the file is stored using a simple C-style array of characters. Nevertheless, for ease of use, methods are defined that convert this information both to and from string values. The class description for the record structure is:

```
class iceCreamRecord {
public:

    // constructors
    iceCreamRecord();
    iceCreamRecord(string & namestr, string & flavorstr);

    // field access
    string name();
    string flavor();

protected:
    // data fields for name and flavor
    char nameField[20];
    char flavorField[20];
};
```

The equality operator, used by the add method and by the includes method, tests only the name field. We can search for a record matching a given name, and the remaining field will be set as a side effect by the includes method. Following a successful search, the argument record will be replaced by the value found in the file, which will include the remaining fields.

```
int operator == (iceCreamRecord & left, iceCreamRecord & right)
    // equality between records based only on name
{
    return left.name() == right.name();
}
```

```
bool isEmpty (iceCreamRecord & s)
    // true if record is empty
{
    return s.name() == "";
}
```

A program to create the database might be written like this:

```
unsigned int hf(iceCreamRecord & x)
{    // hash function for ice cream database
    string name(x.name());
    return name[2] - 'a';
}


void createIceCreamDatabase()
{
    openHashTable<iceCreamRecord> hashtab("iceCreamDatabase", hf);
    hashtab.create(10);

    hashtab.add(iceCreamRecord("Alex", "vanilla"));
    hashtab.add(iceCreamRecord("Amanda", "strawberry"));
    hashtab.add(iceCreamRecord("Albert", "bubblegum"));
    hashtab.add(iceCreamRecord("Alice", "peach"));
    hashtab.add(iceCreamRecord("Amy", "marionberry"));
    hashtab.add(iceCreamRecord("Anne", "chocolate"));
    hashtab.add(iceCreamRecord("Alfred", "blueberry"));
    hashtab.add(iceCreamRecord("Andy", "chocolate"));
    hashtab.add(iceCreamRecord("Arthur", "vanilla"));
    hashtab.add(iceCreamRecord("Abraham", "strawberry"));
}
```

A subsequent program can be written to recover and print the values held in the ice-cream database. The following procedure, for example, takes a name and returns the ice-cream flavor associated with the name. To discover the value, the procedure first makes a new record entry with only the name field filled in. The includes method is then invoked. If the inclusion test is successful, then the flavor field of the record will have been filled in by the includes method. If not, then the name given by the argument is not present in the database and the string "not in database" is returned.

```
string iceCreamFlavor(string name)
    // find the flavor favored by the named individual
{

        // make a new record with name but no flavor
    iceCreamRecord rec(name, " ");
```

```
                    // read the database
         if (hashtab.includes(rec))
              return rec.flavor();
                    // not in database
         return "not in database";
   }
```

20.6 CHAPTER SUMMARY

Key Concepts

- Character stream operations (get, put, peek, putback, getline, read, write)
- Merge sort
- Direct-access files and streams
- Open table hashing

In this chapter we have explored the use of external files, accessed using stream operations, as a mechanism for developing data structures. At the most fundamental level, a file is simply a stream of characters. Many applications, such as lexical analysis, process a file character by character. Because files are not limited in size by the amount of available memory, it is possible to store and process vast amounts of data using a file. We illustrated this by developing the merge sort algorithm, which can operate on collections even if they are larger than will fit in available memory. Finally, using the ability to position a file at any location, we showed how a file could be considered to be a vector of fixed-size elements. Building on this view, we created a new form of hash table, called an open hash table. If provided with a sufficiently good hash function, open hash tables can give very efficient access to large amounts of information.

Further Reading

More information on streams can be found in the books by Stroustrup [Stroustrup 91] and Lippman [Lippman 91].

Lexical analysis is discussed extensively by Aho, Sethi, and Ullman in [Aho 86].

External sorting and hashing are both discussed in Volume 3 of Knuth [Knuth 75]. The merge sort algorithm presented here is adapted from the version described by Brian Kernighan and Peter Plauger [Kernighan 76].

There are many variations on open table hashing. Knuth discusses several of these; careful analysis of running times for various algorithms is presented by Gaston Gonnet and Ricardo Baeza-Yates [Gonnet 91].

Study Questions & Exercises

Exercises

1. The technique used to read a floating-point value in the lexical analysis data abstraction does not check to make sure there is at least one decimal number value following the exponent indication (that is, the character e or E). Modify the procedure to check for this condition, pushing the extraneous character back into the input if a number is not found.

2. Comments can be written either using two slash characters or a slash followed by a star. In the latter form, comments extend (possibly over

many lines) until a matching star–slash pair is found.

```
/*
    this example comment extends over
    many lines
*/
```

Revise the code for the slash character to recognize both types of comments.

3. Simulate the merge sort algorithm using the following data values. Assume that initially a maximum of five values are inserted into each temporary file. Show the contents of each temporary file.

Abel	Abigail	Abraham	Ada
Angela	Anita	Anne	Antonia
Albert	Alex	Alfred	Alice
Adam	Adrian	Adrienne	Agnes
Amanda	Amy	Andrew	Andy
Arnold	Arthur	Audrey	

4. Complete the design of an iterator class for the random access stream data abstraction.

5. We purposely did not include a method to remove an entry from the open table hashing data structure described in Section 20.5.1. To see some of the problems involved with deletion, assume first that when an entry is deleted we simply copy a new blank (uninitialized) value into the emptied location. Delete the value for *Amy* from the full table. Now simulate the execution of the `includes` method with value *Alfred*. What happens? What other values have now "disappeared" from the collection?

6. A solution to the problem uncovered in the previous question is to have two types of empty values. Initially all entries have true empty values. When an entry is deleted, it is replaced by a special record that indicates "deleted," but not "empty." A function `isDeleted` can be used to check for this condition.

a. Write a `delete` method that will create such entries.
b. Modify the `includes` method so that it will skip deleted entries in searching for a match to the argument value.
c. Modify the `add` method so that it will reuse a deleted entry position if it finds either an empty location or a deleted entry during the process of insertion.

7. It is important that the hash function used to examine entries in a hash table is the same as that used to create the entries. To see why, assume that the hash table for Amy's club is saved before all locations have been filled, for example, at the point where eight of the ten positions have been filled (as shown in Section 20.5.1). Now assume a subsequent program tries to use the table, but hashes using the second, rather than the third character in each name. How many entries can be successfully recovered by the `includes` method? How does this situation change if we use the final, completely full, hash table?

8. Develop an iterator for the open hash table data abstraction. Like the iterator for the random access stream, the iterator for the hash table needs to maintain only the index of the current position. When incrementing, the iterator should skip empty or deleted positions. (You will likely want to make the iterator class a friend of the hash table class.)

9. Write a program that allows members of Amy's club to change the value held in the ice-cream database. Your program should prompt for the member name, verify that the member is included in the club (by making sure an entry already exists in the database), and then prompt for the type of ice cream preferred. With this information, your program should then alter the value held in the database.

10. Write a procedure to sort a file represented by a random access stream.

11. Write a procedure to perform a binary search on a sorted random access stream.

Part **IV**

APPENDICES

Appendix A

Common Implementation Difficulties

The definition of the new standard library specifies many features that are difficult for current compilers to support. In time, compiler technology will undoubtedly catch up with the standard definition and these difficulties will disappear. Until then, the features described in this appendix represent some of the more common problems that users of the standard library might encounter.

A.1   THE CLASS BOOL

The class bool is a recent addition to the C/C++ family of languages, not yet supported by all compilers. Many implementations still use the older technique whereby zero represents false and anything nonzero represents true. In most cases, programs that use bool can be correctly compiled by defining bool to be a synonym for int, and true and false as symbolic constants. This is most easily performed using a typedef statement.

```
typedef int bool;
const int true = 1;
const int false = 0;
```

A.2   INTEGRATING THE STRING LIBRARY AND THE CONTAINER CLASSES

The string library was developed independently of the container classes library, and only in the latter stages of the standard process were the two combined. Many implementations still do not provide iterators for the class string, and some do not even provide features such as the definition of the less-than operator.

In some cases, the following class derived from class string can be used to overcome many of these difficulties:

```
class sstring : public string {
public:
        // define iterators
    typedef char * iterator;
    iterator begin () { return c_str(); }
    iterator end () { return begin() + length(); }
};


        // define less than operator
bool operator < (string & left, string & right)
{
    return left.compare(right) < 0;
}
```

A.3   OPTIONAL TEMPLATE ARGUMENTS

Almost all of the standard containers allow an optional argument that can be used to specify the operator to be used in comparing two elements in the collection. Few compilers at present support optional template arguments. Therefore, in most cases the user is forced to specify this argument. However, this task can most easily be accomplished using the standard template function class named less. For example, instead of declaring a new class as:

```
set <int> aSet;
```

the user must specify:

```
set <int, less<int> > aSet;
```

Be careful to ensure that there is a space between the two ending angle brackets, otherwise most compilers will recognize the two characters as one symbol. If reverse comparisons are desired, the function greater can be used.

Classes that permit (or require) such an argument include set, map, stack, queue, and priority_queue.

Another place where optional template arguments occur is the class `istream_iterator`. Here the optional second argument is the type that characterizes the difference between two pointer values. Most commonly, this is a standard type named `ptrdiff_t`, as in:

```
istream_iterator<int, ptrdiff_t> intstream(cin);
```

A.4 ALLOCATORS

The standard library defines a sophisticated system for hiding the underlying machine memory model and allocation. This scheme, termed *allocators*, is intended to be largely hidden from the user. However, some implementations of the standard library force the programmer to specify an allocator when creating instances of standard library classes. In most cases, the default allocator can be used, as in:

```
vector<double, allocator<double> > x(3, 2.5);
```

A.5 TEMPLATE ARGUMENTS ON MEMBER FUNCTIONS

Another feature described in the standard is the ability to add template parameters to member functions that are independent of any template arguments found in the class. This feature, too, is at present seldom supported by compilers.

The most common place this feature occurs is as part of a constructor that permits a container to be initialized using a pair of iterators, as in:

```
template <class value_type>
class list {
public:
    .
    .
    .
    template <class Iterator>
    list (Iterator start, Iterator stop)
        { copy (inserter(begin()), start, stop); }
};
```

I have avoided discussing these functions in my descriptions of the standard container classes. This is because the functionality is easily simulated using other facilities, and also, of all the features described in this appendix, this one is least likely to change in the near future.

In a few other instances it could have been possible to use member functions in place of ordinary functions, had this feature been supported. A notable example is the definition of the assignment operator in the `matrix` class described in Chapter 18.

Summary of Standard Container Operations

The first part of Appendix B will summarize the member functions implemented by each of the standard container classes. The second part will summarize the operation of the various generic algorithms.

B.1   THE STANDARD CONTAINERS

B.1.1   String

Constructors

`string s;`	Default constructor
`string s ("text");`	Initialized with literal string
`string s (aString);`	Copy constructor

Character Access

`s[i]`	subscript access

`s.substr(pos, len)`	Return substring starting at position of given length
`s.c_str()`	Return pointer to internal buffer

Length

`s.length ()`	Number of characters in string
`s.resize (int, char)`	Change size of string, padding with char
`s.empty ()`	True if string has no characters

Assignment

`s = s2;`	Assignment of string
`s += s2;`	Append second string to end of first
`s + s2`	New string containing s followed by s2

Iterators

`string::iterator t`	Declaration of new iterator
`s.begin ()`	Starting iterator
`s.end ()`	Past-the-end iterator

Insertion, Removal, Replacement

`s.insert (pos, str)`	Insert string after given position
`s.remove (start, length)`	Remove length characters after start
`s.replace (start, length, str)`	Insert string, replacing indicated characters

Comparisons

`s = s2  s != s2`	Comparisons for equality/inequality
`s < s2  s <= s2`	Comparisons for relation
`s <= s2  s >= s2`	

Searching Operations

`s.find (str)`	Find start of argument string in receiver string
`s.find (str, pos)`	Find with explicit starting position
`s.find_first_of (str, pos)`	First position of first character from argument
`s.find_first_not_of (str, pos)`	First character not from argument

Input / Output Operations

`stream << str`	Output string on stream
`string >> str`	Read word from stream
`getline(stream, str, char)`	Read line of input from stream

B.1.2   Vector

Constructors

`vector<T> v;`	Default constructor
`vector<T> v (int);`	Initialized with explicit size

`vector<T> v (int, value);`	Size and initial value
`vector<T> v (aVector);`	Copy constructor

Element Access

`v[i]`	Subscript access, can be assignment target
`v.front ()`	First value in collection
`v.back ()`	Last value in collection

Insertion

`v.push_back (value)`	Push element on to back of vector
`v.insert(iterator, value)`	Insert new element after iterator
`v.swap (aVector)`	Swap values with another vector

Removal

`v.pop_back ()`	Pop element from back of vector
`v.erase (iterator)`	Remove single element
`v.erase (iterator, iterator)`	Remove range of values

Size

`v.capacity ()`	Maximum number of elements buffer can hold
`v.size ()`	Number of elements currently held
`v.resize (unsigned, value)`	Change to size, padding with value
`v.reserve (unsigned)`	Set physical buffer size
`v.empty ()`	True if vector is empty

Iterators

`vector<T>::iterator itr`	Declare a new iterator
`v.begin ()`	Starting iterator
`v.end ()`	Ending iterator

B.1.3   List

Constructors and Assignment

`list<T> v;`	Default constructor
`list<T> v (aList);`	Copy constructor
`l = aList`	Assignment
`l.swap (aList)`	Swap values with another list

Element Access

`l.front ()`	First element in list
`l.back ()`	Last element in list

Insertion and Removal

`l.push_front (value)`	Add value to front of list

`l.push_back (value)`	Add value to end of list
`l.insert (iterator, value)`	Insert value at specified location
`l.pop_front ()`	Remove value from front of list
`l.pop_back ()`	Remove value from end of list
`l.erase (iterator)`	Remove referenced element
`l.erase (iterator,iterator)`	Remove range of elements
`l.remove (value)`	Remove all occurrences of value
`l.remove_if (predicate)`	Removal all values that match condition

Size

`l.empty ()`	True if collection is empty
`l.size ()`	Return number of elements in collection

Iterators

`list<T>::iterator itr`	Declare a new iterator
`l.begin ()`	Starting iterator
`l.end ()`	Ending iterator
`l.rbegin ()`	Starting backwards moving iterator
`l.rend ()`	Ending backwards moving iterator

Miscellenous

`l.reverse ()`	Reverse order of elements
`l.sort ()`	Place elements into ascending order
`l.sort (comparison)`	Order elements using comparison function
`l.merge (list)`	Merge with another ordered list

B.1.4   Stack

Insertion and Removal

`s.push (value)`	Push value on front of stack	$O(1)$
`s.top ()`	Access value at front of stack	$O(1)$
`s.pop ()`	Remove value from front of stack	$O(1)$

Size

`s.size ()`	Number of elements in collection	$O(n)$
`s.empty ()`	True if collection is empty	$O(1)$

B.1.5   Queue

Insertion and Removal

`q.push (value)`	Push value on back of queue	$O(1)$
`q.front ()`	Access value at front of queue	$O(1)$

`q.back ()`	Access value at back of queue	$O(1)$
`q.pop ()`	Remove value from front of queue	$O(1)$

Size

`q.size ()`	Number of elements in collection	$O(n)$
`q.empty ()`	True if collection is empty	$O(1)$

B.1.6   Deque

Constructors and Assignment

`deque<T> d;`	Default constructor
`deque<T> d (int);`	Constuct with initial size
`deque<T> d (int, value);`	Constuct with initial size and initial value
`deque<T> d (aDeque);`	Copy constructor
`d = aDeque;`	Assignment of deque from another deque
`d.swap (aDeque);`	Swap contents with another deque

Element Access and Insertion

`d[i]`	Subscript access, can be assignment target
`d.front ()`	First value in collection
`d.back ()`	Final value in collection
`d.insert (iterator, value)`	Insert value before iterator
`d.push_front (value)`	Insert value at front of container
`d.push_back (value)`	Insert value at back of container

Removal

`d.pop_front ()`	Remove element from front of vector
`d.pop_back ()`	Remove element from back of vector
`d.erase (iterator)`	Remove single element
`d.erase (iterator,iterator)`	Remove range of elements

Size

`d.size ()`	Number of elements currently held
`d.empty ()`	True if vector is empty

Iterators

`deque<T>::iterator itr`	Declare a new iterator
`d.begin()`	Starting iterator
`d.end()`	Stopping iterator
`d.rbegin()`	Starting iterator for reverse access
`d.rend()`	Stopping iterator for reverse access

B.1.7   Bit set

Constructors
`bitset<N> s`	Construct bitset for N bits
`bitset<N> s(aBitSet)`	Copy constructor

Bit level operations
`s.flip()`	Flip all bits
`s.flip(i)`	Flip position i
`s.reset()`	Set all bits to false
`s.reset(i)`	Set bit position i to false
`s.set()`	Set all bits to true
`s.set(i)`	Set bit position i to true
`s.test(i)`	Test if bit position i is true

Operations on entire collection
`s.any()`	Return true if any bit is true
`s.none()`	Return true if all bits are false
`s.count()`	Return number of true bits

Combination with other bitsets
`s |= s2`	Set s to union of two sets
`s & s2`	Set s to intersection of two sets
`s = s2`	Set s to symmetric difference of two sets
`s == s2`	Return true if two sets are the same

Other operations
`s << n`	Shift set left by one
`s >> n`	Shift set right by one
`s.to_string()`	Return string representation of set

B.1.8   Set

Constructors
`set<T> s;`	Default constructor
`multiset<T> m;`	Default constructor
`set<T> s (aSet);`	Copy constructor
`multiset<T> m (aMultiset)`	Copy constructor
`s = aSet`	Assignment
`s.swap (aSet)`	Swap elements with argument set

Insertion and Removal

`s.insert (value_type)`	Insert new element
`s.erase (value_type)`	Remove all matching element
`s.erase (iterator)`	Remove element specified by iterator
`s.erase (iterator, iterator)`	Remove range of values

Testing for Inclusion

`s.empty ()`	True if collection is empty
`s.size ()`	Number of elements in collection
`s.count (value_type)`	Count number of occurrences
`s.find (value_type)`	Locate value
`s.lower_bound (value_type)`	First occurrence of value
`s.upper_bound (value_type)`	Next element after value
`s.equal_range (value_type)`	Lower and upper bound pair

Iterators

`set<T>::iterator itr`	Declare a new iterator
`s.begin ()`	Starting iterator
`s.end ()`	Stopping iterator
`s.rbegin ()`	Starting iterator for reverse access
`s.rend ()`	Stopping iterator for reverse access

B.1.9   Priority Queue

Insertion and Removal

`q.push (value)`	Insert new value into queue	$O(\log n)$
`q.top ()`	Access largest element in queue	$O(1)$
`q.pop ()`	Remove largest element in queue	$O(\log n)$

Size

`s.empty()`	True if collection is empty	$O(1)$
`s.size()`	Number of elements in collection	$O(\log n)$

B.1.10   Map

Constructors

`map<T> m;`	Default constructor
`multimap<T> m;`	Default constructor
`map<T> m (aMap)`	Copy constructor
`multimap<T> m (aMultiMap)`	Copy constructor
`m = aMap`	Assignment

Insertion and Removal

`m [ key ]`	Return reference to value with key
`m.insert (value_type)`	Insert given key value pair
`m.erase (key)`	Erase value with given key
`m.erase (iterator)`	Erase value at given iterator

Testing for Inclusion

`m.empty ()`	True if collection is empty
`m.size ()`	Return size of collection
`m.count (key)`	Count number of elements with given key
`m.find (key)`	Locate element with given key
`m.lower_bound (key)`	First occurrence of key
`m.upper_bound (key)`	Next element after key
`m.equal_range (key)`	Lower and upper bound pair

Iterators

`map<T>::iterator itr;`	Declare new iterator
`m.begin ()`	Starting iterator
`m.end ()`	Ending iterator
`m.rbegin ()`	Backwards moving iterator start
`m.rend ()`	Backwards moving iterator end

B.2   GENERIC ALGORITHMS

B.2.1   Initialization Algorithms

The following algorithms are chiefly, although not exclusively, used to initialize a newly created sequence.

```
void fill (iterator start, iterator stop, value)
void fill_n (iterator start, int n, value)
```

The `fill` algorithm copies the indicated value to each location in the specified range. The `fill_n` algorithm writes *n* copies of the given value. The algorithm can be used to insert values into a `list` or `set` by means of an insert iterator (see Section 9.2.1).

```
iterator copy (iterator start, iterator stop, iterator destination)
iterator copy_backward (iterator start, iterator stop, iterator dest)
```

The copy algorithm copies values from the source range into the destination iterator. It is assumed (but not verified) that the destination is large enough to hold the values being copied. The algorithm can be used to insert values into a `list` or `set` by means of an insert iterator (see Section 9.2.1).

The algorithm can be used to output the contents of a container by means of an output stream iterator (see Section 20.2.1).

```
void generate (iterator start, iterator stop, generator)
void generate_n (iterator start, int n, generator)
```

A *generator* is a function that will return a series of values on successive invocations. These algorithms overwrite the given range, invoking the generator function for each new value.

```
iterator swap_ranges (iterator start, iterator stop, iterator destination)
```

This function swaps the values from the input range and the destination. It is assumed (but not verified) that the destination has at least as many values as the source.

B.2.2 Searching Operations

```
iterator find (iterator start, iterator stop, value)
iterator find_if (iterator start, iterator stop, predicate)
```

The algorithm find locates the first occurrence of the given value, returning the end-of-range iterator if no such value is located. The algorithm find_if returns the first value that satisfies the given predicate.

```
iterator adjacent_find (iterator start, iterator stop)
iterator adjacent_find (iterator start, iterator stop, predicate)
```

This algorithm locates the first element that is equal to the next immediately following element. The first form uses the equality operator to perform the comparison, while the second uses the user-supplied binary predicate.

```
iterator search
    (iterator start1, iterator stop1, iterator start2, iterator stop2)
iterator search
    (iterator start1, iterator stop1,
        iterator start2, iterator stop2, compare)
```

This algorithm locates the beginning of a subsequence within a larger sequence. The first pair of iterator values defines the larger sequence, while the second pair defines the pattern being sought. The optional binary predicate can be used in place of the equality operator.

```
iterator min_element (iterator start, iterator stop)
iterator min_element (iterator start, iterator stop, compare)
iterator max_element (iterator start, iterator stop)
iterator max_element (iterator start, iterator stop, compare)
```

These algorithms locate the smallest and largest elements in a sequence. The optional binary predicate can be used in place of the default comparison operator (operator $<$).

```
pair<iterator, iterator> mismatch
     (iterator start, iterator stop, iterator dest)
pair<iterator, iterator> mismatch
     (iterator start, iterator stop, iterator dest, compare)
```

The `mismatch` algorithm compares the two ranges element by element, and returns a pair containing iterators that describe the first mismatched elements. The `pair` data structure was described in Chapter 16. The optional binary predicate can be used in place of the equality-testing operator.

B.2.3   In-Place Transformations

```
void reverse (iterator start, iterator stop)
```

This algorithm reverses in place the elements in the specified range.

```
void replace (iterator start, iterator stop, value, replacement)
void replace_if (iterator start, iterator stop, predicate, replacement)
void replace_copy (iterator start, iterator stop,
     iterator destination, value, replacement)
void replace_copy_if (iterator start, iterator stop,
     iterator destination, predicate, replacement)
```

The first two algorithms replace, in place, the specified values with the given replacement. The second two algorithms are similar, but leave the original collection unchanged and instead copy values to the specified destination.

```
void rotate (iterator start, iterator middle, iterator stop)
```

This algorithm rotates elements around a midpoint. The rotation divides the sequence into two sections, then swaps the order of the sections, maintaining the relative ordering of the elements within the sections. Suppose, for example, that we have the values 1 to 10 in sequence, and the middle iterator points to the value 7. A rotation would produce the values

$$7\ 8\ 9\ 10\ 1\ 2\ 3\ 4\ 5\ 6$$

```
iterator partition (iterator start, iterator stop, predicate)
iterator stable_partition (iterator start, iterator stop, predicate)
```

A partition is formed by moving all the elements that satisfy a predicate to one end of a sequence, and all the elements that fail to satisfy the predicate to the other end. The algorithm returns an iterator that describes the start of the second group. The first form of the algorithm guarantees only that the result is a partition, while the second form preserves the original relative ordering of the elements within each group.

```
bool next_permutation (iterator start, iterator stop)
bool next_permutation (iterator start, iterator stop, compare)
bool prev_permutation (iterator start, iterator stop)
bool prev_permutation (iterator start, iterator stop, compare)
```

A permutation is a rearragement of values. Permutations can be ordered, based on the relative position of the different values (see Section 12.4.3). The `next_permutation` algorithm produces the next permutation of the input values, while the `prev_permutation` algorithm produces the previous permutation.

```
void inplace_merge (iterator start, iterator middle, iterator stop)
void inplace_merge (iterator start, iterator middle, iterator stop, compare)
```

Two adjacent ranges of values are specified by the three iterators. The two ranges are each assumed to be ordered. The values are merged together in place. The optional binary function can be used in place of the comparison operator to define the ordering of values.

```
void random_shuffle (iterator start, iterator stop)
void random_shuffle (iterator start, iterator stop, generator)
```

The `random_shuffle` algorithm randomly rearranges the elements in the sequence. The second form supplies the random number generator to be used in selection values. This function must take as argument a positive value m and return an integer value between 0 and $m - 1$.

B.2.4 Removal Algorithms

The following algorithms can be somewhat confusing to the unwary reader. Both claim to remove certain elements from a sequence, but in fact only copy elements to the front of the sequence, overwriting the removed positions. Both return an iterator that indicates the end of the copied sequence. This iterator can then be used as the beginning of an `erase` operation to actually remove the remaining values.

```
iterator remove (iterator start, iterator stop, value)
iterator remove_if (iterator start, iterator stop, predicate)
```

The first algorithm removes all occurrences of the given value. The second removes all values that satisfy the given predicate. Both return an iterator that indicates the end of the range of unremoved values.

```
iterator unique (iterator start, iterator stop)
iterator unique (iterator start, iterator stop, predicate)
iterator unique_copy (iterator start, iterator stop, iterator destination)
iterator unique_copy (iterator start, iterator stop,
     iterator destination, predicate)
```

This algorithm removes all but the first of any runs of similar values. For example, a sequence such as 1 3 3 2 2 2 4 would be reduced to 1 3 2 4. The optional binary predicate can be used in place of the equality-testing operator for comparing two elements. The copy version of the algorithm leaves the original unchanged, and places the output in the destination sequence.

B.2.5   Scalar-Producing Algorithms

```
void count (iterator start, iterator stop, value, int & Counter)
void count_if (iterator start, iterator stop, predicate, int & counter)
```

These algorithms count the number of occurrences that match the given value, or that satisfy the given predicate. Note that the result is returned through a pass-by-reference integer parameter, and not as the function result.

```
value accumulate (iterator start, iterator stop, value initial)
value accumulate (iterator start, iterator stop, value initial, function)
```

An accumulation is produced by placing a binary operator (by default the addition operator +) between each pair of elements in a sequence. The user can specify both the initial value for this series (typically zero) and the binary operator.

```
value inner_product (iterator start1, iterator stop1,
    iterator start2, value initial)
value inner_product (iterator start1, iterator stop1,
    iterator start2, value initial, function add, function times)
```

An inner product of two sequences is formed by summing the sequence of pairwise products. The user can optionally specify the functions to be used in place of the addition and multiplication operators.

```
bool equal (iterator start1, iterator stop1, iterator start2)
bool equal (iterator start1, iterator stop1, iterator start2, predicate)
```

This algorithm tests two sequences for pairwise equality, returning a boolean true or false value. The user can optionally specify the predicate to be used in place of the equality operator.

```
bool lexicographical_compare (iterator start1, iterator stop1,
    iterator start2, iterator stop2)
bool lexicographical_compare (iterator start1, iterator stop1,
    iterator start2, iterator stop2, predicate)
```

These algorithms compare two sequences lexicographically. A lexicographical comparison is the "dictionary" ordering of the sequences. The user can specify a binary function to be used in place of the comparison operator.

B.2.6   Sequence-Generating Algorithms

```
iterator transform (iterator start, iterator stop,
    iterator destination, UnaryFunction)
iterator transform (iterator start1, iterator stop2, iterator start2,
    iterator destination, BinaryFunction)
```

These algorithms transform a sequence, replacing values with new values. The first replaces every value in a sequence with the result of the unary function. The second operates on two sequences in parallel, and replaces the second with the result of the binary function.

```
iterator partial_sum (iterator start, iterator stop, iterator destination)
iterator partial_sum (iterator start, iterator stop,
    iterator destination, binaryFunction)
```

This algorithm replaces every value in the sequence with the sum of all preceding values. A binary function can be specified to be used in place of the addition operator.

```
iterator adjacent_differernce (iterator start, iterator stop,
    iterator destination)
iterator adjacent_differernce (iterator start, iterator stop,
    iterator destination, BinaryFunction)
```

The adjacent different algorithm computes the sequences of differences between adjacent elements in the sequence. The user can specify a binary function to be used in place of the subtraction operator.

B.2.7   Sorting Algorithms

```
void sort (iterator first, iterator last)
void sort (iterator first, iterator last, compare)
void stable_sort (iterator first, iterator last)
void stable_sort (iterator first, iterator last, compare)
void partial_sort (iterator first, iterator middle, iterator last)
void partial_sort (iterator first, iterator middle, iterator last, compare)
```

These algorithms place the given elements into ascending order. The user can subsitute a different binary function to be used in place of the default comparison function. The first algorithm is the fastest, but is not guaranteed to preserve the relative ordering of equal elements. The second algorithm does preserve this ordering. The `partial_sort` algorithm sorts only the number of elements in the range specified by the first to the middle iterators. The order of elements in the remainder of the sequence is undefined.

```
void nth_element (iterator first, iterator nth, iterator last)
void nth_element (iterator first, iterator nth, iterator last, compare)
```

This algorithm places into the location specified by the nth iterator the value that would appear in this position if the sequence was sorted. However, the order of the other elements in the sequence is undefined.

B.2.8   Binary Search

```
bool binary_search (iterator start, iterator stop, value)
bool binary_search (iterator start, iterator stop, value, compare)
iterator lower_bound (iterator start, iterator stop, value)
iterator lower_bound (iterator start, iterator stop, value, compare)
iterator upper_bound (iterator start, iterator stop, value)
iterator upper_bound (iterator start, iterator stop, value, compare)
pair<iterator, iterator> equal_range (iterator start, iterator stop, value)
pair<iterator, iterator> equal_range (iterator start, iterator stop,
    value, compare)
```

These algorithms perform binary search on the given sequence, which must be ordered in relation to the comparison operator. The first returns a Boolean value that indicates whether the given value is in the collection. The second returns an iterator that indicates the first location where the value could be inserted without violating the ordering property. The third returns the last such location, and the final returns a pair that includes both of these values.

B.2.9   Set Operations

```
iterator merge (iterator start1, iterator stop1,
    iterator start2, iterator stop2, iterator destination)
iterator merge (iterator start1, iterator stop1,
    iterator start2, iterator stop2, iterator destination, compare)
iterator set_union (iterator start1, iterator stop1,
    iterator start2, iterator stop2, iterator destination)
iterator set_union (iterator start1, iterator stop1,
    iterator start2, iterator stop2, iterator destination, compare)
iterator set_intersection (iterator start1, iterator stop1,
    iterator start2, iterator stop2, iterator destination)
iterator set_intersection (iterator start1, iterator stop1,
    iterator start2, iterator stop2, iterator destination, compare)
iterator set_difference (iterator start1, iterator stop1,
    iterator start2, iterator stop2, iterator destination)
iterator set_difference (iterator start1, iterator stop1,
    iterator start2, iterator stop2, iterator destination, compare)
iterator set_symmetric_difference (iterator start1, iterator stop1,
```

```
        iterator start2, iterator stop2, iterator destination)
iterator set_symmetric_difference (iterator start1, iterator stop1,
        iterator start2, iterator stop2, iterator destination, compare)
```

These algorithms perform the indicated set operation, combining the two ordered sequences and copying the result to the destination sequence.

```
bool includes (iterator start1, iterator stop1,
        iterator start2, iterator stop2)
bool includes (iterator start1, iterator stop1,
        iterator start2, iterator stop2, compare)
```

This algorithm returns true if the first set includes all elements from the second set.

B.2.10   Heap Operations

```
void make_heap (iterator start, iterator stop)
void make_heap (iterator start, iterator stop, compare)
void push_heap (iterator start, iterator stop)
void push_heap (iterator start, iterator stop, compare)
void pop_heap  (iterator start, iterator stop)
void pop_heap  (iterator start, iterator stop, compare)
void sort_heap (iterator start, iterator stop)
void sort_heap (iterator start, iterator stop, compare)
```

These algorithms implement operations on a heap data structure. The effect of each operation was described in Chapter 15.

B.2.11   Miscellaneous Algorithms

```
void for_each (iterator first iterator last, unaryFunction)
```

This algorithm executes the given unary function on each element in the given range.

```
void swap (value a, value b)
void iter_swap (iterator a, iterator b)
```

The first function exchanges the contents of the two argument variables. The second is similar, except that the arguments are specified by iterators.

Tables of Various Functions

The tables in Appendix C supply approximate values for several functions. Each line provides values for $\log n$, $\sqrt{n}$, $n \log n$, and n^2. These values are used in the solution of various exercises throughout the book.

$\log n$	$\sqrt{n}$	n	$n \log n$	n^2
0.0	1.0	1	0.0	1.0
1.0	1.4	2	2.0	4.0
1.6	1.7	3	4.8	9.0
2.0	2.0	4	8.0	16.0
2.3	2.2	5	11.6	25.0
2.6	2.4	6	15.5	36.0
2.8	2.6	7	19.7	49.0
3.0	2.8	8	24.0	64.0
3.2	3.0	9	28.5	81.0
3.3	3.2	10	33.2	100.0
4.3	4.5	20	86.4	400.0
4.9	5.5	30	147.2	900.0
5.3	6.3	40	212.9	1600.0

$\log n$	$\sqrt{n}$	n	$n \log n$	n^2
5.6	7.0	50	282.2	2500.0
5.9	7.7	60	354.4	3600.0
6.1	8.4	70	429.1	4900.0
6.3	8.9	80	505.8	6400.0
6.5	9.5	90	584.2	8100.0
6.6	10.0	100	664.4	10000.0
7.6	14.1	200	1528.8	40000.0
8.2	17.3	300	2468.6	90000.0
8.6	20.0	400	3457.5	160000.0
8.9	22.4	500	4482.9	250000.0
9.2	24.5	600	5537.3	360000.0
9.4	26.5	700	6615.9	490000.0
9.6	28.3	800	7715.1	640000.0
9.8	30.0	900	8832.4	810000.0
9.9	31.7	1000	9965.8	1.0×10^6
10.6	38.7	1500	15826.1	2.2×10^6
10.9	44.7	2000	21931.6	4.0×10^6
11.3	50.0	2500	28219.3	6.2×10^6
11.6	54.8	3000	34652.2	9.0×10^6
11.8	59.2	3500	41206.0	1.2×10^7
11.9	63.2	4000	47863.1	1.6×10^7
12.1	67.1	4500	54610.7	2.0×10^7
12.3	70.7	5000	61438.6	2.5×10^7
12.6	77.5	6000	75304.5	3.6×10^7
12.8	83.7	7000	89412.0	4.9×10^7
12.9	89.4	8000	103726.0	6.4×10^7
13.1	94.9	9000	118221.0	8.1×10^7
13.3	100.0	10000	132877.0	1.0×10^8
14.3	141.4	20000	285754.0	4.0×10^8
14.9	173.2	30000	446180.0	9.0×10^8
15.3	200.0	40000	611508.0	1.6×10^9
15.6	223.6	50000	780482.0	2.5×10^9

$\log n$	$\sqrt{n}$	n	$n \log n$	n^2
15.9	244.9	60000	952360.0	3.6×10^9
16.1	264.6	70000	1.1×10^6	4.9×10^9
16.3	282.8	80000	1.3×10^6	6.4×10^9
16.5	300.0	90000	1.5×10^6	8.1×10^9
16.6	316.2	100000	1.7×10^6	1.0×10^{10}

If C++ Is the Solution, Then What Is the Problem?

C++ is a programming language that is rich in a variety of mechanisms used to overcome various difficulties encountered during software development. The language is so rich, in fact, that a programmer first starting to create software using C++ is often hard-pressed to understand the utility or importance of a particular feature, simply because he or she may not understand the problem that the feature is designed to help solve.

In Appendix D we will briefly overview the most commonly used programming mechanisms encountered in C++ programs, and outline the major problem(s) addressed by each feature. These are presented in roughly the same order that they have been introduced in the book.

D.1   CLASS DEFINITIONS

There are two major benefits provided by the class mechanism. These are

▲ Encapsulation

▲ Instansiation

The term *encapsulation* refers to the idea that the class definition can bring together, in a single unit, functions and data areas that are linked by a common purpose. This allows the programmer to think of a class structure as a single conceptual object, not simply a collection of separate functions.

A related aspect of this encapsulation is a reduction in name space congestion. Classes allow a fine degree of control over the exposure or access to names (see Sections D.3 and D.12). Without classes, most data areas that would need to retain values between function invocations would be declared global. This practice results in a large increase in global names, which causes both conceptual and practical problems when names from separate programming units are similar or identical.

The term *instansiation* refers to the ability to create multiple instances of a class. That is, once a class has been defined, it is no more difficult to create ten independent instances of the class than it is to create a single instance. Without the class mechanism, a similar sort of functionality is usually provided using global variables; however, with global variables the creation of multiple independent instances is considerably more difficult.

D.2   MEMBER FUNCTIONS

Member functions are the primary mechanism used to associate behavior (that is, functionality) with classes. Unlike an ordinary function, a member function is always associated with a specific class. To invoke a member function, an instance of the class must be specified. The syntax of member functions reflects this (except where operators are defined as member functions, see Section D.8). The instance being manipulated (called the *receiver* for the function invocation) is described first, followed by a period, followed by the member function name. This illustrates the member function `length` being applied to a vector named `data`:

```
data.length()
```

The code that implements a member function must name both the member function being implemented and the class in which the function is defined. Different classes can, and often do, implement member functions with a common name.

Within a member function, the value of the receiver is available through a pointer variable named `this`.

When a member function is invoked from within another member function, the receiver does not need to be named if it is the same as the receiver for the initial invocation.

D.3   ACCESS CONTROLS (PUBLIC, PRIVATE, AND PROTECTED)

A class can be envisioned as a software component that is designed to provide a specific service. In a software development team composed of several programmers, for any individual class we can divide the team into *users* of the software service and *implementors* of the service. These two different subgroups require different levels of information concerning the class.

Features defined in the *public* portion of a class describe elements of interest to users of the data abstraction provided by the class. Features defined in the *private* portion of a class outline functions and data values of interest only to the implementors of the class, and are not necessary for users of the class. Access control is enforced by the compiler. Private fields can be manipulated only from within member functions associated with the class, or by explicitly designated friends (see Section D.12).

Fields described as *protected* are slightly more accessible than private fields, but are not public. They can be manipulated by member functions associated with the class, or by member functions associated with derived classes (see Section D.13).

D.4   REFERENCES AND POINTERS

A *reference* is an alias, a mechanism to permit access to a single data value under two (or more) different names. The most common use of references is in the implementation of pass-by-reference parameter passing (see Section D.5). References are also used to permit a field in one class to refer to another class or to an individual data value held by another class. This occurs in many iterator structures, where a field in the iterator refers to the structure over which iteration is being performed.

In most cases, the implementation mechanism used to simulate references is the same as the technique used to implement pointers. That is, the value stored in memory is the address of the object referred to by the alias. Thus, a reference can be envisioned as simply a form of pointer. References differ from pointers in three important respects:

1. A reference can never be null; it must always refer to a legitimate object.

2. Once established, a reference can never be changed so that it points to a different object.

3. A reference does not require any explicit mechanism to dereference the memory address and access data values.

D.5   REFERENCE PARAMETERS

The semantics of the C++ programming language require that, unless the programmer specifies otherwise, a *copy* of a data value must be generated whenever a value is passed as an argument. This default parameter passing mechanism is known as *call-by-value*. An alternative mechanism, *call-by-reference*, is indicated by placing an ampersand in the parameter list, as in this example function definition:

```
double sqrt(complex & value)
{
    :
    :
}
```

To implement a call-by-reference parameter, only a reference (that is, a pointer) is passed to the function. This eliminates the necessity of making a copy of the argument. For almost all data types this results in much more rapid execution. Thus, reference parameters are extensively used in the parameter passing of large structures.

Because a reference parameter is simply an alias for the associated argument value, changes to the reference made within a function will be reflected in subsequent changes to the argument value following execution of the procedure. This is not true with call-by-value semantics, because changes to the parameter merely change a copy of the argument value in the current activation record.

Protection of the argument value from undesired modification can be ensured by declaring the parameter as *constant*. This is accomplished by prepending the keyword const to the parameter declaration. The resulting parameter passing mechanism is sometimes then referred to as *call-by-constant* reference.

D.6   CONSTRUCTORS

A *constructor* is a function used to ensure that newly created instances of a class are properly initialized. A constructor is characterized as a member function having the same name as the class. Constructors are never explicitly invoked by the user; instead, constructors are invoked as part of the processing of a declaration statement. Where needed, arguments to a constructor are provided using the same syntax as a function call.

```
Card x;          // invoke constructor with no arguments
Card y(heart, 3);    // invoke constructor with two arguments
```

Note that no parentheses are used in a declaration statement that invokes a constructor with no arguments. The use of parentheses in this situation is a common programming error.

The implementation of a constructor differs from a normal member function implementation in that the return type is not named, and the function heading can be followed by a sequence of initializers. Initializers either provide initial values for class data fields, arguments for constructors of class data fields, or arguments for constructors for parent classes from which the class definition inherits.

```
rational::rational(int numerator, int denominator)
     : top(numerator), bottom(denominator)
{
     normalize();
}
```

Constructors are also one of two mechanisms used by C++ to define conversion operations. A constructor with a single argument implicitly defines how conversions are to be performed from the argument type to the type associated with the class of the constructor. For example, the following constructor defines the conversion from integer to rational number. Conversions will be performed automatically by the C++ compiler to ensure compatibility between the left and right sides of an assignment statement, or between parameters and argument values.

```
rational::rational (int numerator) : top(numerator), bottom(1)
{
     // no further actions needed
}
```

Explicit conversion operators (see Section D.9) provide the second method used to define conversions from one type to another.

D.7   COPY CONSTRUCTOR

Copy constructors are characterized as constructors that take as argument a constant call-by-reference parameter of the same type as the class in which the constructor is defined.

```
rational::rational(rational & value)
  : top(value.numerator()), bottom(value.denominator())
{
     // no further initialization required
}
```

As the name implies, copy constructors are invoked by the C++ compiler whenever it is necessary to form a duplicate copy of a value. Most often this occurs when instances of a class are passed by value to a function or procedure. Copy constructors should therefore do whatever is necessary to form a duplicate copy of a value.

D.8   OPERATORS AS FUNCTIONS AND OPERATORS AS MEMBERS

Operators (built-in, nonalphabetic functions, such as + and ∗) are unique because they can be implemented either as ordinary functions or as member functions associated with a particular class. Differences between these two are:

▲ When defined as an ordinary function, all arguments to the operator are described in the argument list. When defined as a member function, the leftmost argument is treated as the receiver, and is not described in the argument list.

▲ When used as a member function, the leftmost argument can only be an instance of the class in which the member function is defined.

▲ When defined as an ordinary function, automatic conversion will be applied to all arguments in order to match argument types to declared function types. When used as a member function, such conversions will not be applied to the receiver.

▲ Operators defined as member functions are, like all member functions, permitted access to the private components of the class definition in which they appear. Such access is denied to nonmember functions.

Note that the number of operators, the number of arguments they take, and their precedence are fixed by the language definition and cannot be changed by the programmer.

D.9   CONVERSION OPERATORS

Data types can be defined as member function operators. Such a function is then invoked when an instance of the class in which the member function appears is to be converted into the type specified by the operator. For example, the following member function appears in the class `rational`. It is invoked when it is desired to convert a rational number into a double-precision floating-point value.

```
rational::operator double ()
{
        return double(top) / double(bottom);
}
```

Notice that no return type is specified for the conversion operator.

Conversion operators were introduced in conjunction with the string data abstraction described in Chapter 7.

D.10 AUTOMATIC AND DYNAMIC ALLOCATION

Most variables are declared, implicitly, as *automatic*. This means that storage for the variable is allocated when the procedure containing the declaration of the variable is entered, and freed (again, automatically) when the procedure exits. At the other extreme are global variables, which are created when the program begins and are destroyed when the program exits.

The dynamic allocation mechanism permits the programmer to allocate and initialize storage that can outlive the scope in which the storage is created. Most often, this is done for one of three reasons:

▲ The lifetime of a variable is neither local or global, but in-between. Using dynamic allocation, the programmer controls when values come into existence and when they are deleted. This occurs with the allocation of nodes in a linked list. Nodes are created when elements are added to the list, and are deleted when values are removed from the list.

▲ The size of a data value is not known at compile time, but is determined at run time. This occurs in both the string and vector data abstractions, where operations (catenation, setSize) may alter the number of elements held by the data value.

▲ True dynamic polymorphic behavior is possible in C++ only when pointer values (either true pointers or references) are used (see Section D.15). Sometimes dynamic allocation is used simply to make use of this feature.

Dynamic values are created using the operator new. This operator is followed by a type name, which is then optionally followed by arguments used in a constructor to initialize the new value. The following illustrates the dynamic allocation of an instance of Card, the class discussed in Chapter 2. Note that the new operator always returns a pointer.

```
Card * newCard = new Card(heart, 3);
```

An array of values can also be allocated using the operator new. The size of the array is specified after the type name. The following illustrates the allocation of an array of 25 integer values.

```
int * intarray = new int[25];
```

Note that memory that is allocated dynamically must be explicitly freed by the programmer. This is accomplished using the `delete` operator. The second line illustrates the form used to delete a vector of values.

```
delete ratptr;
delete [ ] intarray;
```

Dynamic allocation is used extensively in the string data type described in Chapter 9, the vector data abstraction described in Chapter 8, and the list data structure described in Chapter 9.

D.11   DESTRUCTORS

A *destructor* is simply a function that is invoked implicitly when an instance of a class is destroyed. Values are destroyed when local variables go out of scope, when dynamically allocated values are deleted, or when a value containing data fields is destroyed (in which case, every field is individually destroyed). A destructor, if defined, is executed immediately before the data area occupied by the value is recovered.

A destructor is characterized as a member function named by a tilde followed by the name of the class in which it is defined. Destructors take no arguments, return no values, and are never directly invoked by the programmer. The following illustrates the definition of the destructor for the class `string`:

```
string::~string()
{
    // recover the memory used by the string
    delete [ ] buffer;
}
```

Destructors are defined for the string class described in Chapter 9, for the vector class described in Chapter 8, and for the list class described in Chapter 12.

D.12   FRIENDS

A class definition can specify one or more *friends*. A friend can be either another class or an individual function. By specifying a friend, the designer of a class explicitly permits the friend to access the private and protected fields of the class. The friend mechanism provides the programmer with very precise control over access to features of a class.

Friends are needed to bridge across different classes. They open up protection to a limited extent, without requiring the programmer to make features accessible to the world at large.

BIBL

Friend classes where introduced in Chapter 9, where the classes `list` and `link` were mutual friends of each other.

D.13   DERIVED CLASSES: INHERITANCE

Two major mechanisms for software reuse are composition and inheritance. *Composition* refers to simply using an instance of one class as a data field in a larger structure. *Inheritance* is used when a new data abstraction is a variation or simplification of an existing data structure. Inheritance permits instances of the new class to access member functions and data areas from the older class without requiring any new code to be written.

Inheritance is also used when a parent class provides specification for actions, but no implementation. This was illustrated by the class `iterator` (Chapter 14), and the classes `stack` and `queue` (Chapter 10). Such a class is known as an *abstract* class.

D.14   TEMPLATES

The *template* mechanism is a facility used to parameterize a class description or a function. By use of templates, one or more types can be left unspecified in the class description. Using templates one can create, for example, a list data abstraction without specifying a type for the elements to be held by the list. Without the template facility, each new type of list would require the development of a new class.

Templates were introduced in Chapter 8. Because the majority of classes used in this book are collections of elements, templates are used extensively throughout.

D.15   POLYMORPHISM: VIRTUAL FUNCTIONS

A *polymorphic* variable is one that can hold values of different types. In C++, only references and pointers to class instances can be truly polymorphic. These can refer to instances of the class with which they have been declared, or instances of any *derive class* of that class (see Section D.13). The term *static type* is used to describe the declared type of such a variable, while the term *dynamic type* describes the type of the actual value (which may vary at different times during execution).

A member function invoked using such a value can either be matched to a function body in the class associated with the static type or to the class associated with the dynamic type. If the member function has been declared to be *virtual* in the parent class, then the member function associated with the class of the dynamic type will be executed. Otherwise,

INDEX